Communications in Computer and Information Science 2659

Rationale

The CCIS series is devoted to the publication of proceedings of computer science conferences. Its aim is to efficiently disseminate original research results in informatics in printed and electronic form. While the focus is on publication of peer-reviewed full papers presenting mature work, inclusion of reviewed short papers reporting on work in progress is welcome, too. Besides globally relevant meetings with internationally representative program committees guaranteeing a strict peer-reviewing and paper selection process, conferences run by societies or of high regional or national relevance are also considered for publication.

Topics

The topical scope of CCIS spans the entire spectrum of informatics ranging from foundational topics in the theory of computing to information and communications science and technology and a broad variety of interdisciplinary application fields.

Information for Volume Editors and Authors

Publication in CCIS is free of charge. No royalties are paid, however, we offer registered conference participants temporary free access to the online version of the conference proceedings on SpringerLink (http://link.springer.com) by means of an http referrer from the conference website and/or a number of complimentary printed copies, as specified in the official acceptance email of the event.

CCIS proceedings can be published in time for distribution at conferences or as post-proceedings, and delivered in the form of printed books and/or electronically as USBs and/or e-content licenses for accessing proceedings at SpringerLink. Furthermore, CCIS proceedings are included in the CCIS electronic book series hosted in the SpringerLink digital library at http://link.springer.com/bookseries/7899. Conferences publishing in CCIS are allowed to use our online conference service (Meteor) for managing the whole proceedings lifecycle (from submission and reviewing to preparing for publication) free of charge.

Publication process

The language of publication is exclusively English. Authors publishing in CCIS have to sign the Springer CCIS copyright transfer form, however, they are free to use their material published in CCIS for substantially changed, more elaborate subsequent publications elsewhere. For the preparation of the camera-ready papers/files, authors have to strictly adhere to the Springer CCIS Authors' Instructions and are strongly encouraged to use the CCIS LaTeX style files or templates.

Abstracting/Indexing

CCIS is abstracted/indexed in DBLP, Google Scholar, EI-Compendex, Mathematical Reviews, SCImago, Scopus. CCIS volumes are also submitted for the inclusion in ISI Proceedings.

How to start

To start the evaluation of your proposal for inclusion in the CCIS series, please send an e-mail to ccis@springer.com

Damir Cavar · Vaneet Aggarwal ·
Jerome Busemeyer · Samuel Yen-Chi Chen
Editors

Quantum AI and NLP

First International Conference, QNLPAI 2025
Bloomington, IN, USA, August 6–9, 2025
Proceedings

Springer

Editors
Damir Cavar
Indiana University
Bloomington, IN, USA

Jerome Busemeyer
Indiana University
Bloomington, IN, USA

Vaneet Aggarwal
Purdue University
West Lafayette, IN, USA

Samuel Yen-Chi Chen
Wells Fargo
New York, NY, USA

ISSN 1865-0929 ISSN 1865-0937 (electronic)
Communications in Computer and Information Science
ISBN 978-3-032-13882-8 ISBN 978-3-032-13883-5 (eBook)
https://doi.org/10.1007/978-3-032-13883-5

This Springer imprint is published by the registered company Springer Nature Switzerland AG
The registered company address is: Gewerbestrasse 11, 6330 Cham, Switzerland

Preface

The first Quantum AI and NLP Conference (QNLP.AI 2025) was held at Indiana University in Bloomington from the 6th to 8th of August 2025 (https://qnlp.ai/). It served as a hub for pioneering research at the intersection of quantum computing, artificial intelligence (AI), and natural language processing (NLP). It marked a significant milestone in the evolution of artificial intelligence for quantum computing, quantum computing for AI-based applications and systems, quantum NLP, and quantum-inspired modeling in cognitive science.

The 2025 program brought together scientists, engineers, and domain experts from academic, government, and business organizations. It attracted international participants across many disciplines to present and discuss current research activities and results. Contributions span the four core topics, including:

- AI methods for quantum computing
- Quantum computing for AI applications and intelligent systems
- Quantum Natural Language Processing
- Cognitive Models and Quantum-inspired Formalisms

A total of forty-five (45) papers were submitted for peer review using Microsoft Conference Management Tool (CMT) and Open Review as platforms. We selected twenty (20) papers for presentation and seventeen (17) papers, one (1) short paper, and one (1) abstract for publication in the proceedings. The papers received two (2) double-blind reviews on average. Each reviewer received, on average, four (4) papers to review. Besides the Program Committee members listed below, no other external reviewers were involved.

The papers in these proceedings reflect the exploratory nature of quantum computing and AI in the current state of quantum hardware and experimental platforms. The authors have pushed the boundaries of the fields and provided a deeper understanding of current possibilities to utilize quantum computing in the four domains. The presentations and papers in this volume emphasize the potential future of quantum computing in hybrid environments that facilitate efficient computation using classical and quantum processing units. They also discuss the advantages of quantum-inspired probabilistic or logical models of cognitive processes.

We extend our deepest gratitude to the program committee, reviewers, and editorial team, whose thoughtful comments and suggestions significantly contributed to the quality and coherence of this volume. Special thanks to our keynote speakers and panelists. Their insights into the future of quantum computing as a service, hybrid classical/quantum environments for AI-related computation, cognitive quantum models that improve predictive modeling of high-dimensional data, the role of quantum computing in higher education, and Quantum-NLP applications inspired the general audience and the large number of students participating.

Special thanks to the Center for Quantum Technologies (CQT), which supported this conference under the Industry-University Cooperative Research Center Program at the US National Science Foundation under Grant No. 2224928. Indiana University Research provided the necessary funds for this event, and other units at Indiana University at Bloomington contributed, e.g., the Luddy School of Informatics, Computing, and Engineering, the Linguistics Department, the Quantum Science and Engineering Center (QSEc), the Natural Language Processing Lab and Quantum AI Study Group, the Ostrom Workshop, and the Quantum Technologies for Everyone (QUTE) student club. We are also grateful to the Association for Computing Machinery (ACM) and the ACM Special Interest Group on Artificial Intelligence (ACM SIGAI) for their support and the "In-cooperation" status for this conference.

August 2025

Damir Cavar
Vaneet Aggarwal
Jerome Busemeyer
Samuel Yen-Chi Chen

Organization

General Chair

Damir Cavar	Indiana University Bloomington, USA

Program Committee Chairs

Vaneet Aggarwal	Purdue University, USA
Damir Cavar	Indiana University Bloomington, USA
Samuel Yen-Chi Chen	Wells Fargo, USA
Jerome Busemeyer	Indiana University Bloomington, USA

Steering Commitee

David Baxter	Indiana University Bloomington, USA
Thomas Wesley Burkle	Indiana University Bloomington, USA
Billy G. Dickson	Indiana University Bloomington, USA
Dan-Adrian German	Indiana University Bloomington, USA
Jiaqi Huang	Indiana University Bloomington, USA
Lawrence S. Moss	Indiana University Bloomington, USA
Gerardo Ortiz	Indiana University Bloomington, USA
Koushik Reddy Parukola	Indiana University Bloomington, USA
Timothy J. Pleskac	Indiana University Bloomington, USA
Shane A. Sparks	Indiana University Bloomington, USA
Rong Zheng	Indiana University Bloomington, USA

Program Commitee

Vaneet Aggarwal	Purdue University, USA
Travis Brown	Indiana University Bloomington, USA
Jerome Busemeyer	Indiana University Bloomington, USA
Yudong Cao	Boston Consulting Group, USA
Damir Cavar	Indiana University Bloomington, USA
Fan Chen	Indiana University Bloomington, USA
Samuel Yen-Chi Chen	Wells Fargo, USA

Sophie Choe	qAIntum.ai, USA
Vedran Dunjko	Leiden University, Netherlands
James Brian Graves	Indiana University Bloomington, USA
Mohsen Heidari	Indiana University Bloomington, USA
Jiaqi Huang	Indiana University Bloomington, USA
Lei Jiang	Indiana University Bloomington, USA
Meng Jiang	University of Notre Dame, USA
Dimitrios Kartsaklis	Quantinuum, UK
Peter Kogge	University of Notre Dame, USA
David Kremer	IBM Quantum, USA
Nicholas LaRacuente	Indiana University Bloomington, USA
Martha Lewis	University of Amsterdam, Netherlands
Alessandro Luongo	Center for Quantum Technologies, Singapore
Lawrence S. Moss	Indiana University Bloomington, USA
Gerardo Ortiz	Indiana University Bloomington, USA
Timothy J. Pleskac	Indiana University Bloomington, USA
Mehrnoosh Sadrzadeh	University College London, UK
Keeper L. Sharkey	ODE, L3C, USA
Yiyu Shi	University of Notre Dame, USA
Zoran Tiganj	Indiana University Bloomington, USA
Juan Uriagereka	University of Maryland, USA
Dominic Widdows	AMD, USA

Sponsoring Institutions

- Indiana University Bloomington
  - Research, IN, USA
  - Luddy School of Informatics, Computing, and Engineering, IN, USA
  - Ostrom Workshop, IN, USA
  - Department of Linguistics
  - Quantum Science and Engineering Center (QSEc)
  - Quantum Technologies for Everyone (QUTE)
  - Natural Language Processing Lab and Quantum AI/NLP Study Group
- Center for Quantum Technologies (CQT) (Indiana University, Purdue University, University of Notre Dame)
- Monroe County, Indiana, Airport

Beyond Pairs: Generalizing the Quantum Question Equality to Multiple Observables

Michael Schnabel
Department of Political Science, Vanderbilt University
michael.schnabel@vanderbilt.edu

Abstract. In quantum mechanics, when two observables do not commute, the joint probability of outcomes cannot be uniquely determined as the probabilities depend on the order of measurements. However, the conditional probabilities for different measurement orders are constrained by the projection postulates of quantum theory. The Quantum Question (QQ) Equality, formulated by Wang and Busemeyer [1] provides a non-parametric prediction for the pairwise probabilities of binary questions represented by two non-commutative observables and their associated projection operators. The QQ Equality has been central to quantum cognition research, helping test whether order effects in survey data can be explained as quantum interference, with strong supporting evidence [2]. In this work, I formulate QQ Equalities that extend beyond pairwise comparisons, accommodating situations with $N \geq 3$ binary questions under the assumption that measurements are represented by idempotent projection operators. These results may be applicable to low-dimensional discrete quantum systems, and offer a generalizable framework for understanding order effects in cognitive decision-making across various domains of questionnaire design, experimental psychology and behavioral economics.

Keywords: Quantum Question Equality · Order Effects · Quantum Cognition

References

1. Wang, Z., Busemeyer, J.R.: A quantum question order model supported by empirical tests of an a priori and precise prediction. Top. Cogn. Sci. **5**(4), 689–710 (2013)
2. Wang, Z., Solloway, T., Shiffrin, R.M., Busemeyer, J.R.: Context effects produced by question orders reveal quantum nature of human judgments. Proc. Nat. Acad. Sci. **111**(26), 9431–9436 (2014)

Contents

Artificial Intelligence for Quantum Computing

Enhancing Interpretability of Quantum-Assisted Blockchain Clustering via AI Agent-Based Qualitative Analysis

Yun-Cheng Tsai[1(✉)], Yen-Ku Liu[1], and Samuel Yen-Chi Chen[2]

[1] National Taiwan Normal University, Taipei 10610, Taiwan
{pecu,41171123h}@ntnu.edu.tw
[2] Wells Fargo, New York 10001, USA
ycchen1989@ieee.org

Abstract. Blockchain transaction data is inherently high-dimensional, noisy, and entangled, posing substantial challenges for traditional clustering algorithms. While quantum-enhanced clustering models have demonstrated promising performance gains, their interpretability remains limited, restricting their application in sensitive domains such as financial fraud detection and blockchain governance. To address this gap, we propose a two-stage analysis framework that synergistically combines quantitative clustering evaluation with AI Agent-assisted qualitative interpretation. In the first stage, we employ classical clustering methods and evaluation metrics—including the Silhouette Score, Davies-Bouldin Index, and Calinski-Harabasz Index—to determine the optimal cluster count and baseline partition quality. In the second stage, we integrate an AI Agent to generate human-readable, semantic explanations of clustering results, identifying intra-cluster characteristics and inter-cluster relationships. Our experiments reveal that while fully trained Quantum Neural Networks (QNN) outperform random Quantum Features (QF) in quantitative metrics, the AI Agent further uncovers nuanced differences between these methods, notably exposing the singleton cluster phenomenon in QNN-driven models. The consolidated insights from both stages consistently endorse the three-cluster configuration, demonstrating the practical value of our hybrid approach. This work advances the interpretability frontier in quantum-assisted blockchain analytics and lays the groundwork for future autonomous AI-orchestrated clustering frameworks.

Keywords: Machine Learning · Blockchain Analytics · AI Agent-based Explainability · Hybrid Quantum-Classical Clustering · Explainable Artificial Intelligence (XAI)

1 Introduction

Blockchain analytics has emerged as a critical field for understanding decentralized economic activities and ensuring network security. However, the intrinsic

D. Cavar et al. (Eds.): QNLPAI 2025, CCIS 2659, pp. 3–19, 2026.
https://doi.org/10.1007/978-3-032-13883-5_1

properties of blockchain data—high dimensionality, temporal entanglement, and transactional noise—pose significant challenges for conventional clustering methods, often leading to suboptimal performance and opaque results [1,19]. Recent advancements in quantum machine learning (QML) offer promising avenues to overcome these hurdles by enhancing feature representations through quantum state encoding [3,11]. Yet, these quantum-assisted models primarily optimize for clustering performance metrics and lack transparency, which undermines their adoption in sensitive applications such as anti-money laundering (AML), fraud detection, and decentralized finance (DeFi) ecosystem monitoring [7,14].

To bridge this gap, we propose a **two-stage analysis framework** that unites the rigor of quantitative evaluation with the interpretability of AI Agent-driven qualitative analysis. In the first stage, we systematically evaluate clustering quality across varying cluster counts ($K = 2$ to $K = 6$), utilizing classical metrics like Silhouette Score, Davies-Bouldin Index, and Calinski-Harabasz Index to identify the most promising partitioning strategies [2]. This phase ensures an objective selection of baseline clustering configurations, effectively narrowing the search space for subsequent analysis.

The second stage employs an AI Agent, leveraging large language models to perform semantic analysis on the clustering outputs. The Agent interprets intra-cluster characteristics, reveals cross-cluster relationships, and identifies potential anomalies—providing critical explanations beyond numerical metrics [15]. Furthermore, the AI Agent is more than a passive observer; it evolves toward an active role by proposing adjustments to cluster configurations and offering strategic insights into clustering parameter design.

Our key contributions are fourfold:

1. **Two-stage analysis framework:** We establish a novel hybrid evaluation pipeline combining quantitative clustering assessments with AI Agent-driven qualitative insights.
2. **Enhanced interpretability:** Our approach improves the explainability of quantum-assisted clustering models, particularly in blockchain applications where actionable insights are paramount.
3. **AI Agent as an active participant:** We advance the role of AI Agents from passive explainers to proactive collaborators, capable of suggesting cluster configurations and detecting anomalies.
4. **Empirical validation in blockchain scenarios:** Through comprehensive experiments on carbon credit transaction data, we demonstrate the effectiveness of our method, with both quantitative and qualitative analyses converging on a three-cluster solution as the optimal configuration.

This study addresses the long-standing interpretability challenges in quantum machine learning. It opens new directions for autonomous AI-driven analytics, paving the way toward fully automated, explainable clustering systems in complex data environments.

2 Related Work

2.1 Quantum Feature Engineering in Blockchain Analytics

Quantum-enhanced feature engineering has emerged as a promising solution to tackle high-dimensional and entangled blockchain data [20]. Quantum Neural Networks (QNNs) utilize quantum properties such as superposition and entanglement to project classical data into high-dimensional Hilbert spaces, revealing latent patterns challenging to capture with classical methods [6].

2.2 Hybrid Classical-Quantum Clustering Approaches

Previous research has explored hybrid strategies, combining quantum-generated features with classical clustering algorithms [11]. Untrained quantum circuits (Random QNN) have been used to generate rich feature sets, demonstrating significant improvements in clustering tasks without extensive training overhead [17].

2.3 Explainable AI (XAI) in Quantum Machine Learning

Explainable AI aims to make black-box models more transparent. In quantum machine learning, interpretability remains an under-explored frontier [12,16]. Our work contributes to this field by integrating an AI Agent to transform complex quantum clustering outcomes into digestible insights [8].

2.4 AI Agents for Model Interpretation

AI Agents, particularly those leveraging natural language generation and rule-based reasoning, have effectively summarized complex model behaviors [14]. We enable automated, interpretable reporting of quantum-enhanced clustering results by deploying such an agent in our study.

3 Methodology

This section presents our two-stage analysis framework, designed to enhance blockchain transaction data's clustering quality and interpretability. The proposed approach integrates rigorous quantitative evaluation with AI Agent-assisted qualitative analysis, enabling a holistic understanding of clustering behaviors. The overall workflow is illustrated in Fig. 1.

3.1 Stage 1: Quantitative Clustering Evaluation

Objective. The first stage aims to establish an objective baseline of clustering performance using established evaluation metrics. We systematically evaluate clustering quality across varying cluster counts ($K = 2$ to $K = 6$) to identify optimal configurations for deeper analysis.

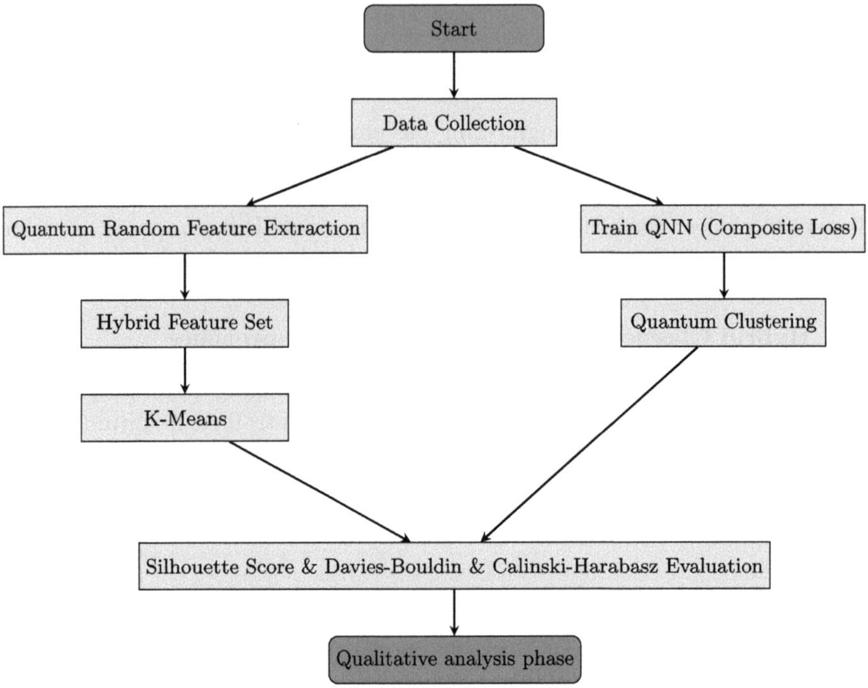

Fig. 1. Overview of the experimental design for quantum-enhanced clustering.

Dataset and Preprocessing. We employ blockchain transaction data from the MCO2 token ecosystem on Ethereum, focusing on carbon credit trading activities involving ten major nodes [10]. The dataset captures essential attributes such as block numbers, timestamps, sender and receiver addresses, token details, transaction values, and gas prices.

A detailed summary of the dataset attributes and preprocessing techniques is provided in Table 1.

Categorical attributes are transformed through label encoding, while numerical variables like `token_value` and `gas_price` undergo robust scaling to mitigate outliers. The `timestamp` is converted into cyclical features (sine and cosine) to capture temporal patterns in transaction behaviors.

This structured preprocessing pipeline ensures the feature set is optimized for quantum feature extraction and clustering.

Quantum Feature Extraction Strategies. We propose two distinct quantum-enhanced feature extraction strategies, each built upon the Quantum-Train (QT) paradigm, which utilizes a QNN with its exponential number of amplitudes to generate the parameters of a classical neural network [13].

- **Random Quantum Features (QF):** The features are extracted from classical neural networks whose parameters are derived from randomly initialized,

Table 1. Dataset Attribute Summary and Preprocessing Techniques

Attribute	Description	Preprocessing
block_number	Block height	Numerical, no scaling
transaction_hash	Transaction ID	Ignored (non-informative)
timestamp	Transaction time	Cyclical encoding (sin/cos)
from_address	Sender address	Label encoding
to_address	Receiver address	Label encoding
token_name	Token name	Label encoding
token_symbol	Token symbol	Label encoding
token_value	Amount transferred	Robust scaling
gas_price	Transaction fee	Robust scaling

untrained QNNs, thereby providing diverse and computationally efficient representations.

- **Fully Trained Quantum Neural Network (QNN):** In contrast, the second strategy trains the QNN end-to-end using the SwAV self-supervised loss to generate parameters for the feature transformation network, thereby optimizing the resulting embeddings for clustering performance.

Both strategies combine quantum features with preprocessed classical features to form hybrid representations. We employ the K-Means algorithm for clustering due to its effectiveness in unsupervised learning tasks [4].

Fully Trained Quantum Neural Network (QNN). In this approach, we further investigate whether optimizing the QNN parameters can enhance clustering performance. Under the hybrid quantum-classical paradigm, the QNN is integrated with a SwAV loss module, forming a unified model. The entire hybrid model is trained end-to-end, utilizing standard backpropagation for optimization. This scheme is illustrated in Fig. 2.

The loss function is defined as:

$$L_{\text{SwAV}} = \text{KL}\left(\text{log1p}(P_1) \,\|\, P_2\right), \tag{1}$$

where P_1 and P_2 are the probability distributions obtained from the QNN outputs with temperature scaling and label smoothing. This loss guides the QNN in learning robust feature representations that are subsequently used for K-means clustering. Training is performed using the Adam optimizer with gradient clipping to mitigate gradient explosion. The Algorithm 1 outlines the fully quantum clustering approach.

Clustering Evaluation Metrics. Clustering performance is assessed using three established internal metrics:

Algorithm 1 Quantum Neural Network Training with SwAV Loss

for each *num_prototypes* in *prototype_range* **do**
  Create output directories for current *num_prototypes*
  for each *quantum_depth* in *quantum_depth_range* **do**
    Initialize base neural network model
    Initialize QNN with given *quantum_depth* using the base model
    Initialize the SwAV loss module with current *num_prototypes*
    Set optimizer with parameters from QNN and SwAV loss
    for each epoch in *num_epochs* **do**
      for each batch in *scaled_features* **do**
        Set QNN to training mode
        $quantum\_output \leftarrow QNN(batch)$
        $aug_1 \leftarrow quantum\_output + \mathcal{N}(0, \sigma^2)$
        $aug_2 \leftarrow quantum\_output + \mathcal{N}(0, \sigma^2)$
        $loss \leftarrow SwAV\_loss(aug_1, aug_2)$
        optimizer.zero_grad()
        Backpropagate *loss*
        Apply gradient clipping
        optimizer.step()
      end for
      Set QNN to evaluation mode
      Initialize empty list *quantum_features*
      for all each batch in *scaled_features* **do**
        $quantum\_output \leftarrow QNN(batch)$ without gradient computation
        Append *quantum_output* to *quantum_features*
      end for
      Concatenate *quantum_features*
    end for
  end for
end for

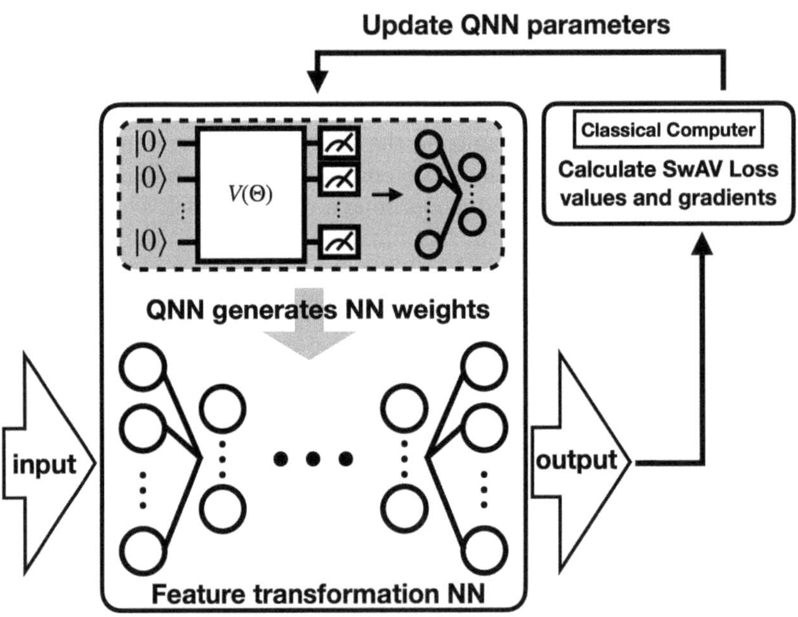

Fig. 2. Trained QNN for generating weights for feature transformation NN.

- **Silhouette Score** [18]: Measures cohesion within clusters and separation between clusters (higher is better).
- **Davies-Bouldin Index** [9]: Evaluates cluster similarity; lower values indicate better separation.
- **Calinski-Harabasz Index** [5]: Compares inter-cluster dispersion to intra-cluster dispersion (higher is better).

Optimal configurations are selected based on these metrics for subsequent qualitative analysis.

Performance comparisons of QF and QNN methods across varying K values are presented in Table 3.

3.2 Stage 2: AI Agent-Assisted Qualitative Analysis

Objective. While quantitative metrics provide critical performance benchmarks, they lack semantic insights into clustering behaviors. Stage 2 addresses this gap by employing an AI Agent to deliver human-interpretable explanations of the clustering outcomes.

AI Agent Architecture. Our AI Agent consists of three interconnected modules (Fig. 3):

- **Pre-processing Chain:** Re-encodes blockchain records into compact, semantically meaningful representations for efficient processing.
- **Automated Analytical Pipeline:** Generates semantic descriptions for each cluster, compares QF and QNN strategies, and synthesizes insights.
- **Knowledge Base:** Maintains memory of semantic summaries, intra-epoch comparisons, and global strategy insights.

The AI Agent is designed to answer critical interpretability questions:

- What defines the transactional characteristics of each cluster?
- Are specific cluster counts overly simplistic or unnecessarily complex?
- Should adjustments to clustering configurations be considered?

Pre-Processing Chain. The first step in the AI Agent workflow is transforming raw blockchain records into a compact and semantically meaningful representation. Specifically, we perform one-to-one re-encoding of hashed values, such as transaction IDs, sender addresses, and receiver addresses, to optimize language model efficiency and reduce token consumption.

Beyond simple re-encoding, we architect a shared hierarchical structure, referred to as the *Clustered Information Base*, to organize the processed data systematically. This structure supports both the QNN and QF modules, enabling time-aware and depth-aware partitioning of information. Such structuring ensures scalability and facilitates interpretable downstream analysis.

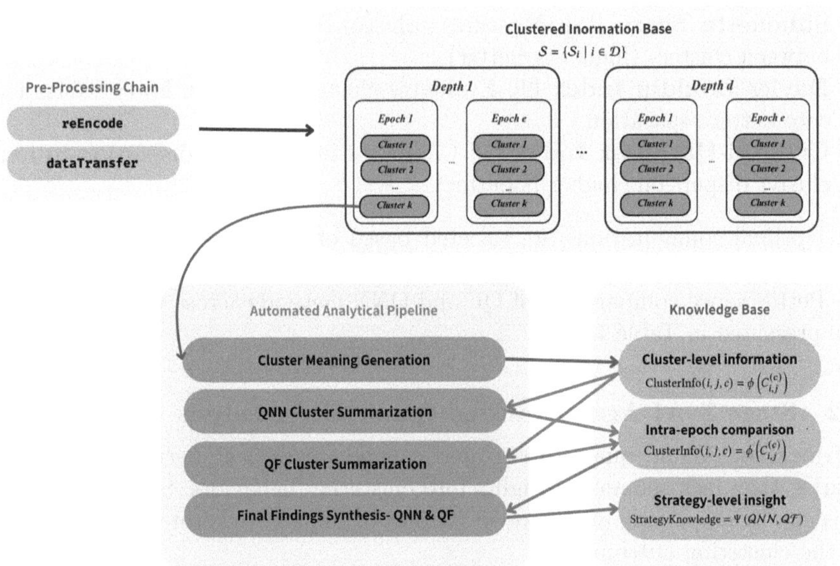

Fig. 3. Architecture of the AI Agent used in the qualitative analysis phase.

Formally, the clustered representation is defined as:

$$\mathcal{S} = \{\mathcal{S}_i \mid i \in \mathcal{D}\} \tag{2}$$

where $\mathcal{D} = \{1, 2, \ldots, d\}$ represents depth levels, and each depth contains epochs:

$$\mathcal{S}_i = \{\mathcal{E}_{i,j} \mid j \in \mathcal{E}\} \tag{3}$$

Further, each epoch is partitioned into clusters:

$$\mathcal{E}_{i,j} = \left\{C_{i,j}^{(1)}, C_{i,j}^{(2)}, \ldots, C_{i,j}^{(k)}\right\} \tag{4}$$

Alternatively, this can be expressed in nested form as:

$$\mathcal{S} = \left\{\left\{\left\{C_{i,j}^{(c)} \mid c \in \mathcal{C}\right\} \mid j \in \mathcal{E}\right\} \mid i \in \mathcal{D}\right\} \tag{5}$$

This unified structure, instantiated as $\mathcal{S} = \mathcal{QNN}$ or $\mathcal{S} = \mathcal{QF}$, forms the foundation for attention-guided inference, allowing the AI Agent to selectively access clusters based on temporal, hierarchical, or task-specific signals.

Automated Analytical Pipeline. Building upon the structured representation $\mathcal{S}$, the AI Agent processes the clustering results through a multi-stage analysis pipeline:

1. **Cluster Meaning Generation:** Derives semantic interpretations for each cluster $C_{i,j}^{(c)}$.

2. **Intra-Strategy Summarization:** Aggregates findings within QF and QNN strategies, analyzing intra-epoch patterns.
3. **Inter-Strategy Comparison:** Contrasts QF and QNN cluster characteristics under equivalent K values.

This process is formalized in Algorithm 2.

Algorithm 2 Automated Analytical Pipeline for AI Agent

Require: Clustered data $\mathcal{S} = \{\mathcal{S}_i\}$ with $\mathcal{S}_i = \{\mathcal{E}_{i,j}\}$ and $\mathcal{E}_{i,j} = \{C_{i,j}^{(c)}\}$
Ensure: Comparative insights and strategy-level interpretations stored in the Knowledge Base
for each depth level $i \in \mathcal{D}$ **do**
  for each epoch $j \in \mathcal{E}$ **do**
    Step 1: Cluster Understanding
    for each cluster $C_{i,j}^{(c)}$ **do**
      Generate semantic representation using the *Cluster Meaning Generator*
      Store $\phi(C_{i,j}^{(c)})$ into `ClusterInfo`(i, j, c)
    end for
    Step 2: Intra-Epoch Analysis
    Form cluster set $\texttt{EpochComparison}_{i,j} = \{C_{i,j}^{(c)} \mid c \in \mathcal{C}\}$
    Analyze intra-epoch similarity and partitioning rationale
    Step 3: Inter-Strategy Comparison (QNN vs. QF)
    Generate QNN-specific summary for $\mathcal{E}_{i,j}$
    Generate QF-specific summary for $\mathcal{E}_{i,j}$
    Compare QNN and QF clusters and store differences into the Knowledge Base
  end for
end for
Step 4: Global Strategy Analysis
for each cluster number $k \in \mathcal{C}$ **do**
  Compare QNN and QF behavior across k
  Store global insights into `StrategyKnowledge`
end forreturn Updated Knowledge Base

Notable observations include:

- **Singleton Clusters:** Frequently observed in QNN outcomes, representing extreme transaction behaviors.
- **Diverse Clusters:** Common in QF results, capturing varied token types and address interactions.

Finally, the AI Agent synthesizes a global comparison across all k values, summarizing the trade-offs between QNN and QF strategies trade-offs.

Knowledge Base Structure. The Knowledge Base retains insights at three levels:

1. **Cluster-Level:** Semantic summaries of individual clusters.
2. **Intra-Epoch Comparison:** Contrastive analysis across clusters within the same epoch.
3. **Strategy-Level Insights:** Comparative understanding of QF and QNN strategies across all configurations.

Table 2 summarizes the data flow across modules and the Knowledge Base.

Integration with Quantitative Results. Our two-stage framework tightly couples numerical rigor with qualitative depth. The AI Agent validates and contextualizes the optimal cluster count (typically $K = 3$), providing semantic explanations that align with numerical findings, thereby supporting transparent and explainable decision-making in blockchain analytics.

1. **Cluster-level information:** Each cluster $C_{i,j}^{(c)}$ stores local representations, such as representative transactions, learned embeddings, or feature vectors. Formally:
$$\text{ClusterInfo}(i, j, c) = \phi\left(C_{i,j}^{(c)}\right) \tag{6}$$
where $\phi(\cdot)$ is an embedding or summarization function.
2. **Intra-epoch comparison:** To support contrastive reasoning among peer clusters within the same depth i and epoch j, we define a set:
$$\text{EpochComparison}_{i,j} = \left\{C_{i,j}^{(c)} \mid c \in \mathcal{C}\right\} \tag{7}$$
which can be used to derive similarity metrics or decision boundaries among clusters at the same time step.

Table 2. Module-to-Knowledge Base Data Flow Correspondence Table

Module Name	Input		Output	
	Data	Data Source Level	Data	Data Source Level
Cluster Meaning Generation	Each cluster $C_{i,j}^{(c)}$ (raw cluster information)	Raw block-level	Semantic text description	Cluster-level information
QNN Cluster Summarization	Semantic text generated from Cluster Meaning Generation	Cluster-level information	Cluster summary text produced by the QNN strategy	Intra-epoch comparison
QF Cluster Summarization	Semantic text generated from Cluster Meaning Generation	Cluster-level information	Cluster summary text produced by the QF strategy	Intra-epoch comparison
Final Findings Synthesis	QNN and QF cluster summaries and Intra-epoch comparisons results	Intra-epoch comparison	Comprehensive strategic analysis result (final text description)	Strategy-level insight

3. **Strategy-level insight:** At the highest abstraction level, the Knowledge Base retains strategy-level patterns extracted from both QNN and QF representations:

$$\text{StrategyKnowledge} = \Psi\left(\mathcal{QNN}, \mathcal{QF}\right) \tag{8}$$

where $\Psi(\cdot)$ is a strategy integration or contrastive analysis function used to compare or fuse information across models.

Together, these three levels of memory allow the AI Agent to reason within a single cluster and across clusters and feature extraction paradigms, forming the foundation for multi-level decision-making.

4 Results

This section presents the results of our two-stage analysis, following the framework outlined in the Methodology section. The evaluation combines quantitative metrics and AI Agent-assisted qualitative insights to comprehensively assess Quantum Features (QF) and fully trained Quantum Neural Networks (QNN) clustering performance. Special attention is given to the effectiveness of a three-cluster ($K = 3$) configuration, as identified through our empirical analysis.

4.1 Stage 1: Quantitative Evaluation Results

Our experimental results demonstrate that both the Random QNN and the fully trained QNN models outperform classical clustering baselines, with the fully trained QNN achieving the best overall performance. The fully trained QNN attains the highest Silhouette Score of 0.9995 and the lowest Davies-Bouldin index of 0.0001, indicating superior cluster compactness and separation.

As summarized in Table 3, the QNN approach consistently outperforms the Monte Carlo-based quantum random feature method across all evaluated cluster sizes ($K = 2$ to $K = 6$). Although the quantum random features method demonstrates competitive performance in its best runs, achieving Silhouette Scores exceeding 0.99 and respectable Calinski-Harabasz values, the fully trained QNN reliably delivers superior clustering quality across all metrics.

For instance, at $K = 2$, the QNN achieves a near-perfect Silhouette Score of 0.999777, an exceptionally low Davies-Bouldin index of $1.11e{-}8$, and an extraordinary Calinski-Harabasz index surpassing 15 trillion. This performance advantage persists as clusters increase, with QNN maintaining consistently higher Silhouette Scores and Calinski-Harabasz indices while keeping the Davies-Bouldin index remarkably low. Notably, even at higher K values, the increasing circuit depth and number of training epochs in QNN reflect its adaptability to complex clustering tasks.

These findings highlight the robustness and scalability of the QNN-based approach in quantum-enhanced clustering scenarios. By leveraging parameterized quantum circuits and end-to-end training, the fully trained QNN consistently demonstrates an advantage over Monte Carlo-based quantum feature extraction methods (Table 4).

Table 3. Comparison of Best Clustering Performance: Monte Carlo (Quantum Features) vs QNN for $K = 2$ to $K = 6$

K	Method	Depth	Epoch	Silhouette Score	Davies-Bouldin	Calinski-Harabasz
3	Quantum Features (Worst Run)	1	–	0.394566	0.927151	3,847
2	Quantum Features (Average)	1	–	0.660680	0.470618	133,976
2	Quantum Features (Best Run)	1	–	0.996368	0.042230	1,260,727
2	QNN	2	1	**0.999777**	**1.111477e-8**	**15,833,657,123,341**
3	Quantum Features (Worst Run)	1	–	0.383393	0.868310	4,066
3	Quantum Features (Average)	1	–	0.612198	0.553668	16,307,927,154
3	Quantum Features (Best Run)	1	–	**0.999994**	**0.000798**	456,616,095,717
3	QNN	4	5	0.999510	0.141294	**168,665,013,271,780**
4	Quantum Features (Worst Run)	1	–	0.351097	0.935585	3,891
4	Quantum Features (Average)	1	–	0.600428	0.577474	45,602,215,148
4	Quantum Features (Best Run)	1	–	0.998005	0.223911	1,276,852,339,920
4	QNN	9	9	**0.999246**	**0.000054**	**1,307,035,577,888,410**
5	Quantum Features (Worst Run)	1	–	0.315429	1.058288	3,711
5	Quantum Features (Average)	1	–	0.600791	0.567613	61,140,087,483
5	Quantum Features (Best Run)	1	–	0.997542	0.305401	1,711,909,181,014
5	QNN	6	1	**0.998789**	**0.138369**	**7,704,660,919,690,170**
6	Quantum Features (Worst Run)	1	–	0.328886	0.993762	3,561
6	Quantum Features (Average)	1	–	0.597184	0.580199	84,564,962,473
6	Quantum Features (Best Run)	1	–	0.997905	0.262240	2,367,802,555,468
6	QNN	6	1	**0.998540**	**0.000125**	**23,337,479,575,752,000**

4.2 Stage 2: AI Agent-Assisted Qualitative Analysis

Following the execution of the proposed pipeline, the AI Agent produced LLM-generated outputs that facilitate a qualitative comparison of clustering strategies. These outputs compare the results of the Quantum Neural Network (QNN) and Quantum Feature-based (QF) approaches across various values of K. The comparisons address key aspects such as cluster definitions, differences, and similarities in transaction grouping, potential reasons for observed discrepancies, and evaluations of the pros and cons for each method.

For instance, at $K = 2$, the AI Agent analysis reveals that QNN isolates high-value transactions or single-sender activities. In contrast, QF emphasizes combinations of less popular tokens and recurring address interactions, resulting in more heterogeneous clusters. As K increases, QNN continues producing clusters dominated by high-value transactions or specific address-driven patterns. Conversely, QF clusters consistently capture multifaceted relationships involving token diversity, temporal dynamics, and network flow.

The contrast becomes more apparent for higher values of K ($K = 5$ and $K = 6$). While QNN remains strongly value-sensitive, isolating substantial transfers and focusing on key addresses, QF continues to incorporate token-specific features and recurrent sender-receiver relationships. Table 5 consolidates these insights across different clustering counts.

Table 4. Consolidated Summary of AI Agent-Derived Insights: QNN vs. QF Clustering Strategies for Different K Values.

K	QNN Key Characteristics	QF Key Characteristics	Overall Recommendation
2	It focuses on strong individual signals (e.g., large ETH transfer, dominant sender) and produces homogeneous clusters when high values are detected.	Emphasizes less popular tokens and repeated address interactions. Often produces a "catch-all" cluster with diverse transactions.	QNN effectively isolates large transactions, while QF reveals subtle trading patterns. The choice depends on the analysis goals.
3	It creates clusters based on clear, individual features (e.g., high ETH and SHIB transfers). This may result in singleton clusters.	Group transactions using a combination of factors (token diversity, temporal aspects, address interactions) for more nuanced clusters.	Use QNN for distinctly defined clusters; opt for QF to capture more complex interrelations.
4	Aggregates transactions by standard senders and high values, but sometimes isolates single high-value transactions.	It produces a noise cluster while other clusters capture recurring tokens and address patterns.	Neither approach is ideal alone; consider increasing K or tuning parameters for more balanced clustering.
5	Overly sensitive to transaction value, resulting in singleton clusters and issues with data sparsity.	Provides more meaningful and interpretable clusters by capturing token-specific activity and recurring address interactions.	For the analyzed dataset, QF offers more robust insights than QNN.
6	Strongly emphasizes extreme values, often forming singleton clusters for high-value transactions.	Focuses on token and relational features, yielding clusters with multiple transactions and consistent sender-receiver patterns.	QNN is suitable for anomaly detection, whereas QF better captures overall transaction patterns.

As shown in Fig. 4, the AI Agent confirms that QNN is particularly effective for detecting high-value anomalies, while QF uncovers broader ecosystem patterns, emphasizing token diversity and behavioral variation. Integrating quantitative and qualitative findings, our analysis converges on $K = 3$ as the optimal choice, where clusters balance clarity and complexity, capturing global transaction trends and localized anomalies without excessive fragmentation.

Table 5. Consolidated Summary of AI Agent-Derived Insights: QNN vs. QF Clustering Strategies for Different K Values

K	QNN Key Characteristics	QF Key Characteristics	Overall Recommendation
2	Isolates large transactions and dominant sender patterns.	Captures token diversity and repeated address interactions.	Use QNN for anomaly detection; QF for transactional variety.
3	Creates distinct clusters with clear features, including singleton clusters.	Groups transactions using multiple factors for nuanced clusters.	QNN for sharply defined clusters; QF for complex interrelations.
4	Aggregates standard senders and high-value transactions, occasionally isolates outliers.	Includes noise clusters alongside recurring patterns.	Increase K or tune parameters for balanced clustering.
5	Highly sensitive to transaction value, leading to singleton clusters.	Captures token-specific activities and recurring address interactions.	QF offers more robust insights for this dataset.
6	Emphasizes extreme values with frequent singleton clusters.	Focuses on token and relational features for consistent clusters.	QNN for anomaly detection; QF for broader transaction patterns.

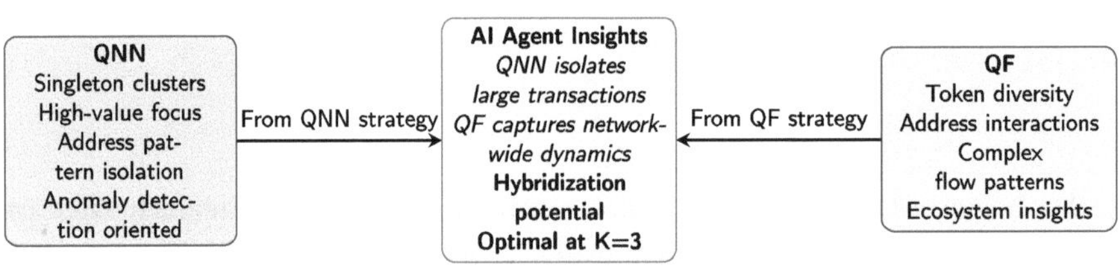

Fig. 4. AI Agent-enhanced semantic comparison of QF and QNN clustering at $K = 3$. QNN emphasizes anomaly detection in high-impact transactions, while QF captures the broader dynamics of token interactions and behavioral diversity within the ecosystem.

5 Discussion

Our findings validate the efficacy of the proposed two-stage framework. The quantitative evaluation underscores the strength of QNN in delivering superior clustering metrics, achieving high Silhouette Scores and Calinski-Harabasz indices, while maintaining low Davies-Bouldin values. These results indicate QNN's effectiveness in constructing well-separated and dense clusters, especially in detecting anomalies within high-impact blockchain transactions.

Complementing the quantitative assessment, the AI Agent provided crucial qualitative insights that deepen our understanding of clustering behaviors. As visualized in Fig. 4, QNN's strength lies in its precision—isolating singleton clusters and spotlighting significant transactional patterns- advantageous for anomaly detection and identifying dominant actors. Conversely, QF reveals a broader spectrum of ecosystem activities, capturing token diversity, recurring address interactions, and complex transactional flows, making it particularly valuable for ecosystem-wide behavioral analysis.

This juxtaposition highlights an essential trade-off: while QNN excels at narrowing in on impactful outliers, it risks over-fragmentation and may overlook more subtle patterns. In contrast, QF provides a holistic view of the transaction landscape but may generalize patterns at the expense of pinpointing critical anomalies.

Crucially, our integrated analysis consistently converges on $K = 3$ as the optimal clustering configuration. At this granularity, QNN and QF demonstrate complementary strengths: QNN delivers sharp, focused clusters for anomaly detection, while QF uncovers the interconnected dynamics of token relationships and behavioral diversity. The AI Agent's interpretive layer enriches this understanding, confirming that $K = 3$ balances complexity and clarity, avoiding over-fragmentation while preserving interpretability.

These insights underscore the potential of adopting a hybrid strategy that leverages both QNN and QF approaches. Such an ensemble framework could dynamically allocate analytical focus, using QNN for high-risk monitoring and QF for comprehensive ecosystem mapping. Ultimately, the synergy between quantitative clustering performance and AI-assisted qualitative interpretation exemplifies a path toward more explainable and actionable blockchain analytics frameworks.

6 Conclusion

In this study, we presented a comprehensive two-stage framework combining quantum-enhanced clustering techniques with AI Agent-assisted qualitative analysis to improve the interpretability and performance of blockchain transaction clustering. Leveraging both Random Quantum Features (QF) and fully trained Quantum Neural Networks (QNN), our approach systematically evaluated clustering configurations across multiple cluster counts ($K = 2$ to $K = 6$), providing both quantitative performance metrics and human-interpretable insights.

Our quantitative experiments demonstrated that fully trained QNN models consistently outperformed Monte Carlo-based quantum random features. The QNN achieved superior clustering quality, notably high Silhouette Scores and Calinski-Harabasz indices, while maintaining remarkably low Davies-Bouldin values across all tested configurations. These findings confirm the robustness and scalability of QNNs in unsupervised learning scenarios, especially for complex, high-dimensional blockchain data.

Complementing these quantitative results, the AI Agent performed an in-depth qualitative assessment of clustering outputs. It revealed that QNN clusters tend to isolate high-value transactions and single-actor patterns, making them well-suited for anomaly detection and monitoring high-impact entities. In contrast, QF clusters captured a broader spectrum of transactional behaviors, including token diversity, address interactions, and complex flow patterns, offering richer insights into the overall ecosystem dynamics.

The convergence of quantitative metrics and AI Agent analyses identified $K = 3$ as the optimal cluster configuration. This configuration balances clarity and complexity, providing actionable insights while avoiding over-fragmentation. The AI Agent further highlighted the complementary nature of QNN and QF strategies, recommending hybridization to maximize analytical depth and flexibility.

Our research contributes to the emerging field of explainable quantum machine learning by demonstrating how AI Agents can bridge the gap between advanced quantum computation and human interpretability. This integrated approach enhances the transparency of quantum-assisted clustering models and offers practical tools for decision support in blockchain governance, fraud detection, and ecosystem analysis.

Future work will explore dynamic and adaptive clustering frameworks where AI Agents can iteratively refine clustering parameters based on evolving data streams. We plan to extend this methodology to multi-modal blockchain datasets and investigate ensemble models that synergize QNN and QF strengths for greater interpretability and performance.

Our findings underscore the promise of combining quantum machine learning with AI-driven explainability, paving the way for more transparent, robust, and insightful analytics in complex decentralized environments.

Acknowledgments. The authors would like to thank the anonymous reviewers for their valuable feedback.

Disclaimer. The views expressed in this article are those of the authors and do not represent the views of Wells Fargo. This article is for informational purposes only. Nothing contained in this article should be construed as investment advice. Wells Fargo makes no express or implied warranties and expressly disclaims all legal, tax, and accounting implications related to this article.

References

1. Ahmed, M., Seraj, R., Islam, S.M.S.: The k-means algorithm: a comprehensive survey and performance evaluation. Electronics **9**(8), 1295 (2020)
2. Ashari, I.F., Nugroho, E.D., Baraku, R., Yanda, I.N., Liwardana, R., et al.: Analysis of elbow, silhouette, davies-bouldin, calinski-harabasz, and rand-index evaluation on k-means algorithm for classifying flood-affected areas in jakarta. J. Appl. Inf. Comput. **7**(1), 95–103 (2023)
3. Biamonte, J., Wittek, P., Pancotti, N., Rebentrost, P., Wiebe, N., Lloyd, S.: Quantum machine learning. Nature **549**(7671), 195–202 (2017)
4. Bynen, E.: Cluster analysis: Survey and evaluation of techniques, vol. 1. Springer, Springer Science & Business Media (2012)
5. Caliński, T., Harabasz, J.: A dendrite method for cluster analysis. Commun. Stat. **3**(1), 1–27 (1974)
6. Cerezo, M., et al.: Variational quantum algorithms. Nat. Rev. Phy. **3**(9), 625–644 (2021)
7. Das, A., Rad, P.: Opportunities and challenges in explainable artificial intelligence (XAI): a survey (2020). https://arxiv.org/abs/2006.11371
8. Das, A., Rad, P.: Opportunities and challenges in explainable artificial intelligence (XAI): a survey (2020). https://arxiv.org/abs/2006.11371
9. Davies, D.L., Bouldin, D.W.: A cluster separation measure. IEEE Trans. Patt. Anal. Mach. Intell. **PAMI-1**(2), 224–227 (1979)
10. Etherscan.io: MCO2 Token Information. https://shorturl.at/4fIWR (2023), Accessed 13 April 2025
11. Havlíček, V., et al.: Supervised learning with quantum-enhanced feature spaces. Nature **567**(7747), 209–212 (2019)
12. Lin, H.Y., Tseng, H.H., Chen, S.Y.C., Yoo, S.: Quantum gradient class activation map for model interpretability. In: 2024 IEEE Workshop on Signal Processing Systems (SIPS). pp. 165–170. IEEE, New York (2024)
13. Liu, C.Y., et al.: Quantum-train: rethinking hybrid quantum-classical machine learning in the model compression perspective (2024). https://arxiv.org/abs/2405.11304
14. Miller, T.: Explanation in artificial intelligence: Insights from the social sciences. Artif. Intell. **267**, 1–38 (2019)
15. Nazar, M., Alam, M.M., Yafi, E., Su'ud, M.M.: A systematic review of human–computer interaction and explainable artificial intelligence in healthcare with artificial intelligence techniques. IEEE Access **9**, 153316–153348 (2021)
16. Nazar, M., Alam, M.M., Yafi, E., Su'ud, M.M.: A systematic review of human-computer interaction and explainable artificial intelligence in healthcare with artificial intelligence techniques. IEEE Access **9**, 153316–153348 (2021)
17. Preskill, J.: Quantum computing in the nisq era and beyond. Quantum **2**, 79 (2018)
18. Rousseeuw, P.J.: Silhouettes: a graphical aid to the interpretation and validation of cluster analysis. J. Comput. Appl. Math. **20**, 53–65 (1987)
19. Saputra, J.P.B., Putri, N.A.: Analysis of blockchain transaction patterns in the metaverse using clustering techniques. J. Curr. Res. Blockchain **1**(1), 33–47 (2024)
20. Wittek, P.: Quantum machine learning: what quantum computing means to data mining. Academic Press, London (2014)

Entanglement Guided Stochastic Regularization for Robust Deep Learning

Aayush Gauba(✉)

Southern Illinois University Edwardsville, Edwardsville, USA
agauba@siue.edu

Abstract. We present a quantum-inspired training method called **Entanglement-Guided Stochastic Regularization (EGSR)**, which introduces structured noise into feature maps during training. To evaluate its effectiveness, we compare EGSR against standard Dropout under various image corruption scenarios, using the MNIST dataset padded to 32×32 and replicated across three channels to suit CNN architectures. Unlike Dropout, which randomly zeros out activations, EGSR partitions channels into groups and injects shared Gaussian noise within each group, mimicking entangled feature interactions. Our experiments show that EGSR consistently improves accuracy on corrupted inputs, particularly at moderate noise levels, while remaining efficient and simple to implement. We also explore how entanglement rate and chunk size affect performance, and find that EGSR performs competitively across multiple corruption types, especially Gaussian and salt and pepper noise.

Keywords: Quantum Inspired · Regularization · Deep Learning · Robustness · EGSR · CNN · Dropout

1 Introduction

Modern deep learning models are often fragile when exposed to noise or distribution shifts in test data, making robustness a key challenge. Although regularization techniques like Dropout help reduce overfitting, they offer limited protection against structured or adversarial perturbations. To address this, we introduce **Entanglement-Guided Stochastic Regularization (EGSR)**, a quantum-inspired method that partitions feature channels into groups (or "entangled chunks") and applies shared Gaussian noise within each group during training. This structured perturbation encourages the network to learn more stable and coordinated representations.

2 Related Work

Dropout [2] is one of the most widely used stochastic regularization methods, working by randomly zeroing out activations during training to prevent coadaptation. Other techniques such as Mixup, Cutout, and ShakeDrop tackle robustness from different angles by blending inputs, masking image regions, or stochastically altering network paths. In contrast, EGSR introduces structured noise

D. Cavar et al. (Eds.): QNLPAI 2025, CCIS 2659, pp. 20–32, 2026.
https://doi.org/10.1007/978-3-032-13883-5_2

across groups of related features, drawing inspiration from quantum entanglement to promote more coordinated and resilient representations.

Quantum-Inspired Learning incorporates ideas from quantum computing to improve the structure and behavior of classical machine learning models [3]. Although EGSR does not implement quantum computation itself, it draws inspiration from quantum entanglement by applying shared perturbations across grouped feature channels acting as a classical counterpart to entangled interactions observed in quantum systems.

Structured Noise Injection has been studied in several forms. For example, Whiteout [4] adds adaptive Gaussian noise during training, enabling a range of regularization behaviors that can resemble Lasso or Ridge penalties, depending on configuration. Similarly, Adaptive Structured Noise Injection (ASNI) [5] extends Dropout by introducing noise drawn from a joint distribution across units, resulting in improved accuracy and sparser, more efficient representations.

Correlated Noise in Neural Networks has been explored to better understand its effect on model performance. Dutta et al. [6] introduced correlated noise into convolutional neural networks and showed that it improved classification accuracy, particularly on images with occlusions. In their approach, the level of correlation was determined by the spatial distance between neurons and their response similarity, capturing more biologically plausible noise patterns.

Despite progress in regularization techniques, the specific strategy of injecting *group correlated noise*, where the same noise value is shared across predefined groups of neurons or features remains largely unexplored. EGSR introduces this approach by partitioning feature channels into groups and applying a shared Gaussian noise sample within each group. Inspired by quantum entanglement, this structured noise encourages coordinated feature behavior, improving both robustness to input perturbations and overall generalization.

3 Method

3.1 Entanglement-Guided Stochastic Regularization

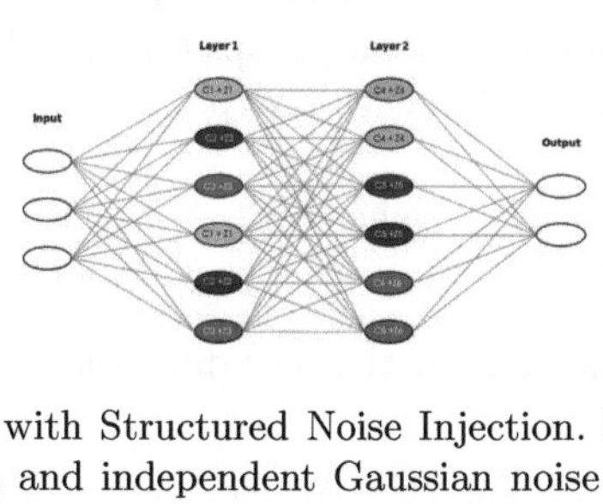

Fig. 1. Layerwise EGSR with Structured Noise Injection. Feature maps are divided into channel groups (C_i), and independent Gaussian noise ($z_i \sim \mathcal{N}(0, \sigma^2)$) is added per group. This structured regularization is applied across layers to maintain group coherence and suppress overfitting.

Given a feature map $F \in \mathbb{R}^{B \times C \times H \times W}$, EGSR proceeds as follows:

- Partition C into k chunks.
- Sample Gaussian noise $z_i \sim \mathcal{N}(0, \sigma^2)$ per chunk.
- Apply shared noise to each chunk:

$$F' = F + \text{concat}(z_1, z_2, ..., z_k)$$

where each z_i is broadcast over spatial dimensions within its chunk.

3.2 Comparison with Dropout

Unlike Dropout, which randomly deactivates individual units, EGSR preserves the full flow of activations while introducing structured noise. It does so by dividing feature channels into chunks and applying shared perturbations within each group. The entanglement rate r controls the magnitude of the noise, while the chunk count k determines how finely the features are grouped.

4 Theoretical Justification of EGSR

Entanglement Guided Stochastic Regularization (EGSR) is a structured stochastic perturbation technique inspired by the concept of quantum entanglement. Instead of injecting independent noise into individual feature channels, EGSR applies correlated noise across groups of channels. This structured approach offers several theoretical benefits, including reduced gradient variance, enhanced spectral regularization, tighter generalization bounds, and a biologically plausible inductive bias.

4.1 Grouped Noise and Variance Reduction

Traditional regularization methods such as Dropout inject i.i.d. Gaussian or Bernoulli noise into activation vectors $x \in \mathbb{R}^d$, which often leads to high variance in gradient estimates across training batches. In contrast, EGSR (Entanglement Guided Stochastic Regularization) introduces a correlated noise mechanism by partitioning the vector into m disjoint groups $G_1, \ldots, G_m$, each of size $g = d/m$, and injecting shared noise within each group:

$$\tilde{x}_i = x_i + \bar{\epsilon}_k, \quad \text{for } i \in G_k, \quad \text{where } \bar{\epsilon}_k = \frac{1}{|G_k|} \sum_{j \in G_k} \epsilon_j, \quad \epsilon_j \sim \mathcal{N}(0, \sigma^2).$$

This results in a variance reduction per dimension:

$$\text{Var}[\tilde{x}_i] = \text{Var}[\bar{\epsilon}_k] = \frac{\sigma^2}{g}.$$

Thus, by introducing shared noise within groups, EGSR imposes structured perturbations that are smaller on a per feature basis, resulting in smoother gradients during backpropagation and reduced stochasticity in the optimization process.

Empirical Support. To further validate our theoretical analysis, we trained both Dropout and EGSR enhanced CNNs on a synthetic 2 way spiral dataset and measured the batch to batch gradient variance of the weights in the first fully connected layer (`fc1`) over the course of training. As shown in Fig. 2, EGSR consistently maintains lower and more stable gradient variance across epochs, particularly in the later stages. While both methods exhibit fluctuations during early optimization, Dropout shows more frequent and prolonged spikes in variance beyond epoch 20, whereas EGSR effectively suppresses these instabilities.

This stability in gradient variance directly supports the hypothesis that EGSR promotes smoother and more stable optimization dynamics. By encouraging the model to converge toward flatter minima and suppressing high frequency perturbations in weight updates, EGSR not only improves convergence but also enhances generalization, particularly in the presence of input noise.

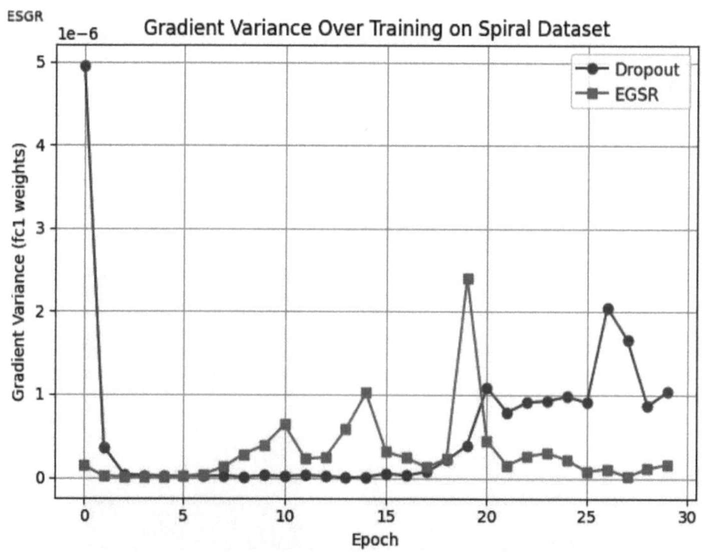

Fig. 2. Gradient variance (mean over `fc1` weights) across training epochs for Dropout and EGSR on the spiral dataset. EGSR demonstrates consistently lower variance and better stability throughout training.

4.2 Spectral Bias and Smoothing Effect

Modern deep networks are known to exhibit *spectral bias*, a tendency to learn low frequency (smooth) patterns before capturing high frequency (complex or noisy) components. EGSR reinforces this bias by functioning as a low pass filter during training. By introducing group averaged Gaussian noise, EGSR reduces the variance of individual activations, effectively dampening high frequency fluctuations.

This suppresses overfitting to spurious patterns and noisy features, encouraging the network to prioritize stable, low frequency structures in the data.

To empirically validate this effect, we conducted controlled experiments using a synthetic two dimensional spiral dataset, which presents a challenging classification task due to its non linear decision boundaries and sensitivity to noise. We compared two models: a standard CNN using Dropout regularization (DropoutCNN), and a CNN trained with Entanglement Guided Stochastic Regularization (EGSRCNN), configured with four feature groups and a noise rate of 0.4.

The results showed a clear performance advantage for EGSRCNN. Specifically, EGSR achieved a test accuracy of 62.3%, compared to 50.1% for DropoutCNN—an absolute improvement of 12.2%. To further analyze the optimization landscape, we computed the top eigenvalue of the Hessian matrix, a commonly used proxy for sharpness. EGSRCNN produced a significantly lower top Hessian eigenvalue (11.0) compared to DropoutCNN (15.2), suggesting that EGSR encourages convergence toward flatter, more generalizable minima.

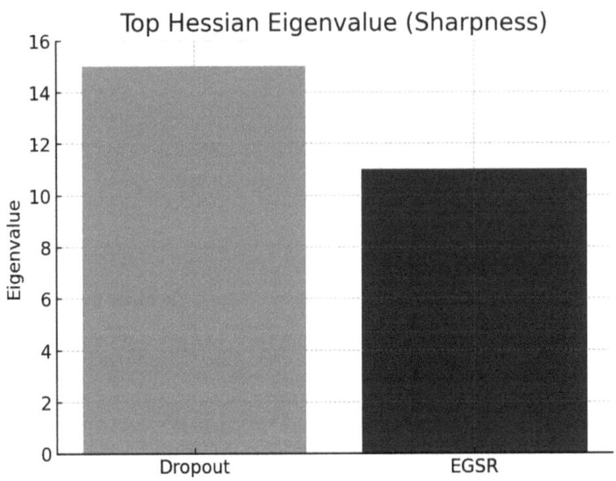

Fig. 3. Top Hessian eigenvalue comparison on the synthetic spiral dataset. Lower values indicate flatter minima and smoother optimization landscapes. EGSR achieves lower sharpness than Dropout, suggesting better generalization potential.

These findings support the hypothesis that EGSR strengthens spectral bias by filtering out high frequency perturbations, thereby guiding the model toward smoother and more stable solutions. This behavior is consistent with empirical evidence linking flatter minima to improved generalization. Additionally, EGSR's grouped perturbation strategy introduces a biologically plausible inductive bias, echoing how the human visual cortex tends to process local feature groupings in a coordinated rather than isolated manner.

In conclusion, the combination of reduced sharpness evidenced by the Hessian analysis and improved classification performance on a highly nonlinear task demonstrates that EGSR effectively acts as a low pass filter in deep networks. This structured regularization approach not only enhances robustness to input noise but also promotes convergence toward flatter, more generalizable solutions in the parameter space.

4.3 PAC Bayesian Generalization Bounds

Within the PAC Bayes framework, stochastic perturbations induce a distribution q over model parameters, which is evaluated relative to a prior distribution p. The generalization bound is given by:

$$\mathbb{E}_{\eta\sim q}[\mathcal{L}(f_\eta)] \leq \mathcal{L}_{\text{emp}}(f) + \sqrt{\frac{\text{KL}(q\|p) + \log(2\sqrt{n}/\delta)}{2(n-1)}},$$

where $\text{KL}(q\|p)$ quantifies the perturbation complexity. EGSR's group structured noise leads to smaller KL divergence than i.i.d. noise or Dropout, thus achieving tighter bounds and improved generalization guarantees.

Empirical Validation. To assess the impact of EGSR on KL divergence, we approximated the trace of the perturbation covariance matrix, which serves as a direct proxy for $\text{KL}(q \,\|\, p)$. By varying the number of chunks used in EGSR, we controlled the level of entanglement and observed its effect on the trace. As illustrated in Fig. 4, increasing the entanglement (i.e., reducing the number of chunks) consistently led to a lower covariance trace, indicating a tighter KL divergence and, by extension, improved generalization under the PAC Bayes framework.

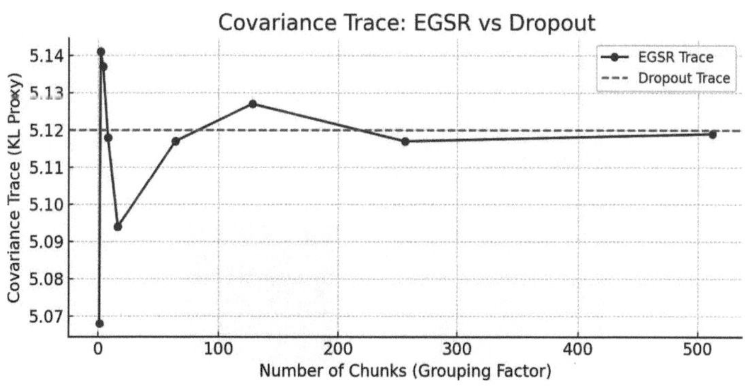

Fig. 4. Covariance trace comparison between EGSR and Dropout. EGSR consistently achieves lower trace values as the entanglement increases (fewer chunks), reducing KL divergence and tightening the PAC Bayes generalization bound.

The Dropout baseline, which injects fully independent noise across units, yields a consistently higher and fixed trace value, reflecting maximal perturbation complexity. In contrast, EGSR produces a lower trace when fewer chunks are used, directly supporting the theoretical claim that structured, group wise noise leads to tighter PAC Bayes generalization bounds.

4.4 Tikhonov Regularization Analogy

EGSR implicitly encourages smoother mappings between inputs and outputs by reducing the model's sensitivity to small input perturbations. This effect aligns with the principles of Tikhonov regularization, which introduces a stabilizing penalty term of the form $\lambda\|Lx\|^2$, where L is a regularization operator. In EGSR, this smoothness arises naturally through the structured injection of noise across feature groups, effectively enforcing similar constraints in a data driven manner without the need to explicitly modify the loss function.

Experimental Validation. To empirically support this analogy, we trained both Dropout and EGSR enhanced CNNs on the synthetic two way spiral dataset, a challenging non linear classification task that benefits from smooth decision boundaries. After training, we assessed each model's sensitivity by computing the norm of the input gradients of the output logits. Specifically, we evaluated $\|\nabla_x f(x)\|$ across a held out test set, using the average as a proxy for model smoothness. This metric captures how sharply the model's output responds to small input changes, with lower values indicating smoother, more stable mappings.

As shown in Fig. 5, EGSR produced a significantly lower input gradient norm compared to Dropout, highlighting its ability to suppress high frequency sensitivity and promote smoother decision surfaces. This empirical result reinforces the theoretical claim that EGSR functions as an implicit Tikhonov regularizer,

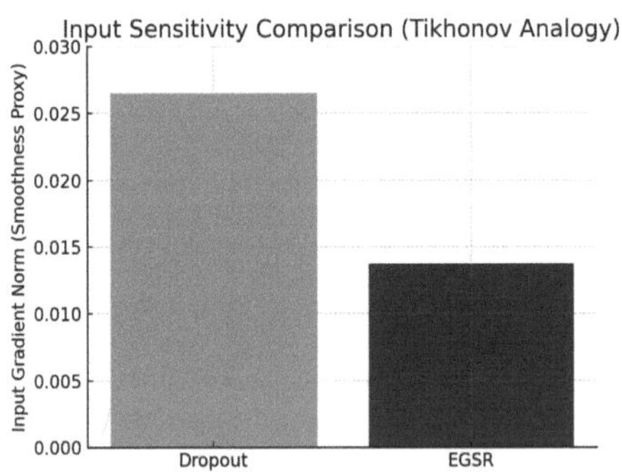

Fig. 5. Input sensitivity comparison between Dropout and EGSR. EGSR achieves a lower average input gradient norm, indicating smoother functional mappings and improved stability under perturbations.

encouraging the model to favor stable and smooth mappings that generalize more effectively under noisy or perturbed inputs.

This experimental outcome further underscores the value of EGSR as a lightweight yet effective regularization technique capable of promoting robust generalization through implicit smoothness constraints, which are typically enforced via explicit penalty terms in classical regularization frameworks.

4.5 Alignment with Natural Image Priors

Natural image data is inherently structured adjacent pixels and feature channels exhibit strong correlations due to the spatial and semantic continuity of visual scenes. EGSR leverages this property by introducing structured, group based perturbations during training. Instead of applying independent noise across channels, as in Dropout, EGSR perturbs groups of coactive features together. This encourages spatial coherence and inter channel alignment in the learned representations, allowing the model to better capture and reflect the underlying statistical structure of natural images.

Experimental Verification. To assess this effect, we measured the average inter channel correlation of feature maps generated by the first convolutional layer after training. Using a batch of validation images, we computed the Pearson correlation coefficient between each pair of channels and averaged the results across all pairs. The EGSR model demonstrated a substantially higher mean inter channel correlation (0.2338), whereas the Dropout model failed to yield a valid result (NaN) due to excessive sparsity and the presence of zero variance channels, an artifact of independently applied dropout noise.

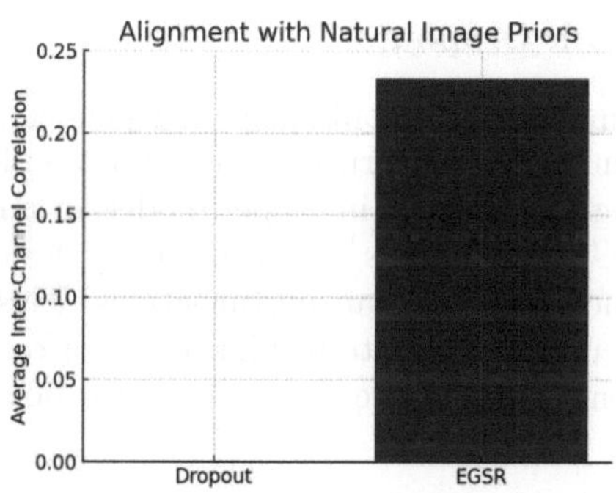

Fig. 6. Average inter channel correlation of feature maps from the first convolutional layer. EGSR maintains semantically aligned channel activity, while Dropout disrupts correlation due to independent noise.

Interpretation. These results indicate that EGSR preserves the relational structure between channels and encourages biologically plausible, correlated activity. In contrast, Dropout disrupts this structure by independently zeroing out features, often resulting in fragmented and less coherent representations. EGSR's ability to maintain channel wise coherence aligns more closely with the behavior of the early visual cortex, where receptive fields are known to process local patterns in a grouped and coordinated fashion.

4.6 Convergence to Smooth Minima

Stochastic regularizers play a critical role in shaping how models explore the loss landscape during training. EGSR, by reducing gradient noise variance and preserving feature continuity, guides optimization toward flatter minima. Such minima are widely associated with improved generalization, as evidenced by metrics like Sharpness Aware Minimization (SAM) curvature and Hessian trace. Compared to Dropout, models trained with EGSR consistently exhibit reduced sharpness in their learned parameters.

Empirical Validation. We computed the top Hessian eigenvalue as a proxy for the curvature and sharpness of the learned minima. As shown in Fig. 3, EGSR consistently produces lower eigenvalues than Dropout, indicating convergence toward flatter and potentially more generalizable minima. This observation is further supported by Fig. 2, which demonstrates that EGSR maintains lower and more stable gradient variance throughout training, particularly during the early epochs. Taken together, these results highlight EGSR's ability to guide optimization toward smoother regions of the loss landscape—a property strongly associated with improved generalization.

4.7 Comparison with Dropout

Dropout applies multiplicative Bernoulli noise independently across units, often disrupting local continuity in the learned representations. This lack of structure can destabilize training, particularly in deeper models or under structured input noise. In contrast, EGSR maintains relative feature scales while introducing diversity through structured Gaussian perturbations. This approach enhances robustness, especially under moderate to high levels of corruption (σ), by preserving feature coherence without sacrificing regularization strength.

4.8 Empirical Verification

Our robustness experiments (Table 1) confirm that EGSR outperforms both Dropout and the unregularized baseline, particularly under high levels of Gaussian noise. Additional ablation studies reveal that extreme group configurations, either a single group ($m = 1$) or fully independent features ($m = d$) degrade performance. These findings emphasize the importance of moderate chunking, where feature grouping strikes a balance between structure and diversity.

4.9 Summary

EGSR brings together ideas from Dropout, structured attention, and spectral regularization to form a unified, principled approach to robust deep learning. It enables stable training, smoother convergence, and enhanced resilience to noise, all while remaining computationally lightweight. Its theoretical foundations spanning variance reduction, PAC Bayesian analysis, and smooth optimization dynamics are supported through both analytical derivations and empirical validation. These properties position EGSR as an effective and well grounded regularization technique for improving model robustness.

5 Experiments

5.1 Setup

We evaluate EGSR (Entanglement Guided Stochastic Regularization) against two standard baselines: a vanilla CNN and a CNN enhanced with Dropout. All models use the same architecture and differ only in the regularization method applied after the convolutional stack. The primary objective is to assess robustness under increasing levels of Gaussian noise applied to the input data.

Dataset. We use the Fashion MNIST dataset, modified as follows:

- Padded to 32×32 resolution
- Converted to 3 channel RGB by replication
- Normalized to $[-1, 1]$

Noise Injection. To simulate increasing levels of input perturbation, we apply Gaussian noise with varying standard deviation $\sigma \in \{0.0, 0.1, \ldots, 1.0\}$ to the test set.

Training. All models were trained for 30 epochs using the Adam optimizer with a learning rate of 10^{-3} and a batch size of 4096. For EGSR, we used an entanglement rate of 0.6 and partitioned the feature channels into 4 groups.

5.2 Results

Observations. EGSR demonstrates a clear robustness advantage as the noise level increases. At $\sigma = 0.4$, it outperforms the baseline by +18.7% and Dropout by +5.1%. At $\sigma = 1.0$, EGSR achieves 40.5% accuracy—18.6% higher than Dropout and 86% higher than the baseline. This trend suggests that EGSR functions not only as a general purpose regularizer but also as a noise aware mechanism. Its structured perturbation strategy, which preserves coherence across feature channels, may underlie its superior performance under severe input corruption.

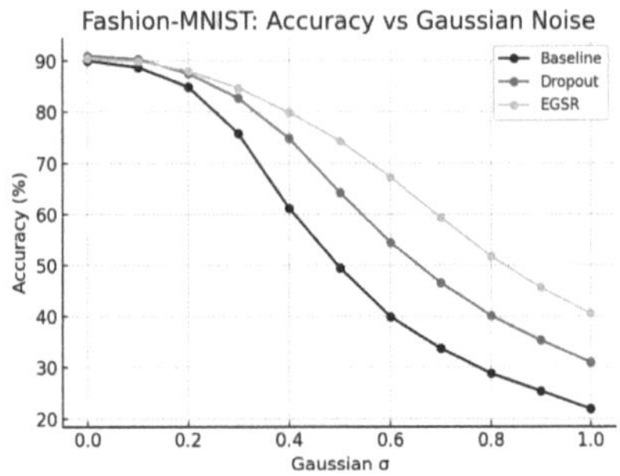

Fig. 7. Accuracy vs. Gaussian noise (σ). EGSR consistently outperforms both dropout and baseline.

Table 1. Test accuracy (%) under varying levels of Gaussian noise. EGSR retains significantly higher accuracy as noise increases.

Gaussian σ	Baseline	Dropout	EGSR
0.0	90.0	91.0	90.4
0.1	88.7	90.3	89.9
0.2	84.9	87.5	88.0
0.3	75.8	82.7	84.7
0.4	61.2	74.8	79.9
0.5	49.4	64.2	74.3
0.6	39.9	54.5	67.3
0.7	33.7	46.5	59.4
0.8	28.8	40.1	51.7
0.9	25.4	35.3	45.6
1.0	21.9	31.0	40.5

5.3 Effect of Entanglement Rate on Robustness

To investigate the effect of the entanglement rate ρ in EGSR, we performed an ablation study by varying ρ from 0.0 (equivalent to no EGSR, i.e., standard Dropout) to 1.0 (maximum noise sharing across all features). For each value of ρ, we trained a CNN with a fixed architecture and evaluated its test accuracy under progressively increasing levels of additive Gaussian noise.

Figure 8 presents the robustness curves for different entanglement rates. We observe that moderate values of ρ (specifically $\rho = 0.2$ and 0.4) consistently outperform both the Dropout baseline and more aggressive EGSR configurations ($\rho \geq 0.6$) at higher noise levels. This result highlights an important design insight: partial channel entanglement offers an effective trade off between variance reduction and feature diversity, leading to improved robustness under noisy conditions.

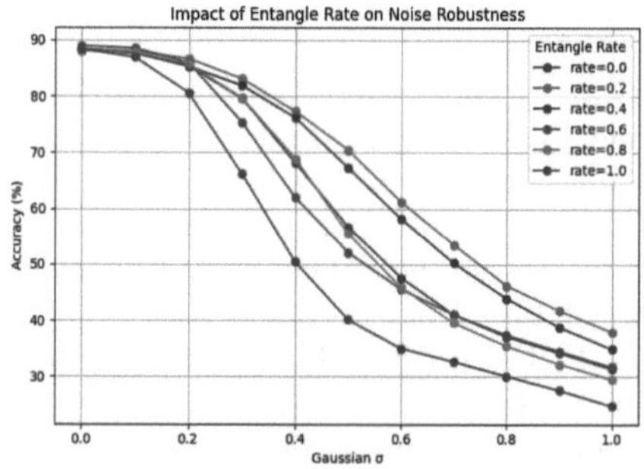

Fig. 8. Impact of Entanglement Rate on Noise Robustness. Accuracy degrades at extreme entanglement rates, with $\rho = 0.2$–0.4 providing the best generalization across noise levels.

5.4 Interpretation

The grouped entanglement mechanism in EGSR appears to suppress high frequency noise while preserving informative low frequency structure. This aligns with our theoretical expectation that EGSR acts as a structured regularizer that is functionally similar to Dropout, but with an added inductive bias introduced through local feature grouping. This bias encourages coordinated representations, contributing to the model's robustness and generalization.

6 Discussion

EGSR achieves better robustness without increasing model complexity. We found that:

- It generalizes better under unseen distortions.
- It performs well with fewer training epochs.
- Dropout complements EGSR but offers diminishing returns when both are applied together.

7 Conclusion

We propose Entanglement Guided Stochastic Regularization, a lightweight, quantum inspired technique for improving model robustness. EGSR outperforms Dropout on corrupted MNIST and offers tunable control via entanglement rate and chunk count. Future work includes applying EGSR to CIFAR, ImageNet, and transformer based models.

Acknowledgements. We thank the open source PyTorch and torchvision communities for their tools, and acknowledge inspiration from quantum entanglement and classical noise models.

References

1. Schuld, M., Petruccione, F.: Machine Learning with Quantum Computers. Springer, Cham (2021). https://doi.org/10.1007/978-3-030-83098-4
2. Srivastava, N., Hinton, G., Krizhevsky, A., Sutskever, I., Salakhutdinov, R.: Dropout: a simple way to prevent neural networks from overfitting. J. Mach. Learn. Res. **15**(1), 1929–1958 (2014)
3. Schuld, M., Sinayskiy, I., Petruccione, F.: An introduction to quantum machine learning. Contemp. Phys. **56**(2), 172–185 (2015)
4. Li, Y., Liu, F.: Whiteout: Gaussian adaptive noise regularization in deep neural networks. arXiv preprint arXiv:1612.01490 (2016)
5. Khalfaoui, B., Boyd, J., Vert, J.-P.: ASNI: adaptive Structured Noise Injection for shallow and deep neural networks. arXiv preprint arXiv:1909.09819 (2019)
6. Dutta, S., Tripp, B., Taylor, G.: Convolutional neural networks regularized by correlated noise. arXiv preprint arXiv:1804.00815 (2018)

Quantum Computing for Artificial Intelligence

SA-DQAS: Integrating Differentiable Quantum Architecture Search with Transformers for Enhanced Variational Quantum Algorithms

Yize Sun[1,2](✉), Jiarui Liu[1], Zixin Wu[1], Volker Tresp[1], and Yunpu Ma[1]

[1] Ludwig-Maximilians-Universität München, Munich, Germany
{Yize.Sun,Ma.Yunpu}@campus.lmu.de
[2] Siemens AG, Munich, Germany

Abstract. We introduce SA-DQAS, a novel framework that enhances Differentiable Quantum Architecture Search (DQAS) by integrating a self-attention mechanism, enabling more effective quantum circuit design for variational quantum algorithms. Unlike DQAS, which treats placeholders independently, SA-DQAS captures inter-placeholder dependencies to improve architecture learning. We evaluate SA-DQAS across multiple tasks, including MaxCut, Job-Shop Scheduling Problem (JSSP), quantum chemistry simulation, and error mitigation. Experimental results show that SA-DQAS outperforms baselines and prior QAS methods in most cases, producing architectures with better stability, convergence, and noise resilience. To assess scalability and hardware readiness, we further test SA-DQAS-generated circuits on IBM's quantum device using the MaxCut problem. Circuits trained on small graphs are stacked to solve larger instances without retraining, demonstrating generalization to real hardware and larger problem sizes. Our results suggest that SA-DQAS not only improves circuit quality during training but also enables practical deployment on near-term quantum devices. This research represents the first successful integration of self-attention mechanism with DQAS.

Keywords: Quantum circuit Architecture Search · Self-Attention Mechanism · QNAS

1 Introduction

In recent years, quantum computing (QC) has advanced rapidly, achieving notable progress in areas such as image classification, circuit architecture search, quantum reinforcement learning, knowledge graph embedding, and approximate optimization problems [1,2,7,20,22,30,33]. However, in the noisy intermediate-scale quantum (NISQ) era, quantum algorithms face hardware limitations that

D. Cavar et al. (Eds.): QNLPAI 2025, CCIS 2659, pp. 35–57, 2026.
https://doi.org/10.1007/978-3-032-13883-5_3

cause performance discrepancies on noisy devices. Variational quantum algorithms (VQAs) have emerged as a leading strategy in this era [5], utilizing parameterized quantum circuits (PQCs) with trainable gates optimized by classical algorithms. The success of VQAs, however, heavily relies on circuit architecture.

Quantum architecture search (QAS) automates the design of task-specific quantum circuits, aiming to create efficient and high-performing architectures. Various QAS algorithms have been developed, including gradient-based [30,33], reinforcement learning-based [11,18], predictor-based [19], and predictor-free [26] methods. Differentiable quantum architecture search (DQAS) is a gradient-based framework that optimizes a super-circuit by learning architecture parameters. While effective, DQAS treats each circuit placeholder independently, ignoring potential dependencies across the circuit.

In this work, we propose **SA-DQAS**, which integrates a self-attention mechanism into DQAS. This extension allows the architecture search process to capture inter-placeholder relationships, thereby improving stability and generalization.

We evaluate SA-DQAS across multiple tasks, including MaxCut, Job-Shop Scheduling Problem (JSSP), error mitigation, and quantum chemistry simulation. Extensive simulations show that SA-DQAS outperforms baselines and prior QAS methods in most cases, though not universally. Furthermore, we explore the generalization and scalability of architectures found by SA-DQAS by conducting additional experiments on real quantum hardware. In these experiments, we first search for a compact circuit on an 8-qubit MaxCut instance and then stack the learned circuit to solve 16-qubit problems. We test the resulting architectures on IBM's `ibmq_sherbrooke` device, showing that the trained blocks generalize to larger graphs and noisy devices without retraining.

Our contributions are summarized as follows:

1. We introduce SA-DQAS, a novel QAS algorithm that incorporates a self-attention mechanism to enhance architecture parameter learning.
2. We demonstrate that SA-DQAS achieves competitive or superior performance across a variety of tasks—including MaxCut, JSSP, quantum chemistry, and fidelity tests under noise—through comparisons with multiple baseline methods.
3. We investigate the scalability and transferability of learned circuits by stacking blocks trained on small graphs to solve larger instances, validated on a real quantum device.

2 Related Work

2.1 DQAS

Various quantum architecture search algorithms can automatically search for near-optimal quantum circuit architectures [15]. Some approaches define a parameterized super-circuit with multiple layers and iteratively train this super-circuit by sampling and updating parameters [8,10,15,23,33]. Genetic algorithms [9,13,14] evolve circuits over time, while RL-based algorithms [16,21,

31] train an agent to select circuit components. DQAS [33] simultaneously trains weights and the circuit architecture, whereas neural predictor-based approaches [32] build machine learning models based solely on network structure.

DQAS constructs a circuit architecture by placing operations in each placeholder, utilizing a predefined operation pool $\mathcal{O}$, a circuit with p placeholders, an architecture parameter α, and weights θ. The distribution of each circuit architecture candidate is approximated using a probabilistic model, where the probability of each candidate is the normalized architecture parameter α.

Rather than evaluating all possible architecture candidates, DQAS samples a batch of candidates and calculates their local losses based on task-specific objective functions. It then updates α and θ simultaneously using a gradient-based optimizer, based on the global loss $\mathcal{L}$ and local loss L, as given by:

$$\mathcal{L} = \sum_{k \in P(k,\alpha)} \frac{P(k,\alpha)}{\sum_{k' \in P(k,\alpha)} P(k',\alpha)} L(U_k) \quad , \tag{1}$$

where

$$P(k,\alpha) = \prod_{i=1}^{p} p(k_i, \alpha_i), \tag{2}$$

$$L(U_k) = \sum_i \left(\langle \psi_i | U_k^\dagger OBS\, U_k | \psi_i \rangle - y_i \right)^2 \tag{3}$$

The symbols ψ_i, OBS, and y_i denote the input data, observable, and corresponding label, respectively, while k determines the circuit structure from the probabilistic model. The local loss is computed by summing the individual losses over all input data points. In some cases—such as the fidelity or MaxCut problems—we consider only a single input ($i = 1$) as a representative example.

2.2 Job Shop Scheduling Problem

JSSP is a combinatorial optimization problem crucial in industrial production environments, where it aims to enhance efficiency. Due to its computational complexity, JSSP quickly becomes intractable for large problem sizes. Various quantum computing approaches, such as quantum gate models and quantum annealing, have been explored to solve JSSP. JSSP can be formulated as a Quadratic Unconstrained Binary Optimization (QUBO) problem, and Variational Quantum Algorithms (VQAs) are employed in quantum gate models to find optimal solutions. It has been demonstrated that algorithms like VQE, QAOA, Var-QITE, F-VQE, particularly F-VQE, can effectively solve JSSP instances with up to 23 qubits [2]. Quantum annealing is emerging as a promising approach for solving combinatorial optimization problems like JSSP [4,28], as it can handle larger-scale problems without being constrained by the number of qubits, unlike quantum gate models.

2.3 Attention Mechanism

Self-attention, as introduced in Transformer architectures [27], has become a key mechanism in modeling dependencies across sequence elements. It enables each position to attend to all others, leading to breakthroughs in fields like natural language processing and image generation. Recent studies have explored the application of attention to quantum models [6], but not specifically in the context of architecture search.

The attention mechanism allows models to focus on the most significant parts of the input. Absolute positional information can be learned as parameters during training. Relative positional embedding is another approach, as demonstrated in [25]. CNN-based models use a multi-step attention mechanism for each decoder layer [17], while RNN-based translation models apply the attention mechanism in the decoder and use bidirectional RNNs in the encoder [3]. The BERT model operates in two stages: pre-training and fine-tuning [12].

3 Methodology

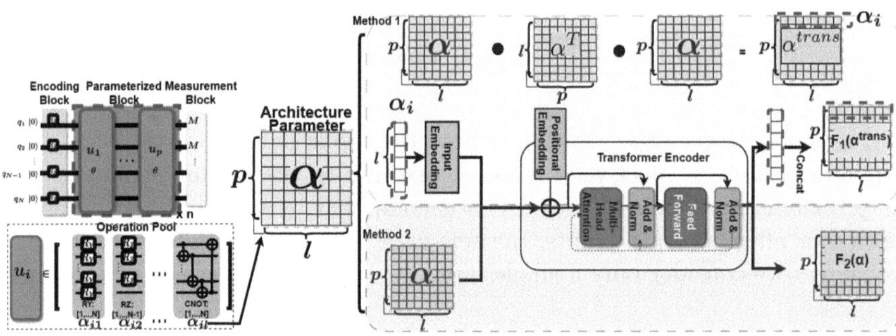

Fig. 1. The illustration of the proposed framework SA-DQAS. On the left side is the common part of both algorithms (Step 1 and Step 2). On the right side, we show the differences between both algorithms. SA-DQAS uses the attention modules F_1 or F_2 to improve the architecture parameters α, such that each operation shares positional and fitness information among operation candidates in different placeholders.

Our work SA-DQAS derives from integrating self-attention mechanism with DQAS, which uses a gradient-based method to construct a quantum circuit by replacing these placeholders with one possible candidate operation from the operation pool. We show our algorithm in Fig 1. We denote the operation pool as $\mathcal{O}$. A circuit is a sequence of p placeholders described as

$$U = \prod_{i=0}^{p} u_i(\theta_i), \tag{4}$$

where u_i stand for unitary placeholder, and θ_i are the parameters of trainable gates. The architecture parameter matrix is $(\alpha_{ij}) \in \mathbb{R}^{p\times l}$ with $l = |\mathcal{O}|$. The probability is calculated by Eq 2 . This setting makes the search process continue and focuses on operations in one placeholder but ignores the relationship among operation candidates placed on different placeholders.

Encoder F1&F2. As shown in Fig 1, each architecture parameters vector α_i is viewed as a word, and the architecture matrix α is viewed as a sentence. The output of the encoder is the architecture parameters, including relationship features, and is added to the original architecture parameter matrix α:

$$\alpha' = \alpha + \beta F(\alpha), \tag{5}$$

where F is the encoder and β is the scaling coefficient.

From different perspectives, by viewing a placeholder as a token, we propose one encoder with two types of input: F_1 and F_2. Regarding the encoder F_1, we use sinusoidal position embedding α_i^{pos} for N layers-encoder. Each layer consists of two sublayers:

$$\alpha_i^{n_1} = \text{LayerNorm}(\alpha_i^{a}), \tag{6}$$
$$\alpha_i^{\text{a}} = \text{MultiHead}(\alpha_i^{pos}, \alpha_i^{pos}, \alpha_i^{pos}) + \alpha_i^{pos}. \tag{7}$$

The second sub-layer is a position-wise fully connected feed-forward network:

$$\alpha_i^{n_2} = \text{LayerNorm}(\alpha_i^{a_2}), \tag{8}$$
$$\alpha_i^{a_2} = \alpha_i^{n_1} + g(\alpha_i^{n_1}), \tag{9}$$
$$g(\alpha_i^{n_1}) = W_2\text{max}(0, W_1\alpha_i^{n_1} + b_1) + b_2. \tag{10}$$

And α is updated by:

$$\alpha_1' = \alpha + \beta F_1(\alpha^{trans}), \tag{11}$$
$$\alpha^{trans} = \alpha \times \alpha^T \times \alpha. \tag{12}$$

For $F2$, we view the original architecture matrix α as an input for the encoder. The output of this method is

$$\alpha_2' = \alpha + \beta F_2(\alpha). \tag{13}$$

We expect that the self-attention mechanism can give us additional features without strongly reducing the effect of the original architecture parameters. As a result, we select a sufficiently small β as a scaling coefficient.

Loss function. The loss function for the whole process of circuit architecture search is described in Eq. 1. In order to get a gradually fixed architecture parameter, we select the distance of the output of the encoder between the current training step and one previous training step as our loss metric. For each training step t, the encoder parameters are updated by

$$w_t = w_t - \eta \Delta_w L_{\text{encoder}} \tag{14}$$

$$L_{\text{encoder}} = \max_{1 \leq i \leq p} \max_{1 \leq j \leq l} |F_{t-m} - F_t(\alpha_{ij}^{trans})|, \tag{15}$$

where F_t is the output matrix of F in training step t. We set $m = 1$ in our experiment and $F(\alpha^0)$ is initialized by 0.

4 Experiments

4.1 Experiment Settings

In our experiments, we evaluate our framework using the JSSP, the Max-cut problem, quantum chemistry and fidelity measurements. We define four different types of operation pools, $\mathcal{O}_1$-$\mathcal{O}_4$, which are used in the Max-cut problem, JSSP and quantum chemistry problem. The basic training settings and the specific types of gates included in $\mathcal{O}_1$-$\mathcal{O}_4$ are given in Table 1. Operation pools:

Table 1. The types of gates in operation pools $\mathcal{O}_1$-$\mathcal{O}_4$

Operation pool	Gate type
$\mathcal{O}_1$	RY, RZ, H, CZ, I
$\mathcal{O}_2$	RY, RZ, H, CNOT, I
$\mathcal{O}_3$	RY, RZ, H, CZ, CNOT, I
$\mathcal{O}_4$	H, U3, CU3, I

The smallest and largest operation pools of $\mathcal{O}_4$ with five qubits in the JSSP for each type are shown as follows:

$$\begin{aligned} \text{op4-1} = \{&\texttt{U3} : [0,1,2,3,4], \\ &\texttt{U3} : [0,1,2,3], \texttt{U3} : [1,2,3,4], \\ &\texttt{U3} : [0,1,2], \texttt{U3} : [1,2,3], \texttt{U3} : [2,3,4], \\ &\texttt{U3} : [0,1], \texttt{U3} : [1,2], \texttt{U3} : [2,3], \texttt{U3} : [3,4], \\ &\texttt{CU3} : [0,1,2,3], \texttt{E} : [0,1,2,3,4]\} \\ \text{op4-4} = \{&\texttt{U3} : [0,1,2,3,4], \texttt{H} : [0,1,2,3,4], \\ &\texttt{CU3} : [0,1,2,3], \texttt{E} : [0,1,2,3,4]\} \end{aligned} \tag{16}$$

The last operation E in the operation pools refers to an identical gate. We adjust the size of the operation pools according to the following rule: each time we reduce the size, we remove all single-gate operations with the current smallest working range. For example, the largest operation pool of $\mathcal{O}_4$ includes the U3 gate, which has a working range length of 2. The smallest pool contains single-qubit gates with a working range length of 5. Consequently, for each type, with

N qubits, we create $N-1$ different sizes of operation pools, numbered in order from largest to smallest.

In addition to the above tasks, we also include a new experiment on real quantum hardware to assess the scalability and practical robustness of our searched circuit architectures. For this evaluation, we focus on the MaxCut problem due to its flexibility in graph size and its widespread use as a quantum benchmark.

In this hardware experiment, we adopt a new operation pool: $\mathcal{O}_{\text{scale}} = \{\texttt{CNOT}, \texttt{RY}, \texttt{RZ}\}$, which provides a minimal yet expressive set of operations suitable for NISQ hardware execution.

To test architectural scalability, we first use SA-DQAS to search for a performant circuit architecture on a small 8-node MaxCut graph. The learned architecture is then transferred to larger problem instances by stacking the learned circuit blocks. Specifically, we evaluate performance on 16-node graphs by repeating the trained block multiple times. This setup allows us to examine whether architectures discovered on small circuits can generalize to larger problems and maintain performance when deployed on real quantum devices.

4.2 Max-Cut Problem

In this section, we address the Max-cut problem using DQAS under various settings. The benchmark graphs, consisting of 8 nodes, along with the baseline circuit, are presented in Fig 2.

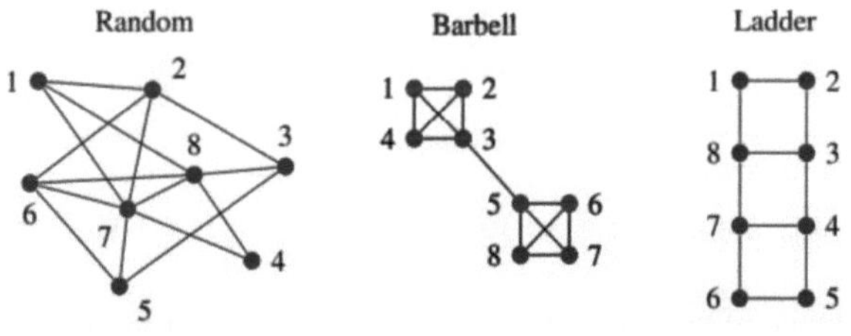

Fig. 2. Benchmark graphs used for Max-cut problem.

We previously discussed incorporating a self-attention mechanism into DQAS comparing with baseline and quantumDarts [30]. SA-DQAS finds circuits using different operation pools, then use these circuits to solve the Max-cut problem on the three graphs. The operation pools op1-* to op4-* are derived from $\mathcal{O}_1$ to $\mathcal{O}_4$. Both controlled gates and single-qubit gates have a maximum working range of [0,1,2,3,4,5,6,7], leading to 28 distinct operation pools. We compare the effectiveness of selected circuits containing controlled gates in solving the Max-cut problem against the baseline.

From the results in Fig. 3, we observe that some circuits quickly converge to the minimum energy, outperforming the baseline, while others show slower convergence. Additionally, the shaded areas representing standard deviation for some circuits are much larger, and their average results fail to reach the exact

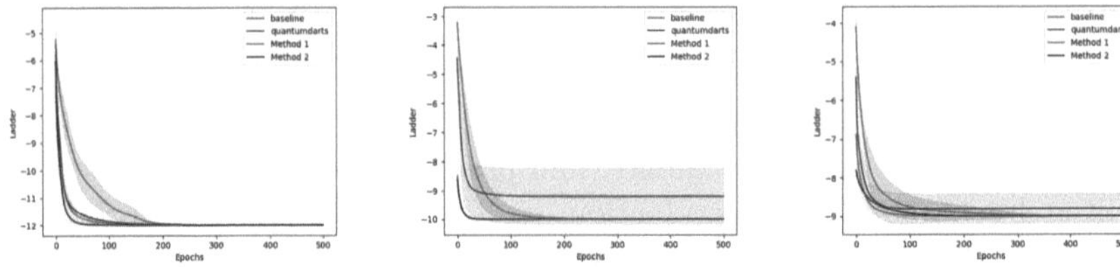

(a) Max-cut Random (b) Max-cut Barbell (c) Max-cut Ladder

Fig. 3. Evaluation of the performance of circuits generated by SA-DQAS and quantumDarts. Method 1 uses the encoder F_1, and Method 2 uses the encoder F_2. The line represents the average results of 5 trials with different initial parameters. The SA-DQAS shows a much more stable performance for Max-cut problem comparing with quantumDarts.

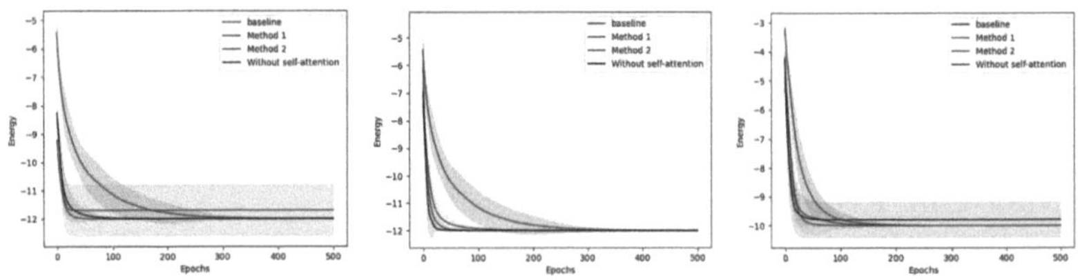

(a) W<WO op2-4_4 (b) W>WO op4-7_4 (c) W≈WO op4-5_4

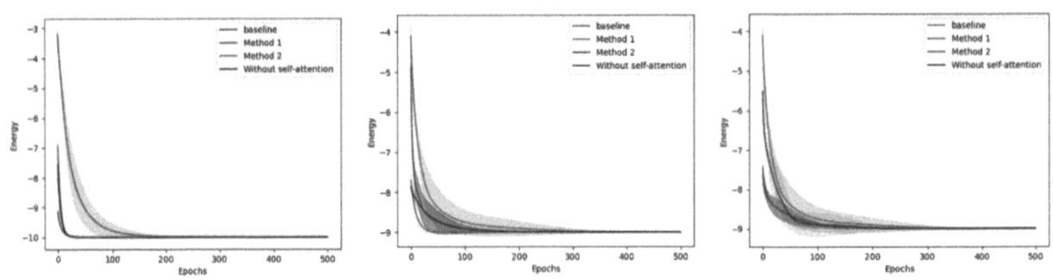

(d) W≈WO op3-3_4 (e) W<WO op3-1_4 (f) W>WO op3-6_4

Fig. 4. Performance of circuits generated with (W) and without (WO) self-attention across different Max-cut problems. (a)–(b) show the evaluation results for Random graphs, (c)–(d) for Ladder graphs, and (e)–(f) for Barbell graphs. Circuits created using method 1 consistently converge faster to the minimum energy than those generated by method 2, as shown in (b), (c), and (e). While some circuits from both methods perform similarly, as seen in (d) and (f), method 2 circuits occasionally exhibit significant deviation, as in (a). Overall, circuits from both methods outperform the baseline, with method 1 generally producing more stable and reliable results, less sensitive to initial parameter variations.

minimum energy, indicating instability in their performance. In some trials, these circuits even reach incorrect solutions, likely due to the limitation of quantumDarts explained in their paper for Max-cut problem. However, all circuits from SA-DQAS converge to the minimum energy faster than the baseline, with no significant standard deviations, and all average results achieve the exact minimum energy.

4.3 Experiments on JSSP

In this section, we conduct experiments using SA-DQAS for the simplest JSSP task, as defined in [2], with five qubits. The manually designed circuit shown in Fig. 12b and the experiment setting are from the paper [2] and used as our baseline. In these experiments, all qubits are initialized to the state $|0\rangle$, and `rx` gates with a rotation angle of π are applied to form the encoding block. There is only one parameterized block containing four placeholders, and all placeholders are updated at each learning step. The energies E are scaled to the range $[0, 1]$:

$$e = \frac{E - E_{\text{min}}}{E_{\text{max}} - E_{\text{min}}} \in [0, 1] \quad , \tag{17}$$

where E_{min} and E_{max} are the minimum and maximum energies, respectively. When $e \approx 0$, the minimal energy is reached, indicating the optimal solution.

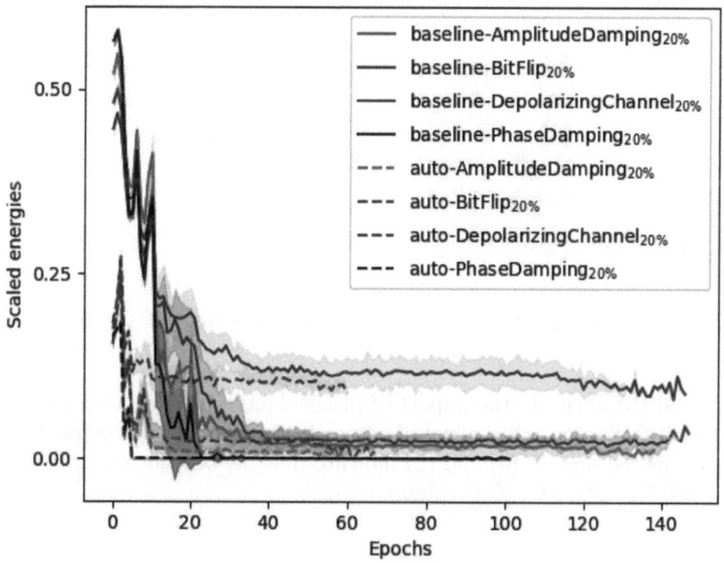

Fig. 5. Performance evaluation in noisy environments: We assess the noise resistance of auto-generated circuits by introducing noise models that add 20% of various noise types to each qubit in the top-performing generated circuit.

In Fig. 5, the shaded standard deviation areas of the designed architectures are significantly smaller than those of the baseline, indicating that the learned circuits produce more consistent outcomes. Under BitFlip noise, both the baseline and the searched circuit yield average results that are considerably higher than the minimum energy. However, the ASP and minimum energies achieved by the designed circuits outperform the baseline across different models. Although neither the learned circuits nor the baseline consistently find the exact minimum energy in some trials due to the influence of noise, the automatically designed circuits are generally more noise-resilient and reliable.

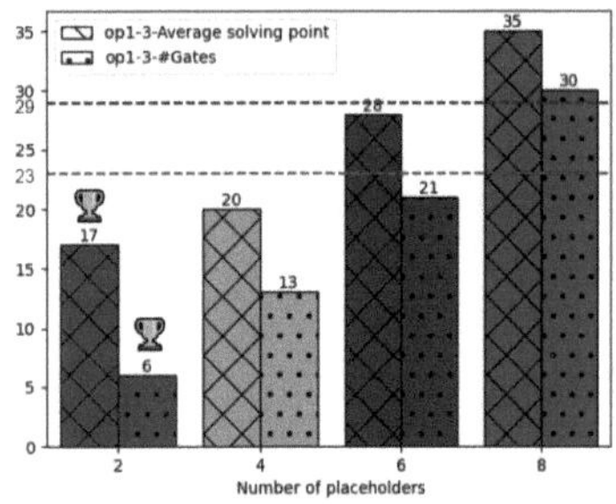

(a) Comparison of placeholders

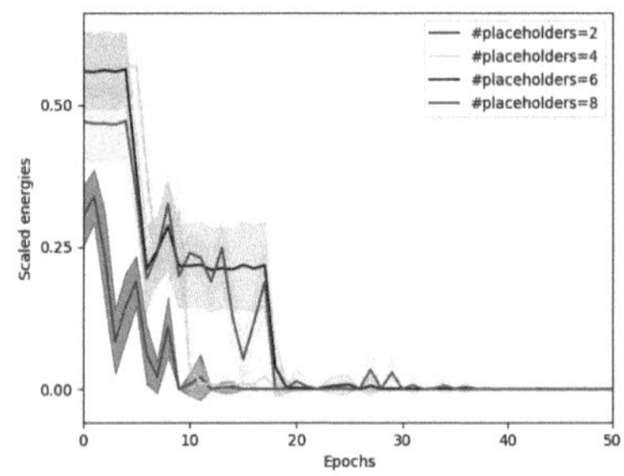

(b) Gates and ASP of auto-generated circuit

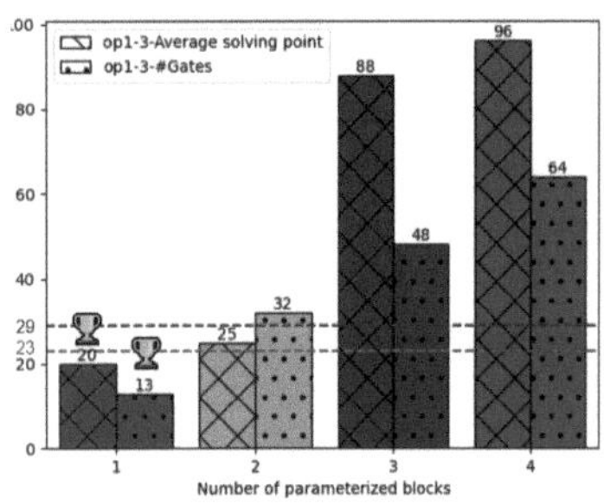

(c) Comparison of parameterized blocks

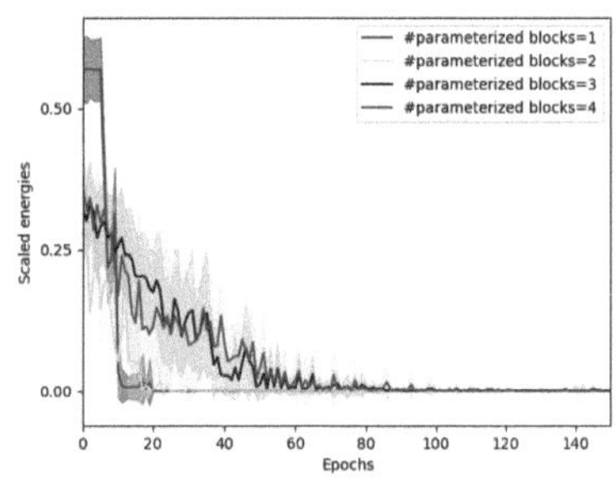

(d) Gates and ASP of auto-generated circuit

Fig. 6. (a) and (b) illustrate the impact of placeholders when generating circuits with op1-3. (c) and (d) illustrate the impact of parameterized blocks when generating circuits with op1-3. The red lines in (a) and (b) indicate that the baseline circuit has 23 gates, while the ASP has 29 gates. (Color figure online)

The impact of placeholders and parameterized blocks during generating circuits is studied in Fig. 6. The evaluation results show that as the number of placeholders and parameterized blocks increases, the number of gates and the depth of the generated circuits also increase, leading to slower convergence when solving a simple JSSP. Deeper circuits require more parameterized gates to be trained, resulting in more complex quantum calculations and, consequently, slower convergence.

We present the comparison of the circuits from op3-3, from which SA-DQAS generates the best-performing circuit. Figure 7a illustrates that the circuit

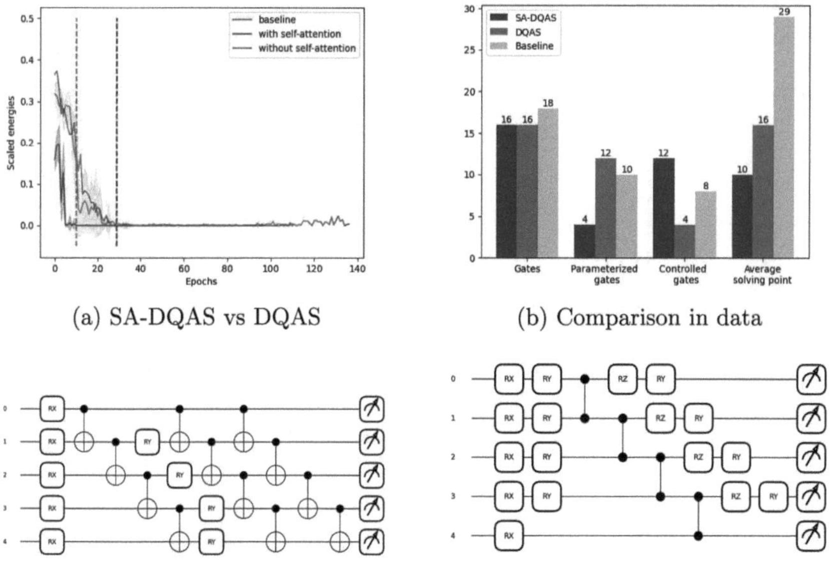

(a) SA-DQAS vs DQAS

(b) Comparison in data

(c) Circuit by SA-DQAS

(d) Circuit by DQAS

Fig. 7. Comparison of generated circuits.

created with SA-DQAS converges much faster than the baseline and circuit generated with DQAS. Comparing the two circuit architectures in Figs. 7c and 7d, they contain the same number of gates, but more controlled gates appear in 7c, meaning that the circuit created with SA-DQAS has fewer trainable parameters, leading to its better performance for JSSP than both the baseline and circuit designed by DQAS. Figure 7b illustrates the advantages of circuits designed with SA-DQAS mentioned above in the data.

By seeing the information in Table 2 in the appendix, we know that nearly all circuits designed with SA-DQAS can find the optimal solution of JSSP faster than those without self-attention. All circuits generated with SA-DQAS have fewer gates than the baseline. When circuits generated with SA-DQAS contain fewer parameterized gates than those with DQAS, they perform better. Nevertheless, there are special cases. The circuit created with SA-DQAS from op1-1 has more parameterized gates but converges faster than with DQAS. They perform fast the same. The circuit created with SA-DQAS from op3-1 performs worse, although it contains less parameterized gates. We can see that it has more controlled gates. This case shows that sometimes controlled gates can reduce training efficiency.

Compared to the structures of circuits generated with different methods, we observe that most circuits created with SA-DQAS contain controlled gates. Controlled gates are essential in quantum circuits because they allow us to create interactions and entanglement between quantum qubits, enabling various quan-

Table 2. Summary of circuits designed with and without self-attention from different operation pools.

Operation pool	#Gates***		#Param. G		#Con. G		Avg. solving point**	
Baseline	18		10		8		29	
	Y*	N*	Y	N	Y	N	Y	N
op1-1	15	14	15	14	0	0	25	26
op1-2	13	9	9	9	4	0	18	11
op1-3	13	19	9	14	4	0	20	39
op1-4	14	20	5	15	4	0	13	38
op2-1	13	9	9	9	4	0	13	16
op2-2	15	16	7	12	8	4	13	28
op2-3	16	18	8	18	8	0	13	40
op2-4	15	18	10	5	0	8	19	14
op3-1	15	13	7	9	8	4	18	15
op3-2	15	13	11	13	4	0	17	32
op3-3	16	16	4	12	12	4	10	16
op3-4	13	20	5	20	8	0	14	39
op4-1	7	12	7	12	0	4	33	72
op4-2	12	15	12	15	8	8	60	108
op4-3	16	16	16	16	8	8	89	96
op4-4	16	17	16	17	16	12	88	91

* Y indicates circuits searched by SA-DQAS and N indicates by DQAS

** Avg. solving point refers to the number of iterations required to find the minimum energy without subsequent fluctuations.

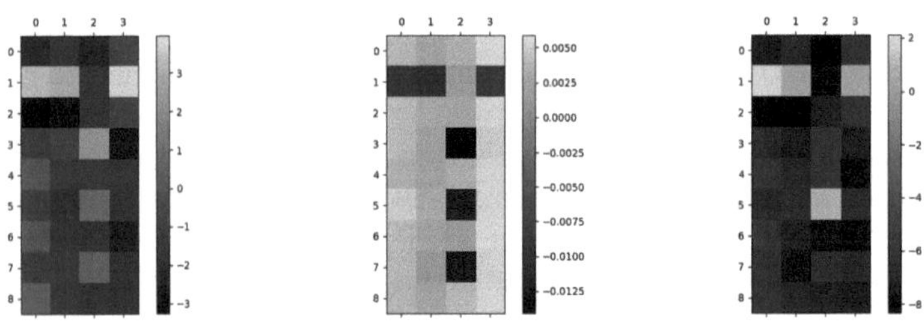

(a) AP-training (b) AP-transformer (c) AP-end

Fig. 8. Illustration of architecture parameters (AP) during training for JSSP problem. In the operation pool there are 9 operation candidates for 4 placeholders, so the architecture parameter matrix here has 9 rows and 4 columns. The subfigure 8a shows the architecture parameter matrix during the training, the lighter the color is, the more likely the operation is to be selected. The subfigure 8b shows the output of transformer encoder which is used to improve the architecture parameters at the same training step. The subfigure 8c shows the architecture parameters after training.

tum computation and quantum information processing tasks. A circuit without controlled gates is indistinguishable from a classical circuit. Self-attention helps us find better and more meaningful quantum circuits.

4.4 Quantum Chemistry

We compared SA-DQAS with different algorithms in terms of minimum energy error of molecules in Table 3. The SA-DQAS can find minimum energy with 10^{-5} error that outperforms QCAS [15], RS or DQAS for molecules H_2, LiH-4 and LiH-6. But, by comparing with quantumDARTS [30], it has similar or slightly lower performance. UCCSD [24] here gives nearly a theoretical bounds for the minimum energy error.

Table 3. Experiments on molecules. We solve the Hamiltonian Error of H_2, LiH-4 and LiH-6 and compare our method to other algorithms. The value indicates the error level compared with ground state energy.

Algorithm	H_2	LiH-4	LiH-6
UCCSD	5.5×10^{-11}	4.0×10^{-5}	4.0×10^{-5}
quantumDARTS	4.3×10^{-6}	1.7×10^{-4}	2.9×10^{-4}
DQAS	3.1×10^{-4}	5.3×10^{-4}	1.5×10^{-3}
QCAS	2.2×10^{-2}	8.6×10^{-2}	7.3×10^{-2}
Randomness	1.9×10^{-2}	1.3×10^{-2}	6.2×10^{-3}
SA-DQAS	1.2×10^{-5}	3.0×10^{-4}	3.0×10^{-4}

4.5 Fidelity Measurement

In this section, we test our algorithm for error mitigation and study the fidelity between pre-defined circuits and those generated by SA-DQAS. A previous experiment in [33] demonstrated that DQAS could be used for error mitigation. The pre-defined circuit is a three-qubit `QFT` circuit as shown in Fig. 9a. During the search process, we set up six placeholders in the circuit—half before and half after the `QFT` part—following the original experimental setup in [33]. The operation pool used in this experiment is $\mathcal{O}_{f1}$ (shown in Appendix A). The noise model assumes 2% BitFlip errors between two gates and 20% BitFlip errors when a qubit is idle. We design circuits using SA-DQAS in an ideal environment and select the one with the highest fidelity to the ideal circuit in a noisy environment. The fidelity between the auto-generated circuit by SA-DQAS (illustrated in Fig. 9a) and the ideal circuit is 0.66, which is slightly higher than the fidelity (0.6) between the ideal circuit from DQAS. This result indicates that SA-DQAS outperforms DQAS in error mitigation.

We build three additional noise models based on BitFlip errors. The first model introduces BitFlip errors with varying probabilities at the end of each qubit. The second model adds 2% BitFlip errors after each operation in non-empty placeholders (where the chosen operation is not "`E`") of the generated circuit, and a 20% BitFlip error to each qubit at the end of the circuit. The third model uses the same noise configuration as provided in [33]. We then calculate

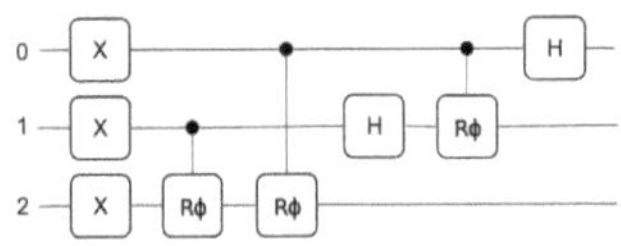

(a) Ideal circuit

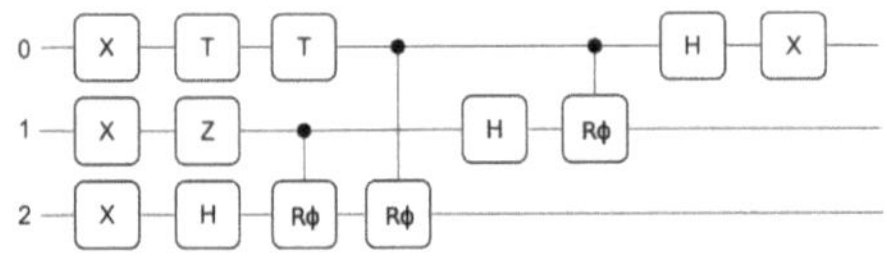

(b) Circuit from SA-DQAS

Fig. 9. Evaluation of newly discovered architectures on a noise-free simulator. The results are averaged over 10 trials with different initial parameters.

the fidelity between the ideal circuit and the generated circuits in environments where BitFlip errors occur with different probabilities.

Table 4. Fidelity between the generated and ideal circuit under different probabilities of BitFlip noise, with placeholders positioned at various locations. Circuits are automatically generated under an ideal environment ($B_{0.0}$) and with 20% BitFlip noise ($B_{0.2}$).

Setting		$B_{0.0}$	$B_{0.1}$	$B_{0.2}$	$B_{0.3}$
Back	$B_{0.0}$	0.94	0.79	0.68	0.57
	$B_{0.2}$	0.97	0.81	0.69	0.57
Back and Front	$B_{0.0}$	0.97	0.79	0.68	0.57
	$B_{0.2}$	0.94	0.78	0.67	0.57
Front	$B_{0.0}$	0.99	0.77	0.65	0.54
	$B_{0.2}$	0.99	0.79	0.66	0.55

From the results in Table 4, we observe that as the probability of BitFlip occurrence increases, the average fidelity decreases. When placeholders are positioned entirely before or after the `QFT` part, circuits generated in a noisy environment exhibit higher average fidelity than those created in an ideal environment. However, when the `QFT` part is in the middle of the circuit, the situation is reversed. Circuits generated in noisy environments tend to be more stable and reliable, with better structures that are less affected by BitFlip noise, making them more noise-resilient. Additionally, the noise resistance of the generated circuits is also influenced by their structural design. In AppendixD, we also show other noise models experiments based on PhaseDamping, AmplitudeDamping, DepolarizingChannel, and other settings.

4.6 Real-Device Evaluation and Scalability via MaxCut

While our previous experiments used quantum simulators and employed smaller circuit sizes, a key question still stands: *How do searched architectures scale to real quantum hardware, and can they scale to bigger problem instances?* To answer this, we have a new, complementary experiment, testing the MaxCut problem, a standard benchmark in quantum combinatorial optimization.

In order to verify searched circuit architectures for scale, we use a stacking method. Precisely, we train circuit block on tiny graphs. We generate each circuit by block which shares the same architecture and represents each edge between two nodes. Subsequently, we examine their performances when stacking these blocks to create deeper circuits for larger graphs. This replicates real-world scenarios in which deep circuits are built from transferable units that have been trained in smaller subproblems.

We examine two graph families, complete bipartite graphs and random graphs, in both $n = 8$ and $n = 16$ nodes. The experiments ran with real quantum hardware `ibmq_sherbrooke` with 10,000 shots per circuit.

Table 5. Performance of Stacked Circuit Architectures on Real Quantum Devices (MaxCut)

Graph Type	#Qubits	Architecture	Cost(Target)	Shots	Device
Complete Bipartite	8	cnot-ry-cnot	16 (16)	10000	`ibmq_sherbrooke`
Complete Bipartite	16	cnot-ry-cnot	64 (64)	10000	`ibmq_sherbrooke`
Random	8	cnot-ry-cnot	12 (12)	10000	`ibmq_sherbrooke`
Random	16	cnot-ry-cnot	20 (20)	10000	`ibmq_sherbrooke`

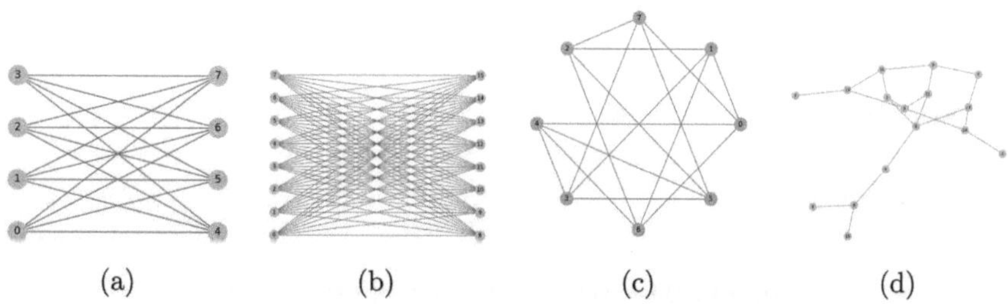

Fig. 10. Graphs used in real-device MaxCut experiments: (a) Bipartite (8 nodes), (b) Bipartite (16 nodes), (c) Random (8 nodes), (d) Random (16 nodes).

The values in Table 5 show that stacked architecture achieves optimal or nearly optimal values of cost even on real hardware as well as on bigger graphs. This showcases that not only do searched architectures generalize over different instances of a problem, but they also scale moderately when applied to bigger circuits by repeated replication. Significantly, it proves the deployability of our NAS-learned circuits to near-term quantum hardware.

5 Conclusion

We have introduced SA-DQAS, which extends Differentiable Quantum Architecture Search (DQAS) to use self-attention to learn interrelations among candidate operations in placeholder positions. This global viewpoint produces more stable, high-performing quantum architectures. Our approach, which we evaluate over a variety of quantum problems including MaxCut, JSSP, quantum chemistry, and fidelity optimization, consistently outperforms DQAS as well as other baselines in terms of convergence speed, quality of the solution, and robustness to noise. Specifically, we introduce real-device evaluation on IBM's hardware via MaxCut, where architecture found in small graph training is stacked and used to tackle large-scale graphs. This scale test demonstrates SA-DQAS's ability to create transferable, hardware-efficient blocks of circuits, pushing its practical applications.

Acknowledgments. The project of this conference paper is based on was supported with funds from the German Federal Ministry of Education and Research in the funding program Quantum Reinforcement Learning for industrial Applications (QLindA) and the Federal Ministry for Economic Affairs and Climate Action in the funding program Quantum-Classical Hybrid Optimization Algorithms for Logistics and Production Line Management (QCHALLenge) - under project number 13N15644 and 01MQ22008B. AI assistance was used during the preparation of this manuscript for tasks such as grammar suggestions, using ChatGPT (OpenAI, 2024). The authors have reviewed and revised all content for accuracy and originality. Due to the iterative nature of writing, we cannot precisely identify individual sentences influenced by AI assistance.

Disclosure of Interests. The authors have no competing interests to declare that are relevant to the content of this article.

A Settings

Experiments settings:

Table 6. Basic settings in different experiments.

Experiments	#Qubits	#Placeholders	#Param. blocks*
Max-cut	8	4	1
JSSP	5	4	1
QC†	4/6	4	1/2
Fidelity	3	6	1

* #Param. blocks indicates the number of parameterized blocks used in the training process.
† QC stands for quantum chemistry.

Operation pools used for study the fidelity:

$$
\begin{aligned}
\mathcal{O}_{f1} = \{&\texttt{X}:[0],\texttt{X}:[1],\texttt{X}:[2],\\
&\texttt{T}:[0],\texttt{T}:[1],\texttt{T}:[2],,\\
&\texttt{E}:[0,1,2]\\
\mathcal{O}_{f2} = \{&\texttt{X}:[0],\texttt{X}:[1],\texttt{X}:[2],\\
&\texttt{T}:[0],\texttt{T}:[1],\texttt{T}:[2],\\
&\texttt{CNOT}:[0],\texttt{CNOT}:[1],\texttt{CNOT}:[2],\texttt{CNOT}:[0,1,2],\\
&\texttt{CZ}:[0],\texttt{CZ}:[1],\texttt{CZ}:[2],\texttt{CZ}:[0,1,2],\\
&,\texttt{E}:[0,1,2,3,4]\}
\end{aligned} \tag{18}
$$

B Experiments on Max-Cut Problem

Baseline in Max-cut problem: In this part, we compare the structural and performing differences between the circuits generated with SA-DQAS and DQAS and the performances in solving different Max-cut problem in the benchmark.

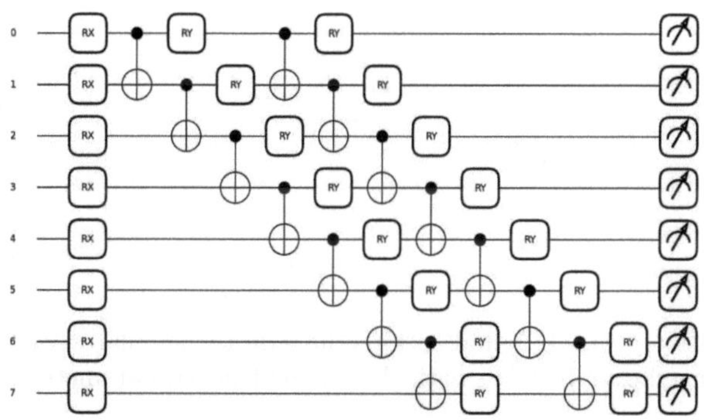

Fig. 11. Baseline used for Max-cut problem.

Table 7. Summary of circuit architectures designed with and without self-attention from various operation pools for solving different Max-Cut problems. M_1 indicates circuits searched by Method 1, M_2 by Method 2, and N by DQAS. #Gate, #Param, and #Con refer to the number of total gates, trainable parameterized gates, and controlled gates in the parameterized blocks, respectively. R, L, and B represent Random, Ladder, and Barbell graphs.

Circuits	#Gate			#Param			#Con		
	M_1	M_2	N	M_1	M_2	N	M_1	M_2	N
$C_{R-\text{op4}-7_4}$	23	22	29	15	6	11	8	16	8
$C_{L-\text{op3}-3_4}$	23	27	22	15	19	14	8	8	8
$C_{B-\text{op3}-6_4}$	29	30	23	21	22	23	8	8	0

According to the Table 7, the circuit $C_{R-\text{op4}-7_4}$ from method 2 has the fewest gates, especially parameterized ones. In the Ladder graph, circuits derived from op3-3 by both methods perform similarly, converging almost simultaneously. For the Barbell graph, the DQAS-generated circuit lacks controlled gates, crucial for quantum entanglement, making it more akin to a classical circuit. In contrast, SA-DQAS circuits, though involving higher hardware costs for entanglement, maintain better quantum properties.

These comparison results indicate that integrating self-attention with DQAS leads to better circuit structures that retain quantum features through entanglement. Such circuits demonstrate greater stability, repeatability, and insensitivity to initial parameters. Additionally, the circuits generated with SA-DQAS have fewer gates, which conserves hardware resources and reduces the errors and noise caused by gates.

C Experiments on JSSP

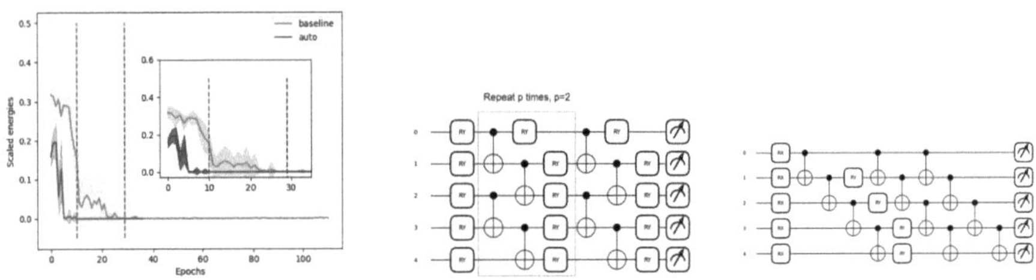

(a) Comparison (b) Baseline (c) Circuit$_{auto}$

Fig. 12. Evaluation of newly found architectures on the simulator without noise. The results are averaged over 10 trials with the different initial parameters.

Figure 12a presents the evaluation of newly discovered architectures on a noise-free simulator. The best-performing automatically designed architectures converge faster than the baseline to the ASP, with average results reaching the optimal schedule within 10 epochs. The shaded areas representing standard deviation are much smaller than the baseline, indicating that these circuits produce consistent outcomes across multiple trials, reflecting the stability, reliability, and reproducibility of the learned architectures. Comparing the top-performing architecture created by SA-DQAS in Fig. 12c with the baseline circuit in Fig. 12b, the former contains no redundant parameterized blocks and ends with repeated `cnot` gates over the range [0,1,2,3], a configuration that rarely appears in manually designed circuits.

In general, more gates, especially controlled gates, increase the cost of building a quantum circuit, although controlled gates are essential for creating quantum entanglement. The circuit discovered by SA-DQAS contains fewer gates

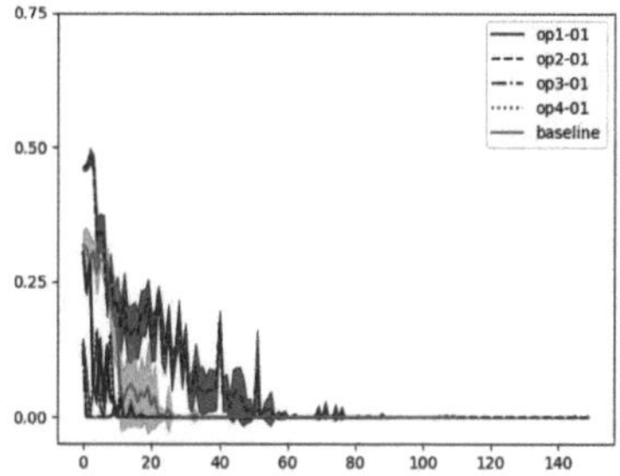

(a) Op*-01

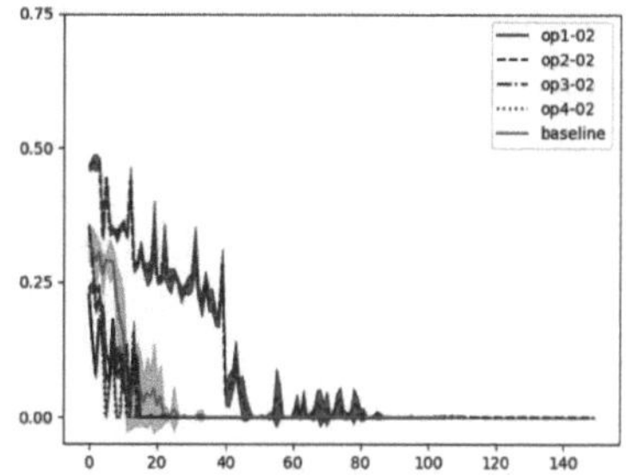

(b) Op*-02

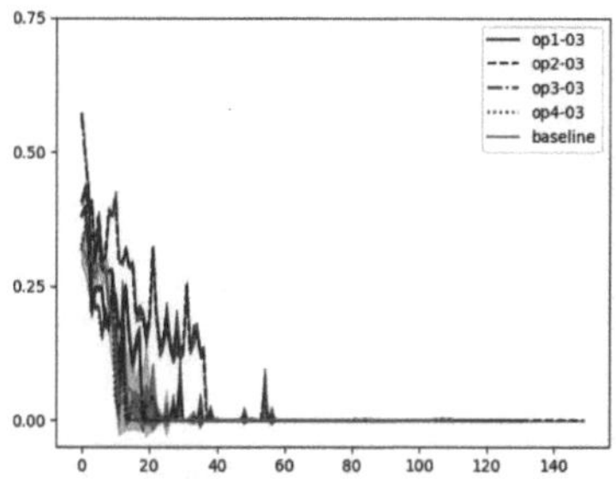

(c) Op*-03

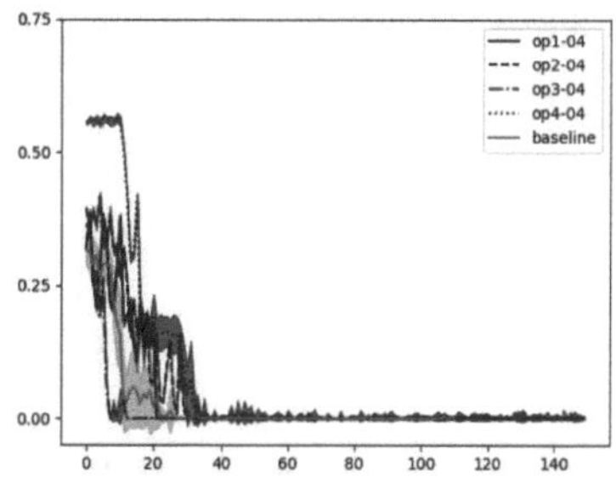

(d) Op*-04

Fig. 13. Comparison of circuits generated using operation pools replacing ry with rx. We also generate operation pools by replacing ry with rx gates.

than the baseline, particularly fewer parameterized gates, reducing the building cost while retaining quantum features. Fewer parameterized gates simplifies the quantum computation process, leading to faster convergence. Additionally, since some noise and errors in quantum circuits are caused by decoherence and gate imperfections, using fewer gates can minimize these issues, resulting in more reliable and stable circuits that converge faster.

We also replace the all Ry gates with Rx gates in all operation pools and comparing them in JSSP problem in Fig 13. Not all operation pools can find a better performing circuit architecture comparing with the baseline. But all of the circuit performance are much more stable than the baseline. The circuit deriving from op3-04 shown in subfigure 13d has the best performance comparing with other operation pools.

D Experiment of Fidelity Measurement

In [33], only single-qubit operations were used in the operation pool. This approach helps mitigate quantum errors by converting coherent errors into more manageable Pauli errors [29,33,34]. We extend this by adding controlled gates to form a new operation pool, $\mathcal{O}_{f2}$ (detailed in Appendix A). This allows the automatically designed parameterized blocks in the circuit architectures to include entangled gates. Using both the original single-qubit pool and the new pool, we generate circuits under ideal conditions and with 20% BitFlip noise added to each qubit at the end of the circuit. The average fidelity of the generated circuits is calculated under these conditions, and the comparisons are presented in Table 8.

Table 8. A table that records the fidelity between the generated circuits from operation pools with and without controlled gates and the ideal circuit under different environments, with placeholders positioned in three locations relative to the QFT part. Y indicates the operation pool contains controlled gates, while N indicates only single-qubit gates are included in the operation pool.

		Ideal		BitFlip 2		BitFlip 3	
		Y	N	Y	N	Y	N
Back	$B_{0.0}$	0.91	0.94	0.66	0.68	0.56	0.65
	$B_{0.2}$	0.94	0.97	0.67	0.69	0.63	0.65
Back and Front	$B_{0.0}$	0.89	0.97	0.63	0.68	0.53	0.66
	$B_{0.2}$	0.89	0.94	0.64	0.67	0.51	0.65
Front	$B_{0.0}$	0.99	0.99	0.65	0.65	0.50	0.64
	$B_{0.2}$	0.99	0.99	0.64	0.66	0.47	0.64

When circuits (excluding the QFT part) contain controlled gates, the average fidelity is lower than circuits with only single-qubit gates, regardless of whether they are in ideal or noisy environments. Controlled gates link multiple qubits, so when one qubit, particularly the control qubit, is affected by an error, it impacts the state of the other qubits. This makes controlled gates more susceptible to noise, leading to lower fidelity in the final circuit. Additionally, circuits with more controlled gates can result in longer idle times for qubits, increasing the likelihood of idling errors.

To further study error mitigation in various noisy environments, we design additional noise models by introducing 20% of different types of errors at the end of each qubit. In our new configurations, the six placeholders can be placed either all before, all after, or half before and half after the QFT part. We continue to use the same operation pool as in the previous experiment. Circuits are automatically generated under both ideal and noisy conditions, and we calculate the fidelity between the ideal circuit and the SA-DQAS-generated circuit in different environments.

Focusing on the results in each table, we observe that the average fidelity between the ideal circuit and the generated circuits, calculated under specific environments, remains nearly the same regardless of whether the circuit was searched in an ideal or noisy environment. The fidelity is close to 1 in the ideal environment, indicating that the generated circuit closely matches the baseline.

Table 9. A table that records the fidelity of the generated circuit under different environments and the baseline when the placeholders are all behind the `QFT` part.

	Ideal	$P_{0.2}$	$A_{0.2}$	$D_{0.2}$
Ideal	0.99	0.85	0.85	0.65
$P^*_{0.2}$	0.99	0.85	0.85	0.81
$A^*_{0.2}$	0.97	0.83	0.83	0.63
$D^*_{0.2}$	0.99	0.85	0.85	0.65

* P indicates PhaseDamping, A is AmplitudeDamping and D is DepolarizingChannel. Their subscripts indicate the probability of noise occurrence, 0.2 is 20%.

Table 10. A table that records the fidelity of the generated circuit under different environments and the baseline when the placeholders are all before the `QFT` part.

	Ideal	$P_{0.2}$	$A_{0.2}$	$D_{0.2}$
Ideal	0.99	0.85	0.85	0.65
$P_{0.2}$	0.99	0.85	0.85	0.65
$A_{0.2}$	0.99	0.85	0.85	0.65
$D_{0.2}$	0.99	0.85	0.85	0.65

Table 11. A table that records the fidelity of the generated circuit under different environments and the baseline when the placeholders are half before and half behind the `QFT` part.

	Ideal	$P_{0.2}$	$A_{0.2}$	$D_{0.2}$
Ideal	0.99	0.85	0.85	0.65
$P_{0.2}$	0.99	0.85	0.85	0.65
$A_{0.2}$	0.99	0.85	0.85	0.65
$D_{0.2}$	0.99	0.85	0.85	0.65

Comparing the results across the three tables, we find that, regardless of the `QFT` part's position, SA-DQAS consistently discovers circuits nearly identical to the baseline, with similar fidelity results. The lowest fidelity is over 60%, demonstrating that SA-DQAS is capable of searching for circuit architectures in noisy environments and finding circuits that are almost identical to the baseline. Furthermore, the automatically generated circuits exhibit strong noise resistance.

References

1. Alam, M., Kundu, S., Topaloglu, R.O., Ghosh, S.: Quantum-classical hybrid machine learning for image classification (ICCAD special session paper). arXiv preprint arXiv:2109.02862 (2021)

2. Amaro, D., Rosenkranz, M., Fitzpatrick, N., Hirano, K., Fiorentini, M.: A case study of variational quantum algorithms for a job shop scheduling problem. EPJ Quantum Technol. **9**(1), 5 (2022)
3. Bahdanau, D., Cho, K., Bengio, Y.: Neural machine translation by jointly learning to align and translate. In: International Conference on Learning Representations (ICLR). ICLR, San Diego, CA, USA (2015). (arXiv preprint arXiv:1409.0473)
4. Carugno, C., Ferrari Dacrema, M., Cremonesi, P.: Evaluating the job shop scheduling problem on a d-wave quantum annealer. Sci. Rep. **12**(1), 6539 (2022)
5. Cerezo, M., et al.: Variational quantum algorithms. Nat. Rev. Phys. **3**(9), 625–644 (2021)
6. Chen, C.S., Kuo, E.J.: Quantum adaptive self-attention for quantum transformer models. arXiv preprint arXiv:2504.05336 (2025)
7. Chen, K.C., Chen, S.Y.C., Liu, C.Y., Leung, K.K.: Quantum-train-based distributed multi-agent reinforcement learning. arXiv preprint arXiv:2412.08845 (2024)
8. Chen, S.Y.C.: Differentiable quantum architecture search in asynchronous quantum reinforcement learning. In: 2024 IEEE International Conference on Quantum Computing and Engineering (QCE), vol. 1, pp. 1516–1524. IEEE, Piscataway, NJ, USA (2024)
9. Chen, S.Y.C.: Differentiable quantum architecture search in asynchronous quantum reinforcement learning (2024). Preprint, arXiv:2407.18202
10. Chen, S.Y.C., Liu, C.Y., Chen, K.C., Huang, W.J., Chang, Y.J., Huang, W.H.: Differentiable quantum architecture search in quantum-enhanced neural network parameter generation. arXiv preprint arXiv:2505.09653 (2025)
11. Dai, X., Wei, T.C., Yoo, S., Chen, S.Y.C.: Quantum machine learning architecture search via deep reinforcement learning. arXiv preprint arXiv:2407.20147 (2024)
12. Devlin, J., Chang, M.W., Lee, K., Toutanova, K.: BERT: pre-training of deep bidirectional transformers for language understanding. arXiv preprint arXiv:1810.04805 (2018)
13. Ding, L., Spector, L.: Evolutionary quantum architecture search for parametrized quantum circuits. In: Proceedings of the Genetic and Evolutionary Computation Conference Companion, pp. 2190–2195. Association for Computing Machinery, New York, NY, USA (2022)
14. Ding, L., Spector, L.: Multi-objective evolutionary architecture search for parameterized quantum circuits. Entropy **25**(1), 93 (2023)
15. Du, Y., Huang, T., You, S., Hsieh, M.H., Tao, D.: Quantum circuit architecture search for variational quantum algorithms. NPJ Quantum Inf. **8**(1), 1–8 (2022)
16. Fösel, T., Niu, M.Y., Marquardt, F., Li, L.: Quantum circuit optimization with deep reinforcement learning. arXiv preprint arXiv:2103.07585 (2021)
17. Gehring, J., Auli, M., Grangier, D., Yarats, D., Dauphin, Y.N.: Convolutional sequence to sequence learning. In: Proceedings of the 34th International Conference on Machine Learning, pp. 1243–1252. PMLR, Sydney, Australia (2017)
18. Giovagnoli, A., Tresp, V., Ma, Y., Schubert, M.: QNEAT: natural evolution of variational quantum circuit architecture. In: Proceedings of the Companion Conference on Genetic and Evolutionary Computation, pp. 647–650 (2023)
19. He, Z., Deng, M., Zheng, S., Li, L., Situ, H.: GSQAS: graph self-supervised quantum architecture search. arXiv preprint arXiv:2303.12381 (2023)
20. Kim, G.S., Lee, S., Cho, I.S., Park, S., Kim, J.: Quantum reinforcement learning for lightweight LEO satellite routing. IEEE Internet of Things J. (2025)
21. Kuo, E.J., Fang, Y.L.L., Chen, S.Y.C.: Quantum architecture search via deep reinforcement learning. arXiv preprint arXiv:2104.07715 (2021)

22. Ma, Y., Tresp, V., Zhao, L., Wang, Y.: Variational quantum circuit model for knowledge graph embedding. Adv. Quantum Technol. **2**(7–8), 1800078 (2019)
23. Meng, F.X., Li, Z.T., Yu, X.T., Zhang, Z.C.: Quantum circuit architecture optimization for variational quantum Eigensolver via Monto Carlo tree search. IEEE Trans. Quantum Eng. **2**, 1–10 (2021)
24. Romero, J., Babbush, R., McClean, J.R., Hempel, C., Love, P.J., Aspuru-Guzik, A.: Strategies for quantum computing molecular energies using the unitary coupled cluster ansatz. Quantum Sci. Technol. **4**(1), 014008 (2018)
25. Shaw, P., Uszkoreit, J., Vaswani, A.: Self-attention with relative position representations. arXiv preprint arXiv:1803.02155 (2018)
26. Sun, Y., Wu, Z., Ma, Y., Tresp, V.: Quantum architecture search with unsupervised representation learning. arXiv preprint arXiv:2401.11576 (2024)
27. Vaswani, A., et al.: Attention is all you need. In: Advances in Neural Information Processing Systems, vol. 30 (2017)
28. Venturelli, D., Marchand, D., Rojo, G.: Job shop scheduling solver based on quantum annealing. In: Proceedings of ICAPS-16 Workshop on Constraint Satisfaction Techniques for Planning and Scheduling (COPLAS), pp. 25–34 (2016)
29. Wallman, J.J., Emerson, J.: Noise tailoring for scalable quantum computation via randomized compiling. Phys. Rev. A **94**(5), 052325 (2016)
30. Wu, W., Yan, G., Lu, X., Pan, K., Yan, J.: QuantumDARTS: differentiable quantum architecture search for variational quantum algorithms. In: Proceedings of the 40th International Conference on Machine Learning. ICML'23, JMLR.org (2023)
31. Ye, E., Chen, S.Y.C.: Quantum architecture search via continual reinforcement learning. arXiv preprint arXiv:2112.05779 (2021)
32. Zhang, S.X., Hsieh, C.Y., Zhang, S., Yao, H.: Neural predictor based quantum architecture search. Mach. Learn. Sci. Technol. **2**(4), 045027 (2021)
33. Zhang, S.X., Hsieh, C.Y., Zhang, S., Yao, H.: Differentiable quantum architecture search. Quantum Sci. Technol. **7**(4), 045023 (2022)
34. Zlokapa, A., Gheorghiu, A.: A deep learning model for noise prediction on near-term quantum devices. In: Proceedings of the ACM/IEEE International Conference for High Performance Computing, Networking, Storage, and Analysis (SC '19), pp. 1–6. Association for Computing Machinery and IEEE Computer Society, Denver, CO, USA (2019). k. Alexander Zlokapa Master's thesis version available as arXiv:2005.10811

Quantum-Inspired Attention for Efficient Face Recognition

Aayush Gauba(✉)

Southern Illinois University Edwardsville, Edwardsville, USA
agauba@siue.edu

Abstract. We present a novel quantum-inspired deep learning model for face recognition that draws key ideas from quantum interference yet operates entirely on standard GPUs. By introducing complex-valued attention mechanisms within a lightweight convolutional neural network (CNN), our approach emulates wave-like interference effects using sinusoidal functions in the complex domain. When trained on the large-scale VGGFace2 dataset, our model achieves 92.8% training accuracy and 91.2% validation accuracy, using only around 8.2M parameters which is substantially fewer than many state of the art approaches. These results suggest that "quantum inspired" design can enhance classical deep learning for face recognition without needing specialized quantum hardware.

Keywords: Quantum-Inspired · Attention Mechanism · Face Recognition · CNN · Quantum Interference · Deep Learning · Triplet Loss

1 Introduction

Face recognition underpins a wide array of applications, from phone unlocking and user authentication to large-scale surveillance systems. Methods like FaceNet [1], ArcFace [2], and VGGFace [3] have led the way in achieving high accuracy, yet they often rely on massive networks with tens of millions of parameters. Such large models can be expensive to train, slow to deploy, and difficult to run on resource-limited or embedded devices.

In parallel, quantum computing research has inspired new computational paradigms that rely on phenomena like superposition and interference. While true quantum neural networks are still largely theoretical, *quantum-inspired* techniques on classical hardware can replicate certain interference-like properties by leveraging complex arithmetic. We adopt this philosophy: **instead of** running on specialized quantum computers, we simulate aspects of quantum interference entirely in a standard deep learning pipeline.

Contributions. Our work introduces:

1. A *quantum-inspired* multi-head attention mechanism that uses complex-valued sinusoidal operations to emulate interference, thus selectively enhancing or suppressing facial features.

D. Cavar et al. (Eds.): QNLPAI 2025, CCIS 2659, pp. 58–66, 2026.
https://doi.org/10.1007/978-3-032-13883-5_4

2. A streamlined CNN architecture requiring only ∼8.2M parameters, trained with triplet loss on VGGFace2, yielding high accuracy for face recognition.
3. A deeper discussion of how wave-like interference can be approximated on classical hardware, offering new directions for "quantum-inspired" deep learning research.

By blending quantum interference ideas with standard CNNs, we open a path to more compact, expressive models, potentially useful across biometric tasks.

2 Related Work

2.1 Deep Face Recognition

Current deep face recognition systems rely on well-established CNN backbones trained on large-scale datasets. FaceNet [1] pioneered the use of triplet loss to produce discriminative embeddings, while ArcFace [2] introduced an angular margin that refines decision boundaries. VGGFace [3] demonstrated the effectiveness of training on millions of face images. Although these models excel at accuracy, their parameter counts often range from 23M (ResNet-50) to over 100M (VGG-16), which complicates deployment on edge devices or cost-sensitive platforms.

2.2 Quantum-Inspired Neural Mechanisms

Quantum neural networks remain somewhat aspirational, given the current immaturity of quantum hardware. However, *quantum-inspired* methods bring elements of quantum mechanics (e.g., interference, phase) into classical deep learning by employing complex arithmetic, phase based transformations, and wave like operations [4]. Our approach fits squarely here: we model certain interference effects through sinusoidal transformations in the complex domain, *without* needing actual quantum systems.

3 Proposed Method

3.1 Overview of the Architecture

Figure 1 outlines our pipeline. We ingest 128×128 face images into a 4-layer CNN backbone, flatten the features, reduce dimensionality to a "quantum dimension", then apply a novel quantum-inspired attention block that simulates interference. Finally, a two-layer MLP maps these enriched features to a 128-d embedding optimized via triplet loss.

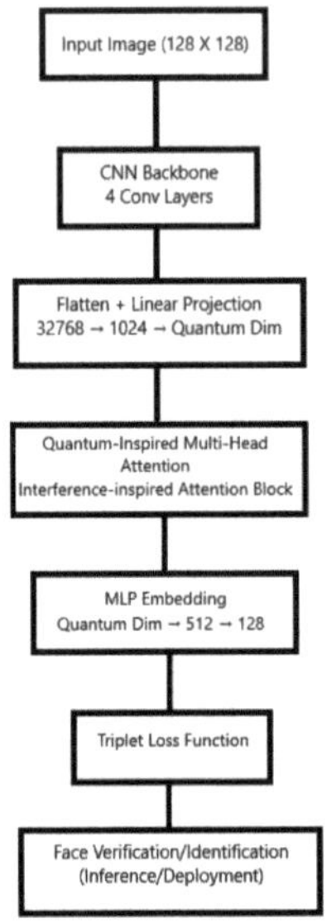

Fig. 1. High level structure of our quantum inspired CNN for face recognition.

3.2 Input and CNN Backbone

We resize each face image to 128×128 to maintain uniformity. The CNN backbone includes:

– Four convolutional layers (3×3 kernels, stride 2, padding 1) to progressively reduce spatial dimensions.

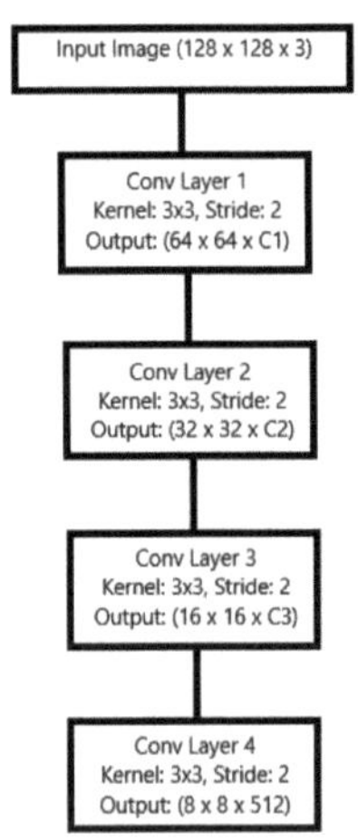

Fig. 2. Our backbone processes a 128×128×3 image into an 8×8×512 feature map.

- Batch normalization and ReLU after each convolution to stabilize gradients.
- Output feature map dimension: $(B, 512, 8, 8)$ for a batch size B.

This lightweight backbone strikes a balance between representation power and parameter efficiency.

3.3 Flattening and Linear Projection

We flatten the $8\times8\times512$ feature map into a 32,768-dimensional vector. Handling such a high dimension can be expensive and prone to overfitting, so we use a two-step linear projection:

1. **FC Layer #1**: 32768→1024, followed by ReLU and dropout ($p = 0.3$).
2. **FC Layer #2**: 1024→'quantum dimension" (e.g., 32).

By distilling essential information into a compact representation, we set the stage for the quantum inspired block to efficiently capture wave like relationships.

3.4 Quantum-Inspired Multi Head Attention

This block is our main innovation. We split the compressed features $x \in \mathbb{R}^{B\times D}$ into multiple heads. Each head operates on a slice of the feature vector and applies a learnable interference transformation of the form:

$$x_{\text{complex}} = x + \sin\Big(\alpha \cdot (\text{scale} \odot x + \text{bias})\Big), \quad \alpha = 0.1,$$

where $\text{scale}, \text{bias} \in \mathbb{C}^{D/H}$ are head specific, learnable complex valued parameters, and $\odot$ denotes elementwise multiplication. The *scale* term adjusts the amplitude of each feature, while the *bias* introduces a learnable phase shift. The sine operation is applied elementwise in the complex domain, simulating wave interference by modulating each feature's phase and intensity. We then take the magnitude of the resulting vector:

$$\text{output} = \Big| x_{\text{complex}} \Big|.$$

By simulating constructive and destructive interference, this transformation selectively enhances or suppresses features in a phase-aware manner. Concatenating outputs from all heads merges multiple interference "perspectives," yielding a more expressive and compact representation. While this mechanism does not implement quantum operations per se, it draws inspiration from quantum interference, where phase alignment determines amplification or cancellation.

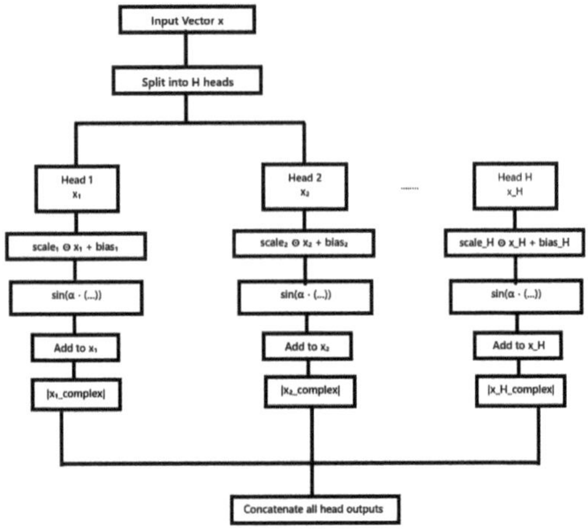

Fig. 3. Illustration of the Quantum-Inspired Multi Head Attention block. The input vector x is split into H heads, and each head applies a sinusoidal interference function based on learnable complex valued scale and bias parameters. The magnitude of each transformed output is computed, and all head outputs are concatenated to form the final representation.

3.5 MLP Embedding and Triplet Loss

An MLP then processes the fused attention outputs:

- **Layer 1**: quantum dimension $\rightarrow$ 512 (with ReLU).
- **Layer 2**: 512 $\rightarrow$ 128, yielding the final face embedding.

We optimize this embedding via a standard triplet margin loss:

$$\mathcal{L}_{\text{triplet}} = \max\Big(0,\ \|f(a) - f(p)\|_2^2\ -\ \|f(a) - f(n)\|_2^2\ +\ m\Big),$$

where a, p, and n are anchor, positive, and negative samples of face images. This ensures embeddings of the same identity are closer than those of different identities by at least a margin $m = 1.0$.

3.6 Quantum Inspiration: Why Interference?

In quantum mechanics, wave interference emerges when two complex exponentials add or subtract, as in:

$$\left| e^{i\theta_1} + e^{i\theta_2} \right|^2 = 2 + 2\cos(\theta_1 - \theta_2).$$

We approximate such behavior using complex sine transformations. Features that "align in phase" can reinforce one another, while out of phase features diminish. Although this is a heuristic approach rather than a formal quantum operation, we find it significantly enriches the representation capacity of a relatively small CNN, helping it discern subtle facial variations.

4 Dataset and Preprocessing

4.1 VGGFace2

We train and evaluate our model on VGGFace2, a large scale dataset of over 3 million images across 9,131 identities, each with about 360 images. This variety tests a model's ability to handle pose, illumination, and other real world variations.

4.2 Data Augmentation

To boost generalization, we apply:

- **Resize**: all images to 128×128
- **RandomResizedCrop**: scale $(0.8, 1.0)$
- **RandomHorizontalFlip**: $p = 0.5$
- **ColorJitter**: brightness=0.2, contrast=0.2, saturation=0.2, hue=0.1
- **Rotation**: up to 15°

5 Training Procedure

5.1 Triplet Loss and Implementation Details

We rely on triplet loss for learning discriminative embeddings. The optimizer is Adam with $(\beta_1, \beta_2) = (0.9, 0.999)$ and learning rate 1×10^{-4}. A StepLR halves the learning rate every 10 epochs to fine tune convergence. We train for 50 epochs on an NVIDIA A100 (40GB VRAM) with PyTorch 1.12. Complex operations use `torch.complex128` to mitigate numerical instability, then convert back to float32 for the remainder of the computations.

5.2 Inference for Face Verification/Identification

At inference time, each image is mapped to a 128-d embedding. Distances (e.g., Euclidean or cosine) between embeddings are used for tasks like face verification (checking if two images match) or face identification (ranking identities in a database).

6 Experimental Results

6.1 Accuracy and Convergence

Table 1 shows training and validation accuracy at several points, demonstrating a steady climb with minimal overfitting. By epoch 150, we reach 92.8% training accuracy and 91.2% validation accuracy.

Table 1. Training and validation accuracy on VGGFace2.

Epoch	Train Acc (%)	Val Acc (%)
1	73.33	74.26
10	83.28	83.63
20	86.45	85.90
30	88.90	87.12
50	91.00	89.00
100	91.71	90.44
150	92.80	91.23

6.2 Parameter Breakdown

Table 2. Parameter counts in each module. Our entire model remains under 8.2M parameters.

Component	Description	# Params
CNN Backbone	4-layer conv stack	$\sim$ 5.2M
Linear Projection	(32768→1024→quantum_dim)	$\sim$ 1.0M
Quantum Blocks	2 stacked multi-head complex attn	$\sim$ 1.2M
Final Embedding	quantum_dim→512→128	$\sim$ 0.8M
Total		$\sim$ 8.2M

Compared to the 23M or more in typical face recognition backbones, our approach is notably smaller. This parameter efficiency is crucial for deployment in real time or on resource constrained devices.

6.3 Validation Accuracy Comparison with Existing Models

To fairly assess the effectiveness of our quantum-inspired architecture, we compare its performance against well-established face embedding models such as FaceNet [5] and ArcFace [6]. While both models are widely cited and evaluated on face verification benchmarks, neither reports direct top-1 classification accuracy on the datasets used for training, such as VGGFace2. Instead, their performance is typically measured on external benchmarks like LFW, CFP-FP, or IJB-C using verification accuracy or true accept rate (TAR) at fixed false accept rates (FAR).

FaceNet reports a validation rate of 87.9% on an internal holdout set at FAR= 10^{-3}, but this is not a direct top-1 accuracy and the dataset used is a private internal collection of 200 million images. ArcFace, although trained on MS1M and VGGFace2, does not report any validation accuracy on these training datasets. Instead, it achieves 99.83% on LFW and similar scores on other verification tasks, which are not directly comparable to classification accuracy.

In contrast, our model is trained and validated on VGGFace2 using a standard 80/20 split. It achieves a top-1 validation accuracy of **90.02%** after 20 epochs, making it one of the few models to report actual validation performance on this widely used dataset. Furthermore, our model achieves this result with fewer than 10 million parameters, offering a lightweight alternative without compromising accuracy.

Table 3. Comparison of models. FaceNet and ArcFace report verification accuracy on external benchmarks, while our model reports direct classification accuracy on VGGFace2.

Model	Train Dataset	Validation Accuracy	Params
FaceNet	Private (200M images)	87.9%@FAR= 10^{-3} (internal)	22M
ArcFace	MS1M + VGGFace2	Not Reported	65M
Ours (Quantum-Inspired)	**VGGFace2**	**90.02%** (Top-1)	**8M**

7 Discussion of "Quantum" Inspiration

Our approach does not implement genuine quantum gates or measurement postulates; rather, it *borrows* the idea of interference to selectively amplify or dampen feature components. This parallels quantum wavefunctions, where constructive and destructive interference depend on relative phases. By mapping features to `complex128` and applying sinusoidal transformations, we approximate that principle, but remain fully on classical hardware.

8 Comparison and Limitations

- **Heuristic Quantum Inspiration**: Critics may note we use "quantum inspired" loosely. True quantum effects like entanglement, superposition, or measurement are not directly modeled. Nonetheless, the analogy to interference helps clarify how phase relationships can enhance feature representation.
- **Stability and Complexity**: Complex arithmetic must be done carefully to avoid numerical issues. Our design uses a modest scaling factor ($\alpha = 0.1$) to keep transformations well behaved.
- **Potential Extensions**: Future efforts could refine these "wave like" operations or even integrate partial quantum hardware accelerators if they become more practical.

9 Conclusion

We presented a compact CNN architecture enriched with quantum-inspired multihead attention for face recognition on the VGGFace2 dataset. By exploiting interference-like effects in complex space, our model reaches 92.8% training accuracy and 91.2% validation accuracy with far fewer parameters than many popular face recognition systems. These findings suggest that wave inspired transformations can enhance classical CNNs without the overhead of genuine quantum hardware. Future directions include exploring more rigorous theoretical grounding, scaling to other biometric tasks, and investigating multi modal data fusion under an interference like paradigm.

Acknowledgements. We gratefully acknowledge open source frameworks (PyTorch, Colab) and the many researchers exploring quantum computing concepts, whose work inspired our approach. Although ours is a purely classical implementation, the notion of interference drives our attempt to capture richer facial features via complex arithmetic.

References

1. Schroff, F., Kalenichenko, D., Philbin, J.: FaceNet: a unified embedding for face recognition and clustering. In: Proceedings of the CVPR (2015)
2. Deng, J., et al.: ArcFace: additive angular margin loss for deep face recognition. In: Proceedings of the CVPR (2019)
3. Parkhi, O.M., Vedaldi, A., Zisserman, A.: Deep Face Recognition. BMVC (2015)
4. Schuld, M., Sinayskiy, I., Petruccione, F.: An introduction to quantum machine learning. Contemp. Phys. (2015)
5. Schroff, F., Kalenichenko, D., Philbin, J.: FaceNet: a unified embedding for face recognition and clustering. In: Proceedings of the IEEE Conference on Computer Vision and Pattern Recognition (CVPR) (2015)
6. Deng, J., Guo, J., Xue, N., Zafeiriou, S.: ArcFace: additive angular margin loss for deep face recognition. In: Proceedings of the IEEE/CVF Conference on Computer Vision and Pattern Recognition (CVPR) (2019)

An Efficient Quantum Classifier Based on Hamiltonian Representations

Federico Tiblias[1(✉)], Anna Schroeder[2], Yue Zhang[3], Mariami Gachechiladze[4], and Iryna Gurevych[1]

[1] UKP Lab, Hessian Center for AI (hessian.AI), Department of Computer Science, Technical University of Darmstadt, Darmstadt, Germany
federico.tiblias@tu-darmstadt.de

[2] Quantum Computing Group, Department of Computer Science, Technical University of Darmstadt, Merck KGaA, Darmstadt, Germany

[3] School of Engineering, Westlake University, Hangzhou, China

[4] Quantum Computing Group, Department of Computer Science, Technical University of Darmstadt, Darmstadt, Germany

Abstract. Quantum machine learning (QML) is a discipline that seeks to transfer the advantages of quantum computing to data-driven tasks. However, many studies rely on toy datasets or heavy feature reduction, raising concerns about their scalability. Progress is further hindered by hardware limitations and the significant costs of encoding dense vector representations on quantum devices. To address these challenges, we propose an efficient approach called *Hamiltonian classifier* that circumvents the costs associated with data encoding by mapping inputs to a finite set of Pauli strings and computing predictions as their expectation values. In addition, we introduce two classifier variants with different scaling in terms of parameters and sample complexity. We evaluate our approach on text and image classification tasks, against well-established classical and quantum models. The Hamiltonian classifier delivers performance comparable to or better than these methods. Notably, our method achieves logarithmic complexity in both qubits *and* quantum gates, making it well-suited for large-scale, real-world applications.

Keywords: Quantum Natural Language Processing · Quantum Machine Learning · Variational Quantum Circuits · Flipped Models

1 Introduction

In recent years, interest in quantum computing has grown significantly due to the provable advantages in computational complexity and memory usage some algorithms exhibit over their best classical analogues [6,38,41]. For instance, efficient algorithms exist that can solve problems such as integer factorization [49], the Fourier transform [8], and specific instances of matrix inversion [23] with an exponential speedup over the fastest known classical methods. Other notable results include Grover's algorithm, which performs an unstructured search, achieving a

D. Cavar et al. (Eds.): QNLPAI 2025, CCIS 2659, pp. 67–89, 2026.
https://doi.org/10.1007/978-3-032-13883-5_5

$\mathcal{O}(\sqrt{n})$ time complexity, a quadratic improvement over the fastest classical approach that scales as $\mathcal{O}(n)$ [20]. In parallel with these theoretical developments, the size of publicly accessible quantum machines has been steadily growing, and several companies have begun offering commercial cloud access to these devices [62].

Quantum machine learning is an offshoot of quantum computing that seeks to extend its advantages to data-driven methods. The leading paradigm revolves around variational quantum circuits (VQCs), quantum algorithms whose parameters can be adjusted with classical optimization to solve a specific problem [10]. This approach is sometimes referred to as quantum neural networks, given the similarities with the classical counterpart [19,28]. Prior works have found some evidence that QML algorithms can offer improvements over their classical analogues in terms of capacity [1], expressive power [18], and generalization [9].

Despite the advancements of VQCs, a large-scale demonstration of *advantage* - the ability of a quantum computer to solve a problem faster, with fewer resources or better performance than any classical counterpart - remains out of reach for QML algorithms. Current quantum machines, referred to as *Noisy Intermediate-Scale Quantum* (NISQ) devices [39], are restricted both in size and complexity of the operations they can perform [63]. *Qubits*, the basic units of quantum computation, are hard to maintain in a state useful for computation, and scaling quantum processors to a size suitable for QML remains a significant challenge. Moreover, the widespread use of dense and unstructured vector representations in modern machine learning architectures [5] makes their translation into quantum equivalents challenging. Specifically, the processes of loading data onto a quantum device, known as *encoding*, and extracting results from it, referred to as *measurement*, can scale rapidly in terms of qubit requirements or computational costs [46]. These costs may grow prohibitively with input size, potentially negating any quantum advantage. As a result, researchers are often forced to down-scale their experiments, making it unclear whether these findings generalize at larger scales [7,36].

Motivated by these limitations, we propose a scheme to efficiently encode and measure classical data from quantum devices and demonstrate its effectiveness across different tasks. The method we propose is a specific instance of a *flipped model* [27], a type of circuit which encodes data as the observable of a quantum circuit rather than as a quantum state, effectively bypassing the need for input encoding. Unstructured input data is mapped onto Pauli strings, which are then combined to construct a Hamiltonian. The classifier prediction is obtained as the expectation value of this Hamiltonian. We present a practical implementation of the standard flipped model by constructing an explicit mapping from classical inputs to quantum observables. This approach not only translates the theoretical flipped model into a concrete, implementable circuit design but does so with favourable resource efficiency, achieving logarithmic scaling in both qubit count *and* gate complexity with respect to input dimensionality. We also introduce two variants that trade some classification performance in exchange for a smaller model size and better sample complexity, respectively. Crucially, the scaling exhibited by these models allows them to be executed on quantum devices and simulated on classical hardware at scales already meaningful for NLP tasks. In brief, this paper provides the following contributions:

C_1 A novel encoding scheme achieving logarithmic qubit and gate complexity;
C_2 Variants of this scheme with different performance-cost tradeoffs;
C_3 A thorough evaluation of our scheme on text and image classification tasks, against established quantum and classical baselines.

2 Hamiltonian Classifier

QML models rely on encoding classical data into quantum states and processing it through VQCs. Existing encoding schemes as well as quantum measurements often pose bottlenecks due to their gate, qubit, and readout costs. This is particularly critical in NLP and CV applications where inputs and outputs are high-dimensional [3,44]. A lengthier discussion into existing techniques and their limitations is provided in Appendix A. To mitigate these challenges, the *flipped model* has been recently conceptualized [27], where quantum resources are only required during training, while inference can happen classically. Flipped models combined with shadow tomography have been proven to outperform classical methods under widely-believed cryptography assumptions [21]. The guarantees of flipped models, as well as their scalability, warrant their exploration in the context of QML.

In the following, we describe a flipped model that improves over previous works by sensibly lowering qubit requirements. To the best of our knowledge, we are the first to apply flipped models to text classification and to provide a thorough evaluation of such methods across multiple datasets, comparing against classical and quantum baselines. We also propose two variants that further reduce model size and sample complexity with minimal impact on performance and extend flipped models to the multi-class scenario.

2.1 Fully-parametrized Hamiltonian (HAM)

Our Hamiltonian classifier takes as input a sequence of embeddings $x = [x_1\, x_2\, \dots\, x_s]$, $x_i \in \mathbb{R}^d$ and outputs a prediction probability $f_{\theta,\phi}$, a real number representing the estimated class the input belongs to.

Similarly to VQCs, gradient descent is used to optimize the classifier parameters θ, ϕ on a given training set $\mathbf{X}$ with binary labels $\mathbf{y}$. The classifier can encode embeddings of size at most $N = 2^n$ with the remaining $N - d$ dimensions padded to 0. The optimization problem can be summarized as:

$$\arg\min_{\theta,\phi} \frac{1}{|\mathbf{X}|} \sum_{x\in\mathbf{X},y\in\mathbf{y}} \mathcal{L}(f_{\theta,\phi}(x), y), \tag{1}$$

$$f_{\theta,\phi}(x) := \sigma(\psi_\theta^\dagger H_\phi(x)\psi_\theta) \tag{2}$$

$$H_\phi(x) := H_\phi^0 + \frac{1}{s}\sum_{i=1}^{s} x_i x_i^\top \tag{3}$$

$$\psi_\theta := U_\theta|0\rangle^{\otimes n} = U_\theta[1\,0\,\cdots\,0]^\top. \tag{4}$$

$H_\phi \in \mathbb{R}^{N\times N}$ is the Hamiltonian of our system, and is constructed from embeddings x and a bias term $H_\phi^0 \in \mathbb{R}^{N\times N}$ (Eq. 3). The bias term is a fully parametrized Hermitian matrix, giving more fine-grained control over the Hamiltonian. $U_\theta \in \mathbb{C}^{N\times N}$ represents a VQC, and ψ_θ is the result of applying said VQC to the starting state (Eq. 4). The specific choice of VQC is application-dependent and we experiment with three qubit-efficient circuits during hyperparameter tuning, which we discuss in Appendix B. The prediction probability $f_{\theta,\phi}$ is regularized using the sigmoid function σ (Eq. 2). Finally, parameters θ, ϕ are optimized classically to minimize the loss function $\mathcal{L}$, the cross entropy. When building U_θ and ψ_θ, they are not explicitly represented as dense matrices in classical form. Instead, they are constructed directly on quantum hardware from a manageable set of parameters, avoiding the need for large-scale classical representations. By encoding inputs of size $d \leq N$ over n qubits, we attain logarithmic scaling in the number of qubits and an overall sample complexity that scales quadratically in the embedding size. We expand on this in Sect. 2.4.

2.2 Parameter-efficient Hamiltonian (PEFF)

The bias term H_ϕ^0 of HAM significantly contributes to its parameter count, resulting in a $\mathcal{O}(N^2)$ scaling. To lower the model size, we experiment with applying a bias term $b_\phi \in \mathbb{R}^d$ directly to the input embeddings as $\tilde{x}_i := x_i + b_\phi$. This term skews the distribution in the vector space while only requiring $\mathcal{O}(d)$ parameters. The Hamiltonian is then constructed as $H_\phi(\tilde{x}) := \frac{1}{s}\sum_{i=1}^{s} \tilde{x}_i\tilde{x}$.

Physically implementing the Hamiltonians of HAM and PEFF requires first decomposing them into observables that the quantum device can measure and then performing measurements for each observable separately. As we detail in Appendix A.1, this process is potentially expensive, requiring an exponential number of operations. In the following, we show how the model can be restructured to drastically reduce this cost.

2.3 Simplified Hamiltonian (SIM) Variant

To address the computational challenges we described above, we propose an extension of PEFF that constructs the Hamiltonian from a small number p of

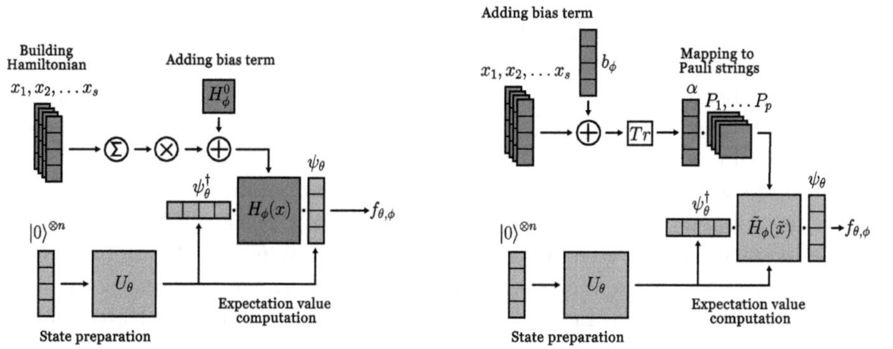

Fig. 1. The HAM (left) and SIM (right) variants of our Hamiltonian Classifier at a glance. In green, parts that are stored classically, in blue, parts that can be represented on quantum computers. (Color figure online)

Pauli strings, circumventing the need for an expensive decomposition and reducing the number of necessary measurements to $\mathcal{O}(p)$ (Fig. 1). More information about Pauli strings can be found in Appendix A.1. We define p Pauli strings $P_1, P_2, \dots P_p \in \mathcal{P}_n$ (in practice, they can be chosen at random) and use them to compute the corresponding coefficients $\alpha_1, \alpha_2, \dots \alpha_p$ from H:

$$\tilde{x} := \frac{1}{s}\sum_{i=1}^{s} x_i + b_\phi \tag{5}$$

$$H_\phi(\tilde{x}) := \tilde{x}\tilde{x}^\top \tag{6}$$

$$\alpha_i = \frac{1}{2^n}\mathrm{Tr}(P_i H_\phi) = \frac{1}{2^n}\tilde{x}^\top P_i \tilde{x} \tag{7}$$

$$\tilde{H}_\phi(\tilde{x}) := \sum_{j=1}^{p} \alpha_j w_j P_j, \tag{8}$$

where $w_j \in \mathbb{R}$ is a learned parameter that re-weights the effect of Pauli strings. P_j and H_ϕ in Eq. 7 are generally large matrices, but several algorithms exist that side-step the costs of full multiplication by exploiting the structure of the Pauli string [22,29]. For this method, we choose to redefine H_ϕ (Eq. 5 and 6) in a way that allows replacing the expensive matrix-matrix product $P_i H_\phi$ with two more efficient vector-matrix products $\tilde{x}^\top P_i \tilde{x}$, thus improving scaling.

The expectation value computation in SIM can be recast as: $f_{\theta,\phi}(\tilde{x}) = \sigma\left(\frac{1}{2^n}\sum_{j=1}^{p} \tilde{x}^\dagger P_j \tilde{x} w_j \psi_\theta^\dagger P_j \psi_\theta\right)$. This shows that SIM computes a weighted sum of several feature maps $\tilde{x}^\dagger P_j \tilde{x}$, where the weights are determined by both the learned term w_j and the factor $\psi_\theta^\dagger P_j \psi_\theta$. These two terms concur to select the feature maps most relevant for solving the problem. During our exploration, we observe that removing w_j significantly degrades performance. We speculate this occurs because $\psi_\theta^\dagger P_j \psi_\theta$ is constrained to the range $[-1, 1]$, whereas the presence of w_j introduces a notion of magnitude that facilitates training. A related approach is discussed in [26], which focuses on improving variational strategies rather than directly addressing the challenges of input encoding. We believe that these two methods could be synergistically combined to further reduce overall computational costs.

All proposed methods output a prediction probability $f_{\theta,\phi}$ to be interpreted as a binary label. We can extend this to a scenario with c distinct classes by using a one-vs-many approach: either U_θ, b_ϕ or w can be tied to a specific class to obtain a class-specific discriminator. We choose a setup that learns c distinct re-weightings $w_1, w_2, \ldots w_c$ and build c separate Hamiltonians $\tilde{H}^1_\phi, \tilde{H}^2_\phi, \ldots \tilde{H}^c_\phi$ so that each one discriminates a single class. For class k, we have $H^k_\phi(\tilde{x}) := \sum_{j=1}^{p} \alpha_j w^k_j P_j$. Parameter count scales as $\mathcal{O}(c)$, although different choices of parameter sharing strongly affect the final number. Since our setup learns different weights for the same Pauli strings across classes, expectation values on a real quantum device can be computed only once and then post-processed to obtain probabilities for all classes.

2.4 Complexity Analysis

In this section, we compare the theoretical qubit count, gate complexity, and sample complexity of our classifier with other established models from the literature. We consider a subset of implementations from the literature that we consider representative of the current discourse. Our three variants all achieve a qubit count that scales as the logarithm of the input dimensionality. This is determined by the number of qubits required to encode a large enough Hamiltonian. For our models, gate complexity depends entirely on the chosen circuit U_θ. The ansätze we consider throughout our experiments result in a linear or quadratic scaling. Sample complexity, defined as the total number of Pauli strings to measure in order to obtain a prediction, both HAM and PEFF necessitate a full evaluation of the Hamiltonian, resulting in a complexity of $\mathcal{O}(4^n)$. Since $4^{\log_2(d)} = 2^{\log_2(d^2)}$, we conclude that the sample complexity is $\mathcal{O}(d^2)$. Notably, SIM combines the logarithmic scaling in qubit and gate complexity of the other variants with a constant sample complexity made possible by simplifying the Hamiltonian, making it a strong candidate for practical implementation on NISQ devices. The full comparison is shown in Table 1. For readability, we omit the precision term arising when running these methods on quantum hardware. All models incur an additional $1/\epsilon^2$ term in sample complexity, where ϵ is the desired precision.

3 Experiments

3.1 Datasets and Pre-Processing

To evaluate the capabilities of our models, we select a diverse set of tasks encompassing both text and image data, covering binary and multi-class scenarios. To facilitate replicability, our scripts automatically download all datasets on the first run.

Table 1. Theoretical scaling comparison of various VQCs, with d input size, l number of layers, and p number of Pauli strings to measure (defined as a hyperparameter).

Model	Reference	Qubit count	Gate complexity	Sample complexity
QCNN	[24]	$\mathcal{O}(d)$	$\mathcal{O}(d^2)$	$\mathcal{O}(2^d)$
	[16]	$\mathcal{O}(\log d)$	$\mathcal{O}(d + l \log d)$	$\mathcal{O}(p)$
QLSTM	[13]	$\mathcal{O}(d)$	$\mathcal{O}(ld)$	$\mathcal{O}(d)$
QNN	[19]	$\mathcal{O}$(d)	$\mathcal{O}$(l)	$\mathcal{O}(1)$
	[37]	$\mathcal{O}(d)$	$\mathcal{O}$(l d)	$\mathcal{O}(1)$
	[45]	$\mathcal{O}(\log d)$	$\mathcal{O}(d + l \log d)$	$\mathcal{O}(1)$
HAM	Ours	$\mathcal{O}(\log d)$	$\mathcal{O}(l \log d)$ or $\mathcal{O}(l \log(d)^2)$	$\mathcal{O}(d^2)$
PEFF	Ours	$\mathcal{O}(\log d)$	$\mathcal{O}(l \log d)$ or $\mathcal{O}(l \log(d)^2)$	$\mathcal{O}(d^2)$
SIM	Ours	$\mathcal{O}(\log d)$	$\mathcal{O}(l \log d)$ or $\mathcal{O}(l \log(d)^2)$	$\mathcal{O}(p)$

Text Datasets. We first consider the GLUE Stanford Sentiment Treebank (SST) dataset as obtained from HuggingFace[1] [51,54]. It consists of $\sim 70k$ single sentences extracted from movie reviews whose sentiment (positive/negative) was annotated by 3 human judges. We then evaluate our method on the IMDb Large Movie Review Dataset [35] containing $50k$ highly polar movie reviews. We also consider the AG News [64] classification task as a benchmark for our multi-class model. AG News consists of $\sim 128k$ news articles divided by topic (world, sports, business, sci/tech). These are commonplace datasets reasonably close to real-world applications. For text datasets, we remove all punctuation, lowercase all text, tokenize with a whitespace strategy, and finally embed tokens with word2vec[2] to obtain a sequence x. The resulting embedding has size $d = 300$ and requires $n = 9$ qubits to be represented in our methods.

Image Datasets. As a sanity check, we consider a binary version of MNIST which only includes digits 0 and 1. We then consider Fashion-MNIST [60], a dataset of $60k$ grayscale images of clothes subdivided into 10 classes. Feeding images directly to our models results in $d = 784$ and $n = 10$. We further experiment on a binarized version of the CIFAR-10 dataset [30], we name CIFAR-2, obtained by grouping the original ten classes into two categories: vehicles and animals. The 32×32 RGB images result in $d = 1024$ features over $n = 10$ qubits. We also note that no further pre-processing or dimensionality reduction is performed to preserve the original properties of the images. MNIST and Fashion-MNIST representations are not sequential and therefore are considered by our model as a special case with $s = 1$, while in CIFAR-2 each channel is considered as a different element of a sequence with $s = 3$.

[1] https://huggingface.co/datasets/stanfordnlp/sst2.

[2] https://code.google.com/archive/p/word2vec/.

3.2 Baselines

We compare our classifiers (HAM, PEFF, SIM) with three quantum baselines: a QLSTM [13], a QCNN [16], and a simple circuit ansatz (CIRC). QLSTM and QCNN have been adapted from implementations of the original papers. CIRC is our implementation and consists of an amplitude encoding for the input, the same hardware-efficient ansätze of HAM, and a linear regression on the circuit's output state. Note that running CIRC in practice would require state tomography, this setup is therefore not meant to be efficient or scalable but rather to give a best-case scenario of a VQC of similar complexity to our classifier. We also compare with out-of-the-box classical baselines: a multi-layer perception (MLP), a logistic regression (LOG), an RNN, an LSTM, and a CNN. MLP and LOG act on the mean-pooled embedding of the sequence.

3.3 Experimental Setting

We first perform a random search on hyperparameters such as learning rate, batch size, number of qubits, and number of layers to identify the best configuration of each architecture. For the sake of brevity, a more detailed discussion is moved to Appendix B. After identifying the best hyperparameters, we train 10 models for each architecture with randomized seeds on the original training split and average their performance on the test split. The only exception is the SST2 dataset, for which no test set is provided. In this case, we select the run achieving the lowest training loss and submit it to GLUE's website to get a test score. Appendix C shows additional experiments in which we further investigate architectural choices such as bias, state preparation, and number of Pauli strings. With the exception of QCNN, which is implemented in PennyLane, all quantum operations are simulated in PyTorch, as it allows batching several Hamiltonians, thus enabling efficient training. We do not simulate noise in order to assess the performance of our approach under an ideal scenario. For all tasks, we use a cross-entropy loss during training.

3.4 Results

In Tables 2 and 3, we report train and test accuracy for the text and image datasets, respectively. MNIST2 is omitted for brevity since all models successfully achieve perfect scores. This validates our setup and confirms that HAM, PEFF, and SIM learn correctly. In the SST2 task, HAM performs competitively with baseline methods using a similar number of parameters, outperforming simpler models like LOG, MLP, and RNN, and ranking just below the LSTM and QLSTM. AG News and IMDb turn out to be easier tasks, with SIM achieving scores comparable to the baselines, and accuracy being high for all models. CIFAR2 proves to be a hard task, likely due to the images being coloured rather than grayscale and having a higher resolution: while HAM and PEFF score relatively higher than the LOG baseline, SIM underperforms, possibly due to its relatively simple decision boundary. We speculate that a higher number of Pauli

Table 2. Accuracies across text datasets. Results are averaged over 10 runs or (*) run achieving lowest training loss.

Model	SST2			IMDb			AG News		
	# Params	Train	Test*	# Params	Train	Test	# Params	Train	Test
LOG	301	84.7	80.4	301	85.8	85.5	1204	90.1	89.2
MLP	180901	97.5	80.2	180901	88.1	85.8	40604	90.2	89.1
LSTM	241701	97.8	84.4	241600	99.3	88.4	242004	91.5	90.5
RNN	40301	89.6	80.1	60501	79.7	78.1	40604	88.8	88.1
CIRC	923	85.2	80.1	923	86.1	85.8	2387	89.7	89.2
QLSTM	2766	89.9	84.4	4679	76.8	67.9	3582	87.2	86.7
HAM	130854	91.2	82.3	130926	91.0	88.1	-	-	-
PEFF	410	81.8	80.0	410	84.0	83.8	-	-	-
SIM	1338	80.6	79.0	1410	86.0	85.3	4416	89.4	88.6

strings would narrow this gap, as more complex transformations would increase the capacity of the model. On Fashion, SIM performs better than LOG but worse than other baselines. Notably, CIRC achieves relatively high performance. Across tasks, PEFF and SIM attain performance comparable with the baseline despite the low parameter count. PEFF confirms our intuition that simply skewing points in the embedding space can substitute the bulky bias term over the whole Hamiltonian, while SIM confirms that performance can be retained even with a Hamiltonian composed of a few Pauli strings. The high parameter count of HAM in MNIST2 and CIFAR2 is necessary to encode full-size images, resulting in large Hamiltonians. Across quantum models, we find no clear link between entangling circuits and performance; non-entangling baselines often perform best, aligning with prior findings [7].

We perform additional experiments in Appendix C and find evidence that the number of Pauli strings is strongly linked with better performance. Specifically, larger models with more Pauli strings exhibit higher accuracy and more stable training dynamics (Fig. 2). Notably, between 500 and 1000 Pauli strings are already sufficient to match the performance of classical baselines on most tasks. This result aligns with our expectations, as increasing the number of Pauli strings enables the model to capture more complex features, as demonstrated in Sect. 2.3. Furthermore, we find that removing the bias term significantly worsens performance, underlining the importance of this component.

4 Discussion and Future Work

This work extends the scalability of flipped models and makes it possible to process significantly larger inputs. Moreover, it demonstrates their importance as a viable quantum method for NLP tasks. The proposed HAM design encodes input

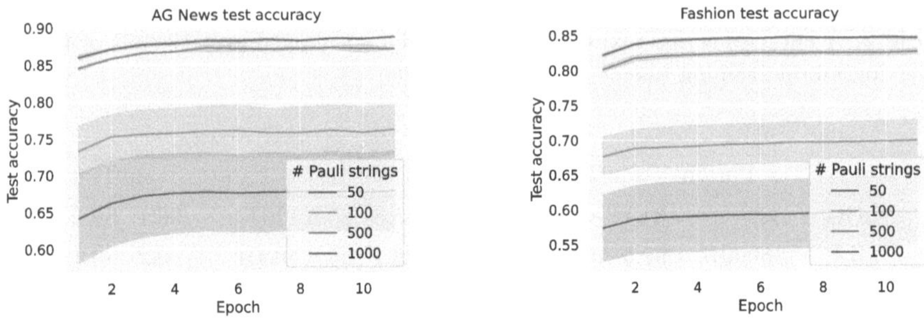

(a) (b)

Fig. 2. Performance on the test sets for different number of Pauli strings in the SIM model. First 10 epochs out of 30 shown.

Table 3. Accuracies across image datasets. Results are averaged over 10 runs.

Model	CIFAR2			Fashion		
	Params	Train	Test	Params	Train	Test
LOG	1025	73.9	72.9	1025	85.5	83.5
MLP	112701	89.0	83.4	89610	87.9	85.8
CNN	75329	96.3	94.1	130250	95.4	90.7
CIRC	2081	85.1	84.6	11094	89.2	86.5
QCNN	169	84.9	84.7	558	76.7	76.3
HAM	523818	89.6	81.0	-	-	-
PEFF	1056	79.3	78.7	-	-	-
SIM	2156	68.9	68.2	10934	87.6	84.4

Table 4. Accuracies of additional variants on SST2. Results are averaged over 10 runs or (*) run achieving best train accuracy.

	# Params	Train	Test*
HAM	130854	91.2	82.3
PEFF	410	81.8	80.0
SIM	9410	84.5	80.1
STATEIN	130854	92.0	80.2
NOBIAS	38	70.0	71.9

data directly as a measurement, obtaining performance comparable with other specialized models. The PEFF variant reduces its parameter complexity, and the SIM variant additionally reduces its sample complexity, offering a scheme that may be more efficiently implemented on quantum hardware. Notably, our method already scales well enough to allow meaningful studies on large datasets using simulators. The Hamiltonian classifier is presently a proof of concept meant to illustrate a novel input scheme for quantum devices with the ultimate goal of expanding the tools available to QML researchers. Future work could characterize the effectiveness of our approach on even larger problems and its integration with existing classical pipelines. Other studies could consider local strings in conjunction with classical shadows techniques to lower sample complexity. A way of learning more complex functions could be to stack several layers of Hamiltonian encoding, possibly performing nonlinear transformations. On the same thread, our Hamiltonian classifier could be reformulated as a feature extractor, allowing in to be integrated into hybrid quantum-classical pipelines. Other directions deserving a paper of their own are noise simulation and physical implementations on real quantum hardware.

Acknowledgment. ChatGPT was used throughout the preparation of this paper solely to assist with language-related tasks, including paraphrasing and polishing the authors' original text. It was not used to generate new content, suggest research ideas, or contribute substantially to the intellectual framing of the work. This usage complies with the ACL 2023 Policy on AI Writing.(https://2023.aclweb.org/blog/ACL-2023-policy/).

Sincere thanks go to Ted Briscoe and Bhiksha Raj for our initial discussions that helped shape this work. We would also like to thank our colleagues from SIG Context and Security/ML for the feedback, allowing us to refine this paper, as well as Prabhav Jain for the many insightful comments. This work has been funded by the LOEWE Distinguished Chair "Ubiquitous Knowledge Processing", LOEWE initiative, Hesse, Germany (Grant Number: 200009-62500000).

A Background

Quantum computers differ fundamentally from classical computers, utilizing the principles of quantum physics rather than binary logic implemented by transistors. In this section, we offer a brief introduction to the notation and formalize the concepts of qubit, gate, measurement, Pauli decomposition, and input encoding. Next, we discuss how these devices have been used to tackle machine learning problems in recent literature, as well as their limitations.

A.1 Quantum Computing Fundamentals

Quantum computers are conceptually and physically different devices from classical computers. Instead of basing their logic on binary data representations implemented by transistors, they utilize the rules of quantum physics as a substrate for computation. For this reason, in what follows, we describe the building blocks of quantum computation.

Dirac Notation. Quantum computing makes extensive use of Dirac notation (also called bra-ket notation) to simplify the representation of linear transformations which are commonplace in the theory. The fundamental elements of this notation are *bras* and *kets*. A ket, denoted as $|\psi\rangle$, represents a column vector ψ in a Hilbert space. A bra, denoted as $\langle\phi|$, represents instead a vector in the dual space (the complex conjugate transpose of a ket). The inner product of two vectors ϕ and ψ, which results in a scalar, is written as $\langle\phi\rangle\,\psi$. Conversely, the outer product $|\psi\rangle\langle\phi|$, forms a matrix or an operator.

Quantum Systems. The basic unit of information in a quantum computer is a two-dimensional quantum bit (qubit) which is mathematically modelled by a normalized column vector, the *state vector*, in a two-dimensional vector space equipped with an inner-product, or Hilbert space. A state vector is usually expressed concisely in Dirac notation as $|\psi\rangle = [\alpha\,\beta]^\top \in \mathbb{C}^2$. We say that a qubit

$|\psi\rangle := \alpha|0\rangle + \beta|1\rangle$ is in a *coherent quantum superposition* of two orthonormal basis states $|0\rangle := [1\,0]^\top$ and $|1\rangle := [0\,1]^\top$, such that the complex coefficients in the basis expansion satisfy normalization constraint $|\alpha|^2 + |\beta|^2 = 1$. This constraint originates from physics: in order to extract any information from a quantum state, we need to *measure* it in a chosen basis, which destroys the superposition in the measured basis by projecting the state $|\psi\rangle$ on one of the basis elements. If we measure state $|\psi\rangle$ in the $\{|0\rangle, |1\rangle\}$ basis, we get outcome"0" with probability $|\alpha|^2$ and the post-measurement state becomes $|0\rangle$, and respectively, we get "1" with probability $|\beta|^2$ and post-measurement state $|1\rangle$.

Multi-qubit Systems. In order to model a quantum system with multiple qubits, we use the so-called *Kronecker product* ($\otimes$) to combine many individual state vectors into a single larger one. An n-qubit system can be represented by a vector of size $N = 2^n$, $|\psi_1 \dots \psi_n\rangle := |\psi_1\rangle \otimes \dots \otimes |\psi_n\rangle$. In a chosen basis, the entries of this vector describe the probability of observing that outcome. Many QML approaches aim to gain a quantum advantage by manipulating only a few qubits to access an exponentially large Hilbert space. To give an example, if two qubits $|\psi_1\rangle$ and $|\psi_2\rangle$ are both initialized in $(|0\rangle + |1\rangle)/\sqrt{2}$, the joint state is given by an equal superposition of all the possible $n = 2$ bit string vectors

$$|\psi_1\rangle \otimes |\psi_2\rangle = \frac{|00\rangle + |01\rangle + |10\rangle + |11\rangle}{2}.$$

In this setup, measurement can performed separately on each qubit, resulting in a n-element bitstring.

Quantum Circuits. Quantum computation is achieved by manipulating qubits. This is done using quantum *gates*. Any n-qubit gate can be represented as a unitary matrix $U \in \mathbb{C}^{N \times N}$ which acts on the n-qubit input state $|\psi\rangle$ via the usual matrix-vector multiplication, giving output $U|\psi\rangle$. Intuitively, quantum gates can be considered as rotations that conserve the length of a state vector. A sequence of gates applied on one or many qubits is called a quantum *circuit*. By construction, unitary circuits perform linear operations. Non-linear computation requires workarounds like running the computation on a larger Hilbert space and measuring output qubits in a subspace or re-uploading input data [28,40,53].

Pauli Decomposition. A concise way of expressing multiple measurements on multiple qubits over multiple bases is through a so-called Hamiltonian. A Hamiltonian H for an n-qubit system is a Hermitian matrix of size $2^n \times 2^n$. The result of a measurement of a state ψ with a specific Hamiltonian H can be expressed as $\langle\psi|H|\psi\rangle$, which is the expectation value of this measurement. The 2×2 Pauli matrices, $\mathcal{P} = \{X, Y, Z, I\}$, or more generally multi-body Pauli operators, also called *Pauli strings*, $\mathcal{P}_n = \{\bigotimes_{i=1}^n O_i | O_i \in \mathcal{P}\}$ form a basis for Hermitian matrices of dimension $2^n \times 2^n$. Consequently, any Hamiltonian can be expressed as a linear combination of Pauli strings:

$$H = \sum_i \alpha_i P_i \quad \text{where} \quad \alpha_i \in \mathbb{R} \quad \text{and} \quad P_i \in \mathcal{P}_n.$$

This decomposition results in $\mathcal{O}(4^n)$ unique Pauli strings, each representing a physical property that can be measured using quantum devices. Generic Hamiltonians are expensive to decompose and measure due to the exponential number of Pauli strings. For this reason, in VQC settings, typical Hamiltonians are constructed from a polynomial number of Pauli strings.

A.2 Data Encoding

The first step for quantum-based ML algorithms is *state preparation*, the process of representing input data as quantum states. Most algorithms share similarities in how they achieve this [42]. The choice of encoding severely impacts the runtime of the circuit as well as its expressivity [50]. *Basis encoding* is the simplest representation analogous to classical bits. An n-element bit string $[x_1\, x_2\, \ldots\, x_n]$ is represented in the basis states of n qubits as $\bigotimes_{i=1}^{n}|x_i\rangle = |x_1 \ldots x_n\rangle$ (e.g. 011 is represented as $|011\rangle$). This representation requires $\mathcal{O}(n)$ qubits. *Angle encoding* represents continuous data as the phase of qubits. A set of n continuous variables $[x_1\, x_2\, \ldots\, x_n]$ can be represented over n qubits as $\bigotimes_{j=1}^{n} R_{\hat{\sigma}}(x_j)|0\rangle$ with $R_{\hat{\sigma}}(x) = e^{-ix\hat{\sigma}}$ a so-called rotation gate, and $\hat{\sigma}$ a Pauli matrix X, Y or Z that specifies the rotation axis. *Amplitude encoding* represents a vector of $N = 2^n$ values $[x_1\, x_2\, \ldots\, x_N]$ over n qubits as $\sum_{i=0}^{N-1} x_i|i\rangle$, where $\{|i\rangle\}_{i=1}^{N}$ corresponds to the canonical orthonormal basis written in a binary representation.

There is a trade-off between ease of encoding and qubit count: basis and angle encoding use $\mathcal{O}(n)$ gates for $\mathcal{O}(n)$ values over $\mathcal{O}(n)$ qubits, while amplitude encoding handles N-dimensional inputs but needs $\mathcal{O}(N)$ gates over $\mathcal{O}(n)$ qubits, an exponential increase in input size but also gates. Angle encoding strategies often embed multiple features onto the same qubit to reduce qubit usage, effectively a form of pooling [18,40]. Amplitude encoding, on the other hand, is often performed using easy-to-prepare quantum states to mitigate its gate complexity [3,18]. In text-related tasks, encoding schemes typically encode words over a set number of qubits [34,59], while in image tasks, pixel values are directly encoded as angles or amplitudes [16,56].

A.3 Variational Quantum Circuits

Once data has been encoded in a quantum computer, it is processed by a quantum circuit to obtain a prediction. One of the leading paradigms for QML revolves around VQCs (also called quantum *ansëtze*, or parametrized quantum circuits), a type of circuit where the action of gates is controlled by classical parameters. The training loop of a VQC closely resembles that of classical neural networks [10]: input data is encoded in the quantum device as a quantum state, several layers of parametrized gates transform this state, a prediction is obtained via quantum measurement, and finally, a specialized but classical optimizer [58] computes a loss and updates the parameters. VQCs have shown better convergence during training [1] as well as better expressive power [18] compared to neural networks of similar size.

Several VQC-based equivalents of classical architectures have been proposed such as auto-encoders [43], GNNs [17], and CNNs [16,24]. Quantum NLP works have focused on implementing VQCs with favourable inductive biases for text, such as quantum RNNs [4,32], quantum LSTMs [13], and quantum attention layers [15,48,65], with recent works showcasing applicability of these methods at scales meaningful for NLP applications [61]

A.4 Quantum Machine Learning Limitations

Despite these achievements, QML applications have yet to demonstrate a practical quantum advantage. Firstly, NISQ devices are limited in terms of the number of qubits in a single device, connectivity between the qubits, noise in the computation, and coherence time [2,63]. Secondly, quantum devices have fundamental difficulties in dealing with the dense and unstructured vector representations around which ML revolves: loading (or encoding) data into a quantum state either requires a large number of qubits (for angle and basis encoding) or a prohibitive amount of gates (for amplitude encoding). Efficient methods for amplitude encoding [3,55] incur trade-offs in the expressivity of vectors that have not been explored sufficiently in the context of QML. Moreover, measurement is an expensive process extracting only one bit of information per qubit measured. Extracting a real-valued vector from a quantum computer generally requires exponentially many measurements [44]. As a result, many current QML experiments are limited in both scale and scope in order to fit within the constraints of NISQ devices and simulators. Small datasets, typically consisting of only a few hundred samples, are often used [14,32,33,47]. Additionally, aggressive dimensionality reduction is commonly performed to reduce data to just a few dozen features [4,65]. In contrast, even "small" classical neural networks by modern standards are several orders of magnitude larger in terms of parameters, dataset size, and representation dimensionality [36]. These limitations have raised concerns about the applicability of QML results to larger, more complex tasks. Some question whether the observed performance is due to the quantum model itself or the upstream pre-processing [12], while others highlight the difficulty of generalizing these results to larger datasets and the challenges of fair benchmarking [7,36]. Several other challenges remain, including barren plateaus [31], development of efficient optimization algorithms for VQCs [57], and error correction [11].

To mitigate the data loading and read-out challenges, the *flipped model* has been recently introduced [27], where quantum resources are only required during training, while inference can happen classically. Although flipped models on NISQ devices are classically simulatable and thus cannot yet achieve quantum advantage, they hold significant promise when combined with shadow techniques [25,52], which allow the prediction of many quantum system properties from a limited number of measurements. There are theoretically provable instances where shadow-flipped models outperform classical methods under widely-believed cryptography assumptions [21]. The guarantees of flipped models, as well as their scalability, warrant their exploration in the context of QML.

[column sep=0.3cm] $\mathrm{R}_X[3, steps = 3, style = dashed, roundedcorners, innerxsep = 2pt, background]R_Y R_Z$ $\mathrm{R}_X R_Y R_Z$ $\mathrm{R}_X R_Y R_Z$

(a)

[column sep=0.3cm] $\mathrm{R}_Y[3, steps = 8, style = dashed, roundedcorners, innerxsep = 2pt, background]1 R_X R_Y 1 R_X$ $\mathrm{R}_Y R_X 1 R_Y R_X 1$ $\mathrm{R}_Y R_X - 2 R_Y R_X - 2$

(b)

[column sep=0.3cm] $\mathrm{R}_X[3, steps = 10, style = dashed, roundedcorners, innerxsep = 2pt, background]R_Z 12 R_X R_X R_X R_Z$ $\mathrm{R}_X R_Z R_X - 11 R_X R_X R_Z$ $\mathrm{R}_X R_Z R_X R_X - 2 - 1 R_X R_Z$

(c)

Fig. 3. Circuit ansätze explored in the experiment. For the sake of visualization, the image shows ansätze for $n = 3$. Since the experiments use different values, we extend the patterns to act on more qubits. (a) Non-entangling ansatz (b) Ring ansatz (c) All-to-all ansatz. (b) and (c) are respectively circuit 14 and 6 from [50].

B Hyperparameter Tuning

For each architecture and for each dataset in our evaluation, we perform a randomised search for the best parameters: we randomly select 50 configurations, train them on the task, and evaluate their performance on the development set. To avoid overfitting, we perform early stopping on the training if the development loss does not decrease for five consecutive epochs. Troughout all experiments, we utilize the *Adam* optimizer provided by PyTorch. Since our largest model HAM has at most $\sim 500k$ parameters (dictated by the embedding space), we limit the random search to configurations with fewer than or equal to the number of parameters to ensure a fair comparison. In practice, we find RNNs, LSTMs and CNNs perform very well with as low as $40k$ parameters. What follows is a list of all hyperparameters we evaluated:

- **Batch size:** [64, 128, 256];
- **Learning rate:** $[10^{-2}, 10^{-3}, 10^{-4}]$;
- **Hidden size:** For RNNs and LSTMs, the size of the hidden representation [100, 300, 500];
- **Layers:** For RNNs and LSTMs, the number of layers of the recurrent block [1, 4, 8]. For MLP, the total number of layers including input and output [3, 4, 5]. For CNNs, the total number of convolutional layers [3, 4, 5]. For HAM, PEFF, SIM and CIRC, the number of repeated applications of the ansatz, analogous to the number of layers [8, 16, 32];
- **Channels:** For CNNs, the number of output channels of each convolutional layer [8, 16, 32, 64, 128];
- **Kernel size:** For CNNs, the kernel dimension of each convolutional layer [3, 5, 7];
- **Circuit:** The ansatz U_θ used to prepare state ψ. We experiment with three hardware-efficient ansätze inspired by circuits from [50] and illustrated in Fig. 3. These ansätze are designed to explore different levels of entanglement (the quantum counterpart of correlation) and gate complexity. The first is a non-entangling circuit composed of single-qubit rotations, exhibiting linear

complexity with respect to the number of qubits. The second is an entangling circuit arranged in a ring configuration, also scaling linearly in gate count. The third is an all-to-all entangling circuit, which scales quadratically. [`Baseline`, `Ring`, `All-to-all`].
- # **Pauli strings:** For SIM, the number of Pauli strings composing the Hamiltonian [50, 100, 500, 1000].

Tables 5 and 6 shows the final selection of best-performing hyperparameters used in the main experiment of Sect. 3.3.

C Supplementary Experiments

C.1 Removing Bias Hurts Performance

To further evaluate our models and assess the impact of key design choices, we conduct an ablation study using the SST2 dataset. As in the main experiment, we begin with the optimal set of hyperparameters identified in Appendix B, apply changes to the architecture, and run 10 separate runs. Finally, we report the test set performance of the run achieving the lowest loss as reported on the GLUE website.

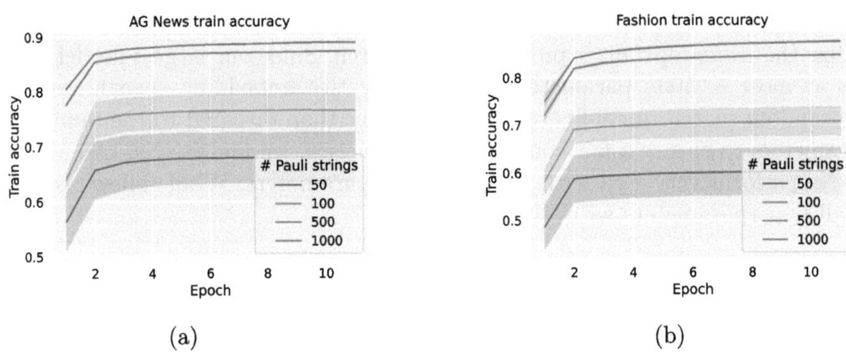

Fig. 4. Performance on the train set for different numbers of Pauli strings in the SIM model. Error bars are shown for all choices, but grow thin for the two largest models. First 10 epochs out of 30 shown.

In this ablation study, we examine the role of the bias term in contributing to downstream performance. Our best-performing model, HAM, delivers strong results but does so with a large number of parameters. In contrast, PEFF offers slightly lower performance but significantly reduces the parameter count, as detailed in Sect. 3.4. To explore the impact of the bias term we completely remove it and assess the performance of the resulting model, referring to this variant as NOBIAS:

$$H_\phi(x) := \frac{1}{s}\sum_{i=1}^{s} x_i x_i^\top. \tag{9}$$

Table 5. Best hyperparameters across all baseline models and tasks

LOG

Dataset	Batch size	Learning rate
SST2	64	10^{-3}
IMDb	64	10^{-2}
AG News	64	10^{-2}
MNIST2	128	10^{-3}
CIFAR2	256	10^{-3}
Fashion	64	10^{-3}

MLP

Dataset	Batch size	Learning rate	Hidden size	Layers
SST2	64	10^{-4}	300	3
IMDb	64	10^{-3}	300	3
AG News	64	10^{-3}	100	3
MNIST2	256	10^{-4}	100	3
CIFAR2	128	10^{-4}	100	3
Fashion	256	10^{-3}	100	3

LSTM

Dataset	Batch size	Learning rate	Hidden size	Layers
SST2	64	10^{-2}	100	2
IMDb	128	10^{-2}	100	2
AG News	128	10^{-3}	100	2

RNN

Dataset	Batch size	Learning rate	Hidden size	Layers
SST2	64	10^{-4}	100	1
IMDb	256	10^{-4}	100	2
AG News	256	10^{-4}	100	1

CNN

Dataset	Batch size	Learning rate	Layers	Channels	Kernel Size
MNIST2	64	10^{-3}	5	16	5
CIFAR2	64	10^{-4}	4	32	5
Fashion	64	10^{-3}	4	16	3

CIRC

Dataset	Batch size	Learning rate	Circuit	Layers
SST2	256	10^{-3}	`All-to-all`	8
AG News	128	10^{-3}	`Baseline`	16
IMDb	128	10^{-3}	`All-to-all`	16
MNIST2	128	10^{-3}	`Baseline`	8
CIFAR2	64	10^{-3}	`Baseline`	8
Fashion	256	10^{-3}	`Ring`	32

Table 6. Best hyperparameters across all Hamiltonian models and tasks

HAM				
Dataset	**Batch size**	**Learning rate**	**Circuit**	**Layers**
SST2	128	10^{-3}	`Ring`	8
IMDb	256	10^{-3}	`All-to-all`	32
MNIST2	256	10^{-2}	`Baseline`	32
CIFAR2	64	10^{-3}	`Ring`	8

PEFF				
Dataset	**Batch size**	**Learning rate**	**Circuit**	**Layers**
SST2	64	10^{-2}	`All-to-all`	8
IMDb	64	10^{-2}	`All-to-all`	8
MNIST2	64	10^{-3}	`All-to-all`	8
CIFAR2	256	10^{-2}	`Baseline`	16

SIM					
Dataset	**Batch size**	**Learning rate**	**Circuit**	**Layers**	**# Pauli strings**
SST2	256	10^{-3}	`Ring`	32	1000
IMDb	256	10^{-2}	`All-to-all`	16	1000
AG News	128	10^{-3}	`All-to-all`	16	1000
MNIST2	256	10^{-2}	`Ring`	32	1000
CIFAR2	64	10^{-3}	`All-to-all`	32	1000
Fashion	256	10^{-2}	`All-to-all`	8	1000

The results, summarized in Table 4, show a marked decrease in performance. The 71.9% accuracy achieved by NOBIAS is nonetheless surprising given the model is stripped of almost all parameters. We hypothesize that, in HAM, the bias term influences the eigenvalues of the Hamiltonian, directly affecting the final expectation value. For PEFF, the bias appears to shift the embeddings into a region more favorable for classification. We further speculate that NOBIAS could achieve results similar to PEFF by simply unfreezing the input embeddings during training; this would allow them to shift as in the other variants.

C.2 Additional State Preparation Leads to Overfitting

In this section we investigate whether combining our HAM architecture with a standard state preparation routine improves model performance. Also, in this experiment, we consider SST2, with the configuration of the main text unchanged but for the additional state preparation. We call this setup STATEIN (short for STATE INput):

$$\tilde{x} := \frac{1}{s}\sum_{i=1}^{s} \tilde{x}_i \tag{10}$$

$$\psi_\theta := U_\theta|\tilde{x}\rangle \tag{11}$$

In this configuration, U_θ acts not on the zero-state, but on an initial state $|\tilde{x}\rangle$ in which the input data has been amplitude-encoded. We hypothesize that applying U_θ directly to the encoded inputs might enable the model to better identify useful features for classification. Results displayed in Table 4 show a slight improvement in training accuracy, with STATEIN achieving an average of 92.0% over 10 runs compared to 91.1% for HAM. However, the test accuracy only marginally exceeds that of PEFF and is noticeably lower than HAM, suggesting that the combination of Hamiltonian encoding and amplitude-encoded inputs may lead to overfitting. While these results provide some insights, a more thorough analysis of the interaction between state preparation and input-encoded measurement is needed, which we leave for future research.

C.3 The Number of Pauli Strings Correlates with Performance

Rewriting the SIM model leads to a bilinear form where each Pauli string acts as a transformation on the input. During hyperparameter tuning, we consistently observe that the best-performing SIM models use 1000 Pauli strings across all experiments. We hypothesize that this is due to the distinct transformation each Pauli string introduces, which enriches the model's feature set. This raises some questions: does increasing the number of Pauli strings, and thus the number of transformations, lead to better performance? Moreover, how does the generalization capability scale with the number of Pauli strings?

To explore this, we use the same configurations found for the AG News and Fashion datasets but vary the number of Pauli strings. Results are displayed in Figs. 2 and 4. Low string count do not perform much better than chance, but accuracy steadily increases and eventually plateaus at 1000 strings, reaching levels comparable to other models like MLP and CIRC. Increasing the number of strings also leads to a more stable training process as highlighted by the error bars growing thin for $p = 500$ and 1000. This suggests the loss landscape may become smoother as more transformations are added, facilitating training. This is a promising outcome: it suggests that transformations induced by Pauli strings actively contribute to learning by creating more complex features. It also indicates that a relatively small number of strings can effectively substitute for a full decomposition. We speculate that increasing the number of Pauli strings beyond 1000 could significantly improve results for more complex datasets like CIFAR2, where performance currently lags.

References

1. Abbas, A., Sutter, D., Zoufal, C., Lucchi, A., Figalli, A., Woerner, S.: The power of quantum neural networks. Nat. Comput. Sci. **1**(6) (2021). https://doi.org/10.1038/s43588-021-00084-1
2. Anschuetz, E.R., Kiani, B.T.: Quantum variational algorithms are swamped with traps. Nat. Commun. **13**(1), 7760 (2022)
3. Ashhab, S.: Quantum state preparation protocol for encoding classical data into the amplitudes of a quantum information processing register's wave function. Phys. Rev. Res. **4**, 013091 (2022). https://doi.org/10.1103/PhysRevResearch.4.013091
4. Bausch, J.: Recurrent quantum neural networks. In: Larochelle, H., Ranzato, M., Hadsell, R., Balcan, M., Lin, H. (eds.) Advances in Neural Information Processing Systems 33: Annual Conference on Neural Information Processing Systems 2020, NeurIPS 2020, December 6-12, 2020, virtual (2020). https://proceedings.neurips.cc/paper/2020/hash/0ec96be397dd6d3cf2fecb4a2d627c1c-Abstract.html
5. Bengio, Y., Ducharme, R., Vincent, P.: A neural probabilistic language model. In: Leen, T.K., Dietterich, T.G., Tresp, V. (eds.) Advances in Neural Information Processing Systems 13, Papers from Neural Information Processing Systems (NIPS) 2000, Denver, pp. 932–938. MIT Press (2000). https://proceedings.neurips.cc/paper/2000/hash/728f206c2a01bf572b5940d7d9a8fa4c-Abstract.html
6. Biamonte, J., Wittek, P., Pancotti, N., Rebentrost, P., Wiebe, N., Lloyd, S.: Quantum machine learning. Nature **549**(7671), 195–202 (2017). https://doi.org/10.1038/nature23474
7. Bowles, J., Ahmed, S., Schuld, M.: Better than classical? the subtle art of benchmarking quantum machine learning models (2024)
8. Camps, D., Van Beeumen, R., Yang, C.: Quantum fourier transform revisited. Numeric. Linear Algebra Appl. **28**(1), e2331 (2021). https://doi.org/10.1002/nla.2331, https://onlinelibrary.wiley.com/doi/abs/10.1002/nla.2331
9. Caro, M.C., et al.: Generalization in quantum machine learning from few training data. Nat. Commun. **13**(1), 4919 (2022). https://doi.org/10.1038/s41467-022-32550-3
10. Cerezo, M., et al.: Variational quantum algorithms. Nat. Rev. Phys. **3**(9) (2021). https://doi.org/10.1038/s42254-021-00348-9
11. Chatterjee, A., Phalak, K., Ghosh, S.: Quantum error correction for dummies. In: Muller, H., Alexev, Y., Delgado, A., Byrd, G. (eds.) Proceedings - 2023 IEEE International Conference on Quantum Computing and Engineering, QCE 2023. pp. 70–81. Proceedings - 2023 IEEE International Conference on Quantum Computing and Engineering, QCE 2023, Institute of Electrical and Electronics Engineers Inc., United States (2023). https://doi.org/10.1109/QCE57702.2023.00017, publisher Copyright: © 2023 IEEE.; 4th IEEE International Conference on Quantum Computing and Engineering, QCE 2023 ; Conference date: 17-09-2023 Through 22-09-2023
12. Chen, S.Y.C., Huang, C.M., Hsing, C.W., Kao, Y.J.: An end-to-end trainable hybrid classical-quantum classifier. Mach. Learn. Sci. Technol. **2**(4), 045021 (2021). https://doi.org/10.1088/2632-2153/ac104d
13. Chen, S.Y.C., Yoo, S., Fang, Y.L.L.: Quantum long short-term memory. In: ICASSP 2022 - 2022 IEEE International Conference on Acoustics, Speech and Signal Processing (ICASSP), pp. 8622–8626 (2022). https://doi.org/10.1109/ICASSP43922.2022.9747369

14. Chen, Y.: Quantum dilated convolutional neural networks. IEEE Access **10**, 20240–20246 (2022). https://doi.org/10.1109/ACCESS.2022.3152213
15. Cherrat, E.A., Kerenidis, I., Mathur, N., Landman, J., Strahm, M., Li, Y.Y.: Quantum vision transformers (2022)
16. Cong, I., Choi, S., Lukin, M.D.: Quantum convolutional neural networks. Nat. Phys. **15**(12) (2019). https://doi.org/10.1038/s41567-019-0648-8
17. Dallaire-Demers, P.L., Killoran, N.: Quantum generative adversarial networks. Phys. Rev. A **98**, 012324 (2018). https://doi.org/10.1103/PhysRevA.98.012324
18. Du, Y., Hsieh, M.H., Liu, T., Tao, D.: Expressive power of parametrized quantum circuits. Phys. Rev. Res. **2**, 033125 (2020). https://doi.org/10.1103/PhysRevResearch.2.033125
19. Farhi, E., Neven, H.: Classification with quantum neural networks on near term processors. arXiv: Quantum Physics (2018). https://api.semanticscholar.org/CorpusID:119037649
20. Grover, L.K.: A fast quantum mechanical algorithm for database search. In: Proceedings of the Twenty-Eighth Annual ACM Symposium on Theory of Computing, pp. 212–219. STOC '96, Association for Computing Machinery, New York (1996). https://doi.org/10.1145/237814.237866
21. Gyurik, C., Dunjko, V.: On establishing learning separations between classical and quantum machine learning with classical data. arXiv preprint arXiv:2208.06339 (2022)
22. Hantzko, L., Binkowski, L., Gupta, S.: Tensorized pauli decomposition algorithm. Phys. Scr. **99**(8), 085128 (2024). https://doi.org/10.1088/1402-4896/ad6499
23. Harrow, A.W., Hassidim, A., Lloyd, S.: Quantum algorithm for linear systems of equations. Phys. Rev. Lett. **103**, 150502 (2009). https://doi.org/10.1103/PhysRevLett.103.150502
24. Henderson, M., Shakya, S., Pradhan, S., Cook, T.: Quanvolutional neural networks: powering image recognition with quantum circuits. Quantum Mach. Intell. **2**(1), 1–9 (2020). https://doi.org/10.1007/s42484-020-00012-y
25. Huang, H.Y., Kueng, R., Preskill, J.: Predicting many properties of a quantum system from very few measurements. Nat. Phys. **16**(10), 1050–1057 (2020)
26. Huang, P.W., Rebentrost, P.: Post-variational quantum neural networks (2024). https://arxiv.org/abs/2307.10560
27. Jerbi, S., Gyurik, C., Marshall, S.C., Molteni, R., Dunjko, V.: Shadows of quantum machine learning. Nat. Commun. **15**(1), 5676 (2024). https://doi.org/10.1038/s41467-024-49877-8
28. Killoran, N., Bromley, T.R., Arrazola, J.M., Schuld, M., Quesada, N., Lloyd, S.: Continuous-variable quantum neural networks. Phys. Rev. Res. **1**(3) (Oct 2019). https://doi.org/10.1103/physrevresearch.1.033063
29. Koska, O., Baboulin, M., Gazda, A.: A tree-approach pauli decomposition algorithm with application to quantum computing. In: ISC High Performance 2024 Research Paper Proceedings (39th International Conference), pp. 1–11 (2024). https://doi.org/10.23919/ISC.2024.10528938
30. Krizhevsky, A.: Learning multiple layers of features from tiny images. University of Toronto (2012)
31. Larocca, M., et al.: A review of barren plateaus in variational quantum computing. arXiv preprint arXiv:2405.00781 (2024)
32. Li, Y., et al.: Quantum recurrent neural networks for sequential learning. Neural Netw. **166**, 148–161 (2023). https://doi.org/10.1016/j.neunet.2023.07.003, https://www.sciencedirect.com/science/article/pii/S089360802300360X

33. Liu, J., Lim, K.H., Wood, K.L., Huang, W., Guo, C., Huang, H.-L.: Hybrid quantum-classical convolutional neural networks. Sci. China Phys. Mech. Astronomy **64**(9), 1–8 (2021). https://doi.org/10.1007/s11433-021-1734-3
34. Lorenz, R., Pearson, A., Meichanetzidis, K., Kartsaklis, D., Coecke, B.: QNLP in practice: running compositional models of meaning on a quantum computer. https://doi.org/10.48550, arXiv preprint arXiv2102.12846 (2021)
35. Maas, A.L., Daly, R.E., Pham, P.T., Huang, D., Ng, A.Y., Potts, C.: Learning word vectors for sentiment analysis. In: Proceedings of the 49th Annual Meeting of the Association for Computational Linguistics: Human Language Technologies, pp. 142–150. Association for Computational Linguistics, Portland (2011). http://www.aclweb.org/anthology/P11-1015
36. Mingard, C., Pointing, J., London, C., Nam, Y., Louis, A.A.: Exploiting the equivalence between quantum neural networks and perceptrons (2024). https://arxiv.org/abs/2407.04371
37. Mitarai, K., Negoro, M., Kitagawa, M., Fujii, K.: Quantum circuit learning. Phys. Rev. A **98**, 032309 (2018). https://doi.org/10.1103/PhysRevA.98.032309
38. Nielsen, M.A., Chuang, I.L.: Quantum Computation and Quantum Information. Cambridge University Press (2000)
39. Preskill, J.: Quantum Computing in the NISQ era and beyond. Quantum **2**, 79 (2018). https://doi.org/10.22331/q-2018-08-06-79
40. Pérez-Salinas, A., Cervera-Lierta, A., Gil-Fuster, E., Latorre, J.I.: Data re-uploading for a universal quantum classifier. Quantum **4**, 226 (2020). https://doi.org/10.22331/q-2020-02-06-226
41. Quetschlich, N., Soeken, M., Murali, P., Wille, R.: Utilizing resource estimation for the development of quantum computing applications (2024)
42. Rath, M., Date, H.: Quantum data encoding: a comparative analysis of classical-to-quantum mapping techniques and their impact on machine learning accuracy (2023). https://arxiv.org/abs/2311.10375
43. Romero, J., Olson, J.P., Aspuru-Guzik, A.: Quantum autoencoders for efficient compression of quantum data. Quantum Sci. Technol. **2**(4) (2017). https://doi.org/10.1088/2058-9565/aa8072
44. Machine Learning with Quantum Computers. QST, Springer, Cham (2021). https://doi.org/10.1007/978-3-030-83098-4_9
45. Schuld, M., Bocharov, A., Svore, K.M., Wiebe, N.: Circuit-centric quantum classifiers. Phys. Rev. A **101**, 032308 (2020). https://doi.org/10.1103/PhysRevA.101.032308
46. Schuld, M., Killoran, N.: Is quantum advantage the right goal for quantum machine learning? PRX Quantum **3**, 030101 (2022). https://doi.org/10.1103/PRXQuantum.3.030101
47. Senokosov, A., Sedykh, A., Sagingalieva, A., Kyriacou, B., Melnikov, A.: Quantum machine learning for image classification. Mach. Learn. Sci. Technol. **5**(1), 015040 (2024). https://doi.org/10.1088/2632-2153/ad2aef
48. Shi, J., Zhao, R.X., Wang, W., Zhang, S., Li, X.: QSAN: a near-term achievable quantum self-attention network (2023)
49. Shor, P.W.: Polynomial-time algorithms for prime factorization and discrete logarithms on a quantum computer. SIAM J. Comput. **26**(5) (1997). https://doi.org/10.1137/s0097539795293172
50. Sim, S., Johnson, P.D., Aspuru-Guzik, A.: Expressibility and entangling capability of parameterized quantum circuits for hybrid quantum-classical algorithms. Adv. Quantum Technol. **2**(12) (Oct 2019). https://doi.org/10.1002/qute.201900070

51. Socher, R., et al.: Recursive deep models for semantic compositionality over a sentiment treebank. In: Proc. of EMNLP, pp. 1631–1642. Association for Computational Linguistics, Seattle, Washington (2013). https://aclanthology.org/D13-1170
52. Song, Y., et al.: A quantum federated learning framework for classical clients (2023). https://arxiv.org/abs/2312.11672
53. Subasi, Y., Holmes, Z., Coble, N., Sornborger, A.: On nonlinear transformations in quantum computation. In: APS March Meeting Abstracts. APS Meeting Abstracts, vol. 2023, p. M64.009 (2023)
54. Wang, A., Singh, A., Michael, J., Hill, F., Levy, O., Bowman, S.R.: GLUE: a multi-task benchmark and analysis platform for natural language understanding. In: Proc. of ICLR. OpenReview.net (2019). https://openreview.net/forum?id=rJ4km2R5t7
55. Wang, H., Ashhab, S., Nori, F.: Efficient quantum algorithm for preparing molecular-system-like states on a quantum computer. Phys. Rev. A **79**(4) (2009). https://doi.org/10.1103/physreva.79.042335
56. Wei, S.J., Chen, Y.H., Zhou, Z.R., Long, G.L.: A quantum convolutional neural network on NISQ devices. AAPPS Bull. **32**(1), 1–11 (2021). https://doi.org/10.1007/s43673-021-00030-3
57. Wiedmann, M., et al.: An empirical comparison of optimizers for quantum machine learning with SPSA-based gradients. In: 2023 IEEE International Conference on Quantum Computing and Engineering (QCE). vol. 1, pp. 450–456. IEEE (2023)
58. Wierichs, D., Izaac, J., Wang, C., Lin, C.Y.Y.: General parameter-shift rules for quantum gradients. Quantum **6**, 677 (2022)
59. Wu, S., Li, J., Zhang, P., Zhang, Y.: Natural language processing meets quantum physics: a survey and categorization. In: Moens, M.F., Huang, X., Specia, L., Yih, S.W.t. (eds.) Proceedings of the 2021 Conference on Empirical Methods in Natural Language Processing, pp. 3172–3182. Association for Computational Linguistics, Online and Punta Cana, Dominican Republic (2021). https://doi.org/10.18653/v1/2021.emnlp-main.254
60. Xiao, H., Rasul, K., Vollgraf, R.: Fashion-MNIST: a novel image dataset for benchmarking machine learning algorithms (2017). https://arxiv.org/abs/1708.07747
61. Xu, W., Clark, S., Brown, D., Matos, G., Meichanetzidis, K.: Quantum recurrent architectures for text classification. In: Al-Onaizan, Y., Bansal, M., Chen, Y.N. (eds.) Proceedings of the 2024 Conference on Empirical Methods in Natural Language Processing, pp. 18020–18027. Association for Computational Linguistics, Miami (2024). https://doi.org/10.18653/v1/2024.emnlp-main.1000
62. Yang, Z., Zolanvari, M., Jain, R.: A survey of important issues in quantum computing and communications. IEEE Commun. Surv. Tutor. **25**(2), 1059–1094 (2023). https://doi.org/10.1109/COMST.2023.3254481
63. Zaman, K., Marchisio, A., Hanif, M.A., Shafique, M.: A survey on quantum machine learning: current trends, challenges, opportunities, and the road ahead (2023)
64. Zhang, X., Zhao, J., LeCun, Y.: Character-level convolutional networks for text classification. In: Cortes, C., Lawrence, N., Lee, D., Sugiyama, M., Garnett, R. (eds.) Advances in Neural Information Processing Systems. vol. 28. Curran Associates, Inc. (2015). https://proceedings.neurips.cc/paper_files/paper/2015/file/250cf8b51c773f3f8dc8b4be867a9a02-Paper.pdf
65. Zhao, R.X., Shi, J., Li, X.: Qksan: A quantum kernel self-attention network. IEEE Trans. Patt. Analy. Mach. Intell. 1–12 (2024). https://doi.org/10.1109/TPAMI.2024.3434974

Quantum Natural Language Processing (Q-NLP)

Cirquitous: A Possible Exploration of Solving Quantum Circuit Challenges Using Human Natural Language

Mithün Paul[1,2(✉)], Tiju Cherian John[1], and Nithin Raveendran[2]

[1] University of Arizona, Tucson, AZ 85719, USA
mithunpaul08@gmail.com, mithun.paul@nau.edu
[2] Northern Arizona University, Flagstaff, AZ 86001, USA

Abstract. Quantum circuit compilation is a challenging task required for the efficient implementation of quantum circuits in a quantum computer. Today, even if the algorithm for a given problem can be conceptually derived, the delicate nature of quantum systems, the high cost, and the limited availability of quantum computing infrastructure create the need for complex gate optimization routines. In this work, we propose to address this problem from a radically novel perspective of using human natural language, for example, English. Specifically, our method uses tools provided by the Quantum Natural Language Processing (QNLP) framework for reducing quantum circuit complexity. This recently invented discipline has identified strong links between human natural language and quantum computing. Given the fact that using QNLP, noisy intermediate scale quantum computing (NISQ) devices are now successfully being used to solve problems in natural language processing (NLP) and Artificial Intelligence (AI), in this work, we propose to ask the converse question: Can QNLP techniques be used to reduce the circuit-size and depth of quantum circuits, in turn contributing to quantum circuit optimization and compilation? We show that this is do-able and present a minimal theoretical proof of concept herewith. Note that this paper is not meant to be a comprehensive experiment results-based work, but instead is meant to be a theoretical vanguard one aimed to introduce the world to the usefulness of QNLP and subsequently initiate research and discussions in this direction.

Keywords: Quantum Natural Language Processing · QNLP · Quantum Compilation · ZX Calculus

1 Introduction

Artificial Intelligence (AI) models like ChatGPT, powered internally by Natural Language Processing (NLP), are already transforming the way we live. On the other hand, Quantum Information Science (QIS) is another rapidly growing field of research with predictions that it will revolutionize technology, the Internet, and computing in the coming decades [38,43].

D. Cavar et al. (Eds.): QNLPAI 2025, CCIS 2659, pp. 93–113, 2026.
https://doi.org/10.1007/978-3-032-13883-5_6

Recently Quantum Natural Language Processing (QNLP), an interdisciplinary field of research, discovered deep connections between human natural language (for example, English) and quantum physics, thus combining both fields in a very effective way. QNLP is a potentially transformative discovery that opens up great possibilities in both fields where QIS can benefit from NLP and vice versa. While QNLP has been proven to be effective in a machine learning and natural language processing setting, the reverse direction of exploring quantum computing problems by projecting them to natural language space has not yet been explored. In this work, we propose exploiting the power of QNLP to solve problems in quantum computing. This paper is meant to be a very theoretical exploratory work exploring the possible uses of the English language to solve certain specific challenges in quantum computing related to quantum circuit compilation routines and quantum error correction tasks. However, the ideology of the proposal is general enough to be applied to a wide variety of problems.

Hence our major contribution is that we introduce a novel way of performing quantum circuit optimization by projecting it into natural language space. This is based on the intuition proven by QNLP that quantum physics and human natural language are deeply correlated. In addition, we plan to explore how to leverage recent state-of-the-art research in classical NLP for this purpose. For example, we will explore if techniques like summarization (which reduces the size of a given big language passage to one or two sentences, while preserving the meaning of it intact) can be used for reduction techniques in quantum circuits, like preparation, manipulation, and optimization of quantum circuits. Further, we also provide this as a general framework for quantum circuit optimization, thus opening an entirely new field of related research.

Specifically, we develop a new framework to optimize a given quantum circuit utilizing the techniques proposed by QNLP. In this framework, the user will first provide a complex quantum circuit as input, which the system will then encode as an equivalent passage in English. This passage will then be provided as input to an interface that will use well-established reduction techniques in NLP, like summarization, to compress its size while maintaining the equivalence in meaning. This summary will then be converted back into the corresponding equivalent quantum circuit using QNLP, which will be verified for equivalence with the original quantum circuit using standard circuit comparison techniques. In other words, the problem of quantum circuit optimization will now be projected into the space of natural language, where established solutions for summarizations and semantic reductions exist.

To the best of our knowledge, this is one of the first works to explore the potential of QNLP in Quantum Circuit Compilation.

2 Background and Related Work

In this section, we will first describe some basics of quantum computation, ZX Calculus, and QNLP, which will form the underlying basis for understanding the technical innovation and research we present in this work.

2.1 Quantum Computation and Quantum Circuits

In classical computation tasks, 0's and 1's are manipulated using logical gates such as AND, OR, XOR, etc. Similarly, handling qubits (quantum states) using reversible (unitary) operations called quantum gates is at the heart of quantum computation. A quantum circuit is a physical model for implementing a quantum algorithm that aims to do a particular computing task, such as integer factorization. Often, an algorithm's sequence of quantum gates is not unique to a given task or hardware. The job of a quantum compiler is to organize the circuit elements or quantum gates in a given quantum algorithm in tune with the available hardware and resources, and there could be multiple ways in which these compilers can be optimized [37]. In fact, this is in itself a challenging task as one needs to be cognizant of the reliability and hardware implementation costs of the chosen gates, as well as the gate count, to make the algorithms realizable. Thus, arriving at the optimal quantum circuit is a multi-faceted optimization problem. For example, a circuit for an integer factorization algorithm is extremely long and complicated, effectively making it useless without an efficient quantum circuit optimization routine to make it amenable to execute in the given available limited quantum computer hardware.

Specifically, in the quantum compilation problem, we want to transform a high-level quantum algorithm into a lower-level sequence of operations that can be executed efficiently on a quantum processor. One way to optimize a quantum circuit is to identify independent operations that can be performed in parallel, thereby optimizing its overall execution time. Multiple approaches used in circuit optimization range from Clifford circuit manipulation through exploiting graph theoretical tools for gate optimization to using ZX calculus [1,10,13,21,23,24,28,29,32,39,45–47]. As explicit use of graph-based tools for optimization, the well-studied Directed Acyclic Graphs (DAGs) are deployed for particular circuit instantiating, graph theory, and quantum gate composition rules. This compilation strategy can help to give smaller circuit instances for a given task. However, these approaches can be challenging when the circuit size scales. To address these problems, we propose to use QNLP, and in-turn ZX calculus, as an alternative methodology for quantum circuit reduction.

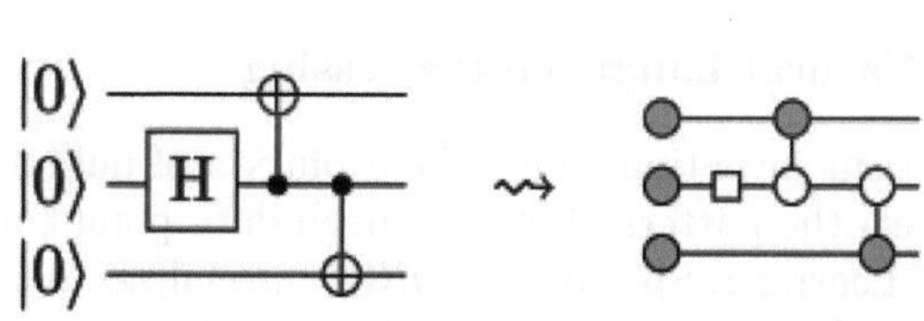

Fig. 1. A simple quantum circuit represented in the ZX diagram form.

2.2 ZX Calculus

As a graphical method used for understanding quantum computation, this approach has gained popularity in various sub-fields like quantum circuit optimization, measurement-based quantum computation, and others [51]. A ZX-diagram typically uses white and grey spherical shapes, with interconnected lines to visually represent a linear relationship between qubits, resembling the circuit diagrams. For example, a quantum circuit can be depicted as a corresponding ZX-diagram, as shown in Fig. 1.

ZX-diagrams come equipped with a compact set of graphical rewrite rules called ZX calculus. Using this, complex quantum equations, which would otherwise take long and involved derivations using the rules of quantum physics, can be easily visualized and proved. For instance, as shown below, using the rules of ZX calculus, we can easily prove diagrammatically that the above circuit implements a GHZ state (we omit the details for brevity):

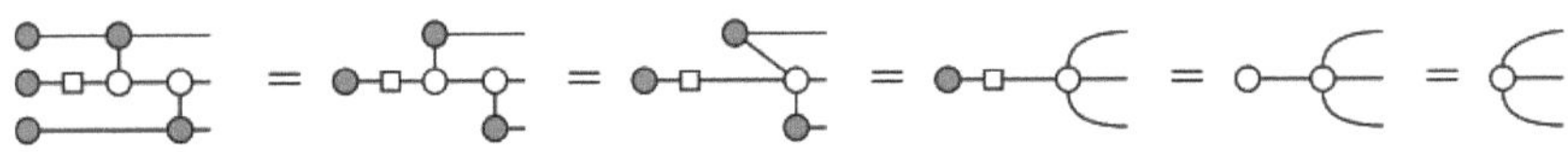

Fig. 2. A visual proof of GHZ state using ZX Calculus.

Since Coecke and Duncan introduced the ZX-calculus in 2008 [16], it has been applied in many quantum computing tasks due to its versatility and ability to easily simplify and visualize complex entities. Initially, it was used in measurement-based quantum computation (MBQC), where graph states can be easily represented as ZX-diagrams [22], making the one-way model and related protocols straightforward to describe [27]. In recent years, the ZX-calculus has been successfully employed in optimizing quantum circuits [2,20], verifying quantum circuit equivalence [28], analyzing surface code quantum computing and lattice surgery [26], and for the design and verification of quantum error-correcting codes [4,5,8,9].

2.3 Quantum Natural Language Processing

QNLP is a very recent invention where the evolution of qubits in quantum circuits is used to learn the patterns between given data points, a task commonly known as Machine Learning. Specifically, QNLP specializes in solving challenges in the human natural language (e.g. classifying text into spam or not spam) by finding patterns and relations between a given pair of data (e.g. a random email and the fact that it belongs to a class called spam) which is then used to predict the class of a hitherto unseen email [14–18]. Even though the practical applications were shown only 2020 onwards, QNLP is the culmination of half a century of theoretical research between grammarians, physicists and mathematicians. Fundamental to QNLP is the idea that there is a strong correlation between human natural language and quantum physics. To understand this, we need to first understand how natural languages function.

There are a few foundational principles in linguistics that most of the human languages that exist today follow. First, a human language typically starts by defining certain fundamental building blocks. Next, more complex structures are built up by combining these fundamental building blocks using certain rules, in many cases, recursively. For example, in the case of English, such fundamental building blocks will typically be parts of speech like nouns, verbs, etc. As we know, these can then be combined to create intermediate structures called noun phrases, prepositional phrases, etc. Next, these structures themselves can be combined, in many cases recursively, to arrive at other complex structures like sentences, paragraphs, discourses, long, drawn research documents, etc. In other words, human natural language is a structure built up from basic building blocks following some rules, which we know as grammar.

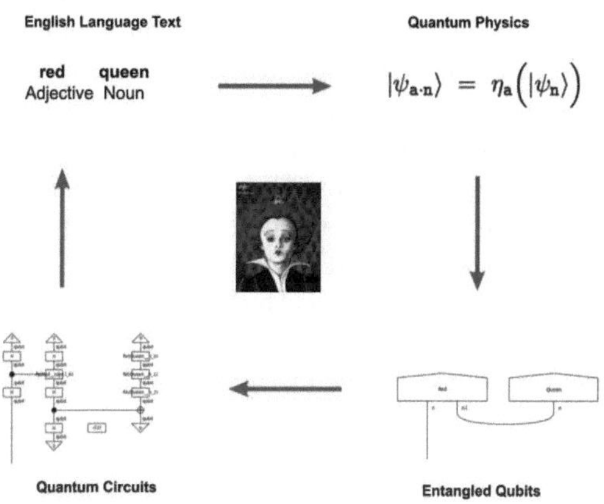

Fig. 3. QNLP connection expressing equivalence of the same English Language phrase in four equivalent ways including quantum circuits.

Typically, multiple mathematical frameworks are used to verify the grammatical correctness of a given complex element of a particular natural language, a process typically known as parsing. For example, the most common methodology used to parse a sentence in English is Context-Free Grammar, which was suggested by Noam Chomsky [11,12]. However, QNLP is built on a not so well known, but similar, mathematical methodology for parsing known as Categorical Grammar [31]. A categorical grammar consists of two parts: a lexicon (or a dictionary), which assigns a set of types (also called categories) to each basic symbol (e.g., nouns), and some type inference rules, which determine how the type of a string of symbols follows from the types of the constituent symbols. However, despite the name and similar properties, categorical grammar was initially considered to be unrelated to category theory in mathematics. In 1989, Lambek (one of the initial proponents of categorical grammar) showed that human natural language belongs to a type of monoid in category theory known as pregroups [30]. Along with being equipped with the standard operations of monoids (e.g., associative binary operation and an identity element), pre-groups also have a unique feature that the elements have left and right inverses. For example, a typical element in the category, a transitive verb (e.g., throws), by definition has to have a subject (its left inverse) and an object (right inverse). Specifically, in the sentence `Alice throws flowers`, the left inverse is `Alice`, and `flowers` is the right inverse of `throws`, respectively. As mentioned earlier this idea was extended by a bunch of physicists, some of whom had already proven the deep correlation between category theory and quantum physics by then, to arrive at the conclusion that human natural language can be represented using quantum physics, a field that came to be then known as QNLP [18].

QNLP can be explained in detail, using an example from the English language as follows: Consider the phrase `red queen`. Here, `queen` is a noun on which the adjective `red` acts to assign it a specific "quality", in this case of being of the color red. In QNLP, the action of an adjective acting on a noun is mathematically modeled as the action of a unitary operator on a qubit, and hence the whole phrase can be represented as a quantum circuit. The various detailed steps of this process are detailed as below, which is also graphically depicted in Fig. 3.

The first assumption of QNLP is that the meaning of words can be modeled as quantum states, which may be represented as qubits of appropriate dimensions. First, the noun `queen` is represented as a 1-qubit state, say $|\psi_{\mathrm{n}}\rangle \in \mathbb{C}^2$. The adjective `red` modifies the noun `queen`. Hence, the action of the adjective `red` on the noun `queen` may be thought of as a unitary operator $\eta_{\mathrm{a}} : \mathbb{C}^2 \to \mathbb{C}^2$ acting on the qubit representing the noun $|\psi_{\mathrm{n}}\rangle$ to produce the modified meaning vector

$$|\psi_{\mathrm{a\cdot n}}\rangle = \eta_{\mathrm{a}}|\psi_{\mathrm{n}}\rangle \in \mathbb{C}^2. \tag{1}$$

This is shown in the top row of Fig. 3. It may be noted that the adjective `red`, which was earlier represented as an operator η_{a} acting on $\mathbb{C}^2$ can also be thought of as a higher dimensional qubit by considering the matrix of η_{a}, as a 2-qubit state. That is, if $\eta_{\mathrm{a}} = \begin{bmatrix} \eta_{00} & \eta_{01} \\ \eta_{10} & \eta_{11} \end{bmatrix}$, then η_{a} can be canonically mapped as a 2-qubit state $|\psi_{\mathrm{a}}\rangle$ as

$$\eta_a \mapsto |\psi_{\mathrm{a}}\rangle := \eta_{00}|00\rangle + \eta_{01}|01\rangle + \eta_{10}|10\rangle + \eta_{11}|11\rangle \in \mathbb{C}^4. \tag{2}$$

The advantage of this mapping is that, in this way, the adjective `red` can also be viewed as a state, in this case, a 2-qubit state. Then the aforementioned process of operator acting on this qubit is achieved by applying a Bell state entanglement between the qubits corresponding to `red` and `queen` as the following easily verifiable fact:

$$|\psi_{\mathrm{a\cdot n}}\rangle = (\mathbb{I} \otimes \langle\ \mathrm{Bell}\ |) \circ (|\psi_{\mathrm{a}}\rangle \otimes |\psi_{\mathrm{n}}\rangle)\,, \tag{3}$$

where $\langle\ \mathrm{Bell}\ | = \frac{1}{\sqrt{2}}\left(\langle 00| + \langle 11|\right)$ and $\mathbb{I}$ is the identity operator. This is shown using the ZX calculus in the bottom right corner of the picture. Next, these

ZX calculus diagrams are converted to quantum circuits with rewrite rules as mentioned in [16] and [18]. This same methodology and intuition are further used to create much bigger sentences, using more complex parts of speech (e.g., transitive verbs live in $\mathbb{C}^6$ since they need a subject and an object to act on), thus mapping the complete hierarchical grammatical structure of human natural language as hierarchical dimensions of qubits.

Next, all the circuits thus generated are used in a standard deep learning-like framework involving feed forward and back propagation loops. The mathematical calculations part of the entire machine learning process (called stochastic gradient descent) is done using a classical computer to conform to the current NISQ paradigm [36,44].

Note that in the first step of converting English language sentences to quantum circuits, a many-to-one mapping exists between syntactically (i.e., through grammatical parsing) similar English language sentences and their corresponding circuits, which then becomes a one-to-one mapping after the machine learning process. For example, if A is a collection of syntactically similar English language sentences, and B is a collection of quantum circuits created by QNLP tools, the mapping from A to B will be many-to-one initially. In the second step, i.e., after the 'training' process, this mapping becomes one-to-one. This is because, after the 'training' process, the angles of the rotational gates uniquely identify and semantically (i.e., meaning-wise) set apart a given sentence from its grammatically equivalent neighbors.

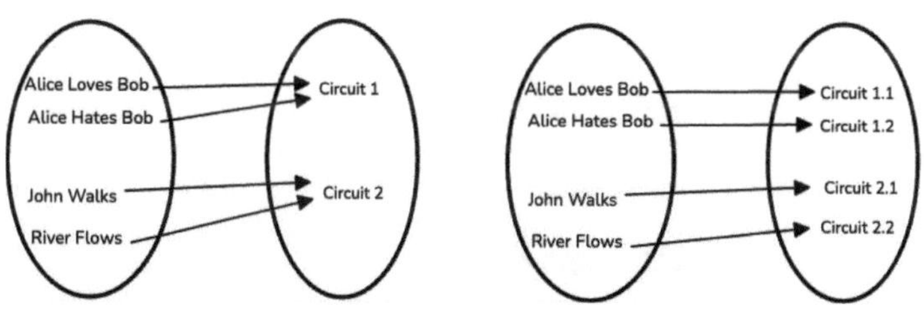

Fig. 4. Mapping from English language sentences to corresponding quantum circuits before and after machine learning. While the gates and structure of the circuit remain the same in both cases, the angles of the rotational gates will be different, indicating a difference in meaning.

In other words, both the sentences `'Alice loves Bob'` and `'Alice hates Bob'` will initially have precisely the same circuit gates and structure so as to reflect the grammatical structural similarity of these two sentences. However, after the entire training process, the angles of each of the rotational gates present in these circuits will be different in each sentence so as to reflect the difference in meaning between the `loves` and `hates`. This is shown in Fig. 4. It is worth remarking that in QNLP, while the grammar of natural language is represented using quantum circuits, as shown above, the flow of meaning between the words is achieved by applying entanglement between their corresponding qubits. Also, note that QNLP internally uses several ZX calculus techniques to reduce the size of the thus created quantum circuits, which would otherwise grow exponentially as the size of the input sentences increases.

To summarize, as shown above, QNLP uses a process of evolution of qubits through its corresponding circuits, to mimic the classical machine learning process. Further, the inventors of QNLP empirically prove that the model is able to understand and 'learn' the meaning of a given complex sentence, well enough to predict it to belong to the right class with very high accuracy, very similar to the functioning of any classical machine learning model currently used in NLP, like neural networks.

3 The Methodology

As shown above, the critical aspects of a quantum circuit are parameters such as the number of qubits and gates, the percentage of two-qubit gates, and depth, along with metrics from the interaction graph (e.g., average node degree) and the gate-dependency graph (e.g., critical path length). Analyzing these parameters helps us understand why certain quantum circuits are better or worse for particular architectures, potentially revealing correlations between circuit structure and performance across different quantum setups. This multi-parameter optimization problem is challenging and of great interest. The major steps we took to investigate and solve this problem are summarized here, which are in-turn detailed below.

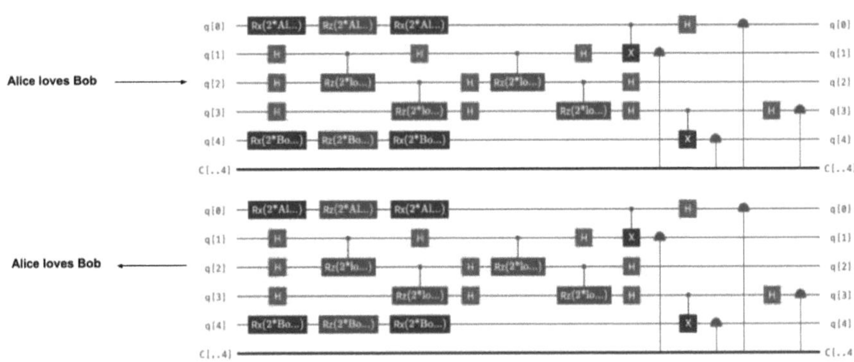

Fig. 5. Difference between QNLP and our proposal. While QNLP converts English language sentences to corresponding quantum circuits, our proposal will investigate the feasibility of converting a given quantum circuit back to the English language and subsequently compressing it in the natural language space.

- **Step 1:** Our first step is to convert a given quantum circuit to an equivalent entity in natural language, in this case English. Note that this entity could be a collection of sentences, a passage, or an entire discourse article, depending on the complexity of the circuit and the vocabulary picked. Then a standard English parser will be used to verify if the thus created English equivalent entity (e.g., a sentence) is grammatically correct, along with a human reader verifying its meaningfulness. If both of these evaluations pass with 95% accuracy or higher, we will consider this step successful. We explain the specific details of the proposed methodologies in Sect. 3.1.

- **Step 2:** Our second step is to use state-of-the-art reduction techniques in classical NLP (e.g., LLM-based summarization) to reduce the language entity (created at the end of step one, say a passage), to a smaller version of itself (e.g., a sentence) while completely preserving its meaning. The techniques mentioned above from QNLP will then be used to convert this reduced English entity back to its corresponding quantum circuit. The newly created smaller circuit will then be compared with the original complex circuit provided as input to step 1 using standard circuit comparison tools. If this comparison evaluation passes with 95% accuracy or higher, we will consider this step to be successful. We explain the specific details of the proposed methodologies in Sect. 3.2.

- **Step 3:** Our third step is to project certain circuit optimization routines recently developed using ZX calculus into the space of natural language. Specifically, this is based on recent research that shows that quantum circuit optimization tasks can be efficiently achieved using the ZX calculus [46,49,51]. Earlier, we mentioned that QNLP internally uses ZX calculus to reduce the size of its circuits. Thus in this step, we will explore if such quantum circuit optimization problems solved by ZX calculus can be projected and solved in natural language space, with possible simplifications inspired by NLP. Specific details of the proposed methodology are explained in Sect. 4.2.

Table 1. Some Quantum Gates and possible linguistic operations that can be depicted by them.

Gate	Linguistic Operation
I	`No Change`
X	`Negate`
Z	`Modify`
Y	`Negative Modification`
H	`Uncertainty`
T	`Subtle Adjustment`
CNOT	`Interaction`
SWAP	`Exchange`

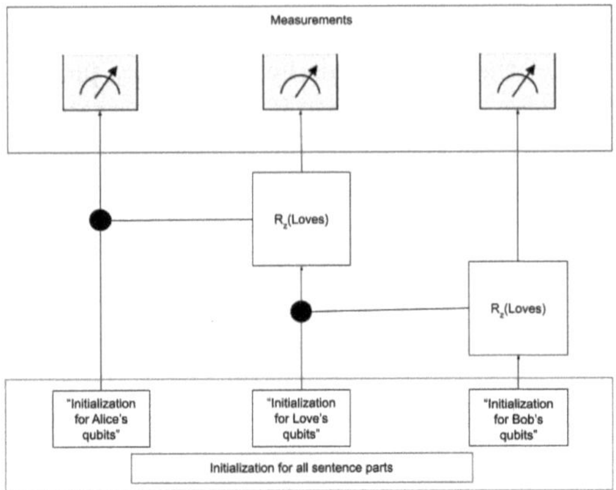

Fig. 6. The phrase `Alice Loves Bob` represented in its simplified circuit form. Observe that the circuit closely resembles the simple GHZ circuit shown in Fig. 1 without the initialization steps, thus demonstrating the power of converting phrases to quantum circuits. The elaborated version of the same circuit can be seen in Fig. 7.

Next we will detail each of the aforementioned steps.

3.1 Step 1: Quantum Gates to Natural Language

As we saw above, QNLP has already devised techniques to convert a given English entity (e.g., a sentence) to a corresponding quantum circuit. Our aim in this step is to investigate the possibility of doing the reverse, i.e., given a quantum circuit, can we create a good corresponding meaningful and grammatically correct entity in English. For example, if we are given the circuits that were created by QNLP for the sentence `Alice loves Bob`, along with the corresponding rotation angles of the gates, (with the assumption that this was created by an oracle like system which we don't know anything about) can we recreate the sentence from it as shown in Fig. 5. Note that this will also open up interesting related questions like what should be the ideal limiting vocabulary of the text to be used for this process, conversion of tenses, can this technique be extrapolated to more extended entities like paragraphs, etc.We will approach this problem by trying to first investigate if mapping quantum gates to some sort of linguistic semantics or processes, along with drawing analogies between quantum operations and language will help to convey the underlying intuition behind the suggested solution. For example, a controlled gate such as CNOT will be used to link the subject and object as in the sentence `Alice loves Bob` as shown in Fig. 6 (A detailed version of the same using only (conditional) rotational gates and Hadamard gates can be seen in Fig. 7).

Similarly, the Pauli gates can be possibly mapped to linguistic structures as follows:

- Pauli X Gate: Analogous to a negation or inversion.
- Pauli Z Gate: Introduces an emphasis or modification of relationships of words.
- Pauli Y Gate: Negative modification.

For example, in the sentence `The cat is not on the mat`, the phrase `is not` inverts the meaning, similar to how the Pauli X gate flips the state of a qubit. Similarly, the Hadamard gate H is a fundamental quantum gate that creates superposition states. For a qubit in state $|0\rangle$ or $|1\rangle$, the Hadamard gate transforms it as follows: $H|0\rangle = \frac{1}{\sqrt{2}}(|0\rangle + |1\rangle)$ and $H|1\rangle = \frac{1}{\sqrt{2}}(|0\rangle - |1\rangle)$. The creation of a superposition state can be analogized to creating a state of ambiguity or potentiality in a sentence.

Similarly the Hadamard gate's effect is to create superposition, which in language might correspond to creating a state where the sentence can be interpreted in multiple ways, or where the meaning is not entirely determined. For example, consider the sentence `The cat might be on the mat.` Here, the predicate `might be on the mat` introduces potentiality/uncertainty in the sentence. More generally, the Hadamard transformation can be mapped to sentences that introduce ambiguity or multiple potential meanings, such as using modal verbs (`"might"`, `"could"`) or constructing sentences with inherent uncertainty.

The T-gate, similarly, is a fundamental quantum gate that applies a phase shift of $\frac{\pi}{4}$ (or 45°) to the state $|1\rangle$. The action of the T gate is: $T|0\rangle = |0\rangle$ and $T|1\rangle = e^{i\pi/4}|1\rangle$. This means that the T gate leaves the $|0\rangle$ state unchanged and adds a complex phase factor to the $|1\rangle$ state. This can be analogized to the introduction of a subtle or nuanced modification, such as adverbs or modals that adjust the tone or certainty of the statement in the meaning of a sentence. For example, consider the sentence '`She almost completed the task`'. Here, `almost completed the task` introduces a certain nuanced modification. In this sentence, the adverb `almost` modifies the verb phrase `completed the task`, similar to how the T gate introduces a phase shift.

Similarly, in sentences, one can also think of the logical transformation of gate operations. For example, with a SWAP gate, we can exchange the states of two qubits. The SWAP gate exchanges states, similar to swapping the positions of elements in a sentence. For instance, `Alice loves Bob` can be swapped to `Bob loves Alice` with a swap gate operation. These connections are summarized in Table 1.

3.2 Step 2: Semantic Summarization for Circuit Reduction

As mentioned before, our second step is to use state-of-the-art reduction techniques in classical NLP, like summarization, to reduce the language entity (created at the end of step one) to a smaller version of itself (e.g., a sentence) while completely preserving its meaning. The intuition here is that the meaning-preserving transformation in the linguistic space will also reflect as an operation-preserving reduction of the corresponding quantum circuits.

In this section, we show a minimal theoretical proof of concept to explain this intuition in detail. To demonstrate this, we start with a toy example. Consider the two toy sentences `Alice loves Bob` and `Alice has deep affection for Bob and holds him in a special place in her heart.` As a human reader, we intuitively understand that these two sentences mean the same, i.e., they both semantically intend to convey the same idea. However, to formally prove that these two sentences are equal, we also need to verify that they are equal at the syntax or grammatical level. We show this below using standard syntactic comparison methodologies in linguistics. Later, we produce the quantum circuits corresponding to these two sentences using the publicly available QNLP tool called LAMBEQ and show that the corresponding circuits are also equivalent. This proves a part of our proposed hypothesis, i.e., that if two sentences are equal in meaning and syntax, they can produce equivalent quantum circuits in QNLP.

Linguistic Proof. To formally confirm the syntactic equivalence of both sentences, we used the linguistics tool of formal semantics notation and reduction, as shown below. Consider the first sentence `Alice loves bob`. In formal semantics, this sentence is represented as

$$\texttt{loves(alice,bob)} \tag{4}$$

where "`loves`" is the predicate indicating the relationship between the two entities "`alice`" and "`bob`". Next, we write the second sentence `Alice has a deep affection for Bob and holds him in a special place in her heart` in the formal notation form as :

$$\begin{aligned} &\texttt{have(alice,for(deep(affection),bob))} \\ &\wedge \texttt{hold(alice,bob,in(special(place),heart))} \end{aligned} \tag{5}$$

Next assume we provide the two meanings `deep(affection) = love` and `having love for someone = loves`. Therefore equation (5) becomes

$$\begin{aligned} &\texttt{have(alice,for(love,bob))} \\ &= \texttt{have(alice,for(deep(affection),bob)} \\ &= \texttt{loves(alice,bob))} \end{aligned} \tag{6}$$

Now we can see that the last part in Eq. (6), `loves(alice,bob)` is exactly the same as Eq. (4) hence proving that given meaning equivalences, these two sentences are syntactically also equivalent.

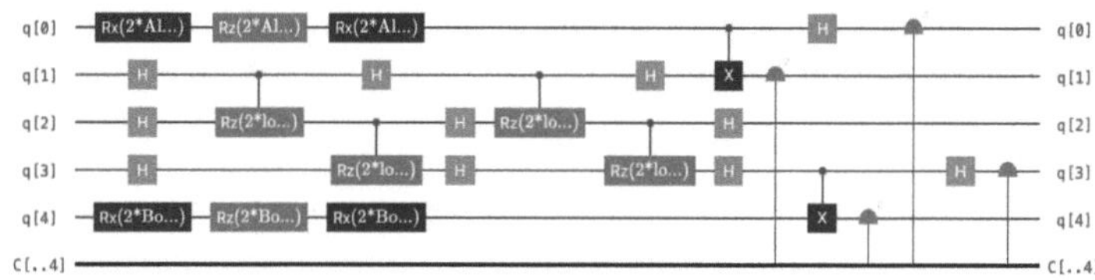

Fig. 7. A quantum circuit produced by the QNLP tool LAMBEQ for the sentence `Alice Loves Bob`.

Quantum Circuit Level Proof. Next, we convert both these sentences to their corresponding quantum circuits using the QNLP tool, LAMBEQ, the corresponding circuits of which are shown in Fig. 7 and Fig. 8 respectively. As you can see, Lambeq builds its circuits with only foundational gates like Rotational, Hadamard, etc.

From a quick visual inspection, both circuits appear to use the same set of rotations and controlled operations, and they measure the qubits after applying the same sequences of gates. Therefore, if all transformations are applied equivalently, the circuits should be theoretically, structurally, and functionally equivalent. Specifically, when comparing the structure of both circuits, we see that they both have the same key components. For example, in the initial step, both circuits initialize qubits in the $|0\rangle$ state and both circuits apply Hadamard gates (H) to the qubits to create superpositions. Next, if we look at the controlled gates and rotations, we can see that both circuits use controlled $-Z(CNOT)$ gates and similar rotational gates. Further, both circuits measure the same qubits at the end, ensuring that the output state is read in the same basis. Given that both circuits apply the same sequence of gates to the same qubits and measure the qubits in the same way, they are indeed equivalent. The operations performed on the qubits in both circuits lead to the same final quantum state, confirming their equivalence, purely from a structural standpoint.

However, to conclusively determine if the two quantum circuits are equivalent, we need to compare each of the individual structure and operations to see if they both produce the same output for any given input as given below. i.e., this is not a comprehensive proof of their equivalence since the placement, parameters, and exact angles of the rotational gates should be verified during and after the evolution, especially during machine learning methodologies, if any. To re-iterate the limitation of this work explicitly, please do note that we did not confirm that these two circuits are equivalent by using standard quantum circuit equivalence approaches such as decision rules [25,35], ZX calculus [7,41] or a tool like Guoq [52] due to time and resource constraints. We leave this as a future work, for us, or other interested parties in the future, since the main purpose of this work is to be a path breaking/shining light into the myriad of possibilities and problems QNLP is capable of potentially solving. Nevertheless, some detailed methods for a comprehensive verification of both circuits is given in the future work section below.

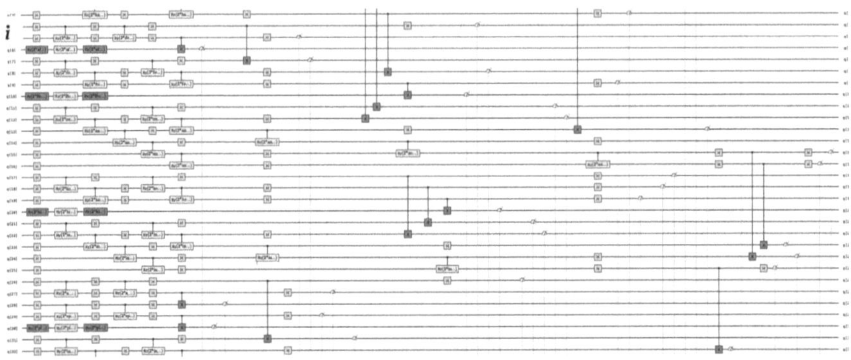

Fig. 8. A complex quantum circuit produced by the QNLP tool LAMBEQ for the sentence `Alice has deep affection for Bob and holds him in a special place in her heart.`

4 Discussion and Future Work

In Sect. 3, we theoretically show that not only are the two sentences `Alice loves Bob` and `Alice has deep affection for Bob and holds him in a special place in her heart` semantically and syntactically equivalent, but their corresponding circuits generated are also equivalent. This preliminary theoretical proof, in our opinion, gives us, and other interested researchers, inspiration to comprehensively investigate this possibility.

Note that the conversion of a given complex circuit to natural language will need deep theoretical investigation, since it has not been done before, along with exploring if any correlations with current quantum circuit compilation methods, including graph theoretic reductions, exist. To summarize, once these individual components are in place, we anticipate our approach from the initial input of a complex circuit through conversion to natural language, summarizing, conversion back to the complex circuit domain, and comparison of newly created circuits, to go in one pass.

Similarly, the two circuits need to be compared comprehensively, especially to ensure the equivalence of initial states, transitions, and state vectors. This can be done using the machine learning methodology specified in [34]. As shown there, a deep learning like methodology involving multiple passes across such circuits generated from a dictionary definition can possibly yield learnings of the meaning of each of the individual words, which will in turn be reflected using the angles of the rotations thus learnt. Once the rotational angles are produced by the machine learning methodology, the equivalence of the two circuits can be established by confirming the equivalence of state vectors, unitary matrices, ancillas, and their respective final measurements. We intend to do this as our future work. Also below, we mention some other future directions we would like to pursue along with this.

Another interesting path of exploration we plan to do is based on the DiscoCirc and related works [19,33,50] of the founders of QNLP, which elaborates possible methodologies for the same.

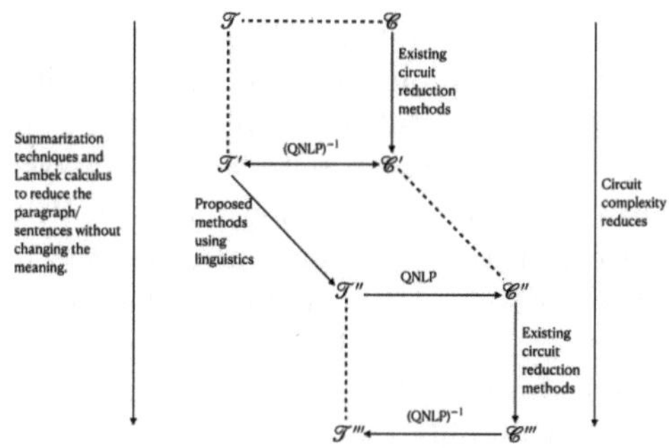

Fig. 9. A ladder approach combining the power of both QNLP and existing state-of-the-art circuit optimization methods.

4.1 Combining With Existing Approaches

We propose that our QNLP-based approach can also be combined with existing state-of-the-art circuit optimization techniques to leverage the power of the existing techniques in the field. The proposed methodology will be as follows, which is also illustrated in Fig. 9.

- Given a circuit $\mathcal{C}$, let $\mathcal{C}'$ be a reduced form of this circuit using the existing circuit optimization routines.
- Corresponding to $\mathcal{C}$ and $\mathcal{C}'$ we have English language texts $\mathcal{T}$ and $\mathcal{T}'$ respectively.
- If $\mathcal{T}'$ can be further reduced using NLP, to get the sentence $\mathcal{T}''$, then we can consider the circuit $\mathcal{C}''$ corresponding to $\mathcal{T}''$.
- The newly obtained obtained circuit $\mathcal{C}''$ should be much more reduced than $\mathcal{C}'$.
- This process may be repeated until we find the most reduced form of the circuit.

4.2 Projecting ZX-Calculus Methods to Natural Language Space

Currently, ZX-calculus is being used as a powerful intermediate tool as a bridge between quantum circuits and graph theoretical tools specifically for reducing qubit count and also for certain circuit optimization tasks [46,49]. The diagrammatic tool one uses therein is referred to as ZX-diagrams as shown in Fig. 2 has exciting applications in QNLP research, instrumental in producing circuits for different sentences/phrases and in obtaining their reductions. In this proposal, we plan to exploit the deep connection that ZX-calculus and QNLP share to incorporate the methodologies from QNLP. This can particularly help in the optimization of the specific tasks that use ZX calculus. Specifically, some of the main questions we plan to investigate are: (1) whether tasks such as degadgetization of Hadamard gates, and qubit reuse with mid-circuit measurements and resets, be performed using NLP tools like paraphrasing and summarization, with QNLP again acting as a bridge between both? (2) it is known that ZX-calculus can be used to perform a variety of operations, such as Pauli fusion computational models [3] (that can further represent lattice surgery operations [4]), and some recently proposed methods [46] for reducing the number of 2-qubit gates and T-gates in a circuit. Here, we would like to investigate whether QNLP can be used to replace the graph theoretical tools in ZX-calculus with natural language equivalents to improve and simplify these protocols.

4.3 Using QNLP Beyond Quantum Compilation

In this step, we will explore the possibility of extending the versatility and utility of QNLP to other quantum computation-related tasks. For example, we will investigate if other standard NLP tasks like text classification can be used for identifying and classifying various components of circuit components (e.g., distinguishing Clifford and non-Clifford parts of a circuit). Or, if an NLP task like part-of-speech tagging can be used to identify corresponding quantum circuit components, which in turn can be used in circuit classification and analysis.

Another such exploration is to use classical NLP ideas of reconstructing passages and texts into coherent yet small chunks of text of manageable size to be used for training in existing NISQ devices. This can mimic the similar idea of circuit cutting and stitching [48] but with semantic equivalency parameters. Note that quantum circuit cutting and stitching are techniques deployed to overcome the limitation of NISQ devices, by breaking up large quantum circuits into manageable sub-circuits employing state-of-the-art machine learning and tensor networks [6,40,42]. This is very similar to the technique of meaning-preserving text chunking in NLP, and hence the possible overlap in intuition. However, this novel approach must be studied in detail to see how to augment existing tensor network-based approaches that minimize errors and classical computational overhead.

A unique thread of exploration that we propose for this step is to use QNLP to obtain error correction constraints embedded in sentence structures. Specifically, in quantum error correction, logical qubits are highly entangled with redundant qubits to protect them from decoherence and unwanted environmental interactions. Recent research using ZX-Calculus has found applications in the unification of existing error correction frameworks and the improvement of specific error correction codes [4,5,8,9]. Based on our observations of porting natural language to quantum circuits, it is intriguing to explore if the grammatical constraints of natural language give logical qubit error correction protection. Further, one can argue that the coherence of passages in any language is dependent on certain key elements or constraints that are present. On the other hand, an erroneous passage can be made coherent based on semantics and such constraints. Then, one can quantify the content of the information using classical and quantum information theoretical tools and construct a more efficient text encoding for quantum information. It is not clear what specific benefits this approach brings at this point. Still, considering how important fault tolerance and error correction are for bringing quantum computers into reality, we propose to pursue this exciting direction as well.

Fig. 10. Word Puzzle To Introduce Quantum Physics.

4.4 Societal Outreach and Broader Impacts

Quantum Information Science (QIS) is currently a rapidly growing field with significant potential to revolutionize technology, computing, and even fundamental understanding of the universe. Hence, we feel this work is thus being proposed at the right time historically to match with the upcoming Quantum Information Science revolution. To add to this we anticipate that QNLP and ZX-calculus, through the usage of only human natural language and graphical diagrams, can easily express and teach concepts in quantum physics and can become a very fruitful pedagogical tool on this front. Here are some directions where we think this project will be able to have a huge, broader impact .

Educational and Pedagogical Purposes. Sometimes in early STEM education (in high school and undergraduate level), otherwise brilliant and motivated students in physics get discouraged due to the heavy mathematics they encounter in the introductory classes to quantum physics. To address this we plan to extend the knowledge gained through this work for educational purposes and encourage further learning of Quantum Physics. For example, we plan to introduce a novel pedagogical methodology of teaching quantum physics using only the English language (internally using QNLP). This methodology will not use heavy mathematics, and instead, the prerequisite will be basic knowledge of at least one human natural language (e.g., English).

Societal Outreach For Creating Quantum Awareness. Currently familiarity with quantum physics has been restricted to the educational and research community. However, for the upcoming quantum revolution, the creation of a quantum-aware society is also essential. Using our fundamental knowledge in QNLP, which was enhanced through this work, we plan to address this problem by creating a user-controlled interactive online word game that will smoothly introduce quantum concepts using very commonly used words. As shown in Fig. 10, the user will be presented with a sentence with hidden parts (similar to the *Wheel of Fortune* TV show), which the user will then have to solve. Eventually, as levels progress, and the complexities of the puzzle increase based on more grammatical components, slowly quantum concepts will also be introduced. Thus, the user can potentially learn, or minimally be aware of, the basic concepts in Quantum Physics, just using English word and sentence building games. Thus, the proposed word game we hope can help create a quantum-aware, if not adept, society.

5 Conclusion

This work introduces a novel, theoretical framework that reframes quantum circuit optimization through human natural language, leveraging and inverting the tools of Quantum Natural Language Processing (QNLP). By translating circuits into language, applying summarization techniques, and reconstructing optimized circuits, we provide an initial proof-of-concept suggesting the feasibility and semantic consistency of this approach. While this proposal is exploratory, it lays foundational groundwork for future research, including rigorous benchmarking and analysis of its applicability across diverse quantum circuits. The potential to integrate QNLP with existing optimization techniques, apply ZX-calculus concepts through language, and extend these ideas to areas like error correction and pedagogy highlights the versatility of this approach. We envision this work as a starting point for interdisciplinary collaboration across quantum computing, NLP, and AI, and invite further exploration into the linguistic structure underlying quantum processes.

Acknowledgments. The authors would like to thank Nirav Merchant, and Robert Henderson for their timely inputs and reviews.

References

1. Aaronson, S., Gottesman, D.: Improved simulation of stabilizer circuits. Phys. Rev. A **70** (2004). https://doi.org/10.1103/PhysRevA.70.052328
2. de Beaudrap, N., Bian, X., Wang, Q.: Techniques to reduce pi/4-parity-phase circuits, motivated by the ZX calculus. Electr. Proc. Theor. Comput. Sci. **318**, 131–149 (2020). https://doi.org/10.4204/eptcs.318.9
3. de Beaudrap, N., Duncan, R., Horsman, D., Perdrix, S.: Pauli fusion: a computational model to realise quantum transformations from ZX terms. Electr. Proc. Theor. Comput. Sci. **318**, 85–105 (2020). https://doi.org/10.4204/eptcs.318.6
4. de Beaudrap, N., Horsman, D.: The ZX Calculus is a Language for Surface Code Lattice Surgery. Quantum **4**, 218 (2020). https://doi.org/10.22331/q-2020-01-09-218
5. Bombin, H., Litinski, D., Nickerson, N., Pastawski, F., Roberts, S.: Unifying flavors of fault tolerance with the ZX calculus. Quantum **8**, 1379 (2024). https://doi.org/10.22331/q-2024-06-18-1379
6. Bravyi, S., Smith, G., Smolin, J.A.: Trading classical and quantum computational resources. Phys. Rev. X **6**, 021043 (2016). https://doi.org/10.1103/PhysRevX.6.021043
7. Burgholzer, L., Wille, R.: Advanced Equivalence Checking for Quantum Circuits. IEEE Trans. Comput. Aided Design Integr. Circuits Syst. **40**(9), 1810–1824 (2020). https://doi.org/10.1109/TCAD.2020.3032630
8. Carette, T., Horsman, D., Perdrix, S.: Szx-calculus: Scalable graphical quantum reasoning. arXiv preprint arXiv:1905.00041 (2019)
9. Chancellor, N., Kissinger, A., Zohren, S., Roffe, J., Horsman, D.: Graphical structures for design and verification of quantum error correction. Quan. Sci. Technol. **8**(4), 045028 (2023). https://doi.org/10.1088/2058-9565/acf157
10. Childs, A.M., Schoute, E., Unsal, C.M.: Circuit Transformations for Quantum Architectures. In: van Dam, W., Mančinska, L. (eds.) 14th Conference on the Theory of Quantum Computation, Communication and Cryptography (TQC 2019). Leibniz International Proceedings in Informatics (LIPIcs), vol. 135, pp. 3:1–3:24. Schloss Dagstuhl – Leibniz-Zentrum für Informatik, Dagstuhl, Germany (2019). https://doi.org/10.4230/LIPIcs.TQC.2019.3
11. Chomsky, N.: Three models for the description of language. IRE Trans. Inf. Theory **2**(3), 113–124 (1956)
12. Chomsky, N.: Aspects of the Theory of Syntax. No. 11, MIT press (2014)
13. Clark, J., Humble, T., Thapliyal, H.: Tdag: Tree-based directed acyclic graph partitioning for quantum circuits. In: Proceedings of the Great Lakes Symposium on VLSI 2023. p. 587–592. GLSVLSI '23, Association for Computing Machinery, New York, NY, USA (2023). https://doi.org/10.1145/3583781.3590234
14. Clark, S., Coecke, B., Sadrzadeh, M.: A compositional distributional model of meaning. In: Proceedings of the Second Quantum Interaction Symposium (QI-2008), pp. 133–140. Oxford (2008)

15. Coecke, B.: The mathematics of text structure. Joachim Lambek: The Interplay of Mathematics, Logic, and Linguistics, pp. 181–217 (2021)
16. Coecke, B., Duncan, R.: Interacting quantum observables: categorical algebra and diagrammatics. New J. Phys. **13**(4), 043016 (2011)
17. Coecke, B., de Felice, G., Meichanetzidis, K., Toumi, A.: Foundations for near-term quantum natural language processing. arXiv preprint arXiv:2012.03755 (2020)
18. Coecke, B., Sadrzadeh, M., Clark, S.: Mathematical foundations for a compositional distributional model of meaning. arXiv preprint arXiv:1003.4394 (2010)
19. Coecke, B., Wang, V.: Distilling grammar into circuits (or, de-humanising grammar for efficient machine use) (2021)
20. Cowtan, A., Dilkes, S., Duncan, R., Simmons, W., Sivarajah, S.: Phase gadget synthesis for shallow circuits. arXiv preprint arXiv:1906.01734 (2019)
21. Duncan, R., Kissinger, A., Perdrix, S., van de Wetering, J.: Graph-theoretic simplification of quantum circuits with the ZX-calculus. Quantum **4**, 279 (2020). https://doi.org/10.22331/q-2020-06-04-279
22. Duncan, R., Perdrix, S.: Rewriting measurement-based quantum computations with generalised flow. In: International Colloquium on Automata, Languages, and Programming, pp. 285–296. Springer (2010)
23. Fösel, T., Niu, M.Y., Marquardt, F., Li, L.: Quantum circuit optimization with deep reinforcement learning (2021)
24. Holker, C.: Causal flow preserving optimisation of quantum circuits in the ZX-calculus (2024). http://arxiv.org/abs/2312.02793
25. Hong, X., Feng, Y., Li, S., Ying, M.: Equivalence checking of dynamic quantum circuits. In: 2022 IEEE/ACM International Conference On Computer Aided Design (ICCAD), pp. 1–8 (2022)
26. Horsman, D.: Quantum picturalism for topological cluster-state computing. New J. Phys. **13**(9), 095011 (2011)
27. Kissinger, A., van de Wetering, J.: Universal MBQC with generalised parity-phase interactions and Pauli measurements. Quantum **3**, 134 (2019)
28. Kissinger, A., van de Wetering, J.: Reducing the number of non-Clifford gates in quantum circuits. Phys. Rev. A **102**, 022406 (2020). https://doi.org/10.1103/PhysRevA.102.022406
29. Kliuchnikov, V., Maslov, D.: Optimization of Clifford circuits. Phys. Rev. **88** (2013). https://doi.org/10.1103/PhysRevA.88.052307
30. Lambek, Joachim, A.: On a connection between algebra, logic and linguistics. Diagrammes **22**, 59–75 (1989)
31. Lambek, J.: The mathematics of sentence structure. Am. Math. Mon. **65**(3), 154–170 (1958)
32. Li, Z., et al.: Quarl: A learning-based quantum circuit optimizer (2023)
33. Liu, J., Shaikh, R.A., Rodatz, B., Yeung, R., Coecke, B.: A pipeline for discourse circuits from ccg. arXiv preprint arXiv:2311.17892 (2023)
34. Lorenz, R., Pearson, A., Meichanetzidis, K., Kartsaklis, D., Coecke, B.: Qnlp in practice: running compositional models of meaning on a quantum computer. J. Artif. Intell. Res. **76**, 1305–1342 (2023)
35. Mei, J., Coopmans, T., Bonsangue, M., Laarman, A.: Equivalence Checking of Quantum Circuits by Model Counting. arXiv (2024)
36. Meichanetzidis, K., Gogioso, S., De Felice, G., Chiappori, N., Toumi, A., Coecke, B.: Quantum natural language processing on near-term quantum computers. arXiv preprint arXiv:2005.04147 (2020)

37. Nash, B., Gheorghiu, V., Mosca, M.: Quantum circuit optimizations for NISQ architectures. Quantum Science and Technology **5** (2020). https://doi.org/10.1088/2058-9565/ab79b1
38. Nielsen, M.A., Chuang, I.L.: Quantum Computation and Quantum Information: 10th Anniversary Edition. Cambridge University Press (2010)
39. Nogue, J.: Reinforcement Learning based Circuit Compilation via ZX-calculus. Master's thesis, Universitat de Barcelona (2023). https://diposit.ub.edu/dspace/bitstream/2445/202911/1/Memoria_TFM-JanNogue.pdf
40. Paler, A., Sasu, L., Florea, A.C., Andonie, R.: Machine learning optimization of quantum circuit layouts. ACM Trans. Quan. Comput. **4**(2) (2023). https://doi.org/10.1145/3565271
41. Peham, T., Burgholzer, L., Wille, R.: Equivalence checking of quantum circuits with the ZX-calculus. IEEE J. Emerg. Sel. Top. Circ. Syst. **12**(3), 662–675 (2022). https://doi.org/10.1109/jetcas.2022.3202204
42. Peng, T., Harrow, A.W., Ozols, M., Wu, X.: Simulating large quantum circuits on a small quantum computer. Phys. Rev. Lett. **125**, 150504 (2020). https://doi.org/10.1103/PhysRevLett.125.150504
43. Preskill, J.: Quantum Computing in the NISQ era and beyond. Quantum **2**, 79 (2018). https://doi.org/10.22331/q-2018-08-06-79
44. Preskill, J.: Quantum computing in the Nisq era and beyond. Quantum **2**, 79 (2018)
45. Schulman, J., Wolski, F., Dhariwal, P., Radford, A., Klimov, O.: Proximal policy optimization algorithms (2017)
46. Staudacher, K., Guggemos, T., Gehrke, W., Grundner-Culemann, S.: Reducing 2-qubit gate count for ZX-calculus based quantum circuit optimization. In: Quantum Processing and Languages (QPL22), pp. 1–17 (2022). https://elib.dlr.de/188470/
47. Sutton, R.S., Barto, A.G.: Reinforcement learning: An introduction. The MIT Press, second edn. (2018)
48. Tang, W., Tomesh, T., Suchara, M., Larson, J., Martonosi, M.: Cutqc: Using small quantum computers for large quantum circuit evaluations. In: Proceedings of the 26th ACM International Conference on Architectural Support for Programming Languages and Operating Systems, pp. 473–486. ASPLOS '21, Association for Computing Machinery, New York, NY, USA (2021). https://doi.org/10.1145/3445814.3446758
49. Vandaele, V.: Qubit-count optimization using ZX-calculus (2024). https://arxiv.org/abs/2407.10171
50. Wang-Mascianica, V., Liu, J., Coecke, B.: Distilling text into circuits. arXiv preprint arXiv:2301.10595 (2023)
51. van de Wetering, J.: ZX-calculus for the working quantum computer scientist (2020). http://arxiv.org/abs/2012.13966
52. Xu, A., Molavi, A., Tannu, S., Albarghouthi, A.: Optimizing quantum circuits, fast and slow. In: Proceedings of the 30th ACM International Conference on Architectural Support for Programming Languages and Operating Systems, Volume 1, pp. 777–793 (2025)

Quantum NLP Models on Natural Language Inference

Ling Sun, Peter Sullivan(✉), Michael Martin, and Yun Zhou

Indiana University, Bloomington, IN 47405, USA
petesullivanis@gmail.com

Abstract. Quantum natural language processing (QNLP) offers a novel approach to semantic modeling by embedding compositional structure directly into quantum circuits. This paper investigates the application of QNLP models to the task of Natural Language Inference (NLI), comparing quantum, hybrid, and classical transformer-based models under a constrained few-shot setting. Using the lambeq library and the DisCoCat framework, we construct parameterized quantum circuits for sentence pairs and train them for both semantic relatedness and inference classification. To assess efficiency, we introduce a novel information-theoretic metric—Information Gain per Parameter (IGPP)—which quantifies learning dynamics independent of model size. Our results demonstrate that quantum models achieve performance comparable to classical baselines while operating with dramatically fewer parameters. The Quantum-based models outperform randomly initialized transformers in inference and achieve lower test error on relatedness tasks. Moreover, quantum models exhibit significantly higher per-parameter learning efficiency—up to five orders of magnitude more than classical counterparts—highlighting the promise of QNLP in low-resource, structure-sensitive settings. To address circuit-level isolation and promote parameter sharing, we also propose a novel cluster-based architecture that improves generalization by tying gate parameters to learned word clusters rather than individual tokens.

Keywords: Quantum NLP · Natural Language Inference · Categorical Compositionality

1 Introduction

Natural Language Inference (NLI) is a fundamental challenge in natural language processing, requiring models to determine whether one sentence logically follows from, contradicts, or is unrelated to another Hu et al., 2019; Richardson et al., 2020). Solving NLI demands not just lexical understanding but also compositional reasoning—the ability to understand how meanings of phrases combine.

Inference is inherently compositional, yet most classical models—especially transformers—lack explicit mechanisms to model compositional structure. While

D. Cavar et al. (Eds.): QNLPAI 2025, CCIS 2659, pp. 114–133, 2026.
https://doi.org/10.1007/978-3-032-13883-5_7

it is possible to improve classical models by augmenting them with annotated data that captures world knowledge and compositional semantics, this process is resource-intensive and does not guarantee generalization. Quantum circuit models, in contrast, offer a novel approach: by leveraging compositional frameworks such as DisCoCat (Coecke et al., 2010; Bradley et al., 2018; Miranda et al., 2022), they natively encode syntactic and semantic structure into circuit form. Yet, the application of these models to practical language tasks remains underexplored.

In this work, we introduce a few-shot benchmark for quantum NLI, designed to reflect the constraints of near-term quantum devices.[1] We limit both data and circuit size—training on only 100 sentence pairs using 1 qubit per word in classical simulation—to assess whether quantum models can learn structured meaning efficiently under resource constraints (Sect. 3).

We propose and evaluate a new information-theoretic metric, Information Gain per Parameter (IGPP), to quantify learning efficiency independent of model size. Our experiments show that quantum models, even in such constrained settings, demonstrate competitive inference performance and dramatically higher learning efficiency, outperforming random-initialized transformers and approaching pretrained baselines (Sect. 4).

However, we identify a key obstacle to quantum generalization: circuit isolation, where each unique input generates a distinct, unshared circuit. To address this, we introduce a novel Cluster model that groups similar circuit boxes and promotes parameter sharing. Our preliminary results show this approach improves macro F1 and mitigates isolation effects (Sect. 5).

Finally, we discuss the limits of current quantum models in generalizing to word- and composition-level patterns, pointing toward future work in shared parameterization and scalable architectures (Sects. 6-8).

2 Preliminaries and Previous Work

NLI tasks require models to determine the logical relationship between sentences. Successful approaches often rely not only on world knowledge but also on an understanding of compositional structures (see Sect. 2.1). Quantum circuit models, such as those based on the DisCoCat framework (Coecke et al. 2010), offer promising capabilities for naturally integrating compositional and syntactic information relevant to NLI tasks (see Sect. 2.2). However, this area remains largely underexplored.

2.1 Natural Language Inference Task

NLI is the task of determining the logical relationship between two sentences. For example, given the premise "Mary ate an apple," one can infer that "Mary ate some fruit" is also true. This type of relationship is known as entailment. A common diagnostic in semantics is the cancellation test: native speakers typically

[1] Our codes is available at https://github.com/LingSyrina/QNLP.

judge the sentence "Mary ate an apple but did not eat any fruit" as contradictory, since the first clause entails the second. Most datasets designed for NLI tasks include three core types of sentence pair relations (MacCartney and Manning, 2008): entailment (2.1), neutral (2.1), and contradiction (2.1). Importantly, these relations are not necessarily symmetric. As illustrated in (2.1), "The cat is sleeping on the mat" entails "The cat is on the mat", but not vice versa. If "The cat is on the mat" serves as the premise, then "The cat is sleeping on the mat" may be true or false, resulting in a neutral relationship.

a **Entailment**
"The cat is sleeping on the mat." *entails* "The cat is on the mat."
b **Neutral**
"The man is eating an apple." is *neutral* with respect to "The man is sitting in a park."
c **Contradiction**
"The dog is barking loudly." *contradicts* "The dog is completely silent."

NLI has long been regarded as a fundamental task in NLP, attracting significant research interest (e.g., Hu et al., 2019; Richardson et al., 2020). This is not only due to its relevance for downstream applications such as question answering (Demszky et al., 2018), dialogue systems (Dziri et al., 2019), and information retrieval (Samarinas et al., 2020), but also because it poses unique challenges to traditional generative and encoder–decoder models. Unlike tasks that rely primarily on sentential syntax or distributional semantics, NLI demands both lexical knowledge and the ability to perform complex compositional reasoning. For example, to correctly infer the relationship between "Mary ate an apple" and "Mary ate some fruit," a model must recognize that an apple is a type of fruit—a fact that requires external commonsense world knowledge. Furthermore, understanding how phrases compose semantically is crucial. The difference between "some apples" and "all apples" illustrates how quantifiers affect inference: "some apples" entails "some fruits," while "all fruits" entails "all apples". The quantifiers "some" and "all" influence the directionality of entailment, demonstrating the need for reasoning over compositional structure.

Many of the most effective models in NLI incorporate world knowledge and compositional reasoning by leveraging grammatical annotations such as categorical grammar (Bernardi et al., 2007), dependency structures (Yusuf et al., 2017), and monotonicity information (Hu et al., 2019; Chen et al. 2021). One notable example is the work by Chen et al. 2021, which utilizes monotonicity annotations to implement compositional inference rules, supported by a word-level monotonicity corpus. Their best-performing model achieved an accuracy of 0.903 on the Sentences Involving Compositional Knowledge (SICK) dataset (Marelli et al., 2014), outperforming other models. This result highlights the importance of incorporating semantic and logical structures beyond surface-level syntax and lexical patterns in NLI systems.

2.2 Categorical Compositional Distributional Framework

The Categorical Compositional Distributional framework (DisCoCat) (Coecke et al., 2010) offers a principled approach to embedding linguistic structure directly into model architecture. Grounded in category theory, DisCoCat distinguishes between words based on their syntactic roles—for example, treating nouns and verbs as different types of tensors or quantum states. This allows for structured composition: verbs and other relational words act as operations that combine or transform arguments. For instance, in the sentence "I like quantum," the verb "like" takes two arguments ("I" and "quantum") and is modeled as a unitary operation acting on their corresponding quantum states. This compositional encoding enables the model to reflect grammatical structure and semantic interactions in a mathematically grounded way, which is particularly well-suited for implementation as a quantum circuit.

The diagram in Fig. 1 illustrates the DisCoCat quantum circuit representation of the sentence "Schrödinger walks in the park." This diagram shows how a sentence can be composed diagrammatically from its parts using quantum circuits. The nouns "Schrödinger" and "park" serve as inputs—each assigned a noun qubit. The verb "walks" acts as an operator on "Schrödinger", transforming the noun state and initiating a sentence-level meaning. Next, the preposition

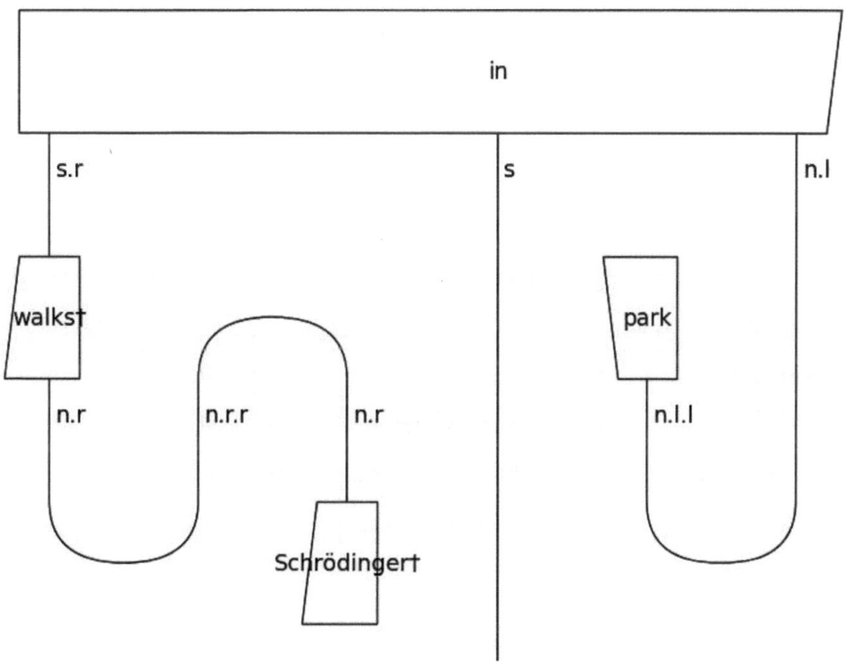

Fig. 1. Diagram representing "Schrödinger walks in the park."

"in" combines the partial meaning "Schrödinger walks" with "park", producing a complete sentence representation.

Formally, the diagram in Fig. 1 distinguishes between atomic types, such as noun and sentence, by assigning each a defined set of qubits in the circuit. Content words like "walks" and "in" are implemented as unitary operations that act on and often entangle these qubits to encode semantic composition. For example, "walks" consumes a noun input and produces a sentence output via a controlled gate, entangling the corresponding qubits. The final meaning of the sentence is encoded in the amplitude of the sentence qubit, which can be interpreted algebraically or approximated through quantum measurement. This quantum state serves as a compact, compositional representation of meaning and can be compared to other sentence states for tasks like semantic inference.

To construct such circuits, we define an ansatz—a template that determines the circuit's structure and expressiveness. The ansatz specifies how word-level quantum subsystems are initialized and how interactions (e.g., entangling gates) are applied to model compositional semantics. Each word in the sentence is mapped to one or more qubits and encoded using parameterized rotation and entangling gates. These parameters are optimized during training. The result is a parameterized quantum circuit in which each gate corresponds to a linguistic transformation, and the sentence meaning emerges as a distributed quantum state optimized for inference, as in Fig. 2. Due to the exponential scaling of classical simulation, we limit our implementation to one qubit per word, which balances representational capacity with tractability.

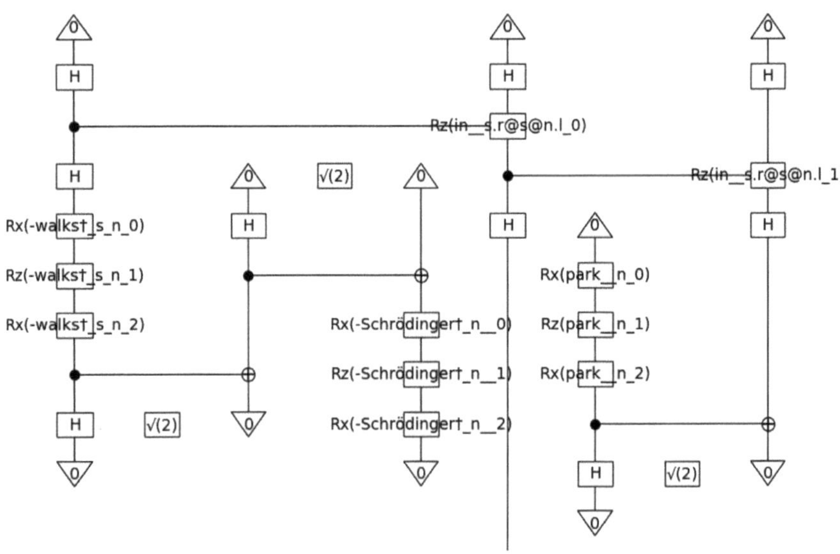

Fig. 2. Quantum circuit representing "Schrödinger walks in the park."

3 Experiments

Our experiments investigate two core tasks: *semantic relatedness* and *natural language inference* (see Sect. 3.1), evaluated across three categories of models—quantum, hybrid, and classical (Sect. 3.3). The objective is to assess each model's ability to learn compositional meaning and generalize under limited supervision.

3.1 Dataset

We use the **Sentences Involving Compositional Knowledge (SICK)** dataset (Marelli et al., 2014), a widely adopted benchmark in natural language inference (NLI), including by Hu et al. 2019.[2] The full dataset contains approximately 9,840 English sentence pairs, derived from existing corpora. For this study, we extract a subset of 100 sentence pairs, filtering to ensure each sentence contains no more than 11 words. This constraint reflects the computational limits of classical simulation of quantum circuits, while also creating a genuine few-shot learning scenario. Our train–dev–test split is set to 70:15:15.

The SICK dataset includes human-annotated labels for:

Semantic relatedness: A continuous score from 1 to 5, which we normalize to the [0, 1] range.

Inference labels: Categorical values indicating whether the hypothesis entails, contradicts, or is neutral with respect to the premise. Since entailment is not a symmetric relation, we evaluate both directions of each sentence pair. For instance, if sentence A entails sentence B but not the reverse, we label the pair *entailment*, and add a second instance with the order reversed, labeled *neutral.* This bidirectional expansion encourages the model to learn the asymmetry of inference relations.

3.2 Metrics

Performance Evaluation Metrics. We use different evaluation metrics for the two tasks in our benchmark to better reflect their distinct objectives:

Mean Squared Error (MSE) is used for the *semantic relatedness* task, as it involves predicting a continuous similarity score. This metric enables a unified comparison across models by measuring how closely predicted scores match the normalized human ratings.

Macro-averaged F1 score is used for the *inference classification* task, where the goal is to predict categorical labels (entailment, neutral, contradiction). Macro F1 provides a class-balanced view of performance by averaging F1 scores across all classes, regardless of label frequency.

As a result, our evaluation combines regression-based and classification-based metrics to provide a fuller picture of model behavior across tasks.

---

[2] https://huggingface.co/datasets/RobZamp/sick.

Information-Theoretic Efficiency Metrics. To quantify how much useful information a model gains per parameter update, we define the Information Gain per Parameter (IGPP) and its gradient-normalized variant (IGGP) as follows:

$$I(Y;\hat{Y}) = \sum_{y,\hat{y}} p(y,\hat{y}) \log \frac{p(y,\hat{y})}{p(y)\,p(\hat{y})} \tag{1}$$

$$IGPP_t = \frac{\Delta I_t}{P} \tag{2}$$

$$IGGP_t = \frac{\Delta I_t}{P\left\|\nabla_\theta L_t\right\|_2} \tag{3}$$

Here, I_t is the mutual information between predicted and true labels at epoch t, P is the number of trainable parameters, and $\|\nabla_\theta L_t\|$ is the L2 norm of model gradients. This allows fair comparison between quantum (qubit-limited) and classical (parameter-rich) models.

3.3 Model Architecture

This experiment evaluates three types of models: classical transformer model, hybrid quantum-classical model, and pure quantum model

Transformer Baseline (SBERT). As a classical baseline, we employ the **Sentence-BERT (SBERT)** architecture, which modifies BERT for sentence-pair tasks by adding a pooling operation to produce fixed-length sentence embeddings (Reimers and Gurevych, 2019). We evaluate two variants of this model:

- **SBERT-pretrained:** A MiniLM-L6-v2 model pretrained on large-scale sentence similarity datasets, fine-tuned on our relatedness and inference tasks.
- **SBERT-random:** The same architecture with randomly initialized weights and no pretraining, trained from scratch on our 100-example dataset.

Both versions take sentence pairs as input, encode them using a transformer encoder, and extract pooled embeddings from the [CLS] token. These embeddings are passed through a lightweight feedforward classification or regression head, depending on the task. The same architecture is used for both semantic relatedness (regression) and inference (classification).

While the pretrained model offers a strong upper bound for small-scale NLI tasks, the random model serves a different purpose: it acts as a fair baseline for comparison with quantum models, which lack pretraining and operate under similarly low-resource constraints. This setup allows us to assess not only absolute task performance but also learning efficiency and generalization in the few-shot regime.

Hybrid Quantum-Classical Model (XOR Pipeline). The hybrid model integrates a compositional quantum circuit with a lightweight classical neural network, enabling joint learning over symbolic structure and data-driven inference. Each sentence is parsed using a categorical grammar and converted into a parameterized quantum circuit via the lambeq-to-PennyLane pipeline. The circuit encodes sentence semantics based on the DisCoCat framework, where each word corresponds to a subcircuit defined by a chosen ansatz (e.g., IQPAnsatz). Atomic types such as *Noun* and *Sentence* are mapped to dedicated qubits, and functional words (e.g., verbs, prepositions) act as entangling gates that combine their inputs.

The quantum circuits are executed in simulation using PennyLane, with expectation values measured at designated wires. These measurements form a fixed-length quantum embedding for the input sentence or sentence pair. This embedding is passed to a classical feedforward network, XORNet, which maps the quantum outputs to a scalar prediction. The network consists of one or two dense layers with non-linear activations and is trained jointly with the quantum parameters via the Adam optimizer.

This hybrid architecture allows the quantum circuit to serve as a semantic feature extractor—capturing structural and entangled representations—while the classical component introduces non-linearity and flexibility. The model is used for both regression (relatedness) and classification (inference) tasks, with a unified architecture across tasks.

Pure Quantum Model (KL Divergence). The KL model is a fully quantum, compositional architecture designed to perform the NLI task directly, with no classical post-processing. Following the framework proposed by Sadrzadeh et al. 2018, the model interprets entailment as a containment relation between quantum representations of sentence meaning. Each sentence is first parsed into a string diagram using lambeq and compiled into a parameterized quantum circuit via an ansatz such as IQPAnsatz. Words are mapped to sequences of quantum gates, and their syntactic roles determine how they act on sentence-level or noun-level qubits. Functional words like verbs and prepositions are implemented as entangling operations, enabling the circuit to encode compositional semantics.

Once compiled and simulated using PennyLane, the circuit produces a quantum state ρ for each sentence. Given a sentence pair (s_1, s_2), their quantum states ρ_1 and ρ_2 are interpreted as probabilistic encodings over measurement outcomes (i.e., bitstring distributions). The degree to which ρ_1 entails ρ_2 is then operationalized by computing the Kullback–Leibler (KL) divergence between the two distributions:

$$D_{KL}(P_{\rho_2} \| P_{\rho_1}) = \sum_i P_{\rho_2}(i) \log \frac{P_{\rho_2}(i)}{P_{\rho_1}(i)}$$

A lower KL divergence indicates that ρ_1 captures most of the probability mass of ρ_2, thus supporting an entailment relation.

Training is conducted by minimizing a cross-entropy loss between predicted and target labels, with the KL divergence serving as the core similarity signal. While originally designed for inference, we extend this model to support both classification (entailment) and regression (relatedness) tasks by mapping the divergence output to either categorical labels or continuous similarity scores. The model remains fully quantum—without classical neural components—providing a semantically grounded and interpretable approach to meaning comparison directly through quantum state relationships.

4 Results

Our results demonstrate that quantum-based models achieve comparable performance to classical baselines on both semantic relatedness and inference tasks (see Sect. 4.1). Despite having significantly fewer parameters, the quantum and hybrid models exhibit strong learning capabilities. Notably, they achieve orders-of-magnitude greater efficiency, as measured by our proposed metric—Information Gain per Parameter (IGPP)—with some models propagating up to 10^5 times more information per parameter during training compared to classical transformers (see Sect. 4.2). However, the training dynamics reveal that quantum circuit models struggle with generalization, largely due to circuit isolation—the lack of shared parameters across input circuits (see Sect. 4.3).

4.1 Model Performance

Table 1 summarizes the performance of all models across the two tasks.

On the semantic relatedness task, the Q-XOR model outperforms all others, including pretrained SBERT, with the lowest test MSE of 0.009. This suggests that quantum circuits can capture fine-grained semantic similarity effectively, especially in low-resource settings. Interestingly, even SBERT with random initialization performs well on relatedness (MSE = 0.017), indicating that the task may require less compositional structure than inference.

The inference task, however, proves more challenging and reveals a clearer separation in generalization ability. As expected, the pretrained SBERT model performs best on the inference task, achieving a macro F1 score of 0.690. However, this comes at the cost of massive scale, with over 100 million trainable parameters. While both Q-XOR and Q-KL match the random SBERT baseline (F1 = 0.232), they fail to surpass it, highlighting the difficulty of achieving robust generalization using circuit-isolated quantum models. These results suggest that while quantum models are highly efficient and promising for tasks requiring localized semantic encoding, their generalization remains limited without mechanisms for broader structural reuse or parameter sharing.

4.2 Information Gain During Training

Table 2 presents the peak Information Gain per Parameter (IGPP) achieved by each model during training. The results highlight a stark contrast in learning efficiency between quantum and classical architectures. The Quantum XOR model

Table 1. Model size (trainable DoF), training epochs, and test MSE for Relatedness and test macro F1 for Inference.

Model	Embed	DoF	Relatedness	Inference
SBERT	Pretrained	~109M	0.014	**0.690**
SBERT	Random	~109M	0.017	0.232
Q-XOR	N/A	1,042	**0.009**	0.232
Q-KL	N/A	981	0.038	0.232
Q-Cluster	N/A	799	0.012	0.467

achieves the highest IGPP value, indicating that it extracts the most information per trainable parameter per epoch. It is closely followed by the Quantum KL model, which also demonstrates strong efficiency.

In comparison, the SBERT model with random embeddings performs significantly worse, achieving an IGPP score that is four to five orders of magnitude lower. Despite having over 100 million parameters, the classical model exhibits early saturation and contributes negligible incremental information after initial epochs. This suggests that quantum architectures are vastly more efficient at propagating and encoding useful information per parameter, particularly in low-resource settings. The high IGPP values observed in the quantum models support the hypothesis that entangled quantum representations can capture structured semantic relationships more compactly and efficiently than classical models. These findings emphasize the promise of quantum NLP models in tasks requiring semantic generalization under parameter and data constraints.

Table 2. Peak information gain per parameter ($\max_t IGPP_t$) across models. Quantum models show orders of magnitude higher parameter efficiency compared to the classical baseline.

Model	$\boldsymbol{\max_t IGPP_t}$
Classical SBERT (random embeddings)	3×10^{-9}
Quantum XOR circuit	$\mathbf{1.5 \times 10^{-4}}$
Quantum KL model	9×10^{-5}

Appendix Fig. 5 presents the epoch-wise evolution of two key metrics—IGPP and IGGP—which quantify learning efficiency per parameter during training on the inference task. These curves provide insight into how effectively different models propagate information, independent of their final accuracy. As expected, the SBERT model with random initialization exhibits consistently low IGPP values, fluctuating around 10^{-9}, indicating weak learning dynamics in the few-shot regime. Most of its high-capacity parameter space remains underutilized when trained from scratch on limited data.

In contrast, the quantum models show substantially higher and more dynamic IGPP and IGGP values, reflecting stronger parameter updates and more efficient learning. The Quantum-XOR model achieves the sharpest peaks, in line with its highest IGPP score reported in Table 2, though it also displays greater volatility. The Quantum-KL model shows comparatively smoother curves, suggesting more stable information flow throughout training. These trends reinforce the notion that quantum models, despite their compact parameter count, are highly information-efficient. Moreover, the correlation between IGPP and IGGP indicates that the observed gains arise not merely from gradient magnitude, but from structurally meaningful updates enabled by quantum entanglement and compositional architecture.

Table 3. Validation MSE, log-likelihood (LogL), AIC, and BIC. Lower AIC/BIC = better fit-complexity trade-off.

Model	MSE	LogL	AIC	BIC
SBERT-random	0.0168	62.5	$2.19e + 08$	$5.05e + 08$
SBERT-pretrained	0.0145	69.8	$2.19e + 08$	$5.05e + 08$
Quantum-XOR	0.0094	91.5	$1.90e + 03$	$4.62e + 03$
Quantum-KL	0.0382	21.4	$1.92e + 03$	$4.47e + 03$

Table 4. Test Cross-Entropy (CE), log-likelihood (LogL), AIC, and BIC for classification models. Lower AIC/BIC = better fit-complexity trade-off.

Model	CE	LogL	AIC	BIC
SBERT-random	1.1651	-116.5	$2.19e + 08$	$5.05e + 08$
SBERT-pretrained	0.6648	-66.5	$2.19e + 08$	$5.05e + 08$
Quantum-XOR	1.1446	-114.5	$2.36e + 03$	$5.13e + 03$
Quantum-KL	1.0091	-100.9	$\mathbf{2.19e + 03}$	$\mathbf{4.77e + 03}$

These efficiency trends are further supported by model selection criteria based on information theory. As shown in Tables 3 and 4, quantum models—despite their drastically smaller parameter counts—achieve significantly lower Akaike Information Criterion (AIC) and Bayesian Information Criterion (BIC) scores compared to classical baselines. For the relatedness task, Quantum-XOR achieves a validation MSE of 0.0094 and an AIC of just $1.90e + 03$, whereas both SBERT variants yield AICs exceeding $2.19e + 08$—highlighting the inefficiency of over-parameterized models in few-shot settings. Similarly, for the inference classification task, Quantum-KL produces the lowest AIC ($2.19e$+03) and BIC ($4.77e$+03) among all evaluated models, despite not having the best cross-entropy score. These findings reinforce the conclusion that quantum models offer a superior trade-off between fit and complexity, with architectures like Quantum-KL and XOR able to extract semantically meaningful representations efficiently—even under tight data and parameter constraints. This supports the hypothesis that entangled quantum encodings not only propagate more meaningful gradients but also result in structurally leaner, more generalizable models.

4.3 Training Dynamics

The training dynamics for both semantic relatedness and inference tasks reveal notable differences across models, particularly in terms of convergence stability and generalization.

As shown in Appendix Fig. 3, all models perform relatively well on the relatedness task, with validation loss remaining low and stable throughout training. Notably, the Q-XOR model exhibits the fastest and smoothest convergence, with both training and validation loss decreasing consistently. SBERT (random) achieves stable, low validation loss despite a relatively high training loss, suggesting that its pretrained embeddings—even when unfrozen—provide useful inductive biases in few-shot settings.

In contrast, the inference task (Appendix Fig. 4) presents a greater challenge. All models show more fluctuation in training and validation loss, particularly the quantum circuits. Both Q-KL and Q-XOR exhibit noisy and non-monotonic training behavior, highlighting the sensitivity of quantum models to gradient instability, circuit-specific variance, and the structural demands of NLI tasks. SBERT (random) fails to show meaningful convergence, with both training and validation losses remaining flat and high throughout.

These trends support our central observation: quantum models, while highly parameter-efficient and capable of capturing structured semantics, are more vulnerable to instability and generalization limits in low-data regimes—especially when no parameter sharing or structural smoothing is applied.

5 Cluster-Based Parameter Sharing

We introduce a novel **cluster-based quantum architecture** designed to address a core limitation of existing QNLP models: *circuit isolation*. In conventional quantum NLP pipelines, each sentence is compiled into a unique quantum circuit, with no parameter sharing between inputs. This prevents generalization across structurally similar examples and severely restricts learning efficiency. Our model tackles this problem by introducing a mechanism for parameter sharing through **word-level clustering**, allowing related words to share circuit parameter distributions during training.

5.1 Proposed Cluster-Based Quantum Model

The architecture begins by extracting contextual word embeddings using a classical language model—specifically, a pretrained SBERT encoder. Each word is also assigned a syntactic type via DisCoCat string diagrams, ensuring structural consistency with the Categorical Compositional Distributional framework. We then apply a K-nearest neighbors (KNN) algorithm to cluster words based on their SBERT embeddings and syntactic roles. This creates a mapping from words to shared *semantic clusters*, serving as a computationally efficient way to leverage large classical LLM representations without directly translating dense embeddings to quantum gates, which remains resource-prohibitive on current quantum hardware.

Each sentence is then converted into a quantum circuit, where word-level subcircuits reference their assigned clusters rather than using unique parameter sets. Gate parameters within the circuit are no longer trainable directly, but are **sampled from learned distributions**—specifically, a Gaussian parameterized by cluster-level mean μ_c and variance ρ_c. This design enables circuits to remain fully compositional while promoting *parameter sharing* across structurally or semantically similar words.

The circuit output, as in previous quantum models, is a 2-dimensional amplitude vector obtained via measurement. This output is passed to a downstream **order embedding layer**, which projects the state into a partially ordered latent space. The embedding is then mapped to a scalar prediction for the semantic relatedness task or a 3-dimensional output for classification (entailment, contradiction, neutral). Importantly, the only trainable parameters in the model are the cluster-level distribution parameters (μ, ρ) and the weights of the order embedding layer.

This design offers three major advantages: (1) it enables **parameter efficiency** by reducing redundancy across sentence-specific circuits; (2) it introduces **generalization through homogeneity**, allowing unseen combinations of familiar elements to be composed from shared latent spaces; and (3) it provides a scalable way to incorporate classical semantic structure into quantum models without incurring the cost of direct quantum translation of large embedding vectors.

5.2 Cluster Model Performance and Efficiency

Task Performance. As shown in Table 5, the Quantum-Cluster model achieves a macro F1 score of **0.467** on the inference task— substantially outperforming other quantum variants (Q-XOR and Q-KL, both at 0.232) and narrowing the gap with the pretrained SBERT baseline (0.690). On the semantic relatedness task, it also performs well, with a test MSE of 0.012—competitive with SBERT and outperforming the Q-KL model. These results demonstrate that parameter sharing via clustering significantly improves task-level generalization in low-resource quantum settings.

Table 5. Summary of Q-Cluster model performance, with best value among other models (SBERT-random, Q-XOR, Q-KL) for reference.

Metric	Q-Cluster	Best (Others)
Model Size		
DoF	799	981 (Q-KL)
Task Performance		
MSE (Rel)	0.012	**0.009** (Q-XOR)
F1 (Inf)	**0.467**	0.232 (Q-XOR / Q-KL)
CE (Inf)	1.10	**1.01** (Q-KL)
Information Efficiency		
$IGPP_{max}$	8×10^{-5}	1.5×10^{-4} (Q-XOR)
Model Fit (Relatedness)		
LogL	78.4	**91.5** (Q-XOR)
AIC	**1.44e3**	1.90e3 (Q-XOR)
BIC	**3.52e3**	4.62e3 (Q-XOR)
Model Fit (Inference)		
LogL	-110.2	**-100.9** (Q-KL)
AIC	**1.82e3**	2.19e3 (Q-KL)
BIC	**3.90e3**	4.77e3 (Q-KL)

Training Dynamics. The training curves in Appendix Fig. 3 and 4 reveal that the Quantum-Cluster model exhibits moderately noisy convergence. While its training loss decreases consistently, the validation loss on the inference task shows non-monotonic fluctuations, especially in early epochs. This instability is expected in few-shot scenarios and may reflect inter-cluster variability or early overfitting before convergence stabilizes. Still, the final validation loss remains lower than in the Q-KL model, and the relatedness task converges stably.

Information Efficiency. Efficiency metrics in Appendix Fig. 5 highlight the strength of the Cluster model. It achieves a peak IGPP of 8×10^{-5}, and its epoch-wise IGPP and IGGP curves are relatively smooth compared to Q-XOR, indicating more stable learning. These dynamics suggest that parameter sharing through clustering not only improves generalization but also leads to more consistent information flow during training. The cluster model is the most balanced of the quantum architectures, combining improved inference performance with high training efficiency and moderate gradient stability.

Taken together, these results show that the Cluster model provides a promising strategy for overcoming structural limitations in quantum NLP pipelines, offering better generalization without sacrificing the representational power of compositional quantum circuits.

6 Discussion

To further assess the generalization abilities of our models beyond standard evaluation metrics, we conduct targeted probing on two key linguistic dimensions:

lexical entailment and compositional inference. Table 6 presents predictions on word and phrase pairs involving subset or hyponymic relations, such as "children" and "kids", designed to test whether models capture hierarchical semantic relationships at the lexical level. Following this, Table 7 examines model behavior on sentence pairs constructed to isolate compositional phenomena–including negation, adverbial modification, and argument structure. These tasks go beyond surface-level similarity, requiring models to reason about meaning in structured and often asymmetric ways. Together, they provide insight into how well quantum models internalize linguistic structure and whether architectural innovations like clustering improve generalization across different levels of language.

Word-Level Relations. Table 6 examines model predictions on word and phrase pairs involving lexical entailment and subset relations, such as hypernyms (e.g., "children" is a hypernym of "boys") and hyponyms (e.g., "tree" is a hyponyms of "plant"). The gold labels reflect hyponyms (2) or hypernyms (1), corresponding to entailment (2) and neutral (1) in an upward entailment environment. The results show that most models fail to capture these fine-grained lexical relations. SBERT and XOR consistently predict hypernym (1) across nearly all examples, suggesting that without explicit lexical training or external knowledge sources, they struggle to infer subset relationships from few-shot data. The KL model, however, displays slightly more variability: it correctly identifies some hyponym pairs (e.g., "little boys" → "kids") and appears more sensitive to hierarchical lexical structures. Still, it also overgeneralizes in several cases, labeling hypernym relations (1) like "children" → "boys" or "kids" → "boys" as hyponyms (2). These findings reinforce a key limitation: current quantum models lack robust lexical generalization, particularly in the absence of large-scale pretraining. While the KL model shows the most promising lexical behavior, it remains constrained by data sparsity and the absence of structured lexical priors.

Table 6. Predictions for word-level subset relations.

A	B	G	BERT	Xor	KL	Cluster
children	kids	2	1	1	2	1
children	boys	1	1	1	2	1
kids	boys	1	1	1	2	1
young boys	little boys	2	1	1	2	1
young boys	boys	2	1	1	1	1
little boys	boys	2	1	1	2	1
little boys	kids	2	1	1	2	1
tree	plant	2	2	1	1	1

Compositional patterns Table 7 presents model predictions on controlled sentence pairs designed to test compositional inference abilities—specifically, how well models handle logical relationships involving negation, adverbial modification, and semantic containment. The ground-truth labels reflect entailment (2), contradiction (0), or neutrality (1). Overall, the results reveal clear differences in compositional generalization. SBERT and the XOR model consistently predict neutral scores (1), suggesting limited sensitivity to fine-grained compositional shifts. The KL model frequently overpredicts entailment (label 2), particularly in cases involving negation (e.g., "fence is playing" vs. "fence isn't playing"), indicating that while it detects some structural asymmetry, it struggles with semantic nuance. Notably, the Cluster model provides a slightly more diverse response pattern, correctly predicting a neutral label in the entailment-reducing pair ("fence is riding the tree dangerously" vs. "fence is riding the tree"). However, its predictions still tend to gravitate toward neutrality, revealing an under-generalization bias. These results suggest that while none of the models demonstrate strong compositional reasoning, the Cluster model shows emerging sensitivity to structural differences—highlighting the promise of parameter sharing as a path toward improved generalization in quantum NLI systems.

Table 7. Predictions for compositional sentence-level relations.

A	B	Gold	SBERT	XOR	KL	Cluster
fence is riding the tree	fence isn't riding the tree	0	1	1	2	1
fence is playing	fence isn't playing	0	1	1	2	2
fence is playing dangerously	fence isn't playing dangerously	0	1	1	2	1
fence isn't playing dangerously	fence isn't playing	1	1	1	1	1
fence isn't playing	fence isn't playing dangerously	2	1	1	1	1

Data Homogeneity. A persistent challenge in our experiments is the lack of data homogeneity, particularly in the quantum setting. Because each sentence is compiled into a structurally unique circuit, there is little to no parameter sharing across inputs. This limits the model's ability to generalize: training on one sentence offers no direct benefit for unseen ones, even when they are semantically similar. The result is highly variable validation performance despite steady training loss improvements. Our proposed cluster model addresses this partially by promoting shared circuit parameter distributions. Further work is needed to enable more robust parameter reuse across structurally or lexically similar inputs.

Simulation Bottlenecks. Quantum circuit simulation remains a major computational bottleneck. Even with modest sentence lengths and limited qubit allocations, classical simulation incurs exponential time and memory costs due to the tensor-product structure of quantum states. This restricts model scale and batch throughput during training. However, on actual quantum hardware, these operations would be performed in parallel via quantum superposition, with time complexity driven primarily by gate depth and width—often polynomial for practical ansätze. Real hardware deployment is thus key to unlocking the true scalability of QNLP models.

7 Conclusion

This work presents a comprehensive study of quantum and hybrid models for Natural Language Inference (NLI) under realistic constraints—limited data and qubit resources. We introduced a few-shot benchmark using only 100 training examples, enabling fair comparisons between classical and quantum approaches. Across this setting, our experiments demonstrate that quantum models can achieve performance comparable to classical transformers while operating with orders-of-magnitude fewer parameters. Through our proposed metric, *Information Gain per Parameter* (IGPP), we show that quantum models are significantly more efficient in propagating learning signal, reflecting their potential for high structural expressiveness even in low-data regimes.

We further identify a critical bottleneck in existing quantum NLP models: *circuit isolation*, which limits generalization by preventing parameter sharing across inputs. To address this, we propose a novel cluster-based quantum model that introduces shared parameter distributions over clustered word embeddings. Our Cluster model achieves the best macro F1 among all quantum models and demonstrates improved generalization while preserving compositional structure. Importantly, it provides a scalable pathway for integrating classical semantic information into quantum circuits without incurring prohibitive translation costs.

Taken together, these results highlight the promise of quantum models—especially when compositional and parameter-sharing strategies are explicitly designed—to perform structured language tasks efficiently. Our findings suggest that with continued refinement, quantum NLP can offer not just theoretical novelty but also practical value in low-resource, structure-sensitive settings. Future work will focus on extending these methods to richer datasets and deploying models on real quantum hardware to explore their true computational advantages.

8 Limitations and Future Work

While our results highlight the promise of quantum and hybrid models for semantic inference, several limitations remain—both practical and methodological.

Quantum Hardware Deployment. All experiments in this work are performed via classical simulation, which imposes strict limits on circuit size and batch throughput. Realizing these models on actual quantum hardware is a critical next step to validate their efficiency claims and unlock their potential for scalability.

Generalization and Circuit Isolation. Although our proposed cluster-based model improves generalization by introducing parameter sharing, circuit-level isolation remains a structural bottleneck in quantum NLP. Future work will explore complementary strategies such as *circuit stratification*—pre-grouping inputs with similar grammatical or semantic structure to promote shared computation paths.

Parameter Sharing and Structural Priors. Our findings suggest that shared representations (e.g., cluster-level parameter distributions) are essential for learning generalizable patterns from few-shot data. Further architectural innovations—such as hierarchical parameter templates or dynamically constructed ansätze—may improve the model's ability to internalize linguistic structure.

Overall, future research will focus on integrating symbolic priors, scaling circuit design, and leveraging quantum hardware to extend the practical viability of QNLP systems in real-world language understanding tasks.

Acknowledgement. This work was developed as part of a course project for a class taught by Dr. Mohsen Heidari. The authors would like to thank him for his valuable advice and insightful suggestions, which were instrumental in shaping the direction of this project.

Declaration on the Use of AI. This paper includes content generated with the assistance of AI tools, primarily for language refinement and code formatting. All model design, experimental work, data analysis, and interpretative conclusions were carried out and verified solely by the authors.

A Complementary Figures

Below are complementary figures for our experiments and implementation.

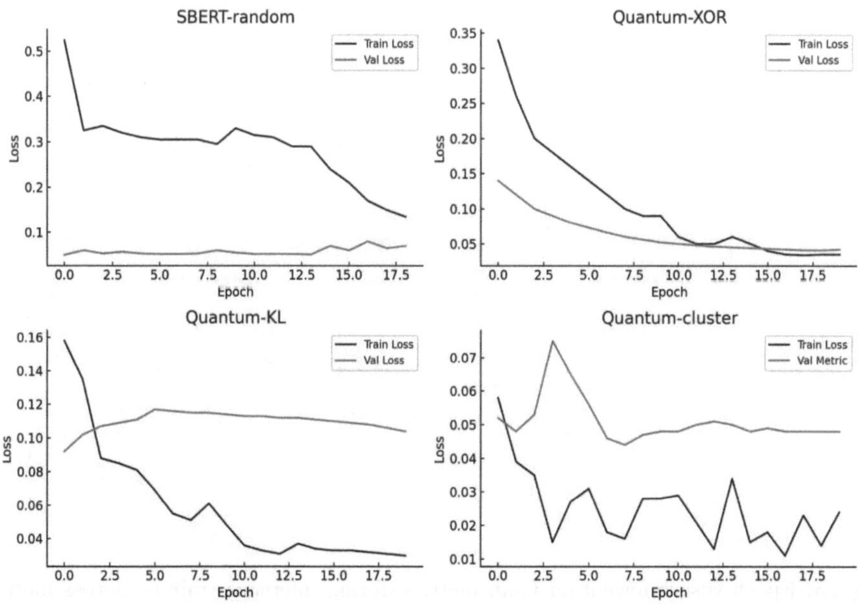

Fig. 3. Training dynamics of quantum, hybrid, and transformer models on relatedness tasks. (a) SBERT-random model, (b) Quantum-XOR model, (c) Quantum-KL model, (d) Quantum-cluster model.

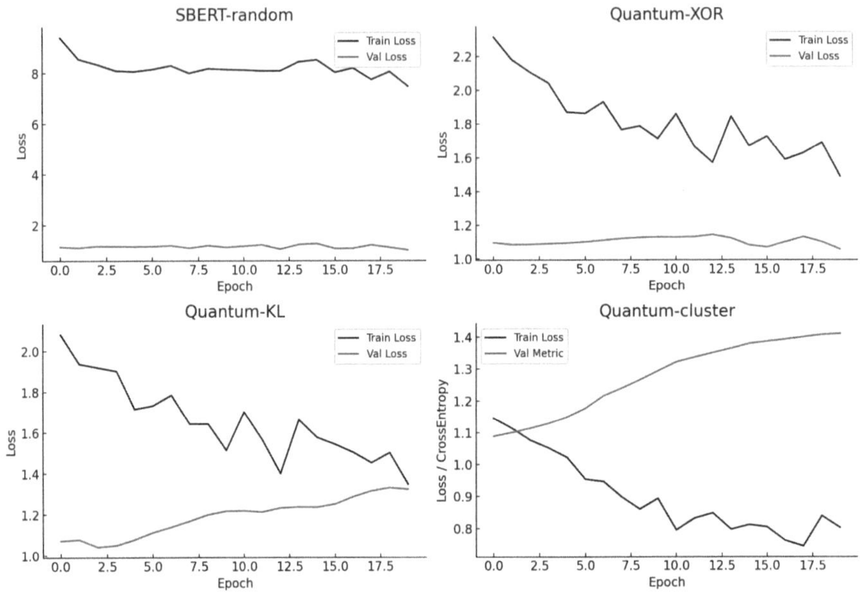

Fig. 4. Training dynamics of quantum, hybrid, and transformer models on inference tasks. (a) SBERT-random model, (b) Quantum-XOR model, (c) Quantum-KL model, (d) Quantum-cluster model.

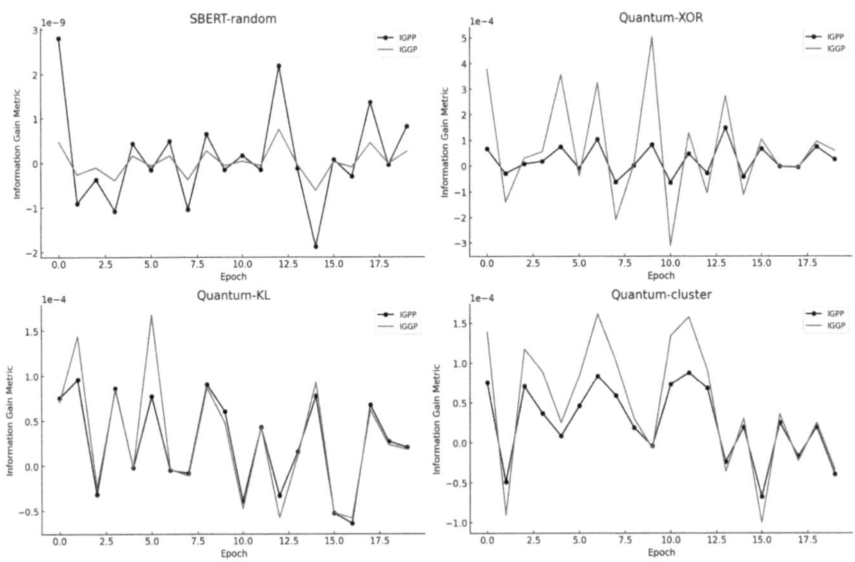

Fig. 5. Epoch-wise Information Gain metrics during inference training across model types: (a) SBERT-random model, (b) Quantum-XOR model, (c) Quantum-KL model, (d) Quantum-cluster model.

References

Bernardi, R., Calvanese, D., Thorne, C.: Lite natural language. In: Proceedings of the 7th International Workshop on Computational Semantics (IWCS-7), vol. 217 (2007)

Bradley, T.-D., Lewis, M., Master, J., Theilman, B.: Translating and Evolving: towards a model of language change in DisCoCat. arXiv preprint arXiv:1811.11041 (2018)

Chen, Z., Gao, Q., Moss, L.S.: NeuralLog: natural language inference with joint neural and logical reasoning. In: Proceedings of* SEM 2021: The Tenth Joint Conference on Lexical and Computational Semantics, pp. 78–88 (2021)

Coecke, B., Sadrzadeh, M., Clark, S.: Mathematical foundations for a compositional distributional model of meaning. arXiv preprint arXiv:1003.4394 (2010)

Demszky, D., Guu, K., Liang, P.: Transforming question answering datasets into natural language inference datasets. arXiv preprint arXiv:1809.02922 (2018)

Dziri, N., Kamalloo, E., Mathewson, K.W., Zaiane, O.: Evaluating coherence in dialogue systems using entailment. arXiv preprint arXiv:1904.03371 (2019)

Hu, H., Chen, Q., Richardson, K., Mukherjee, A., Moss, L.S., Kuebler, S.: MonaLog: a lightweight system for natural language inference based on monotonicity. arXiv preprint arXiv:1910.08772 (2019)

MacCartney, B., Manning, C.D.: Modeling semantic containment and exclusion in natural language inference. In: Scott, D., Uszkoreit, H. (Eds.) Proceedings of the 22nd International Conference on Computational Linguistics (Coling 2008). Coling 2008 Organizing Committee, Manchester, UK, pp. 521–528 (2008). https://aclanthology.org/C08-1066/

Marelli, M., Menini, S., Baroni, M., Bentivogli, L., Bernardi, R., Zamparelli, R.: A SICK cure for the evaluation of compositional distributional semantic models. In: Proceedings of the Ninth International Conference on Language Resources and Evaluation (LREC'14). European Language Resources Association (ELRA), Reykjavik, Iceland, pp. 216–223 (2014). http://www.lrec-conf.org/proceedings/lrec2014/pdf/363_Paper.pdf

Miranda, E.R., Yeung, R., Pearson, A., Meichanetzidis, K., Coecke, B.: A quantum natural language processing approach to musical intelligence, pp. 313–356. Foundations, Methods and Advanced Concepts. Springer, In Quantum Computer Music, Cham (2022). https://doi.org/10.1007/978-3-031-13909-3_13

Reimers, N., Gurevych, I.: Sentence-BERT: sentence embeddings using Siamese bert-networks. arXiv preprint arXiv:1908.10084 (2019)

Richardson, K., Hai, H., Moss, L., Sabharwal, A.: Probing natural language inference models through semantic fragments. In: Proceedings of the AAAI Conference on Artificial Intelligence, vol. 34, pp. 8713–8721 (2020)

Sadrzadeh, M., Kartsaklis, D., Balkır, E.: Sentence entailment in compositional distributional semantics. Ann. Math. Artif. Intell. **82**(4), 189–218 (2018). https://doi.org/10.1007/s10472-017-9570-x

Samarinas, C., Hsu, W., Lee, M.L.: Latent retrieval for large-scale fact-checking and question answering with NLI training. In: 2020 IEEE 32nd International Conference on Tools with Artificial Intelligence (ICTAI), pp. 941–948. IEEE (2020)

Yusuf, A.A., Nwojo, N.A., Boukar, M.M.: Basic dependency parsing in natural language inference. In: 2017 13th International Conference on Electronics, Computer and Computation (ICECCO), pp. 1–4. IEEE (2017)

A Quantum Semantic Framework for Natural Language Processing

Christopher J. Agostino[1(✉)], Quan Le Thien[2,3], Molly Apsel[4,5], Denizhan Pak[4,6], Elina Lesyk[7], and Ashabari Majumdar[1,8]

[1] NPC Worldwide, Bloomington, IN 47403, USA
info@npcworldwi.de
[2] Department of Physics, Indiana University, Bloomington, IN 47405, USA
[3] Quantum Science and Engineering Center (QSEC), Indiana University, Bloomington, IN 47405, USA
[4] Cognitive Science Program, Indiana University, Bloomington, IN 47405, USA
[5] Department of Psychological and Brain Sciences, Indiana University, Bloomington, IN 47405, USA
[6] Luddy School of Informatics, Computing, and Engineering, Indiana University, Bloomington, IN 47405, USA
[7] Independent Consultant, Munich 81549, Germany
info@elinalesyk.com
[8] Department of Physics, University of Notre Dame, Notre Dame, IN 46556, USA

Abstract. Semantic degeneracy represents a fundamental property of natural language that extends beyond simple polysemy to encompass the combinatorial explosion of potential interpretations that emerges as semantic expressions increase in complexity. In this work, we argue that this property imposes fundamental limitations on Large Language Models (LLMs) and other modern NLP systems, precisely because they operate within natural language itself. Using Kolmogorov complexity, we demonstrate that as an expression's complexity grows, the amount of contextual information required to reliably resolve its ambiguity explodes combinatorially. The computational intractability of recovering a single intended meaning for complex or ambiguous text, therefore, suggests that the classical view that linguistic forms possess intrinsic meaning in and of themselves is conceptually inadequate. We argue instead that meaning is dynamically actualized through an observer-dependent interpretive act, a process whose non-deterministic nature is most appropriately described by a non-classical, quantum-like logic. To test this hypothesis, we conducted a semantic Bell inequality test using diverse LLM agents. Our experiments yielded average CHSH expectation values from 1.2 to 2.8, with several runs producing values (e.g., 2.3–2.4) in significant violation of the classical boundary ($|S| \leq 2$), demonstrating that linguistic interpretation under ambiguity can exhibit non-classical contextuality, consistent with results from human cognition experiments. These results inherently imply that classical frequentist-based analytical approaches for natural language are necessarily lossy. Instead, we propose that Bayesian-style repeated sampling approaches can provide more practically useful and appropriate characterizations of linguistic meaning in context.

D. Cavar et al. (Eds.): QNLPAI 2025, CCIS 2659, pp. 134–155, 2026.
https://doi.org/10.1007/978-3-032-13883-5_8

1 Introduction

Prior to the deep-learning revolution of the 2010s, there was a prolonged AI winter spanning from the mid-1980s to the early 2000s. During this period, most researchers in natural language processing and artificial intelligence contended—based on the promises of AI that were unmet in the 1960s and 1970s—that computers on their own would never be capable of producing any kind of general intelligence or simulating the phenomenon that is described as natural language. AI researchers who tried often found themselves drowning in heuristics that broke down with edge cases, usually abandoning the tasks for more readily-solvable problems. See Dreyfus' *What Computers Still Can't Do* [29] to better understand the logical and semantic limitations of artificial reason perceived by researchers prior to the successes of tools making extensive use of large neural networks like Google Translate and others that followed (e.g., transformers, large language models). Such large neural networks that have now become commonplace for consumer products are often termed Distributional Semantic Models (DSMs) [27,34,37,53,59]. DSMs, in effect, infer relevance and meaning from statistical co-occurrences, and they have enabled a variety of highly practical natural language processing (NLP) applications, including topic models, sentiment classification, and large language models [17,28,68,82]. By construction, DSMs like BERT-style topic models presuppose that documents possess singular, intrinsic semantic compositions (e.g., early bag-of-words models; see Harris 1954 [37] for contrast with dynamic view.

Because of the practical successes of DSMs in many domains, some researchers have forgotten or not considered many of the initial criticisms of artificial reason that to this day remain sound, instead assuming that these limitations too will be solved by more computing or more data. However, consider the following salient problems in the current field of Natural Language Processing:

1. DSM-powered approaches still exhibit limitations, particularly when dealing with complex, ambiguous, or context-rich texts [42,48].
2. The apparent lack of much progress seen in the latest generation of frontier large language models (LLMs)—compared to the leaps seen in prior model releases—appears to have revealed a fundamental barrier in the reliability of semantic problem solving that more compute/data have not alleviated (e.g., GPT-4.5, Llama 4, Gemini 2.5, Claude 3.7 Sonnet). Likewise, many frontier researchers have shifted away from prioritizing progress in LLMs in favor of more dynamically capable models (e.g., JEPA [8], MAMBA [35], CTM [26], or modifications to LLMs that allow them to self-improve [72,74]).

These issues and the evolving research landscape suggest that the challenges faced by DSM-based approaches may stem from a more fundamental issue in linguistics: the problem of semantic degeneracy. This concept, extending beyond simple polysemy, refers to the inherent multiplicity of potential interpretations that arise when processing complex linguistic expressions [15,69,75].

Indeed, the concept intuitively makes sense: empirical observation reveals to any observer that natural language meaning is not fixed or absolute [37,58] and interpretation itself is radically context-dependent [10,39,89]. Thus, any semantic meaning realized by an agent interpreting a natural language expression depends crucially on a combinatorially explosive set of potential factors. These factors include, but are not limited to:

- the surrounding sentential and discourse context [14,49]
- the agent's current attentional focus and task demands, which can selectively highlight specific conceptual features, [13,41,44,54,81,88]
- the agent's background knowledge, cultural milieu [9,47,76],
- transient psychological states [23][1]
- the specific language being used, as different languages carve up semantic space differently [57].

This profound context dependence implies that meaning is not merely decoded from the specific words in and of themselves independently, but that meaning is actively constructed or realized by an interpretive agent within a specific situation—[11,16,63]. The same expression presented to different agents—or to the same agent under different conditions—can yield different interpretations [25,60]. Critically, this highlights the *observer-dependent* nature of the actualization of semantic meaning through direct interpretation, providing a quantum mechanical analog to an observable acting upon a state, which we will explore the implications of more thoroughly in Sect. 3. This kind of co-creative process has been posited to be mediated by a process called Relevance Realization (RR)—a core cognitive capacity enabling individuals to efficiently navigate vast semantic spaces by employing context-sensitive attentional mechanisms to identify relevant information and filter out the irrelevant [6,45,83]. Crucially, RR is non-algorithmic in the standard computational sense [45], and as such is more adept at handling challenges like problem framing and indefinite search spaces that are intractable for purely formal systems operating in "small worlds" [84]. This embodied, observer-dependent, and contextually situated view of meaning construction challenges any notion of semantic expressions possessing intrinsic, context- or observer-independent meaning, aligning with dynamic models of semantic memory [10,11,25,40,46,54,79,80].

The inherent uncertainties and deep context-dependencies of this dynamic process suggest that classical probabilistic and logical frameworks are insufficient. Consequently, researchers have turned to non-classical frameworks—such

[1] While many consider LLMs simply statistical machines that are completely disconnected from the material reality of the physical world, it is certainly possible that real-world physical variations in the environment that they inhabit or other random phenomena like cosmic rays could induce transient states. Additionally, when a model like Claude from Anthropic possesses knowledge of the time of the year, its having a French name, and the training and system prompting of Claude reinforce a French mindset onto the model to the point that its response patterns and willingness to put in effort vary depending on whether the time of year coincides with French holidays.

as those employing principles from quantum theory—to find more suitable mathematical tools. Such approaches have been adopted to model a wide range of cognitive phenomena, including concept combinations, decision-making, and memory [1,18,20,21,32,65,87]. The utility of these quantum-inspired models is not merely theoretical but is demonstrated in empirical studies. For instance, [5] identified quantum-like contextuality effects when analyzing concept co-occurrence statistics for the "Pet-Fish problem" on the World-Wide Web, showing that meaning construction at this scale deviates from classical probabilistic assumptions. In a similar vein, other work has applied Bell's [12] theorem to human cognition, uncovering non-classical correlations that violate classical bounds in both information retrieval judgments [78] and cognitive decision-making tasks [2–4].

More recent work provides a crucial conceptual refinement by distinguishing between two types of contextual influence. In experiments on facial trait judgments, [19] delineate between *context-sensitivity*, a standard causal influence of context, and true *contextuality*. The latter is defined as an acausal form of context dependence where a property may be genuinely indeterminate prior to measurement. They argue that if a cognitive phenomenon is found to be contextual, the underlying cognitive properties do not possess well-defined, pre-existing values. Instead, the property is actualized in the moment of judgment—a phenomenon that non-classical models are uniquely equipped to formalize.

Given the state of affairs, we aim in this work to accomplish two primary tasks: (1) identify the combinatorial problems that have stalled the apparent progress of frontier LLMs and (2) provide a practical path forward for understanding and studying natural language using a non-classical framework. To this end, in Sect. 2, we provide an information-theoretic exploration of the role of semantic degeneracy in single-turn problem-solving tasks. Then, in Sect. 3, we formulate a quantum semantic theoretical framework for the act of interpretation. Following this, we detail our experimental methodology in Sect. 4 to test whether natural language interpretation may exhibit non-classical behavior, leveraging LLMs as interpretative stand-ins. Section 5 presents our findings, and Sect. 6 discusses their broader implications for the future of computational linguistics and our understanding of cognitive science.

2 Kolmogorov Complexity, Semantic Degeneracy, and the Challenge of Interpretation

The concept of Kolmogorov complexity (KC) [51] provides a powerful lens through which to understand the fundamental limitations of natural language interpretation, particularly pertinent with respect to LLMs, which are expected to reliably solve problems for users. Kolmogorov Complexity, $K(s)$, of a string s is formally defined as the length of the shortest computer program (in a fixed universal description language) that produces s as output. While KC strictly applies to finite strings, its underlying principle—the quantity of information required for minimal description—can be extended to the domain of semantics.

For some semantic expression S_E, we can conceptualize $K(M(S_E))$ as the minimum number of bits required to unambiguously specify the *intended meaning* $M(S_E)$ of a given semantic expression S_E. This specification must capture not only the identities of the concepts involved but also their precise contextual nuances and the intricate web of relationships binding them into a coherent whole. For instance, the KC of specifying a single, coherent interpretation of 'I just went to the animal shelter and I brought a dog home' is low, whereas for a passage from a work as complicated and inter-connected as James Joyce's *Finnegans Wake* e.g.,

> And what sensitive coin I'd be possessed of at Latouche's, begor, I'd sink it sumtotal, every dolly farting, in vestments of subdominal poteen at prime cost and I bait you my chancey oldcoat against the whole ounce you half on your backboard (if madamaud strips mesdamines may cold strafe illglandsl) that I'm the gogetter that'd make it pay like cash registers as sure as there's a pot on a pole. And, what with one man's fish and a dozen men's poissons, sowing my wild plums to reap ripe plentihorns mead, lashings of erbole and hydromel and bragget, I'd come out with my magic fluke in close time, fair, free and frolicky, zooming tophole on the mart as a factor.

the KC would be extraordinarily high to the extent that the amount of constraints from context needed to disambiguate the 'intended meaning' of the passage might require a program that is orders of magnitude longer than the original expression, reflecting the vast amount of information needed to resolve its multifaceted ambiguities into one particular reading.

Thus, the informational burden, $K(M(S_E))$, necessary to constrain interpretations to those closely aligned with an author's original intention, scales dramatically with the number and interconnectedness of the concepts and relationships within an expression S_E. While the constituent concepts c_i form the foundation, each requires a number of bits for contextual instantiation. This linear relationship might be tractable on its own, but it is the relationships $r_{i,j}$ between concepts that contribute to actualizing the intended meaning, and specifying the interrelational constraints requires specifying an $O(N^2_{Concepts})$ number of bits to have a shot at disambiguating potential interpretations and reproducing the intended one. Because of this, the KC for an expression can be written as an inequality with a lower bound based on the number

$$K(M(S_E)) \geq \sum_{i}^{N} c_i + \sum_{i,j}^{N} \cdot c_{i,j}^2 \tag{1}$$

As can be seen, $K(M(S_E))$ increases at least superlinearly as the complexity of an expression increases. Each of the $K(M(S_E))$ bits represents an informational specificity or a semantic choice point (e.g., deciding to interpret 'bat' as an animal instead of a wooden stick used for baseball) that an interpreting agent must successfully reconstruct. Crucially, at each such decision point, there is a potential opportunity for degenerate solutions as many words have multiple meanings, and so we specify some degeneracy per bit d_b (Note that this essentially serves as an error rate, but we employ it in this way to maintain the conceptual notion). Consequently, the probability of an interpreter correctly actualizing *all* $K(M(S_E))$ bits to arrive at the precise intended meaning is the product of the probabilities of getting each bit right,

$$P(\text{perfect interpretation}) = \frac{1}{N!} \prod_{k=1}^{K(M(S_E))} (\frac{1}{d}) \tag{2}$$

If we assume an average degeneracy per bit, $\bar{d_b}$

$$P(\text{perfect interpretation}) \approx \frac{1}{N!} (\frac{1}{\bar{d_b}})^{K(M(S_E))} \tag{3}$$

a relationship which we illustrate graphically in Figure 1. As $K(M(S_E))$ grows in Fig. 1, the probability of a perfect (or otherwise similar enough) interpretation diminishes exponentially, rapidly approaching zero for expressions of moderate complexity. This result provides a clear demonstration of semantic degeneracy in action: the combinatorial explosion of alternative, plausible interpretations surrounding any expression S_E. At this point, it is worth mentioning that this situation bears an analogy to concepts in statistical mechanics, wherein S_E is like an ensemble of micro-states. An error in inferring even one bit (a constraint on a degree of freedom) leads to a different microstate, and, with the high dimensionality $(K(M(S_E)))$, it becomes overwhelmingly probable that an interpreter will rarely, if ever, reproduce the specific set of micro-states (which we will argue in Sect. 3 are themselves unknowable a priori) that make up the ensemble, resulting in high 'semantic entropy'. This KC-based analysis highlights a fundamental limitation for NLP systems and explains the persistent difficulties in LLM-assisted tasks requiring deep, unambiguous understanding or translation of semantically degenerate expressions: the LLM generates a *plausible* meaning—one of many accessible microstates—but almost never the *singularly intended* one. This result on its own highlights the need to move beyond training artificially intelligent systems that prioritize single-shot response success and to prioritize research on alternative models that can successfully simulate natural language in the way that LLMs have while also being able to dynamically update and adapt itself accordingly. It is our hope that these lessons here, coupled with the quantum semantic approach, can provide a clearer fundamental basis upon which future methods and models can be trained, tested, and evaluated.

3 A Theory of Quantum Semantics

The foundational premise of this work is that meaning is not an intrinsic, static property of a semantic expression, but rather an emergent phenomenon actualized through the dynamic interaction between the expression and an interpretive agent situated within a specific context. As described, this framework naturally

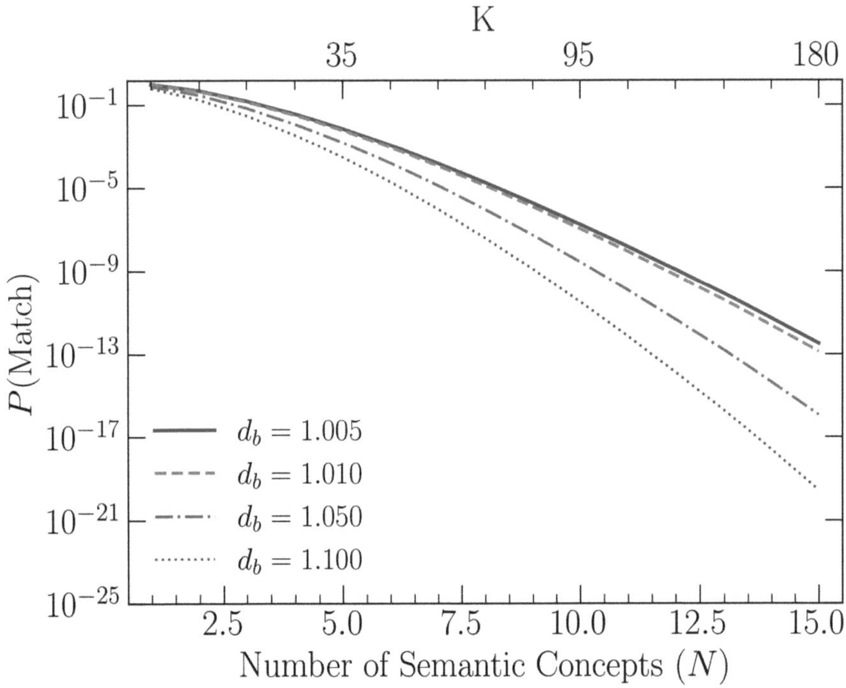

Fig. 1. Probability of perfect semantic interpretation versus the number of core semantic concepts ($N_{concepts}$) in an expression, illustrating the impact of superlinear growth in semantic complexity. The total semantic bits (K, shown on the top x-axis) are modeled as the sum of information required for individual concepts and their pairwise relationships, here assuming $c_{concept} = 5$ bits per concept and $c_{relationship} = 1$ bit per relationship. Different curves represent varying average probabilities of error per bit (p_e). The superlinear increase in K with $N_{concepts}$ leads to a dramatically faster exponential decrease in the probability of flawless interpretation, underscoring the profound challenge posed by semantic degeneracy as inter-concept dependencies proliferate.

challenges the assumption of realism, which historically arose in classical physics. To formally model this observer-dependent and contextual nature of meaning, we propose a quantum semantic framework that mirrors the difference between quantum and classical physics. Semantic expressions are separated from syntax and instead treated as observables, mirroring how physical measurement outcomes in quantum systems are detached from the system as opposed to the realism as assumed in classical systems. We hope that the processes of interpretation and meaning actualization are elucidated clearly under this quantum logical structure.

We begin by positing that a semantic expression, denoted S_E, does not possess a pre-defined, inherent meaning. Instead, it functions as a symbol that affords a spectrum of possible interpretations when engaged by an agent. To represent this capacity for interaction, S_E is associated with a state vector $|\psi_{S_E}\rangle$ in a complex Hilbert space $\mathcal{H}_S$, the semantic state space. This vector is a linear superposition of basis states, $|\psi_{S_E}\rangle = \sum_i c_i|e_i\rangle$. A crucial aspect of this proposal is that the basis states $\{|e_i\rangle\}$ themselves are not assumed to be known or fixed a priori, nor are they necessarily interpretable as a universal set of predefined semantic primitives. Instead, they may represent abstract dimensions of potential semantic differentiation that only become operationally relevant or partially discernible through specific interpretive acts (measurements), where $\{|e_i\rangle\}$ is the set of eigenbasis of an observable $\hat{\text{も}}$—here denoted by a Japanese character which is pronounced 'mo'— as posited by the agent performing the measurement, i.e. interpreting the syntax. The Hilbert space $\mathcal{H}_S$ is thus a formal construct whose basis is defined by the set of all possible ways an expression can be distinctively engaged with, rather than by a pre-enumerated list of fundamental meanings. The coefficients c_i are complex numbers ($c_i \in \mathbb{C}$), determined by how the semantic expression S_E can be decomposed as a superposition of the semantic bases $|e_i\rangle$. While the squared moduli $|c_i|^2$ relate to probabilities of outcomes upon measurement with respect to a chosen observable, the complex phase of these coefficients holds additional information with no direct analogue in classical probabilistic models, and so it is impossible to derive any analogical particular meaning from these coefficients as one might consider weights in a language model. Indeed, the complex nature is fundamental for modeling potential interference and entanglement effects in semantic processing. The full interpretive significance of c_i is only realized through the associated interpretive axis $|e_i\rangle$ set by an agent, i.e., there is no notion of pre-existing and isolated probabilities of meaning.

An agent A engages S_E through an interpretive observable, $\hat{\text{も}}_A(t)$, which is dynamically constituted from its semantic memory (comprising goals, persona, knowledge, attentional state) as activated by the current context $C_A(t)$. The act of interpretation to ascertain a specific semantic aspect is represented by applying a Hermitian operator, denoted $\hat{\text{も}}_A(t)$ to $|\psi_{S_E}\rangle$. This operator $\hat{\text{も}}_A(t)$ embodies the specific semantic probe. The eigenvalues $\{m_i\}$ of $\hat{\text{も}}_A(t)$ encompass all possible outcomes of agent A's semantic measurement, specifically, they represent all possible distinct interpretations actualized by the agent, even though they cannot be explicitly enumerated. The probability of actualizing interpretation m_i is thus given by

$$P(m_i) = |\langle c_i|\psi_{S_E}\rangle|^2 = \langle\psi_{S_E}|\hat{P}_i|\psi_{S_E}\rangle \tag{4}$$

where $\hat{P}_i = |e_i\rangle\langle e_i|$ is the projection operator onto the eigenspace of m_i. This interaction is analogous to a quantum measurement.

With such formulation, semantic measurements by different agents can now possess non-commutativity, similar to quantum observables. If two distinct interpretive operations, $\hat{\text{も}}_1$ and $\hat{\text{も}}_2$, do not commute, i.e. $[\hat{\text{も}}_1, \hat{\text{も}}_2] \neq 0$, then the semantic aspects they probe cannot generally possess simultaneous, definite, pre-existing values.

The dynamics of meaning actualization extends to the time evolution of the interpretive process. The agent's interpretive observable $\hat{\text{も}}(t)$ and the semantic expression $|\psi_{S_E}(t)\rangle$ are generally not static. While $\hat{\mathfrak{t}}(t)$ as an observable can vary explicitly in time, $|\psi_{S_E}(t)\rangle$'s dynamics can, in analogy to quantum mechanics, be governed by a semantic Schrödinger equation:

$$i\hbar_{sem}\frac{\partial}{\partial t}|\psi_{S_E}(t)\rangle = \hat{H}_{sem}(t)|\psi_{S_E}(t)\rangle \tag{5}$$

where the semantic Hamiltonian, $\hat{H}_{sem}(t)$, generates this evolution, encapsulating drivers such as shifts in context $C_A(t)$, sequential information processing from S_E, and the agent's internal cognitive dynamics. The constant $\hbar_{sem}$ sets the scale for these semantic dynamics, where quantum coherence between the bases $|e\rangle_i$ is important. This formalism allows for agents' interpretive engagement evolution. The dependence of $\hat{H}_{sem}(t)$ on t allows for modeling changes in this evolution as the agent navigates different semantic loci. In this work, however, we set aside the time evolution component of our framework and focus more on certifying the quantum state nature of the semantic expression S_E through sampling exploration by way of a Semantic Bell Test, thus adapting a logic that has previously been employed in cognitive psychological experiments to reveal non-classical contextuality in human judgements across diverse domains, including decision-making, information retrieval, and assessments of concepts [2–4, 78].

4 Experimental Design

This section outlines the experimental methodology designed to test for non-classical correlations in semantic interpretation, analogous to a CHSH-type Bell test in quantum physics [12, 24]. In particular, this experiment focuses on how Large Language Model (LLM) agents interpret ambiguous word pairs within simple sentence structures, under varying contextual (persona-based) settings.

4.1 LLMs as Observers

In this work, LLM agents serve as the "observers" in this semantic Bell test. To mitigate potential model-specific biases and enhance the robustness of our findings, each agent instantiation is randomly selected from a predefined pool of diverse, state-of-the-art foundation models and providers. This pool includes models such as variants of Gemini (e.g., 'gemini-1.5-flash', 'gemini-2.0-flash-lite', 'gemini-2.0-flash'), Anthropic's Claude series (e.g., 'claude-3-5-sonnet-latest', 'claude-3-5-haiku-latest', and 'claude-3-7-sonnet-latest'), DeepSeek's 'deepseek-chat', as well as various models from OpenAI (e.g., 'gpt-4o', 'gpt-4o-mini', 'gpt-4.1-mini', 'gpt-4.1-nano', 'gpt-4.1-nano'). This approach aligns with recommendations for multi-model triangulation to ensure fairness and generalizability of results [33, 36, 62, 71] and to ensure that any potential correlations we find are not restricted only to a single model's weights. For each experimental trial, two primary base personas, "Alice" and "Bob" are generated. These personas are characterized by randomly assigned attributes such as age (e.g., 25–70 years) and location (e.g., Bloomington, IN; Detroit, MI), which implicitly defines their primary language (English, in this setup). These attributes inform the agent's base semantic memory profile for the trial.

It should be noted here that, paradoxically, while LLMs exhibit limitations on complex tasks because of semantic degeneracy, their internal mechanisms—specifically their attention architectures—function as a kind of black box which—like the brain—collapses the state of potential interpretations into a specific one that they use when responding to user inquiries. Although the underlying mechanism is of course distinct from the biological and cognitive underpinnings of human linguistic interpretation, the similarity of the two 'observing' a specific state suggests that LLMs do indeed effectively reproduce this function of language understanding and cognition. Thus, these models can serve as experimental interpretative probes in natural language tasks. In addition, it has also been demonstrated that LLMs can generate responses that can to first order mimic human linguistic behavior in various contexts (e.g. example surveys [50,70,77][2] [50] also note the power of personas in improving the verisimilitude of the responses, an important facet that we make use of as well. Thus, we argue that one can and should use LLMs to probe the statistical patterns of semantic interpretations under diverse conditions (e.g., persona and context variations). By observing how LLMs grapple with semantic ambiguity and context-dependent meaning, we can gain insights into the mechanisms of interpretation and the types of computational strategies that are more or less successful in navigating tasks with high semantic degeneracy [52,64].

4.2 Bell Test

The core of our semantic Bell test involves presenting sentences containing two ambiguous words to LLM agents. The agents are then tasked with choosing a singular, unambiguous meanings for each of the words in the pair. Stimuli are constructed by embedding ambiguous word pairs (e.g., "trunk" with meanings 'A' for storage/tree vs. "bow" with meanings 'A' for ship front/knot) into simple sentence templates (e.g., "The word1 was settled near the word2"). Four distinct interpretive settings are defined for agents Alice (A, A') and Bob (B, B'), created by providing their base personas with additional, distinct short textual prompts designed to prime semantically orthogonal different contextual perspectives (e.g., "You are a surgeon..." vs. "You are a bus driver..."). For each of these four settings, the corresponding LLM agent provides a singular simultaneous interpretation for both ambiguous words. Alice and Bob are not shown the definitions under consideration so as to avoid biasing them or limiting the semantic search space, and

[2] The last of these references, [77], actually describes the performance of LLMs in this regard as poor as they note they are subject to perturbations that humans in a similar survey would not be as strongly affected. We note here that their findings here fit neatly within the framework of this work and that, if one additionally considers the role of relevance realization for the human subject (context-rich by way of physical embeddedness) versus the LLM (context-poor and disembodied), it appears clear that the main 'problem' with the LLM responses in their experiment was due to a drastic contextual disadvantage.

so a separate LLM call is required to then determine if each interpretation aligns with predefined meaning 'α' or 'β', triggering a re-interpretation if the choice is unclear (e.g. if the two options for meaning for the word 'chair' are 'leader of a group' or 'furniture to sit on' and the interpretation says 'furniture or leader') or outside these options (e.g. for the chair example if it decides the sentence is referring to an execution by 'electric chair', it would be considered outside of the definitional scope and a re-interpretation is carried out).[3] These classified interpretations are mapped to numerical values (A $\rightarrow$ +1, B $\rightarrow$ −1), yielding a 2-element outcome vector for each setting. Finally, the outcome vectors ($\hat{\mathfrak{v}}_A$, $\hat{\mathfrak{v}}_{A'}$, $\hat{\mathfrak{v}}_B$, $\hat{\mathfrak{v}}_{B'}$) are normalized, and expectation values $E(XY)$ are calculated as the average dot product of corresponding pairs of (α, β), which are then used to compute the CHSH S-value $S = E(A,B) - E(A,B') + E(A',B) + E(A',B')$. However, a critical assumption in this standard CHSH formulation is that of marginal consistency, also known as 'no-signaling' [22,30], which posits that the marginal probability for one agent's outcome is independent of the measurement setting of the other agent. As [30] have extensively discussed, this assumption is often violated in cognitive and behavioral experiments. Such violations, termed 'inconsistent connectedness' can complicate the interpretation of Bell-type inequalities. Therefore, while a result of $|S| > 2$ suggests a violation of local realism, it must be interpreted with caution, as the excess correlation could potentially arise from these direct contextual influences rather than true contextuality.

All agent definitions and LLM response handling are carried out using the open-source `npcpy` package[4].

Table 1. Calculated $|S|$ values for the CHSH inequality from different experimental runs, with slight variations between the persona configurations (age, location) as well as the total number of trials (N) per experiment. Values $|S| > 2$ indicate a violation of the classical Bell-CHSH inequality.

Experiment	N Trials	|S|
1	5	2.8
2	5	1.2
3	10	2.0
4	10	2.44
5	20	2.32
6	20	2.0
7	50	2.33
8	200	1.83

[3] It is possible to imagine this experiment can be carried out with word choice sets with more than 2 meanings, and we plan to explore that in future work as this would allow us to further explore the qubit-style logic we might consider in more practical applications, but that is outside of the scope of this work.

[4] https://github.com/NPC-Worldwide/npcpy.

5 Results

In this short section, we highlight and discuss the results of our Semantic Bell test.

In our experimentation, we conducted 8 experiments where we varied the number of trials in the individual experiments from 5–200 and instantiated different persona combinations, and we show the various $|S|$ values for the experiments in Table 1. For illustrative purposes, we show in Fig. 2 the evolution of the |S| value's evolution across trial number for experiment #7 with $N = 50$ trials. To be clear, there is no particular meaning to be derived from the variation in $|S|$ as it progresses with trial number as the $|S|$ value itself ought to be derived from an infinite number of trials. This illustration simply serves as a visual aid to show the stabilization of the $|S|$ value for a non-negligible number of trials.

Importantly, in these results, we find a rich variety of correlation structures ranging from classical behavior to non-classical quantum logical. Theoretically, the upper bound for quantum systems in the Bell experiment is $|S| \leq 2\sqrt{2}$. It is interesting then that one of our experiments (albeit $N = 5$), the $|S|$ value reached 2.8, providing an empirical upper bound for these experiments that can be consistent with quantum computational frameworks.

6 Discussion

The arguments presented in this work, concerning the fundamental limitations imposed by semantic degeneracy and the potential of a quantum semantic framework, offer a new lens through which to re-evaluate several core debates and prevailing methodologies in natural language processing and cognitive science. This discussion will first address how the information-theoretic challenge of semantic degeneracy, as quantified by Kolmogorov complexity, impacts the capabilities of distributional semantic models (DSMs) and Large Language Models (LLMs) in tasks requiring deep contextual understanding (Sect. 6.1). Subsequently, we will explore how a quantum semantic framework, emphasizing observer-dependent meaning actualization, engages with and offers alternatives to classical theories of meaning and interpretation (Sect. 6.2). We will then connect these ideas to specific cognitive phenomena and psycholinguistic findings (Sect. 6.3), and finally, consider the broader implications for NLP research (Sect. 6.4) and practical industrial applications (Sect. 6.5).

6.1 Semantic Degeneracy: Implications for DSMs and LLMs

Distributional Semantic Models, including contemporary Large Language Models (LLMs), have achieved remarkable success by learning statistical co-occurrences from vast text corpora [17,28,37,59]. These models implicitly operate under the assumption that sufficient statistical exposure can lead to robust representations of meaning. However, the principle of semantic degeneracy, particularly when analyzed through Kolmogorov complexity (KC) as detailed in

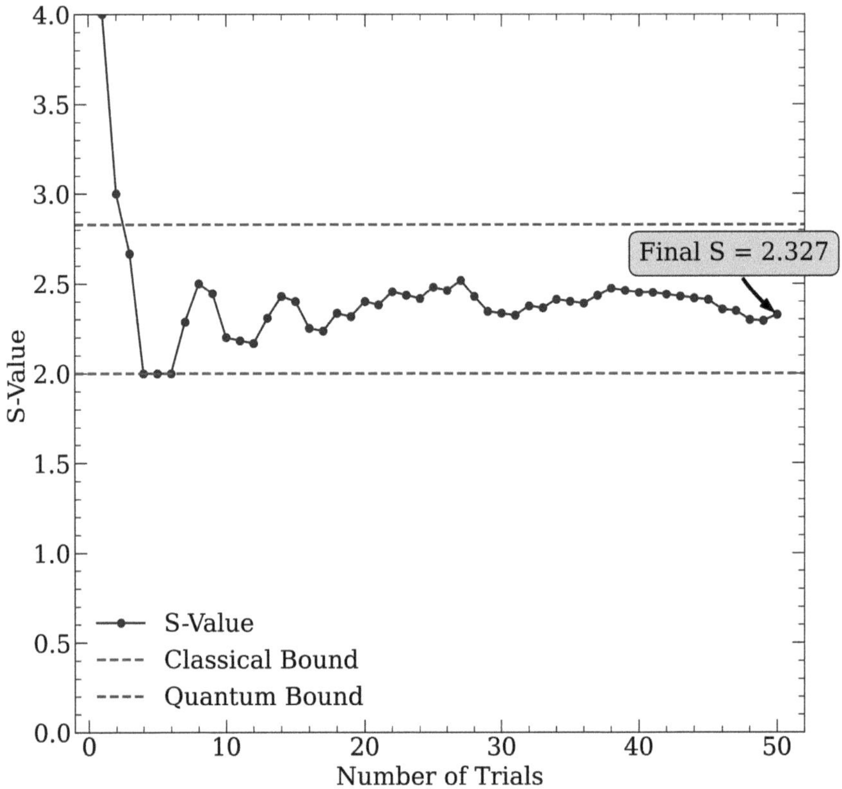

Fig. 2. Example evolution of the calculated CHSH S-value as the trial number progressed for an experiment run with a total of 50 trials, eventually settling at 2.327 (Experiment #7 from Table 1). The dashed red line at $S = \pm 2$ indicates the classical bounds of the CHSH inequality, and the dashed green line indicates the proposed quantum bound at $S=2\sqrt{2}$.

Sect. 2, reveals a fundamental challenge to this assumption for tasks demanding precise, contextually-specific interpretations, as we have shown that as the complexity of a semantic expression and its required contextual disambiguation increases, the KC of specifying the singularly intended meaning grows superlinearly. This implies that any DSM or LLM—trained on finite sets of data and with fixed weights—will more likely than not provide solutions and interpretations that are not aligned with the 'intended' one on some critical aspects, resulting in a complete breakdown in understanding. These information-theoretic limits stem from the combinatorial explosion of potential interpretations and can adequately explain the observed plateaus in LLM performance on complex reasoning tasks and the persistent difficulties DSMs face with ambiguous or context-rich texts [42,48] despite increasing model size and data. Indeed, it appears that the limitations of DSMs at navigating tasks with high ambiguity likely preclude them from ever achieving the status of 'strong' AI. It appears likely that alternative methods or ensemble approaches (e.g., where LLMs are used as reasoning engines along with an alternative, more dynamic model) will prevail.

6.2 Quantum Semantics Versus Classical Theories of Meaning

The limitations highlighted by semantic degeneracy motivate the exploration of alternative frameworks for meaning. Our proposed quantum semantic framework (Sect. 3), which posits that meaning is not an intrinsic property of text but is actualized through an observer-dependent interpretive act, directly confronts the classical assumptions of semantic realism and locality often implicit in DSMs and traditional linguistic theories. Classical realism assumes pre-existing, definite meanings, while locality assumes semantic components can be independently determined. A quantum semantic approach, by contrast, treats expressions as affording a spectrum of potential interpretations (a superposition), with a specific meaning being 'collapsed' or actualized by an agent's interpretive 'measurement' within a given context. This aligns with constructivist theories in cognitive science that view understanding as an active, situated process [10,31,49]. Philosophical critiques of essentialist views of meaning [67,85] also resonate with our results as meaning becomes tied to use and interaction rather than inhering statically in symbols. The non-commutativity of interpretive operations—a feature of the quantum semantic model—implies that the order of contextual probing can affect the realized meaning, a phenomenon difficult to capture in purely classical additive models but observed in human cognition, e.g., order effects in judgment [43] and quantum-like contextuality effects such as the 'Pet-Fish' problem [5].

6.3 Quantum Semantics: Connections to Cognitive and Psycholinguistic Phenomena

The observer-dependent actualization central to quantum semantics provides a compelling explanatory framework for a range of established cognitive and psycholinguistic findings. The profound influence of an agent's current context, goals, and primed semantic memory on interpretation [7,11,25,40,46,60] is naturally accommodated if meaning is not fixed but realized in interaction. This quantum concept of 'measurement contextuality' aligns with models of dynamic semantic memory [54,79,80], accounts of attentional focus [41,81,88], the non-algorithmic nature of Relevance Realization [45], and even cross-linguistic variations in semantic categorization [9,57,76].

This notion of measurement contextuality finds strong empirical parallels in human judgment research. For instance, work by [19,21] on facial judgments extends contextuality beyond language to perception, arguing that such properties are indeterminate and constructed in the moment of judgment. This reinforces our core premise: if concrete perceptual traits are indeterminate, then abstract semantic meaning is even more likely to require an interpretive act to become actualized. Our experimental findings provide direct quantitative support for this view. The violation of the CHSH inequality we observed is comparable in magnitude to results from cognitive experiments with humans, such as the work by [4] on conceptual entanglement. This parallel suggests that LLMs tap into the same non-classical probabilistic structures inherent in human semantic processing.

This convergence of findings positions our LLM experiments as a novel methodology for investigating the fundamental nature of semantic contextuality itself. In this light, LLMs serve as sophisticated "computational cognitive systems" capable of bridging the gap between the macro-level statistical phenomena found in collective human data and the micro-level interpretive acts of an individual agent. The contextuality we observe, therefore, suggests this non-classical behavior is not a quirk of human psychology or a specific LLM architecture, but a pervasive feature of how semantic meaning is structured and processed in any complex, interconnected system.

6.4 Methodological Shifts: Bayesian Exploration and Quantum Cognition Analogies

The dual arguments—the limitations imposed by semantic degeneracy on classical systems and the potential of a quantum semantic framework—strongly suggest a paradigm shift in NLP methodologies towards non-classical, Bayesian-informed approaches. Instead of pursuing a single, definitive interpretation, techniques involving Monte Carlo sampling of interpretations under diverse contextual conditions, combined with dynamic explorations of semantic space (e.g., through Markovian random walks), may offer more practically useful and robust characterizations of text. This is particularly relevant for tasks such as nuanced translation, novel discovery, and complex single-turn completion where LLMs currently face inherent difficulties due to the Kolmogorov complexity challenge; a system designed to explore a wide distribution of plausible actualizations, effectively navigating many potential paths from problem to solution, while slower, would likely prove more effective at approximating an understanding of the requirements of the semantic expression. Adopting such a Bayesian-informed perspective allows systems to treat ambiguity not as an error to be eliminated, but as an inherent and informative feature of the semantic landscape. This approach directly addresses the computational intractability posed by semantic degeneracy, offering a practical path toward building more resilient and contextually-aware language technologies that better reflect the probabilistic nature of meaning itself.

6.5 Practical Architectures and the Role of Human Oversight

Translating these conceptual shifts into practical applications, especially for complex scenarios such as multi-agent systems [56,86], or large-scale enterprise environments demanding dynamic document understanding [38,73], necessitates the development of novel and adaptable system architectures for models attempting to approach intelligence. These architectures must be capable of managing and leveraging contextual variability rather than attempting to eliminate it. Crucially, the observer-dependent nature of meaning actualization, as posited by the quantum semantic framework, underscores the enduring and fundamental importance of Human-in-the-Loop (HITL) systems. Far from being a temporary measure until AI achieves perfect autonomy, HITL will remain an integral component for navigating inherent semantic ambiguity, validating interpretations, and ensuring that system outputs align with human goals and ethical considerations, particularly in safety-critical domains [55,61,66] like healthcare, defense, and finance. The explicit recognition of both the fundamental limits of purely automated interpretation in open contexts and the potential of alternative, context-aware frameworks can guide the development of more realistic, robust, and ultimately more capable language technologies.

7 Conclusions

In this work, we have used a theoretical framework based on Kolmogorov complexity and a novel experimental design using Large Language Model agents to investigate the fundamental, non-classical nature of semantic meaning. We have approached this analysis by identifying the information-theoretic limits inherent in any act of linguistic interpretation and have provided the first known test of contextuality in the interpretive acts of diverse LLM-powered AI agents. Our major conclusions are the following:

1. Semantic degeneracy is a fundamental property of natural language that imposes an information-theoretic limit on interpretation; our analysis using Kolmogorov complexity (Sect. 2) formalizes how this makes the recovery of a single intended meaning from a complex expression computationally intractable for any system, thereby providing a clear explanation for the observed performance plateaus in LLMs.
2. Linguistic interpretation under ambiguity exhibits non-classical contextuality, as demonstrated by frequent and significant violations of the CHSH inequality ($|S| > 2$) in our semantic Bell test experiments with LLM agents (Sects. 4, 5).
3. The contextuality measured in the interpretive acts of LLMs is consistent with a broader pattern of non-classical findings across human cognitive science, indicating that observer-dependence and indeterminacy are general principles of information processing and not simply artifacts of human psychology.
4. The observer-dependent nature of meaning, confirmed by our experiment, reveals that there is no absolute, fundamental meaning to be found, only contextualized interpretations; consequently, the only viable scientific methodology is to shift from seeking any single "correct" answer and instead use repeated Bayesian-style sampling to characterize how these conditional interpretations interconnect within a possibility space.
5. The consistent emergence of non-classical contextuality across a diverse pool of non-biological LLM agents, when considered alongside similar findings in human cognition, indicates that these statistical properties are not artifacts of any specific interpretive system but are objective, structural features of natural language itself.

References

1. Aerts, D.: Quantum structure in cognition. J. Math. Psychol. **53**(5), 314–348 (2009). Special Issue: Quantum Cognition. https://doi.org/10.1016/j.jmp.2009.04.005. https://www.sciencedirect.com/science/article/pii/S0022249609000558
2. Aerts, D., Aerts, S., Broekaert, J., Gabora, L.: The violation of bell inequalities in the macroworld. Found. Phys. **30**(9), 1387–1414 (2000). https://doi.org/10.1023/a:1026449716544
3. Aerts, D., et al.: Spin and wind directions ii: a bell state quantum model. Found. Sci. **23**, 337–365 (2018)
4. Aerts, D., et al.: Spin and wind directions i: identifying entanglement in nature and cognition. Found. Sci. **23**(2), 323–335 (2018). https://doi.org/10.1007/s10699-017-9528-9
5. Aerts, D., Czachor, M., D'Hooghe, B., Sozzo, S., et al.: The pet-fish problem on the world-wide web. In: AAAI Fall Symposium: Quantum Informatics for Cognitive, Social, and Semantic Processes (2010)
6. Andersen, B.P., Miller, M., Vervaeke, J.: Predictive processing and relevance realization: exploring convergent solutions to the frame problem. Phenomenol. Cogn. Sci., 1–22 (forthcoming). https://doi.org/10.1007/s11097-022-09850-6
7. Anderson, J.R., Milson, R.: Human memory: an adaptive perspective. Psychol. Rev. **96**(4), 703 (1989)
8. Assran, M., et al.: Self-supervised learning from images with a joint-embedding predictive architecture. In: Proceedings of the IEEE/CVF Conference on Computer Vision and Pattern Recognition (CVPR), June 2023. pp. 15619–15629 (2023)
9. Athanasopoulos, P.: Cognitive representation of colour in bilinguals: the case of Greek Blues. Bilingualism Lang. Cogn. **12**(1), 83–95 (2009). https://doi.org/10.1017/S136672890800388X
10. Barsalou, L.W.: Situated simulation in the human conceptual system. Lang. Cognit. Process. **18**(5–6), 513–562 (2003). https://doi.org/10.1080/01690960344000026
11. Barsalou, L.W.: Simulation, situated conceptualization, and prediction. Philos. Trans. R. Soc. B Biol. Sci. **364**(1521), 1281–1289 (2009). https://doi.org/10.1098/rstb.2008.0319
12. Bell, J.S.: On the Einstein Podolsky Rosen paradox. Physics Physique Fizika **1**, 195–200 (1964). https://doi.org/10.1103/PhysicsPhysiqueFizika.1.195. https://link.aps.org/doi/10.1103/PhysicsPhysiqueFizika.1.195
13. Bermeitinger, C., Wentura, D., Frings, C.: How to switch on and switch off semantic priming effects: activation processes in category memory depend on focusing specific feature dimensions. Psychon. Bull. Rev. **18**, 579–585 (2011)
14. Bicknell, K., Elman, J.L., Hare, M., McRae, K., Kutas, M.: Effects of event knowledge in processing verbal arguments. J. Mem. Lang. **63**(4), 489–505 (2010). https://doi.org/10.1016/j.jml.2010.08.004
15. Binder, K.S., Rayner, K.: Contextual strength does not modulate the subordinate bias effect: evidence from eye fixations and self-paced reading. Psychon. Bull. Rev. **5**(2), 271–276 (1998). https://doi.org/10.3758/BF03212950
16. Borghi, A.M., Glenberg, A.M., Kaschak, M.P.: Putting words in perspective. Mem. Cogn. **32**(6), 863–873 (2004). https://doi.org/10.3758/BF03196865
17. Brown, T., et al.: Language models are few-shot learners. In: Larochelle, H., Ranzato, M., Hadsell, R., Balcan, M.F., Lin, H. (eds.) Advances in Neural Information Processing Systems 33 (NeurIPS 2020), pp. 1877–1901. Curran Associates, Inc. (2020)

18. Bruza, P., Kitto, K., Ramm, B., Sitbon, L., Song, D.: Quantum-like non-separability of concept combinations, emergent associates and abduction. Logic J. IGPL **20**(2), 445–457 (2012). https://doi.org/10.1093/jigpal/jzq049
19. Bruza, P., et al.: Contextuality and context-sensitivity in probabilistic models of cognition. Cogn. Psychol. **140**, 101529 (2023). https://doi.org/10.1016/j.cogpsych.2022.101529. https://www.sciencedirect.com/science/article/pii/S0010028522000652
20. Bruza, P., Busemeyer, J.R., Gabora, L.: Introduction to the special issue on quantum cognition. J. Math. Psychol. **53**(5), 303–305 (2009). Special Issue: Quantum Cognition. https://doi.org/10.1016/j.jmp.2009.06.002. https://www.sciencedirect.com/science/article/pii/S0022249609000637
21. Bruza, P., Kitto, K., Ramm, B., Sitbon, L.: A probabilistic framework for analysing the compositionality of conceptual combinations. J. Math. Psychol. **67**, 26–38 (2015)
22. Cervantes, V.H., Dzhafarov, E.N.: Advanced analysis of quantum contextuality in a psychophysical double-detection experiment. J. Math. Psychol. **79**, 77–84 (2017)
23. Cesario, J., Plaks, J.E., Hagiwara, N., Navarrete, C.D., Higgins, E.T.: The ecology of automaticity: how situational contingencies shape action semantics and social behavior. Psychol. Sci. **21**(9), 1311–1317 (2010). https://doi.org/10.1177/0956797610378685
24. Clauser, J.F., Horne, M.A., Shimony, A., Holt, R.A.: Proposed experiment to test local hidden-variable theories. Phys. Rev. Lett. **23**, 880–884 (1969). https://doi.org/10.1103/PhysRevLett.23.880. https://link.aps.org/doi/10.1103/PhysRevLett.23.880
25. Connell, L., Lynott, D.: Principles of representation: why you can't represent the same concept twice. Top. Cogn. Sci. **6**(3), 390–406 (2014). https://doi.org/10.1111/tops.12097
26. Darlow, L., Regan, C., Risi, S., Seely, J., Jones, L.: Continuous thought machines. arXiv e-prints arXiv:2505.05522, May 2025. https://doi.org/10.48550/arXiv.2505.05522
27. Deerwester, S.C., Dumais, S.T., Furnas, G.W., Landauer, T.K., Harshman, R.A.: Indexing by latent semantic analysis. J. Am. Soc. Inf. Sci. **41**(6), 391–407 (1990)
28. Devlin, J., Chang, M.W., Lee, K., Toutanova, K.: BERT: pre-training of deep bidirectional transformers for language understanding. arXiv Preprint arXiv:1810.04805 (2018)
29. Dreyfus, H.L.: What Computers Still Can?T Do: A Critique of Artificial Reason. MIT Press (1992)
30. Dzhafarov, E.N., Kujala, J.V., Cervantes, V.H.: Contextuality-by-default: a brief overview of ideas, concepts, and terminology. In: Quantum Interaction: 9th International Conference, QI 2015, Filzbach, Switzerland, 15–17 July 2015, Revised Selected Papers 9, pp. 12–23. Springer, Heidelberg (2016)
31. Elman, J.L.: Finding structure in time. Cogn. Sci. **14**(2), 179–211 (1990). https://doi.org/10.1207/s15516709cog1402_1
32. Gabora, L., Aerts, D.: Contextualizing concepts using a mathematical generalization of the quantum formalism. J. Exp. Theor. Artif. Intell. **14**(4), 327–358 (2002). https://doi.org/10.1080/09528130210162253. https://doi.org/10.1080/09528130210162253
33. Gallegos, I.O., et al.: Bias and fairness in large language models: a survey. arXiv preprint arXiv:2309.00770 (2023). https://arxiv.org/abs/2309.00770

34. Griffiths, T.L., Steyvers, M., Tenenbaum, J.B.: Topics in semantic representation. Psychol. Rev. **114**(2), 211–244 (2007). https://doi.org/10.1037/0033-295X.114.2.211
35. Gu, A., Dao, T.: Mamba: linear-time sequence modeling with selective state spaces. arXiv e-prints arXiv:2312.00752, December 2023. https://doi.org/10.48550/arXiv.2312.00752
36. Guo, W., Caliskan, A.: Detecting emergent intersectional biases: contextualized word embeddings contain a distribution of human-like biases. In: Proceedings of the 2021 AAAI/ACM Conference on AI, Ethics, and Society, pp. 122–133 (2021). https://doi.org/10.1145/3461702.3462536
37. Harris, Z.S.: Distributional structure. WORD **10**(2-3), 146–162 (1954). https://doi.org/10.1080/00437956.1954.11659520
38. Herzig, P.: SAP's new ai innovations and partnerships deliver real-world results, June 2024. https://news.sap.com/2024/06/ai-innovations-partnerships-sap-sapphire/
39. Higgins, E.T.: Knowledge activation: accessibility, applicability, and salience. In: Higgins, E.T., Kruglanski, A.W. (eds.) Social Psychology: Handbook of Basic Principles, pp. 133–168. Guilford Press (1996)
40. Hintzman, D.L.: MINERVA 2: a simulation model of human memory. Behav. Res. Meth. Instrum. Comput. **16**(2), 96–101 (1984)
41. Hoenig, K., Sim, E.J., Bochev, V., Herrnberger, B., Kiefer, M.: Conceptual flexibility in the human brain: dynamic recruitment of semantic maps from visual, motor, and motion-related areas. J. Cogn. Neurosci. **20**(10), 1799–1814 (2008). https://doi.org/10.1162/jocn.2008.20123
42. Hoffman, P., Lambon Ralph, M.A., Rogers, T.T.: Semantic diversity: a measure of semantic ambiguity based on variability in the contextual usage of words. Behav. Res. Meth. **45**(3), 718–730 (2013). https://doi.org/10.3758/s13428-012-0278-x
43. Hogarth, R.M., Einhorn, H.J.: Order effects in belief updating: the belief-adjustment model. Cogn. Psychol. **24**(1), 1–55 (1992). https://doi.org/10.1016/0010-0285(92)90002-J. https://www.sciencedirect.com/science/article/pii/001002859290002J
44. Hsu, N.S., Kraemer, D.J.M., Oliver, R.T., Schlichting, M.L., Thompson-Schill, S.L.: Color, context, and cognitive style: variations in color knowledge retrieval as a function of task and subject variables. J. Cogn. Neurosci. **23**(9), 2544–2557 (2011). https://doi.org/10.1162/jocn.2011.21619
45. Jaeger, J., Riedl, A., Djedovic, A., Vervaeke, J., Walsh, D.: Naturalizing relevance realization: why agency and cognition are fundamentally not computational, December 2023. https://doi.org/10.3389/fpsyg.2024.1362658, osf.io/pr42k_v1
46. Jamieson, R.K., Avery, J.E., Johns, B.T., Jones, M.N.: An instance theory of semantic memory. Comput. Brain Behav. **1**(2), 119–136 (2018). https://doi.org/10.1007/s42113-018-0008-2
47. Johns, B.T.: Distributional social semantics: inferring word meanings from communication patterns. Cogn. Psychol. **131**, 101441 (2021). https://doi.org/10.1016/j.cogpsych.2021.101441
48. Jones, M.N.: When does abstraction occur in semantic memory: insights from distributional models. Lang. Cogn. Neurosci. **34**(10), 1338–1346 (2018)
49. Kintsch, W.: Predication. Cogn. Sci. **25**(2), 173–202 (2001). https://doi.org/10.1207/s15516709cog2502_1
50. Kitadai, A., Ogawa, K., Nishino, N.: Examining the feasibility of large language models as survey respondents. In: 2024 IEEE International Conference

on Big Data (BigData), pp. 3858–3864, December 2024. https://doi.org/10.1109/BigData62323.2024.10825497
51. Kolmogorov, A.N.: Three approaches to the quantitative definition of information. Probl. Inf. Transm. **1**, 1–7 (1965)
52. Lampinen, A., et al.: Can language models learn from explanations in context? In: Goldberg, Y., Kozareva, Z., Zhang, Y. (eds.) Findings of the Association for Computational Linguistics, EMNLP 2022, Abu Dhabi, United Arab Emirates, December 2022, pp. 537–563. Association for Computational Linguistics (2022). https://doi.org/10.18653/v1/2022.findings-emnlp.38. https://aclanthology.org/2022.findings-emnlp.38/
53. Landauer, T.K., Dumais, S.T.: A solution to Plato's problem: the latent semantic analysis theory of acquisition, induction, and representation of knowledge. Psychol. Rev. **104**(2), 211–240 (1997). https://doi.org/10.1037/0033-295X.104.2.211
54. Lebois, L.A.M., Wilson-Mendenhall, C.D., Barsalou, L.W.: Are automatic conceptual cores the gold standard of semantic processing? The context-dependence of spatial meaning in grounded congruency effects. Cogn. Sci. **39**(8), 1764–1801 (2015). https://doi.org/10.1111/cogs.12174
55. Li, Z., Wu, W., Wang, Y., Xu, Y., Hunt, W., Stein, S.: HMCF: a human-in-the-loop multi-robot collaboration framework based on large language models. arXiv preprint arXiv:2505.00820 (2025). https://arxiv.org/abs/2505.00820
56. LlamaIndex Contributors: Multi-Agent Workflows—LlamaIndex Documentation (2025). https://docs.llamaindex.ai/en/stable/understanding/agent/multi_agent/
57. Marian, V., Kaushanskaya, M.: Language context guides memory content. Psychon. Bull. Rev. **14**(5), 925–933 (2007). https://doi.org/10.3758/BF03194123
58. McDonald, S.A., Shillcock, R.C.: Rethinking the word frequency effect: the neglected role of distributional information in lexical processing. Lang. Speech **44**(3), 295–322 (2001). https://doi.org/10.1177/00238309010440030101
59. Mikolov, T., Sutskever, I., Chen, K., Corrado, G.S., Dean, J.: Distributed representations of words and phrases and their compositionality. arXiv preprint arXiv:1310.4546 (2013)
60. Musz, E., Thompson-Schill, S.L.: Semantic variability predicts neural variability of object concepts. Neuropsychologia **76**, 41–51 (2015). https://doi.org/10.1016/j.neuropsychologia.2014.11.029
61. Naminas, K.: Human in the loop machine learning: the key to better models (2025). https://labelyourdata.com/articles/human-in-the-loop-in-machine-learning
62. Payne, B.K., Vuletich, H.A., Lundberg, K.B.: The bias of crowds: how implicit bias bridges personal and systemic prejudice. Psychol. Inq. **28**(4), 233–248 (2017). https://doi.org/10.1080/1047840X.2017.1335568
63. Pecher, D., Zeelenberg, R., Raaijmakers, J.G.W.: Does pizza prime coin? Perceptual priming in lexical decision and pronunciation. J. Mem. Lang. **38**(4), 401–418 (1998). https://doi.org/10.1006/jmla.1997.2557
64. Piantadosi, S.T., Hill, F.: Meaning without reference in large language models. arXiv preprint arXiv:2208.02957 (2022)
65. Pothos, E.M., Busemeyer, J.R.: Quantum cognition. Ann. Rev. Psychol. **73**, 749–778 (2022). https://doi.org/10.1146/annurev-psych-033020-123501. https://www.annualreviews.org/content/journals/10.1146/annurev-psych-033020-123501
66. Quach, V., et al.: Conformal language modeling. arXiv preprint arXiv:2306.10193 (2023). https://arxiv.org/abs/2306.10193
67. Quine, W.V.O.: Word & Object. MIT Press (1960)

68. Radford, A., Wu, J., Child, R., Luan, D., Amodei, D., Sutskever, I.: Language models are unsupervised multitask learners. OpenAI Blog (2019). openAI technical report, Version 1
69. Rayner, K., Cook, A.E., Juhasz, B.J., Frazier, L.: Immediate disambiguation of lexically ambiguous words during reading: evidence from eye movements. Br. J. Psychol. **97**(4), 467–482 (2006). https://doi.org/10.1348/000712605X89363
70. Salecha, A., Ireland, M.E., Subrahmanya, S., Sedoc, J., Ungar, L.H., Eichstaedt, J.C.: Large language models display human-like social desirability biases in big five personality surveys. PNAS Nexus **3**(12), 533 (2024). https://doi.org/10.1093/pnasnexus/pgae533
71. Siddique, Z., Khalid, I., Turner, L.D., Espinosa-Anke, L.: Shifting perspectives: steering vector ensembles for robust bias mitigation in LLMs. arXiv preprint arXiv:2503.05371 (2025)
72. Simonds, T., Yoshiyama, A.: LADDER: self-improving LLMs through recursive problem decomposition. arXiv e-prints arXiv:2503.00735, March 2025.https://doi.org/10.48550/arXiv.2503.00735
73. Srivastava, J., et al.: GenAI can revolutionize ERP transformations. Boston Consulting Group Insight, April 2025. https://www.bcg.com/gen-ai-can-revolutionize-erp-transformations
74. Sun, Q., Cetin, E., Tang, Y.: Transformer-squared: self-adaptive LLMs. arXiv e-prints arXiv:2501.06252, January 2025. https://doi.org/10.48550/arXiv.2501.06252
75. Tabossi, P., Colombo, L., Job, R.: Accessing lexical ambiguity: effects of context and dominance. Psychol. Res. **49**(2–3), 161–167 (1987). https://doi.org/10.1007/BF00308682
76. Thompson, B., Roberts, S.G., Lupyan, G.: Cultural influences on word meanings revealed through large-scale semantic alignment. Nat. Hum. Behav. **4**(10), 1029–1038 (2020). https://doi.org/10.1038/s41562-020-0924-8
77. Tjuatja, L., Chen, V., Wu, T., Talwalkwar, A., Neubig, G.: Do LLMs exhibit human-like response biases? A case study in survey design. Trans. Assoc. Comput. Linguist. **12**, 1011–1026 (2024). https://doi.org/10.1162/tacl_a_00685
78. Uprety, S.: Investigation and modelling of quantum-like user cognitive behaviour in information access and retrieval (2020)
79. Van Dam, W.O., Rueschemeyer, S.A., Lindemann, O., Bekkering, H.: Context effects in embodied lexical-semantic processing. Front. Psychol. **1**, 150 (2010). https://doi.org/10.3389/fpsyg.2010.00150
80. Van Dam, W.O., Van Dijk, M., Bekkering, H., Rueschemeyer, S.A.: Flexibility in embodied lexical-semantic representations. Hum. Brain Mapp. **33**(10), 2322–2333 (2012)
81. Van Dantzig, S., Pecher, D., Zeelenberg, R., Barsalou, L.W.: Perceptual processing affects conceptual processing. Cogn. Sci. **32**(3), 579–590 (2008). https://doi.org/10.1080/03640210802035365
82. Vaswani, A., et al.: Attention is all you need. arXiv preprint arXiv:1706.03762 (2017)
83. Vervaeke, J., Ferraro, L.: Relevance, meaning and the cognitive science of wisdom, pp. 21–51, November 2013. https://doi.org/10.1007/978-94-007-7987-7_2
84. Vervaeke, J., Ferraro, L.: Relevance realization and the neurodynamics and neuroconnectivity of general intelligence. In: Harvey, I., Cavoukian, A., Tomko, G., Borrett, D., Kwan, H., Hatzinakos, D. (eds.) SmartData, pp. 57–68. Springer, New York (2013)

85. Wittgenstein, L.: Philosophical Investigations. Basil Blackwell, Oxford (1953)
86. Wu, Q., et al.: AutoGen: enabling next-gen large language model applications via multi-agent conversation. arXiv preprint arXiv:2308.08155 (2023). https://arxiv.org/abs/2308.08155
87. Yearsley, J.M., Busemeyer, J.R.: Quantum cognition and decision theories: a tutorial. J. Math. Psychol. **74**, 99–116 (2016). Foundations of Probability Theory in Psychology and Beyond. https://doi.org/10.1016/j.jmp.2015.11.005. https://www.sciencedirect.com/science/article/pii/S0022249615000772
88. Yee, E., Ahmed, S.Z., Thompson-Schill, S.L.: Colorless green ideas (can) prime furiously. Psychol. Sci. **23**(4), 364–369 (2012)
89. Yeh, W., Barsalou, L.W.: The situated nature of concepts. Am. J. Psychol. **119**(3), 349–384 (2006). https://doi.org/10.2307/20445349

Old Wine in New Bottles: Using Classical Word Embeddings in Gate-Based Quantum NLP Systems

Damir Cavar(✉), Koushik Reddy Parukola, James Bryan Graves, and Shane A. Sparks

Indiana University, Bloomington, IN 47405, USA
dcavar@iu.edu

Abstract. Vector representations as embeddings of words, text, or images in n-dimensional semantic space are essential for neural models in state-of-the-art (SOTA) Natural Language Processing (NLP) and AI systems. Such embedding models are engineered and trained using classical computers and large amounts of data. Given the current technical limitations, we are unaware of a method to achieve the same task on a quantum computer alone. In this report, we discuss experimental results related to hybrid systems utilizing classical models in quantum algorithms for common NLP and AI inferencing. We demonstrate how word and text embeddings as n-dimensional dense vectors of real numbers, as used in current classical SOTA AI systems, can be mapped to quantum states using $log_2(n)$ and $log_2(n/2)$ qubits. The quantum encoding strategies used for this task include amplitude encoding of real and complex word embeddings to quantum state vectors, as well as reductions of Hamiltonian representations of quantum states to further reduce the number of required qubits, the number of gates, and the circuit depth. We show that the mapping results in a linear number of circuit gates. The high correlation coefficient between the classical and quantum embedding similarity scores indicates that there is no significant information loss that would affect the semantic space distribution of words in the tested quantum encoding strategies. The results show that existing NLP embedding models in classical computing environments can be used efficiently in quantum computing. We discuss how improvements of classical embedding models could significantly improve the classical to quantum computing interface for popular systems, such as Generative AI and Large Language Models (LLM).

Keywords: Quantum Computing · Natural Language Processing · Word Embeddings · Computational Semantics

---

Supported by the Center for Quantum Technologies and the Indiana University Pervasive Technology Institute.

D. Cavar et al. (Eds.): QNLPAI 2025, CCIS 2659, pp. 156–171, 2026.
https://doi.org/10.1007/978-3-032-13883-5_9

1 Introduction

Generative AI and Large Language Models (LLMs) rely on vector representations of linguistic units, for example, subword tokens or entire words. Such vectors or embeddings are crucial for all SOTA NLP and AI algorithms based on a neural architecture or transformer models. From a technical perspective, using fixed-length vector representations of words or text eliminates the issue of handling variable-length input. It also reduces the problem of handling words and text that have not been included in the training data of the NLP and AI models.

Neural network architectures and trained models have a predefined architecture for input and output that cannot be altered in the training phase of the models or in the final application and induction phases. Currently, all SOTA neural models require input vectors with a specific dimensionality. Since natural language expressions vary in length, encoding them as fixed-length vectors simplifies their use in neural models, in particular, in current SOTA LLMs.

Vectors that act as embedded approximations of word meanings in a semantic vector space are typically trained using distributional semantic assumptions [17]. The distributional properties of words extracted from text corpora provide the empirical basis for training dense vector representations in a self-supervised setting, capturing aspects of word meanings such as similarity in common contexts.

The idea of using contextual and distributional properties of words can be traced back to several publications. According to [13], the distributional properties of the linguistic units can be derived from their contextual usage. [11] suggested that the context of an ambiguous word can be used for word sense disambiguation. [30] proposed performing word sense disambiguation leveraging the distributional properties of ambiguous words in large corpora.

Using vector spaces to model the semantic properties of lexical items is much older than current technical implementations. [27], for example, suggested a model based on multidimensional Euclidean space. Analogies in such a model would correlate with the relative distances of the terms measured as the vector distances.

Current SOTA word embedding models thus provide vector representations for linguistic units that are geometrically similar to other word embeddings if they share similar contexts in text corpora used for training. For example, *cat* and *dog* share more contexts than *cat* and *moon*, and thus the vector representations for *cat* and *dog* should be closer in Euclidean space than *cat* and *moon*. In the early phases of vector space modeling of linguistic units, these vectors were, for example, handcrafted and encoded specific features that are geared towards optimization in specific NLP or AI applications, e.g., text classification, sentiment analysis, or grammar checking.

To train such word embeddings, the frequencies of terms and co-occurrence in fixed-size context windows in documents are used. Some models are trained to predict context words from specific target words [3,20,23], while others are trained to predict a masked word given a specific context [9]. In LLMs, embeddings are trained to predict the next word given a previous context of n words [4]. The distributional properties and frequencies of contextual collocations of words are mapped into probability distributions to train the word embeddings. These frequency-based vectorization approaches found their application in the lexical-semantic modeling of words and lexical units in NLP applications. Instead of using a specific vector length of arbitrary real values or some weighting model over frequency and collocation distributions of words, such vectors are trained using Distributional Semantics [17], as described above.

That is, the vectorized representations of words in the form of dense vectors are optimized to reflect semantic properties that can be measured in terms of similarity by using term or word collocations in close proximity. In such models, semantically related words are closer to each other than semantically unrelated words, which are measured using linear algebra concepts. The similarity in these linguistic units can be measured using, for example, *cosine similarity* or *inner product* between dense vectors (i.e., word embeddings).

Figure 1 shows the similarity and analogy relations between word pairs in the GloVe [23] embedding space:

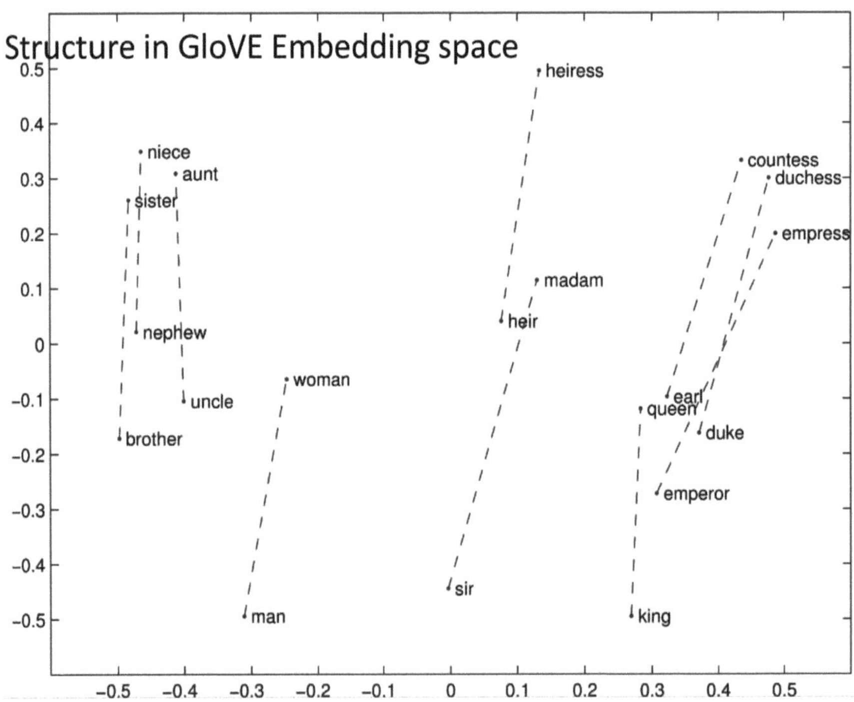

Fig. 1. Similarity and Analogy in the GloVe Embedding Space [23]

One of the goals in the GloVe model was to add distributions reflecting analogy to the semantic space as discussed in [28]. Analogy in this approach could be understood as the spacial distance of two parallels, e.g., "brother is to sister what nephew is to X" with X being identified as the approximately equidistant concept on the parallel to the "brother - sister" vector.

Such embedding models are limited to n-dimensional vectors in classical computing environments. In Quantum Natural Language Processing (QNLP) or Quantum Machine Learning (QML) [25], such models could be based on much more sophisticated mathematical grounds. In particular, we could think of predicates from a theoretical semantic perspective as different from referential nominal entities or objects. In our models, we treat predicates as quantum gates, i.e., as matrices rather than vectors (see, for example, [2]).

In QNLP, a potential quantum advantage might be achieved for semantic vector space models using the extended modeling possibilities that quantum computing environments provide [8].

Classical NLP approaches use n-dimensional vectors as word embeddings. Such embeddings could be used in a quantum computer to perform common NLP tasks, such as text classification. However, quantum vector spaces, being physical Hilbert spaces of quantum states [10], provide a much broader framework for modeling semantic properties of natural language units. In NLP, vector space modeling for semantic properties [16] does not use this broad capacity of quantum computing environments.

While our research goal aims at these extended modeling opportunities for quantum embeddings and linguistic semantics, we focus our work here on experiments related to the interface between classical and quantum computers and how machine learning models from classical computers could be transferred into the quantum environment by minimizing loss of information and maximizing usability for NLP and AI applications.

Given the effort and costs associated with generating language models and word embeddings, reusing existing models is naturally a priority if it is technically feasible and if no significant information loss in the embedding model is associated with the transfer from classical to quantum computers. The work here focuses on exactly that, i.e., evaluating the semantic loss involved in encoding classical word embeddings as quantum states.

2 Previous Work

[26] demonstrate that encoding methods that map dense classical vectors to quantum embeddings, e.g., basis encoding, angle encoding, or amplitude encoding used in popular machine learning algorithms, can not only be used successfully in quantum computing, but that the resulting quantum embeddings can in fact "contribute to improved classification accuracy and F1 scores" in the relevant applications.

[18] use amplitude encoding for words in a binary sentence classification task, deriving the word meaning using two different quantum-inspired models. They utilize the Hilbert Space representation of particles in Quantum Mechanics, assigning a relative phase (a complex number) to each word.

A recent paper discusses quantum embeddings in the context of computer vision [34]. While this is similar to our work here only with respect to using quantum embeddings for semantic representations, it is not using quantum embeddings for words or text representations.

Although encoding methods such as amplitude encoding or angle encoding have been reported to be adequate for QML applications [26], to the best of our knowledge, there are no experimental results measuring information loss related to semantic similarity in the different encoding methods used to transfer machine learning models such as classical embedding vectors to a quantum computer that encodes word embeddings as quantum states.

Previous experiments of quantum embeddings from classical embeddings have shown that there is a strong correlation between the similarity scores for classical word pair embeddings and their quantum embedding counterparts using amplitude encoding, e.g., [6,7]. The similarity scores in this study were computed for a few arbitrarily selected nouns.

3 Quantum Word Similarities: Methodology

Classical word embeddings are n-dimensional vectors of real numbers. To compare the similarities of two words in the classical environment within one model, we use linear algebra computations based on the embedding vectors for those words. Transferring classical vectors to quantum environments requires an encoding strategy, such as basis encoding, angle encoding, or amplitude encoding [21,26] used in popular machine learning algorithms [19].

For the comparison between vector similarities in classical and quantum environments, we use classical word embedding models. We extract vector representations for individual words using all these models. Our particular focus is on GPT embeddings offered by OpenAI, and VoyageAI embeddings as used in Claude 3.x AI models by Anthropic. The vectors from these models are used to compute the similarity score on classical computers. Subsequently, we encode these vectors as quantum embeddings using amplitude encoding alongside two different vector reduction approaches to reduce the vector dimensionality to 50% of its original size. We then measure the quantum similarity between two quantum embeddings using the SWAP test [1,5].

The classical similarity between two words was computed in our experiments using cosine similarity and, if not normalized, also the model-specific embedding vectors for those words; see Eq. 1.

$$cos(\vec{v}, \vec{w}) = \frac{\vec{v} \cdot \vec{w}}{|\vec{v}||\vec{w}|} = \frac{\sum_{i=1}^{N} v_i w_i}{\sqrt{\sum_{i=1}^{N} v_i^2} \sqrt{\sqrt{\sum_{i=1}^{N} w_i^2}}} \tag{1}$$

Some models, e.g., the *voyage-3* embeddings by VoyageAI (as recommended by Anthropic, Claude-3.x), are normalized. Thus, the dot product similarity score with *voyage-3* embeddings was computed; see Eq. 2. In the classical computing environment, the vectors were not manipulated, normalized, or padded.

$$\vec{v} \cdot \vec{w} = \sum_{i=1}^{N} v_i w_i \tag{2}$$

For quantum embedding of the classical word vectors, the vectors were normalized and padded to a length that is a power of 2. All word vector models used have been preprocessed in this way for the quantum similarity experiments, as to reduce the computational effort in the quantum embedding computations.

Given the normalized and padded word embedding vectors, the quantum encoding was performed using amplitude encoding. With a normalized and 0-padded vector v of real numbers and 4 dimensions, each scalar is used to specify one amplitude of a qubit superposition.

$$\vec{v} = \begin{pmatrix} 0.27 \; 0.54 \; 0.81 \; 0.0 \end{pmatrix} \tag{3}$$

With one qubit represented as in Eq. 4, we have two basis states 0 and 1, each associated with one complex amplitude α and β respectively. For n qubits there are exactly 2^n basis states and one corresponding amplitude for each basis state.

$$|\Psi\rangle = \alpha|0\rangle + \beta|1\rangle \tag{4}$$

With each additional qubit, the number of amplitudes grows exponentially. With two qubits, as in Eq. 5, there are four amplitudes.

$$|\psi\rangle = \alpha|00\rangle + \beta|01\rangle + \gamma|10\rangle + \delta|11\rangle \tag{5}$$

The amplitude encoding of normalized real vectors replaces each amplitude with a dimension from the vector in sequence, as in Eq. 6 for vector v.

$$|\psi\rangle = 0.27|00\rangle + 0.54|01\rangle + 0.81|10\rangle + 0.0|11\rangle \tag{6}$$

While the binary encoding of such vectors in classical computers usually requires $n \times 32$ *bits*, i.e., 4×32 *bits* $= 128$ *bits* in our example above, such a 128 *bit* classical representation can be encoded and significantly compressed in just two or even only one qubit, as explained in the following.

As mentioned above, the amplitudes of qubits are complex numbers. In Eq. 6, we ignore the imaginary part by setting it to $0i$. This method achieves a compression of n-dimensional real vectors to $log_2(n)$ qubits. Encoding the dimensions of a real vector as complex amplitudes can be achieved by setting every second dimension as the imaginary part of one amplitude. Thus, our vector in Eq. 3 could be encoded in just one qubit since we only need $log_2(n/2)$ qubits, as shown in Eq. 7.

$$|\psi\rangle = (0.27 + 0.54i)|0\rangle + (0.81 + 0.0i)|1\rangle \tag{7}$$

Using this encoding strategy and word embeddings from OpenAI's model *text-embedding-ada-002* with 1536 dimensions, the real-number amplitude encoding would require 11 qubits (since $\lceil \log_2(1536) \rceil = 11$), while the complex-number amplitude encoding would require 10 qubits (since $\lceil \log_2(1536/2) \rceil = 10$).

Saving only one qubit in the complex-amplitude encoding approaches does not seem to be significant. However, with an input vector length of N, the circuit depth and the number of gates are $O(N)$. For each dimension of an embedding vector, we might need a time step in a quantum circuit, which corresponds to the circuit depth. Along the same line, for each amplitude, we need a gate to set it in the circuit. This means that the number of gates and the circuit depth both scale linearly with the length of the embedding vector. The complex-number amplitude encoding reduces the number of amplitudes that need to be set by half. This significantly reduces the number of gates and the circuit depth required for amplitude encoding. Given that current qubit coherence times are challenging, and the probability of errors grows with the accumulation of errors as the circuit evolves, the complex-number amplitude encoding would be a more desirable encoding approach.

The experiments described in the following aim to clarify whether these quantum encoding methods are problematic in maintaining the semantic properties of the word embeddings from the different AI models.

Our approach to defining the quantum similarity between two words is based on the SWAP test [1,5]. The SWAP test can be performed between any two circuits S and T of the same number of qubits and can measure the difference between S and T. It requires one additional ancilla qubit and a classical bit for the measure. This test measures the similarity between two quantum states $|\psi\rangle$ and $|\phi\rangle$ by estimating the squared inner product of the two quantum states. The central object of the SWAP test is the SWAP operator, a time-evolution operator under the Heisenberg exchange Hamiltonian $H = X \otimes X + Y \otimes Y + Z \otimes Z$, for a time $t = \pi/4$ (up to a global phase), or $SWAP = e^{-iH\frac{\pi}{4}}$. This SWAP can be controlled, $H_{CSWAP} = |1\rangle\langle 1| \otimes H$. Thus quantum dynamics are leveraged in our experiment by means of the SWAP tests, which are fundamentally interferometric measurement of overlap, implemented via controlled exchange dynamics.

Applying the SWAP test in our experiment means that we generate two quantum states for the two word vectors `word1` and `word2`. We denote the corresponding quantum circuits `circuit(word1)` and `circuit(word2)`, we define the SWAP distance `swap_dist(word1, word2)` between `word1` and `word2` to be

$$\begin{aligned} &\texttt{swap\_dist(word1, word2)} \\ &= P(1; \texttt{circuit(word1), circuit(word2)} \end{aligned} \tag{8}$$

which is the probability of measuring 1 from q_0 with $S = $ `circ(word1)` and $T = $ `circ(word2)`

In the following, we describe in more detail the selection of words from the different classical word embedding models used in the evaluation.

4 Data and Experiments

The data set that we used in the experiments consists of nouns from the SimLex-999 dataset [14]. SimLex-999 contains 999 word pairs with human-assigned similarity scores, with two-thirds of these being noun pairs. With this, there are

666 noun pairs in use for this experiment. We computed the similarity scores for these noun pairs using a variety of embedding models and quantum embeddings.

We restricted the selection of words and the corresponding embeddings from the different models to only nouns, of which there are a unique 751 within SimLex-999, as some nouns are present multiple times in different pairs. The reason for restricting the selection is that we assume predicates to be more accurately modeled not as vectors but rather as functions, operators, or, in our context, as quantum gates.

Measuring a vector embedding of nouns is more reasonable from the perspective of a classical set-theoretic semantic theory, even though the embedding models are trained using a simplified distributed semantics assumption, which does not differentiate between predicates with an argument structure and contextual arguments. Because of this method of training, the experiment and its results, we argue, are independent of the choice of words and our restriction to nouns only.

The approach in this experiment is to pick words from a model and compute similarity scores for word pairs using the embeddings of these words. After encoding the embeddings into quantum states, we measure the similarity scores of the quantum states using the SWAP test. We analyze the correlation coefficient between the classical similarity scores of word pairs and the quantum similarity scores. A high correlation coefficient would indicate little information loss.

We picked the 666 noun pairs from SimLex-999 since we could use the individual word embedding vectors from the different models. Some embedding models are static, i.e., there will be no embedding for out-of-vocabulary (OOV) words. Other models can compose an embedding for OOV words from tokens that are common subword tokens of words (see, for example, [9]). Current SOTA LLMs use byte-pair encoding (BPE) that is not based on common linguistic intuitions about morphemes, subword elements, or complete words. Such BPE-based models can generate embeddings as a composition of multiple subword tokens based on BPE tokenization.

For the experiments, we used all 666 noun pairs from SimLex-999, instead of using the complete set of 576,081 possible noun pairs from the Cartesian product. We decided to pick this existing subset with human similarity scores to reduce the huge computational effort associated with similarity computation, in particular when using quantum simulators or real quantum computers.

We computed the cosine similarity and the quantum state similarity for all pairs using the vector representations from the models listed below, as well as using the complex amplitude encoding. The quantum state in this experiment represents the quantum embeddings for two nouns using the amplitude encoding of a classical embedding vector.

We used the following models in previous studies to select word pairs and measure classical similarities (through cosine similarity) using the model embeddings. All models except ConceptNet Numberbatch [31] were English word lists, but many of those contained non-English words and non-words or non-linguistic expressions. The Numberbatch model, trained on the ConceptNet knowledge graph, is multilingual. BERT is not a model consisting of word and vector pairs, but rather a transformer [33], which is a deep learning [12] model that generates a vector representation for some input text. We used BERT word embeddings without providing any context words.

- word2vec, 300-dim. word vectors, [20]
- GloVe, 840 billion tokens, 300-dim. word vectors, 2.1 mil. words, [24]
- fastText, 300-dim. word vectors, 2.5 mil. words, [3,15]
- Numberbatch, 300-dim. vectors, 516,783 words, [31]
- BERT, 768-dim. word vectors, [9]
- GPT embeddings, 3072-dim. *text-embedding-3-large* and 1536-dim. *text--embedding-3-small* model, see https://platform.openai.com/docs/guides/embeddings
- Anthropic/VoyageAI embeddings, model *voyage-3*, 1,024-dim.,[1] see https://docs.voyageai.com/docs/embeddings

We expect differences in these models with respect to word similarities, as reflected in the geometric distance of the embedding vectors. Meanwhile, word2vec vectors were generated using continuous bag-of-words (CBOW) and continuous skip-gram to train the word embeddings. In the CBOW algorithm, a specific word is predicted given the context, while in the skip-gram algorithm, the words in a local surrounding context are predicted. The resulting word embeddings are not disambiguated, in that the word *bank* just has one vector representation which carries all potential meanings for the word, with these different meanings occurring in differing contexts. For example, the meaning *financial institution* might occur in a context mentioning *money*, *account*, or *customer*, while the meaning *river bank* would more frequently be surrounded by words like *river* and other terms of nature. The GloVe model improves this approach by learning word embeddings from global co-occurrence statistics of words in a large corpus. It improves word analogy learning compared to word2vec, as shown in Fig. 1.

The fastText model further improves the embeddings by adding subword embeddings. Subword embeddings provide vector representations for morphemes that are segments in words. For example, the word *unlockable* would have the sequence of *un*, *lock*, and *able* as subwords. This approach seems to improve the embedding properties for rare words or out-of-vocabulary words for which an embedding can be computed from the word segments.

The Numberbatch word embeddings are built using ConceptNet, which is a knowledge graph representation of common sense concepts and terms, and embeddings from word2vec and GloVe. Since ConceptNet provides relations between concepts (or words that represent concepts) such as hypernym, synonym, or related edges, this information significantly improves the semantic properties of the Numberbatch embeddings, outperforming word2vec and GloVe

[1] *voyage-3* vectors are normalized to length 1, thus dot product for classical similarity was used.

with respect to word similarity metrics measured in terms of geometrical vector distances.

BERT is trained using the masked word approach. This approach is comparable to a cloze test [32], where a human language learner must guess a masked or missing word in a specific context. One of the core advantages of the BERT model is that word embeddings for specific words are dynamically computed depending on the context, providing *contextually informed word embeddings.* Since we are not using context in our experiments here, we always generate the same vector representation for a word using BERT. In subsequent experiments, we intend to test multiword expressions and more complex utterances, which would benefit from this specific property of BERT.

Another crucial difference between BERT and other discussed embedding models is that BERT uses the subword tokenization algorithm WordPiece to generate embeddings for subwords. A word like *locking* could be tokenized as *lock* and *##ing*, and embeddings would be provided for both word segments (or tokens). The special markup of the token *##ing* indicates that *ing* should be treated as a word continuation in the sense of a dependent morpheme in the linguistic sense. This way, BERT reduces the unknown word problem and increases the coverage at the lexical level. The WordPiece algorithm was first laid out in [29] as a method to cope with out-of-vocabulary words and improve the general performance of machine learning and NLP tasks.

Given the fundamentally different underlying machine learning approaches and significant differences in the amount of data and text corpora used to train the different models, we also expect a very different overall similarity score in the classical and quantum embeddings.

None of the classical vectors was reduced or, in other ways, manipulated. We did not fine-tune any of the models and restricted ourselves to the raw models as pre-trained by the providers. The goal here is not to tune or improve the embeddings for specific tasks but rather to evaluate whether their properties can be transferred to a quantum computing environment with minimal loss.

5 Evaluation of Similarities

The evaluation steps in this experiment involve:

- Generating cosine similarity (or dot product) scores for all word pairs using all the different models.
- Using amplitude encoding to convert word embedding vectors from the classical computing environment to quantum states.
  - Using real-number amplitude encoding
  - Using complex-number amplitude encoding with two different real-to-complex conversion strategies
- Generating the quantum state similarity scores using SWAP-test-based quantum circuit/state similarities.
- Computing the correlation coefficient between the classical similarity scores and the quantum similarity scores.

There were multiple variables that we could control. Due to the complexity of the experiment and the computing time for the interface between classical and quantum computing, we ran only one variable setting. The quantum measures were based on the similarity calculation of 1,000 shots per word pair. We only used the `qasm_simulator` from `qiskit-aer 0.16.1` in the initial phase of the experiment. Currently, we are preparing to run the same experiments on the IBM Quantum computers.

As mentioned earlier, given the amplitude encoding approach, we can compress a 300-dimensional word embedding vector with real number values to eight or nine qubits, depending on the strategy. This means that, on average, a $300 * 32\ bit = 9,600\ bit$ vector can be compressed to just nine qubits. The corresponding 768-dimensional BERT vectors can be represented as ten-qubit embeddings. Even a 3,072-dimensional GPT *text-embedding-3-large* embedding can be converted to an 11- or 12-qubit quantum state. This compression rate is highly significant. Existing quantum computers allow us to experiment on real hardware with these embeddings, given that the SWAP test requires a maximum of 25 qubits. Our goal is to evaluate whether there is some information loss as measured by similarity after mapping classical vectors to quantum states.[2]

6 Results

When interpreting the correlation results between the classical similarity scores with one embedding model and its quantum counterpart, we should be aware of some correlation coefficients between the classical models. For example, if we compare the correlation coefficients for the same word pair similarity scores between fastText and Glove vectors, we achieve a correlation coefficient of 0.84.

For the selected 666 noun pairs and quantum-to-classical similarity correlations, we focus on SOTA embeddings from OpenAI for GPT and from VoyageAI.

The first correlation coefficients that we compare are for OpenAI's GPT embeddings. Table 1 shows the correlation coefficients for the different similarity scores.

Table 1. GPT embeddings correlation coefficients

	Classic	Q Real	Q Comp.int.	Q Comp.split
Classic		0.9485	0.9076	0.9099
Q Real			0.8914	0.8821
Q Comp.int.				0.8590

Classical similarities (*Classic*) using cosine similarity for the GPT embeddings correlate closest to the quantum embeddings generated using amplitude

[2] See the Limitations section for some problems with quantum embeddings based on amplitude encoding.

encoding with real numbers. The correlations are also very high between the classical embeddings and the quantum complex embeddings. The given correlation coefficient above 0.9 means that the semantic similarities between the words in the word pairs are mostly preserved. The quantum real-number encoded states show a correlation coefficient less than 0.90, implying that there is some loss between the real and complex-number quantum encoding strategies.

For VoyageAI embeddings, the correlation coefficients are given in Table 2.

Table 2. VoyageAI embeddings correlation coefficients

	Classic	Q Real	Q Comp.int.	Q Comp.split
Classic		0.9756	0.9755	0.9731
Q Real			0.9535	0.9543
Q Comp.int.				0.9570

The correlation coefficients are obviously much higher in all cases. There is no significant difference between the classical and all versions of quantum embeddings.

We find little or no significant information loss using the quantum encoding approaches we suggest. It is important to note that any of the complex amplitude encoding strategies result in acceptable coefficients, in particular when using the Voyage embeddings.

Some loss in the mapping process can be located in all the operations performed. We expect a loss in the mapping from classical to quantum embeddings using amplitude encoding. [22] discuss the loss when using different encoding techniques, in particular amplitude encoding, using simulators and hardware quantum computers.

6.1 Availability

All code and data discussed in this article are available on the GitHub repository https://github.com/dcavar/nlqk as part of the Natural Language Qu Kit (NLQK) Python module. The models used are all freely available online. A link to the download sites is made available in the GitHub repo.

7 Conclusion

We show that the embeddings based on dense vectors with more than 1,000 dimensions and real numbers can be compressed to 12 qubits or less. The correlation coefficient was calculated using the classical similarity scores, and the SWAP-test scores of the quantum circuit representing the amplitude encoded embedding vectors show that there is a strong correlation between the classical and quantum similarities using these methods. This high correlation score allows us to conclude that there is minimal information loss when mapping classical embeddings to quantum states. This means that classical word embedding models could potentially be used in quantum computing environments in NLP applications.

In some future quantum computing environments, the generation of new embedding models might still be necessary to exploit advanced vector space modeling potentials provided by the nature of qubits and potential embedding encodings. Current limitations and the lack of quantum memory or adequate ways for persistent storage of states prevent us from training purely quantum-based embedding models.

The possibility of using mappings of real numbers from embedding vectors to complex amplitudes in quantum states appears to be acceptable for semantic similarity computations in quantum computing. It provides an instrument to reduce the number of gates and the circuit depth even further. Using complex number encoding of embedding vectors reduces the linear scaling of input vectors to quantum circuits by 50%. Given the results from the similarity correlation coefficients, with some vector models, i.e., VoyageAI vectors, the loss is minimal when compared to the real-number amplitude encoding.

On the other hand, the interface between classical and quantum computing is still problematic. Data transfer of classical embedding vectors to amplitude-encoded quantum states is time-consuming and costly.

8 Limitations

We must emphasize that this work currently has various limitations. While the insight into the potential use of classical NLP and AI resources and models in quantum computers is highly relevant to our work, the limitations restrict the potential benefit in QNLP, given the current state of quantum computers.

Quantum computers still produce significant error rates that limit evaluations and experiments with NLP and AI algorithms in general on existing quantum hardware. Most work in the field is performed using quantum simulators, or it lacks a practical and empirical component. This error rate can affect amplitude encoding in particular. In addition to error rates, there are hardware limits on how precise the preparation of quantum states using amplitudes can be and how precise the reading of amplitudes can be. These are hardware and implementation restrictions that are beyond our control and beyond the scope of this work.

The amplitude encoding approach converts n-dimensional vectors of real numbers into quantum circuits with $log_2(n)$ or $log_2(n/2)$ qubits. However, the worst-case scenario is that the computed quantum circuit, to prepare the quantum state of these $log_2(n)$ qubits, will require a n number of quantum gates to set the state of the qubits. Given the mentioned error rate of current quantum computers, this is not desirable since every quantum gate might, and in fact, on current hardware will increase the error of the computation. A considerable depth of quantum circuits in terms of quantum gates might result in decoherence effects and high error rates. It also consumes computation time in quantum computers. However, this problem can be partially remedied by using the complex number amplitude encoding strategy that reduces the number of gates and the circuit depth by 50%.

When mapping classical vectors to quantum states using only real-number amplitude encoding, we map vectors of real numbers to amplitudes that consequently stay real. That is, the imaginary part of complex amplitudes in qubits will be zero in this encoding strategy. If we were able to tune and train embeddings on a quantum computer, we would be able to use the full potential of complex number amplitude-encoded embeddings. To be able to apply any repetitive optimization cycle on quantum states, quantum RAM is needed, in addition to sufficient fault-tolerant qubits and persistence of states over longer time periods. Current quantum computer environments do not offer this.

Acknowledgement. This material is based upon work supported by the Center for Quantum Technologies under the Industry-University Cooperative Research Center Program at the US National Science Foundation under Grant No. 2224928.

This research was supported in part by Lilly Endowment, Inc., through its support for the Indiana University Pervasive Technology Institute.

References

1. Barenco, A., Berthiaume, A., Deutsch, D., Ekert, A., Jozsa, R., Macchiavello, C.: Stabilisation of quantum computations by symmetrisation (1996). https://arxiv.org/abs/quant-ph/9604028
2. Baroni, M., Zamparelli, R.: Nouns are vectors, adjectives are matrices: representing adjective-noun constructions in semantic space. In: Proceedings of the 2010 Conference on Empirical Methods in Natural Language Processing, EMNLP '10, pp. 1183–1193. Association for Computational Linguistics, USA (2010)
3. Bojanowski, P., Grave, E., Joulin, A., Mikolov, T.: Enriching word vectors with subword information. Trans. Assoc. Comput. Linguist. **5**, 135–146 (2017)
4. Brown, T.B., .: Language models are few-shot learners (2020). https://arxiv.org/abs/2005.14165
5. Buhrman, H., Cleve, R., Watrous, J., De Wolf, R.: Quantum fingerprinting. Phys. Rev. Lett. **87**(16), 167902 (2001). https://doi.org/10.1103/PhysRevLett.87.167902
6. Cavar, D., Parukola, K.R.: Word and text similarity using classical word embeddings in quantum NLP systems. In: 2025 IEEE International Conference on Acoustics, Speech, and Signal Processing Workshops (ICASSPW), pp. 1–5 (2025). https://doi.org/10.1109/ICASSPW65056.2025.11010999
7. Cavar, D., Zhang, C.: Semantic similarities using classical embeddings in quantum NLP. In: 2024 IEEE International Conference on Quantum Computing and Engineering (QCE), vol. 02, pp. 450–451 (2024). https://doi.org/10.1109/QCE60285.2024.10350
8. Coecke, B., de Felice, G., Meichanetzidis, K., Toumi, A.: Foundations for near-term quantum natural language processing (2020). https://doi.org/10.48550/arXiv.2012.03755

9. Devlin, J., Chang, M.W., Lee, K., Toutanova, K.: BERT: pre-training of deep bidirectional transformers for language understanding. In: Burstein, J., et al. (eds.) Proceedings of the 2019 Conference of the North American Chapter of the Association for Computational Linguistics: Human Language Technologies, Volume 1 (Long and Short Papers), pp. 4171–4186. Association for Computational Linguistics (2019)
10. Dirac, P.A.M.: The Principles of Quantum Mechanics. International Series of Monographs on Physics. Oxford University Press, Oxford, New York (1982)
11. Firth, J.R.: A synopsis of linguistic theory 1930–1955. In: Palmer, F.R. (ed.) Selected Papers of J.R. Firth 1952–1959. Longman, London (1968)
12. Goodfellow, I., Bengio, Y., Courville, A.: Deep Learning. MIT Press (2016). http://www.deeplearningbook.org
13. Harris, Z.: Distributional structure. Word **10**(23), 146–162 (1954)
14. Hill, F., Reichart, R., Korhonen, A.: SimLex-999: evaluating semantic models with (genuine) similarity estimation. Comput. Linguist. **41**(4), 665–695 (2015)
15. Joulin, A., Bojanowski, P., Mikolov, T., Jégou, H., Grave, E.: Loss in translation: learning bilingual word mapping with a retrieval criterion. In: Proceedings of the 2018 Conference on Empirical Methods in Natural Language Processing (2018)
16. Jurafsky, D., Martin, J.H.: Speech and Language Processing, 2nd edn. Prentice-Hall Inc., Upper Saddle River, NJ, USA (2009)
17. Lenci, A., Sahlgren, M.: Distributional Semantics. Studies in Natural Language Processing. Cambridge University Press (2023). https://doi.org/10.1017/9780511783692
18. Li, Q., Uprety, S., Wang, B., Song, D.: Quantum-inspired complex word embedding. In: Augenstein, I., et al. (eds.) Proceedings of the Third Workshop on Representation Learning for NLP, pp. 50–57. Association for Computational Linguistics, Melbourne, Australia (2018). https://doi.org/10.18653/v1/W18-3006. https://aclanthology.org/W18-3006
19. Maria Schuld, I.S., Petruccione, F.: An introduction to quantum machine learning. Contem. Phys. **56**(2), 172–185 (2015). https://doi.org/10.1080/00107514.2014.964942
20. Mikolov, T., Chen, K., Corrado, G., Dean, J.: Efficient estimation of word representations in vector space (2013). https://arxiv.org/abs/1301.3781
21. Mitsuda, N., et al.: Approximate complex amplitude encoding algorithm and its application to data classification problems. Phys. Rev. A **109**(5) (2024). https://doi.org/10.1103/physreva.109.052423
22. Munikote, N., Li, A., Liu, C., Stein, S.: Comparing quantum encoding techniques (2024). https://arxiv.org/abs/2410.09121
23. Pennington, J., Socher, R., Manning, C.: GloVe: global vectors for word representation. In: Moschitti, A., Pang, B., Daelemans, W. (eds.) Proceedings of the 2014 Conference on Empirical Methods in Natural Language Processing (EMNLP), Doha, Qatar, pp. 1532–1543. Association for Computational Linguistics (2014). https://doi.org/10.3115/v1/D14-1162
24. Pennington, J., Socher, R., Manning, C.D.: GloVe: global vectors for word representation. In: Empirical Methods in Natural Language Processing (EMNLP), pp. 1532–1543 (2014). http://www.aclweb.org/anthology/D14-1162
25. Peral-García, D., Cruz-Benito, J., García-Peñalvo, F.J.: Comparing Natural Language Processing and Quantum Natural Processing approaches in text classification tasks. Exp. Syst. Appl. **254**, 124427 (2024). https://doi.org/10.1016/j.eswa.2024.124427

26. Rath, M., Date, H.: Quantum data encoding: a comparative analysis of classical-to-quantum mapping techniques and their impact on machine learning accuracy. arXiv arXiv:2311.10375 (2023). https://api.semanticscholar.org/CorpusID:265281517
27. Rumelhart, D.E., Abrahamson, A.A.: A model for analogical reasoning. Cogn. Psychol. **5**(1), 1–28 (1973). https://doi.org/10.1016/0010-0285(73)90023-6
28. Rumelhart, D.E., Todd, P.M.: Learning and connectionist representations. In: Meyer, D.E., Kornblum, S. (eds.) Attention and Performance 14: Synergies in Experimental Psychology, Artificial Intelligence, and Cognitive Neuroscience, pp. 3–30. The MIT Press (1993)
29. Schuster, M., Nakajima, K.: Japanese and Korean voice search. In: International Conference on Acoustics, Speech and Signal Processing, pp. 5149–5152 (2012)
30. Schütze, H.: Automatic word sense discrimination. Comput. Linguist. **24**(1), 97–124 (1998)
31. Speer, R., Chin, J., Havasi, C.: ConceptNet 5.5: an open multilingual graph of general knowledge. In: Proceedings of the Thirty-First AAAI Conference on Artificial Intelligence, pp. 4444–4451. AAAI'17. AAAI Press (2017)
32. Taylor, W.L.: "cloze procedure": a new tool for measuring readability. J. Mass Commun. Q. **30**, 415–433 (1953). https://api.semanticscholar.org/CorpusID:206666846
33. Vaswani, A., et al.: Attention is all you need (2023). https://arxiv.org/abs/1706.03762
34. Zhang, J., et al.: Applications of quantum embedding in computer vision. In: Luo, B., Cheng, L., Wu, Z.G., Li, Hongyi ad Li, C. (eds.) Neural Information Processing, pp. 165–177. Springer Nature Singapore, Singapore (2024)

Extending the Frontiers of QNLP Beyond English: Grammar-Sensitive Pipeline for Hindi Sentiment Classification Using Compositional Quantum Models

Gautami Sanjay Naik[1(✉)], Rishi Koushik Reddy Thippireddy[1], Naman Srivastava[2], Parishri Shah[1], Ravi Raj[1], Sunil Saumya[1], and H. Aswath Babu[1]

[1] Indian Institute of Information Technology, Dharwad, Dharwad, Karnataka, India
gautaminaik2000@gmail.com, {sunil.saumya,aswath}@iiitdwd.ac.in
[2] Indian Institute of Science, Bengaluru, Karnataka, India

Abstract. Advancements in Natural Language Processing (NLP) have predominantly focused on English due to its global usage and the abundance of linguistic resources, whether via classical or quantum platforms. Although English remains the most studied language in computational linguistics, Hindi, the third most spoken language worldwide after Mandarin, has received comparatively limited attention. Spoken primarily in India, Hindi differs significantly from English in its script, syntactic structure, and cultural-linguistic context. Linguistically, English belongs to the Germanic branch of the Indo-European family, whereas Hindi, derived from Sanskrit, is part of the Indo-Aryan branch. It uses the Devanagari script, exhibits rich morphological inflection, and follows a subject-object-verb (SOV) order, in contrast to English's relatively simpler morphology and subject-verb-object (SVO) structure. These typological differences make Hindi a compelling candidate for exploring the generalization capacity of quantum-enhanced NLP models. Motivated by Hindi's syntactic and morphological complexity and its underrepresentation in both classical and quantum NLP research, we propose a grammar-aware Quantum NLP (QNLP) pipeline for Hindi sentiment classification. A key focus is on handling sentential negation, a linguistic feature inadequately addressed in current models. Most QNLP implementations are limited to English and lack grammar-sensitive methods for morphologically rich and syntactically flexible languages. We use a manually annotated dataset of Hindi sentences labeled as positive, negative, or neutral, and encode them using pregroup grammar types. Sentences are processed through Lambeq, generating quantum circuits using a novel, negation-aware compositional grammar. We train Hybrid Quantum Neural Networks (HQNNs) for both binary and ternary sentiment classification. Our results demonstrate successful classification performance and showcase QNLP's potential for typologically diverse languages.

Keywords: Quantum Natural Language Processing · Quantum Computing · AI

D. Cavar et al. (Eds.): QNLPAI 2025, CCIS 2659, pp. 172–185, 2026.
https://doi.org/10.1007/978-3-032-13883-5_10

1 Introduction

Quantum Natural Language Processing (QNLP) represents an emerging paradigm that combines quantum computing with natural language processing (NLP) to encode linguistic meaning into quantum states for language task execution [15]. The Distributional Compositional Categorical (DisCoCat) model of meaning developed by Coecke et al. (2010) [6] serves as the foundation for QNLP to create a mathematical system that unites grammatical structures with semantic meaning. The DisCoCat framework uses Lambek pregroups as grammar types to determine how word representations (in terms of quantum states or tensors) merge and evolve as sentence meanings [12]. The compositional nature of this approach aligns perfectly with quantum principles as tensor mathematics for meaning directly corresponds to quantum mechanics formalism. Theoretical research at an early stage indicated that QNLP could achieve algorithmic benefits through quadratic speed-up for particular operations by representing the linguistic structure as quantum states.

The field of QNLP has transitioned from theoretical development to practical implementation through recent advancements. The availability of noisy intermediate-scale quantum (NISQ) hardware allows researchers to conduct initial experiments that run NLP models as quantum circuits [10]. Lorenz *et al.* (2021) [13] achieved the first execution of small QNLP models on operational quantum computers, wherein the authors used an IBM quantum device to run their QNLP pipeline, for basic sentence meaning binary classification while demonstrating positive results despite hardware constraints. So far research on using QNLP to analyze sentiment in English language content has been perceived [8,17]. The two-class sentiment classification system developed by Lorenz et al. [13] was expanded by Martínez et al. (2022) [14] to perform emotion classification on a bigger dataset with four emotional categories. The DisCoCat QNLP framework demonstrated its ability to handle real-world applications by achieving high accuracy on small test datasets.

Most previous QNLP implementations have focused on English-language datasets, but multilingual adaptation has been minimally researched. Previous studies were insufficient in addressing the computational complexities encountered after selection due to the necessity of precise measurement outcomes for quantum circuits in order to achieve reliable results.

This paper presents an application of the QNLP method for Hindi sentiment classification. The Hindi language has a head-final structure with a Subject-Object-Verb (SOV) order, complex morphology, and flexible word order, which makes it difficult for QNLP pipelines that were originally designed for English (SVO order). To address this, we manually developed a Hindi pregroup grammar resource, assigning types to words such that sentences are reduced grammatically. While there are preliminary efforts to formalize Hindi grammar using pregroups [1], there was no off-the-shelf parser available for Hindi. We used the open-source Lambeq toolkit [15] to convert the manually typed Hindi sentences into quantum tensor networks and parameterized quantum circuits.

The syntactic structure of each Hindi sentence is converted into string diagrams, which are then translated into parameterized quantum circuits using the Lambeq toolkit. The Hybrid Quantum Neural Network (HQNN) architecture is used to classify the sentiment of each sentence into two categories: positive and neutral. The circuit construction and training procedure are explained in detail in the Methodology section.

2 Background

2.1 Foundations of QNLP

QNLP receives its foundation from the categorical compositional model of meaning developed by Coecke et al. (2010) [6], which demonstrated how grammatical composition can be translated into linear algebra and tensor products. The semantic vector space contains each word of a sentence as a vector that functions as a quantum state, while pregroup or categorial grammar determines the vector combination rules for sentence-level vector creation. The connection between grammar and quantum mechanics emerges because grammatical reductions can be expressed through string diagrams that equal quantum circuits in the mathematics of the tensor network [10]. The DisCoCat framework allows compositional meaning computation as it uses tensor contractions (via quantum circuits) to calculate sentence meanings based on syntactical word meaning interactions. The work of Coecke et al. introduced a new approach to handling natural language semantics through quantum formalisms, which showed that quantum computers would execute these operations naturally. The concept received further development through the Foundations for Near-Term QNLP by Coecke and coworkers (2020) [15], who adapted DisCoCat to NISQ device-friendly quantum circuits while discussing the integration of quantum machine learning with compositional linguistics.

2.2 QNLP Tooling (DisCoPy and Lambeq)

Research has been undertaken to come up with software frameworks to automate the process of converting sentences into quantum computations for practical QNLP model implementation. DisCoPy (Distributional Compositional Python) is a library for string diagrams and monoidal categories that offers a formal method to work with the graphical structures that underpin QNLP [14]. It enables the representation of grammatical reductions through diagrammatic operations and enables the connection to quantum circuit libraries. Kartsaklis *et al.* (2021) [10] developed Lambeq as a high-level QNLP toolkit. The QNLP pipeline is fully supported by Lambeq, which starts with sentence parsing through A Combinatory Categorial Grammar (CCG) parser via pregroup grammar, which further leads to string diagram generation and parameterized quantum circuit creation. The Lambeq generates quantum circuit ansatze from the syntax trees of sentences through qubit assignment and rotation gate allocation for words and entangling operations for grammatical connections. The toolkit provides "QNLP-in-practice" experiments through its ability to hide technical details while following the same processing sequence as Meichanetzidis et al. and Lorenz et al. in their first QNLP hardware experiments. Our research work uses Lambeq together with DisCoPy to process Hindi sentences by inputting manually parsed Hindi sentences into Lambeq, which produces simplified string diagrams and quantum circuits that we modify for our HQNN model.

2.3 Prior QNLP Experiments on English

The first demonstrations of QNLP focused on English as parsing tools are readily available for this language. Lorenz *et al.* (2021) performed binary sentiment classification on real quantum hardware using Lambeq-generated circuits, but they heavily depended on post-selection and templated English sentences [13]. Ganguly et al. (2023) employed Lambeq for binary sentiment classification on a small dataset [5], and Martinez and Leroy-Méline (2022) expanded QNLP to four emotion classes using synthetic English data [14]. These early implementations primarily addressed English-based datasets without extending the framework to structurally diverse languages.

2.4 Pregroup Grammar

The algebraic framework of pregroup grammar was first introduced by Lambek [12]. The system includes atomic types and their adjoint (left/right) counterparts, which enable the recognition of grammatical sentences through the cancellation of matching adjoint types. The formalism has been used to represent the syntax of many languages, including English, French, Japanese, and Sanskrit, Arabic as a single uniform system [2–5]. Coecke *et al.* (2010) showed that pregroups function as compositional building blocks for semantic models, including quantum natural language processing, through type alignment with tensor structures [7,11].

With regards to Hindi, the analysis of the formal structure faces multiple challenges because of its typological features. Here the language structure features head-finality and follows an SOV pattern with postpositional case markers. The word order follows the Subject-Object-Verb, while determiners and case markers (postpositions) occur after the noun, and verbs (including auxiliaries) appear at the end of the clause. The postpositional structure with the SOV word order makes it difficult to directly use the grammatical frameworks that were developed for English (SVO and prepositional). The word order of Hindi shows flexibility because constituents can be rearranged for emphasis or topicalization, but these rearrangements follow specific grammatical rules. These properties require a grammar system that can process meaningful word-order changes while maintaining proper syntactic relationships [7].

Shrivastava and Debnath (2021) proposed a pregroup formalization for Hindi using Paninian karaka roles [11]. Each case-marked noun phrase is typed according to its syntactic function: subjects as k_1, objects as k_2, and so on. These combine with postpositions and verbal arguments to reduce to the sentence types

[16]. Further taking inference from these references, we have come up with a Pregroup Grammar Types for Hindi-English Compositional Semantics as shown in the Table. 1.

Table 1. Pregroup Grammar Types for Hindi-English Compositional Semantics

Symbol	Category	Meaning
s	Sentence	Complete sentence
n	Noun	General noun type
o	Object	Object of verb
p	Predicate	Verb or verb phrase
$\pi_{11}, \pi_{12}, \pi_{13}$	Pronoun (Singular)	First, Second, Third person pronouns
$\pi_{21}, \pi_{22}, \pi_{23}$	Pronoun (Plural)	First, Second, Third person plural pronouns
τ_1, τ_2, τ_3	Tense Marker	Past, Present, Future
κ_1 to κ_8	Karaka Marker	*ne*, *ko* (object), *se*, *ko* (dative), *ke liye*, *se* (source), *me*, *par*
ρ_1, ρ_2	Sambandha Marker	Masculine, Feminine agreement
$\alpha_1, \alpha_2, \alpha_3$	Aspect Marker	Perfect, Imperfect, Continuous
n_{11}, n_{12}	Singular Nouns	Masculine, Feminine
n_{21}, n_{22}	Plural Nouns	Masculine, Feminine

Hindi's verb phrases are complex, often involving aspect markers (such as *raha, chuka*) and tense auxiliaries (such as *hai, tha*) as shown in the Table 2. The pregroup system handles this via intermediate types like *aspect* and *tense* denoted as α and τ, respectively. A typical transitive verb like khata ("eats") would take subject and object roles as inputs and expect a tense marker to yield sentences 's'. For instance, take a Hindi sentence"main seb khata hu" (*I eat an apple*), the structure reduces to "s" through valid contractions [7].

$$\pi \ o \ o^r @ \pi^r @ s @ \tau^l \ \tau. \tag{1}$$

3 Dataset Collection

Table 2. Hindi Sentence Structures Demonstrating Placement of *Nahi* and Associated Pregroup Types. Note: superscripts 'r' and 'l' stand for right and left adjoints (inverses) of the pregroup types. The curved brackets and simple '@' are used for grouping multiple pregroup types that interact and evolve into a single output.

Sentence Structure	Example (Hindi → English)	Pregroup Type Sequence
Simple Affirmative (SOV)	Ram gaya. ("Ram went.")	$n_{11} \quad n_{11}^r @ s$
Simple Negation (SOV)	Ram nahi gaya. ("Ram did not go.")	$n_{11} \quad (n_{11}^r @ s) @ (n_{11}^r @ s)^l \quad n_{11}^r @ s$
With Auxiliary (Affirmative)	Main seb khata hu. ("I eat an apple.")	$\pi_{11} \quad o \quad o^r @ \pi_{11}^r @ s @ \tau_2^l \quad \tau_2$
With Auxiliary (Negation)	Main seb nahi khata hu. ("I do not eat an apple.")	$\pi_{11} \quad o \quad (o^r @ \pi_{11}^r @ s @ \tau_2^l) @ (o^r @ \pi_{11}^r @ s @ \tau_2^l)^l \quad o^r @ \pi_{11}^r @ s @ \tau_2^l \quad \tau_2$
Progressive Negation (Pre-verb)	Main nahi kha raha hu. ("I am not eating.")	$\pi_{11} \quad (o^r @ \pi_{11}^r @ p @ \alpha_3^l) @ (o^r @ \pi_{11}^r @ p @ \alpha_3^l)^l \quad o^r @ \pi_{11}^r @ p @ \alpha_3^l \quad \alpha \quad \tau^l \quad \tau$
Progressive Negation (Pre-auxiliary)	Main kha nahi raha hu. ("I am not eating.")	$\pi_{11} \quad o^r @ \pi_{11}^r @ p @ \alpha_3^l \quad (\alpha_3 \alpha_3^l)^l \quad \alpha_3 \quad \tau_2^l \quad \tau_2$

3.1 Incorporating the Negation Particle *Nahi* in Hindi QNLP

Sentiment analysis relies heavily on sentiment negation as one of its essential construction elements. The Hindi language uses the negation particle *nahi* ("not"), which comes before the main verb of the clause [9]. The finite verb receives *nahi* immediately before it in basic sentence structures.

For example, the sentence *Ram nahi gaya* means "Ram did not go," in contrast to the positive statement *Ram gaya* which means "Ram went."

The pregroup representation allows the negation word to function as an adverbial modifier that maintains the original type reductions. The negation word *nahi* operates by inserting itself into a specific verb phrase type and producing a verb phrase of the same type without modifying the required arguments of the verb.

Negation can be incorporated by assigning *nahi* a compound type of $xx.l$, where x represents the type of the verb phrase it modifies so that *nahi* x maintains type x. The sentence *Ram nahi gaya* receives the pregroup type sequence:

$$n \; ((n^r @ s)(n^r @ s)^l) \; n.r \; s, \tag{2}$$

which reduces to 's' in the same way as $n \; n.r \; s$ for affirmative cases.

The placement of *nahi* appears before the main verb or participates in complex verb phrases that include auxiliaries. Table 2 presents various Hindi sentence structures with and without negation to demonstrate *nahi* placement and the associated pregroup types.

3.2 Manually Curated Hindi Dataset for Quantum Sentiment Classification

We created a specific dataset for this study to evaluate sentiment classification using a QNLP framework for Hindi. The dataset contains 250 Hindi sentences that were manually created and annotated with positive, negative, or neutral sentiment labels.

The dataset was constructed and verified entirely by hand, keeping its size small to maintain high linguistic quality and structural accuracy. This method enabled strict grammatical accuracy and exact sentiment representation, validated by native Hindi speakers. The dataset functions as a proof-of-concept to demonstrate the QNLP pipeline, rather than striving for state-of-the-art performance on extensive corpora.

The vocabulary distribution across the sentiment classes was balanced to eliminate lexical bias, ensuring that classification depends on structural and semantic features rather than surface word frequency. The sentences contain between 5 to 7 words on average, making them suitable for building efficient quantum circuits.

3.3 Sentence Composition

The sentences were designed to reflect everyday statements that carry clear sentiment, including emotionally expressive and neutral factual expressions:

- **Positive Sentences:** Expressions of praise, happiness, etc.
  Example: *Mujhe tumari saari baatein pasand hai* ("I like everything about you.")
- **Negative Sentences:** Expressions of complaints, sadness, etc.
  Example: *Ve farsh nahi saaf kar rahe* ("They are not cleaning the floor.")
- **Neutral Sentences:** Objective or emotionless factual statements.
  Example: *Gautami ne khana banaya* ("Gautami cooked food.")

These sentences ensure that the model learns to distinguish between emotional and non-emotional content based on structure and semantics, not just keywords.

The pregroup type assignments accompany each sentence through the Hindi grammar lexicon described in the methodology section. The dataset includes syntactic diversity across common constructions, such as copula forms, transitive verb phrases, and negated predicates.

Given its size, the dataset was not intended to train a high-capacity model but to serve as a proof-of-concept corpus. Every sentence was manually checked by native Hindi speakers to confirm grammatical accuracy and correct sentiment expression. Vocabulary distribution remained equal among sentiment classes to avoid lexical bias and ensure that classification relied on compositional structure.

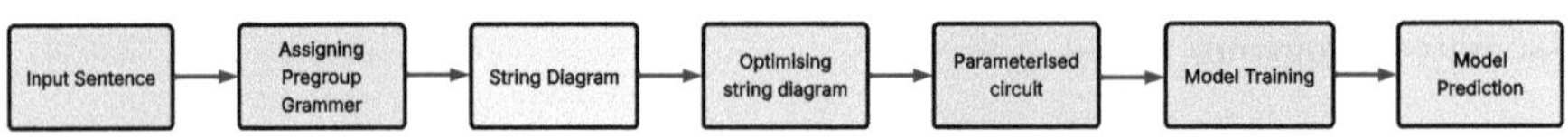

Fig. 1. Lambeq Pipeline

4 Methodology

4.1 Dataset

The dataset contains a collection of sentences with varying sentiments, including both positive, negative, and neutral examples. The dataset was divided into training, validation, and test sets in a ratio of 70:10:20. The dataset comprised entirely single, grammatically complete sentences. A restricted vocabulary was employed to decrease the number of unfamiliar words within the test sets without total elimination. This approach ensures some degree of generalisability over the test words while maintaining a wealth of common vocabulary.

4.2 QNLP Pipeline

The QNLP pipeline for the Hindi sentiment classification is shown in Fig. 1. The pipeline starts with a Hindi sentence as input, parses it into a pregroup grammar representation, converts it into a string diagram, translates the diagram into a parameterized quantum circuit, and finally integrates the circuit into a hybrid quantum-classical model. In summary, our pipeline comprises four main stages (illustrated in Fig. 1):

1. Sentence to String Diagram: The process begins by applying the Hindi pregroup grammar to each sentence to assign atomic types to every word. The grammar assigns the noun type denoted as 'n' to all noun words, while transitive verbs receive compound types that transform two noun inputs into a sentence output 's'. The DisCoCat parser from Lambeq transforms grammar reductions into string diagrams that depict word types as wires and implement noun-adjoint type contractions through cup-shaped connections. The cups exist as entangled wire pairs that connect the words in the diagram [18].

2. Diagram Simplification: The Lambeq tool simplifies diagrams through its application of rewrite rules to optimize string diagrams. The optimization process removes superfluous cups and decreases the wire complexity (such as removing duplicate noun wires) while preserving the original sentence meaning. The reduction of unnecessary cups helps decrease the quantum state dimensionality, which leads to fewer qubits and gates required in the circuit.

3. String Diagram to Quantum Circuit: The simplified diagram is then converted into a parameterized quantum circuit (PQC) using a chosen ansatz. We employ Lambeq's built-in Instantaneous Quantum Polynomial (IQP) ansatz for this conversion. In this step, each wire in the diagram (of types like 'n' or 's') is mapped to one or more qubits, and each diagrammatic operation (ex. each word or cup) is mapped to a sequence of quantum gates. For example, each word state is prepared by a parameterized gate sequence on its qubit(s), and each cup (which connects a noun to a verb's adjoint type) is implemented by an entangling gate (such as a controlled-Z rotation) between the corresponding qubits. The result is a variational quantum circuit whose adjustable gate parameters θ_i correspond to the weights of the word meanings in the sentence.

4. Hybrid Model Training: The hybrid model training process uses generated circuits for each sentence as part of a sentiment classification system. The quantum circuit receives trainable parameters for each sentence before its execution (simulation) to generate output results such as measurement probabilities or expectation values. The quantum output data flows into a classical post-processing layer (Sect. 3.3) to generate the final prediction. The model receives its end-to-end training through the evaluation of predicted sentiment against actual sentiment labels and the calculation of loss. The circuit parameters receive updates through gradient descent using a classical optimizer from Lambeq's PyTorch backend with the Adam optimizer until the model achieves convergence [10].

Example: Pregroup Parsing and Circuit

We demonstrate the approach by analyzing the Hindi sentence **"Gautami faal khati hai"**, which means *"Gautami eats fruit."* The sentence contains a subject (Gautami) and an object (fruit) together with a verb phrase ("eats").

We begin by assigning each word its corresponding type from the Hindi pregroup grammar as shown below:
Sentence: "Gautami faal khati hai"
Types:

$$\text{Gautami} \rightarrow \pi_{13}$$
$$\text{faal} \rightarrow o$$
$$\text{khati} \rightarrow o^r \cdot \pi_{13}^r \cdot s \cdot \tau_2^l$$
$$\text{hai} \rightarrow \tau_2$$

$$\text{Gautami} \rightarrow \pi_{13}$$
$$\text{faal} \rightarrow o$$
$$\text{khati} \rightarrow o^r \cdot \pi_{13}^r \cdot s \cdot \tau_2^l$$
$$\text{hai} \rightarrow \tau_2$$

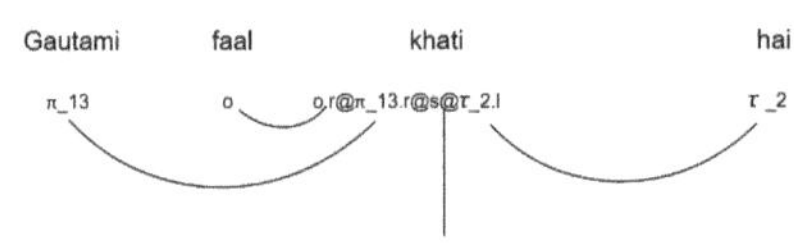

Fig. 2. Pregroup. Note: Labels like π_{13}, τ_{21} are generated from the Lambeq code, and appear here as π_13 and τ_21, same is with other labels.

Step 1: Creating the Sentence Diagram. Using pregroup notation and word connections, we apply the pregroup grammar framework to describe Hindi. Sentence diagrams are created for the given sentences as shown in the sentence diagram of Fig. 2. As stated in Sect. 4.1, the sentence yields the corresponding string diagram shown in Fig. 3.

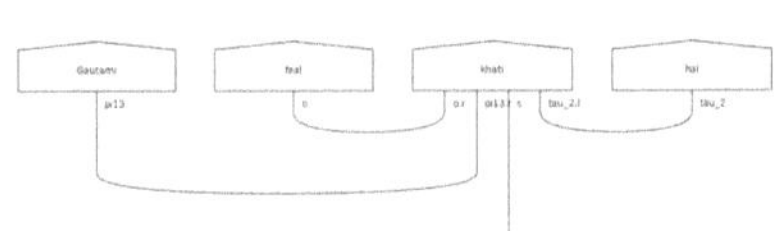

Fig. 3. String Diagram. Note: Labels like π_{13}, τ_{21} are generated from the Lambeq code, and appear here as pi13 and tau_21, same is with other labels.

Step 2: Building the Parameterized Quantum Circuit. The simplified diagram is translated into a parameterized quantum circuit through Lambeq's circuit compiler. The atomic wires (such as π_{13}, o, and τ_2) function as qubits in the system, and the word boxes transform into parameterized unitary blocks that contain trainable quantum gate operations.

The process involves:

- The embedding of *Gautami* and *faal* occurs through $R_z(\theta)$ layers, which perform single-qubit state preparation.
- The *khati* operation functions as a multi-qubit block that creates entanglement between the qubits representing π_{13}, o, and τ_2.
- The operator *hai* functions as a one-qubit operator that targets τ_2.
- The diagram's cups are implemented through entangling gates (typically CZ gates) that connect the corresponding qubits according to grammatical rules.

The resulting quantum circuit maintains the compositional meaning of the sentence while incorporating trainable parameters $\{\theta_i\}$, which are optimized during the classification process.

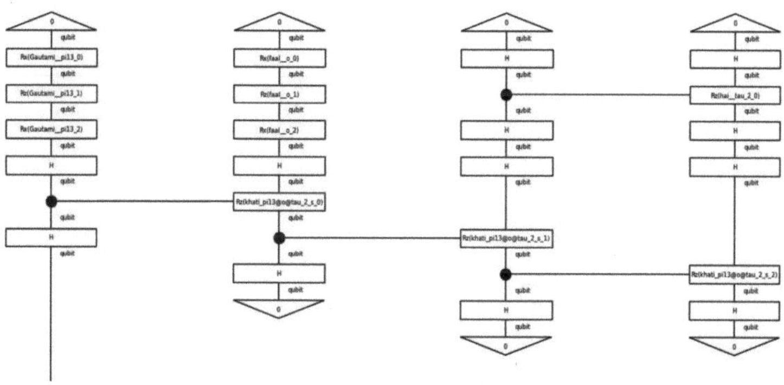

Fig. 4. Quantum Circuit. Note: Labels like π_{13}, τ_{21} are generated from the Lambeq code, and appear here as pi_13 and tau_21, same is with other labels.

Step 3: IQP Ansatz. The IQP (Instantaneous Quantum Polynomial-time) ansatz built into Lambeq is used to construct the circuits. This ansatz consists of:

- Hadamard gates applied to all qubits
- Followed by parameterized R_z rotations
- Entangling CZ gates between qubits as dictated by the grammatical cups

Each word contributes a local subcircuit, and the entire circuit is variational, with parameters trained to encode the sentiment meaning of the sentence. See Fig. 4 for the circuit corresponding to the example sentence

5 Results and Discussion

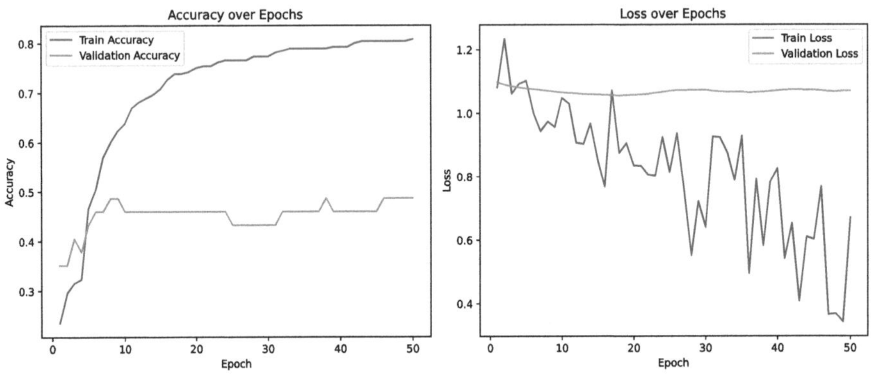

Fig. 5. Ternary Class Classification. Left: Accuracy Vs Epoch, Right: Loss Vs Epoch.

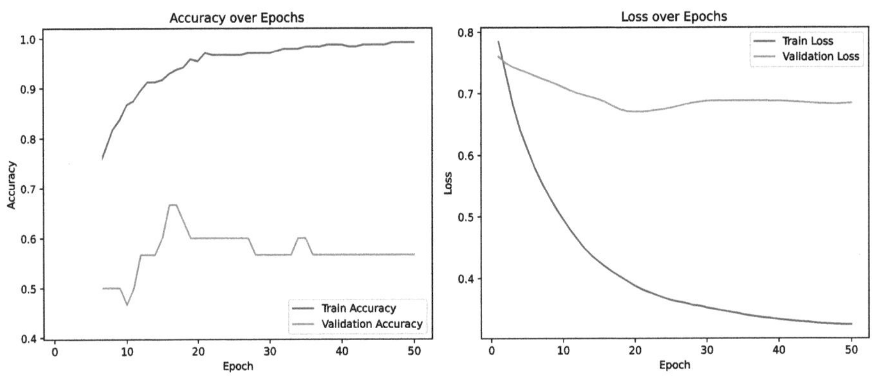

Fig. 6. Binary Class Classification. Left: Accuracy Vs Epoch, Right: Loss Vs Epoch.

The performance of the proposed hybrid quantum-classical model was evaluated across two sentiment classification tasks: a **Ternary-class task** (positive, negative, neutral) and a **Binary-class task** (positive, negative). Additionally, experiments were conducted using two data split configurations: **70:10:20** and **80:10:10** (train: validation: test). All models were trained and tested using simulated quantum circuits.

The dataset used in this study contained a highly diverse vocabulary, with many words appearing only once or a few times. While this variety proves the working of the model, it also presents challenges for learning and generalization. The model was particularly affected in the Ternary-class classification setting,

Table 3. Sentiment Classification Accuracy (%)

Task Type	70:10:20 Split	80:10:10 Split
Ternary-Class Classification	55.0	61.0
Binary-Class Classification	68.0	73.0

where low-frequency words offered limited learning opportunities for embedding representations. As shown in Table 3, performance in the Binary-class classification task was consistently stronger than in the Ternary-class version, highlighting the difficulty in accurately detecting neutral sentiment, which often lacks distinctive emotional or grammatical features. Additionally, the comparison of dataset splits reveals that the 80:10:10 configuration yielded higher accuracy than the 70:10:20 split for both tasks. These results are substantiated in the Accuracy and Loss Vs Epoch plots shown in the Figs. 5 and 6. This suggests that a larger training set provides greater stability during quantum parameter optimization, indicating that hybrid quantum models are notably sensitive to training data volume and may underfit with limited samples.

6 Conclusion

The research presented a grammar-aware QNLP pipeline for Hindi sentiment classification via the application of compositional quantum models to complex morphological languages. The pregroup grammar framework enabled us to construct sentence diagrams that integrated the Hindi negation particle *"nahi"* directly into the syntactic structure. The Lambeq toolkit converts these diagrams into parameterized quantum circuits. The hybrid quantum-classical neural network (HQNN) demonstrated promising accuracy in both binary (positive/negative) and ternary (positive/negative/neutral) sentiment classification tasks when evaluated on a manually annotated corpus of 250 Hindi sentences. The compositional QNLP method successfully detects Hindi semantic features, including intricate morphological patterns and negation-induced semantic transformations.

This research presents the initial implementation of complete compositional QNLP methods for Hindi that possess complex morphology and adaptable word arrangement. The proposed model successfully handles the *"nahi"* negation particle, which represents a significant achievement because negation has traditionally been difficult to analyze in sentiment analysis. The proposed approach has the advantage of grammar-informed quantum models, which structurally represent negation in quantum circuits to properly detect changes in sentiment polarity. The proposed Hindi QNLP sentiment classifier demonstrates that compositional quantum techniques can be applied to complex linguistic structures beyond English language boundaries. The research expands QNLP applications and demonstrates how sentiment analysis models can become more transparent through linguistic foundations.

7 Future Scope

We have several plans to extend this research. First, we increase the size and diversity of the Hindi dataset to improve the model's generalizability. A larger corpus with more varied vocabulary and syntactic constructions, including interrogatives, imperatives, and complex compound sentences, will allow the proposed HQNN to learn a broader range of linguistic patterns and better handle edge cases. The inclusion of more diverse sentence types and grammatical structures (e.g., different word orders or embedded clauses) will further strengthen the compositional framework and ensure its robustness in capturing Hindi's rich syntax.

Second, we plan to apply the proposed QNLP pipeline to other Indian languages, such as Telugu, Kannada, and Marathi. These languages belong to different linguistic families and feature distinct grammatical features. By adapting the pregroup grammar diagrams and quantum circuit ansätze to these languages, we can evaluate the generality of our approach across diverse morphosyntactic settings. The successful implementation of multiple languages demonstrates that compositional QNLP techniques are broadly applicable and not limited to a single linguistic context.

Finally, the ultimate goal is to deploy and test the proposed model on actual quantum hardware. To date, all experiments have been conducted on simulated or hybrid quantum platforms; running the sentiment classification circuits on real quantum processors is a crucial step toward validating the practicality of the proposed approach. As quantum computing technology matures, we aim to assess the performance of the proposed HQNN on noisy intermediate-scale quantum (NISQ) devices and identify any quantum-specific advantages or challenges. This transition from simulation to physical quantum hardware provides deeper insights into the feasibility of QNLP for real-world applications and helps guide further refinement of the model.

References

1. Akshar, B., Chaitanya, V., et al.: Natural Language Processing: A Paninian Perspective. PHI Learning Pvt., Ltd. (1995)
2. Bargelli, D., Lambek, J.: An algebraic approach to Arabic sentence structure. Linguis. Anal. **31**(3), 301–315 (2001)
3. Cardinal, K.: An algebraic study of Japanese grammar (2002)
4. Casadio, C., Sadrzadeh, M.: Clitic movement in pregroup grammar: a cross-linguistic approach. In: International Tbilisi Symposium on Logic, Language, and Computation, pp. 197–214. Springer, Heidelberg (2009). https://doi.org/10.1007/978-3-642-22303-7_13
5. Casadio, C., Sadrzadeh, M.: Word order alternation in Sanskrit via precyclicity in pregroup grammars. In: Horizons of the Mind. A Tribute to Prakash Panangaden: Essays Dedicated to Prakash Panangaden on the Occasion of His 60th Birthday, pp. 229–249. Springer, Heidelberg (2014). https://doi.org/10.1007/978-3-319-06880-0_12
6. Coecke, B., Sadrzadeh, M., Clark, S.: Mathematical foundations for a compositional distributional model of meaning. arXiv preprint arXiv:1003.4394 (2010)

7. Debanth, A., Shrivastava, M.: A computational algebraic analysis of Hindi syntax. J. Logic Lang. Inform. **32**(5), 759–776 (2023)
8. Ganguly, S., Morapakula, S.N., Coronado, L.M.P.: Quantum natural language processing based sentiment analysis using lambeq toolkit. In: 2022 Second International Conference on Power, Control and Computing Technologies (ICPC2T), pp. 1–6 (2022). https://doi.org/10.1109/ICPC2T53885.2022.9776836
9. HindiPod101.com: Negation in Hindi: how to make negative sentences (2021). https://www.hindipod101.com/blog/2021/08/10/hindi-negation/. Accessed 18 May 2025
10. Kartsaklis, D., et al.: lambeq: an efficient high-level python library for quantum NLP (2021). https://arxiv.org/abs/2110.04236
11. Lambek, J.: Type grammar revisited. In: Lecomte, A., Lamarche, F., Perrier, G. (eds.) Logical Aspects of Computational Linguistics, pp. 1–27. Springer, Heidelberg (1999). https://doi.org/10.1007/3-540-48975-4_1
12. Lambek, J.: Pregroups and natural language processing. Mathe. Intelligencer **28**(2) (2006)
13. Lorenz, R., Pearson, A., Meichanetzidis, K., Kartsaklis, D., Coecke, B.: QNLP in practice: running compositional models of meaning on a quantum computer. J. Artif. Int. Res. **76** (2023). https://doi.org/10.1613/jair.1.14329
14. Martinez, V., Leroy-Meline, G.: A multiclass Q-NLP sentiment analysis experiment using discocat. arXiv preprint arXiv:2209.03152 (2022)
15. Meichanetzidis, K., Gogioso, S., de Felice, G., Chiappori, N., Toumi, A., Coecke, B.: Quantum natural language processing on near-term quantum computers. Electron. Proc. Theor. Comput. Sci. **340**, 213–229 (2021). https://doi.org/10.4204/eptcs.340.11
16. Palmer, M., Bhatt, R., Narasimhan, B., Rambow, O., Sharma, D.M., Xia, F.: Hindi syntax: annotating dependency, lexical predicate-argument structure, and phrase structure. In: The 7th International Conference on Natural Language Processing, pp. 14–17 (2009)
17. Ruskanda, F.Z., Abiwardani, M.R., Syafalni, I., Larasati, H.T., Mulyawan, R.: Simple sentiment analysis ansatz for sentiment classification in quantum natural language processing. IEEE Access **11**, 120612–120627 (2023)
18. Srivastava, N., Belekar, G., Saumya, S., et al.: Enabling quantum natural language processing for Hindi language. arXiv preprint arXiv:2312.01221 (2023)

Compact Quantum Circuits for Martinican Creole LID: A Typologically Informed Proof-of-Concept

Ludovic Mompelat[(✉)]

University of Miami, Coral Gables, FL 33146, USA
lvm861@miami.edu

Abstract. We present the first Quantum-Natural-Language-Processing (QNLP) proof of concept for token-level language identification in Martinican Creole, a low-resource language with substantial lexical overlap with French. Our approach compares: (1) a character-bigram baseline, (2) a classical logistic regression model trained on three interpretable intra-token features (entropy, vowel ratio, syllable complexity), and (3) a compact three-qubit variational circuit embedding the same features in product-state and entangled configurations.

On token-level macro-F_1 and accuracy, the classical model performs slightly better than the entangled variant, reflecting its robustness on high-frequency items where individual features are most discriminative. However, a type-level analysis shows a different pattern: the entangled embedding reduces the number of distinct misclassified types and uniquely corrects a sizable subset that both the classical and product-state models miss. The rescued set is heterogeneous (i.e., mixing frequent Creole items and proper names with cross-lingual orthography), and some gains are dataset-contingent serendipitous effects, since the models are context-blind and rely only on intra-token features.

Our findings demonstrate that even minimal quantum embeddings can capture non-linear interactions between interpretable features in ways that simple linear models and product mappings cannot. The results highlight the potential of hardware-efficient QNLP for fine-grained, low-resource language identification, especially in settings where context is unavailable but token-internal cues are strong. We conclude with a roadmap for extending this work to richer feature sets, context-aware hybrid architectures, and cross-lingual transfer to other Creole and closely related language pairs.

Keywords: QNLP · Martinican Creole · Token-level Language Identification · Low-Resource Language Modeling

1 Introduction

Automatic language identification for Creole text at the token level presents a uniquely challenging problem, especially when discriminating between a Creole

D. Cavar et al. (Eds.): QNLPAI 2025, CCIS 2659, pp. 186–203, 2026.
https://doi.org/10.1007/978-3-032-13883-5_11

language and its lexifier. In varieties such as Martinican Creole, constant contact with French gives rise to pervasive code-switching and mixing—both between sentences (intersentential) and within a single clause (intrasentential) [7,8]. While sentence-level language identification can exploit large context windows and strong distributional cues, intrasentential token-level identification must decide on very short strings, often a single word, clitic, or affix whose orthographic and phonotactic properties can overlap entirely across both languages.

To isolate and amplify the subtle structural signals that distinguish Creole from French at this fine granularity, we present the first QNLP proof of concept for token-level Creole identification. By deliberately restricting ourselves to token-internal features, we keep our quantum circuits within the size limits of today's noisy intermediate-scale devices and can pinpoint exactly which interpretable features benefit from quantum interference and entanglement. Each token is mapped to a compact three–dimensional feature vector consisting of: (1) Shannon entropy over the character sequence, (2) vowel-to-consonant ratio, and (3) a simple syllable-complexity measure.

We compare three end-to-end pipelines:

1. A purely classical structural-feature model in which the three–dimensional feature vector is passed into a logistic-regression classifier (with z-score scaling).
2. A product-state quantum pipeline in which the features are embedded into a 3–qubit variational circuit without entanglement, followed by a logistic-regression head.
3. An entangled quantum pipeline in which the same embedding is passed through a 3–qubit variational circuit with Ising entanglers, also decoded with logistic regression.

Linguistic typology and information theory both motivate our choice of features. Creoles typically favor simple (CV) syllable structure without complex clusters [9], and exhibit lower symbol-sequence entropy than typologically related lexifiers [2,10]. Likewise, Creoles cluster around roughly 20 consonants but only 6–8 basic vowels, whereas French employs a similarly sized consonant inventory alongside a much richer vocalic system [4,5]. These cross-linguistic patterns directly inform our entropy, C/V-ratio, and syllable-complexity measures.

In this paper we make three contributions:

1. We establish a robust, interpretable classical baseline for token-level Creole identification using three compact, linguistically motivated features.
2. We perform a systematic QNLP comparison of product-state and entangled 3–qubit variational circuits as the first token-level benchmark for Martinican Creole identification.
3. We provide a comprehensive evaluation (precision, recall, F_1, confusion matrices) and an in-depth type-level, class-conditioned error overlap analysis, highlighting both shared and model-specific misclassifications.

Our overlap analysis shows that the product-state model makes nearly all of the errors made by the classical model, while introducing many more of its own, whereas the entangled model substantially reduces the total number of unique error types. Crucially, entanglement "rescues" a large set of errors shared by the other two models, including frequent, monosyllabic Creole tokens, even though it introduces a small set of unique errors on rare French borrowings. This pattern underscores entanglement's power to capture subtle joint-feature interactions in a compact circuit, while pointing to morphological or contextual augmentations to curb its remaining misclassification.

2 Background

2.1 Token-Level Language Identification

Fine-grained, token-level language identification (LID) is markedly more challenging than document- or sentence-level LID due to extremely short contexts (often 1–7 characters), orthographic overlap between varieties, and severe class imbalance (in our case, far more Creole tokens than French borrowings). Early work on token-level LID in code-switched settings relied on lexicons, character n-gram log-linear models, and simple sequence models (CRFs), achieving F_1 scores in the 60–80% range but suffering high confusion on closely related or shared-orthography tokens.

Molina et al. [6] provide a comprehensive overview of the 2016 shared task on language identification in code-switched data. In their summary of the 2016 evaluation, the best-performing Spanish–English system achieves a token-level F_1 of 0.973, whereas on the typologically closer pair of Modern Standard Arabic vs. Dialectal Arabic the top token-level F_1 falls to 0.876. Neural architectures that learn character- and contextualized word-level embeddings show improvements on social-media text, yet they still underperform on extremely short or out-of-domain tokens [3].

Our work departs from these standard n-gram and lexicon-heavy approaches by systematically evaluating three progressively richer classifiers on a 9k-token Martinican Creole test set, all using the same compact, interpretable token-internal features: entropy, vowel ratio, and syllable complexity. First, a character-bigram baseline model classifies each token via a softmax over their log-likelihoods. Second, we establish a classical logistic-regression baseline trained on these features (with z-score scaling). Third, we embed the same features into a 3-qubit variational circuit in a product-state configuration, and then introduce entanglement via interleaved CNOT gates to capture higher-order joint-feature correlations.

Our type-level, class-conditioned error overlap analysis reveals a clear hierarchy: the product-state model reproduces nearly all errors made by the classical model while adding its own, whereas the entangled model substantially reduces the total number of unique error types and "rescues" many frequent, monosyllabic Creole tokens misclassified by both baselines. These gains come alongside a small set of unique entangled-only errors, mostly rare French borrowings, highlighting both the promise and the current limits of compact entangled circuits for this task.

2.2 Structural Token Features

Creole syllable structure is uniformly simple, a fact we capture in our *syllable_complexity* feature. Typological surveys show that most Martinican Creole syllables conform to CV or VC templates, systematically shedding complex codas and avoiding onset clusters. As Bonan [1] observes, Guadeloupean (and by close analogy Martinican) Creole reduces many French CVC syllables by deleting the coda or inserting a vowel to yield CV rhythm, and most Creole words are one syllable shorter than their French counterparts (p. 72). For example, French *lavable* [lavabl](washable) surfaces in Creole as *lavab* [la.vab] via apocope (therefore erasing the final consonant cluster), while *heure* [œʁ] (hour) becomes *lè* [lɛ] with coda reduction [ʁ → ø] and initial consonant epenthesis giving us a CV sequence. Such systematic simplification and normalization directly motivates a metric of syllable count and consonant-cluster weight per token.

From an information-theoretic standpoint, we quantify character-sequence unpredictability via Shannon entropy, forming our `entropy` feature. Shannon's original formulation defines entropy as the expected information per symbol, and subsequent work has shown that languages with reduced phonotactic constraints tend to exhibit higher local entropy than their lexifiers [2,10]. In Creole orthography, this often manifests in short, morphologically stable function words like *an*, *pa*, or *sé*, whose limited character options yield low entropy, contrasting with longer, morphologically variable French forms such as *ajouter* or *régulièrement*, whose richer orthotactic patterns raise entropy. By measuring entropy at the token level after normalizing case and punctuation, we ensure the feature captures orthographic–phonotactic complexity rather than stylistic variation.

Finally, Creoles exhibit systematically different consonant–to–vowel balances, which we encode in our `vowel_ratio` feature. Large-scale phonological surveys report that Creoles cluster around roughly twenty consonants but maintain fewer vowel qualities (often seven to ten), whereas French combines a similar consonant inventory with twelve to sixteen vowel phonemes [4,5]. This difference influences the segmental makeup of words: Creole tokens such as *mango* or *pou* typically have a high vowel proportion relative to consonants, while French items like *prendre* or *structure* are consonant-heavy. This distributional cue, when combined with syllable complexity and entropy, provides a complementary dimension for distinguishing Creole from French tokens without relying on contextual information.

In our updated workflow, these three compact, interpretable features form the sole input to *both* classical and quantum pipelines. By design, we strip all contextual information, balance the Creole/Not-Creole training sets by type, and apply identical punctuation filtering to gold and predicted data. We compute features after lowercasing and canonicalizing quotes/dashes. For entropy, we retain only letters plus apostrophe and hyphen (to capture orthographic structure); for vowel ratio and syllable complexity, we use letters only, removing punctuation and digits. Punctuation-only tokens are excluded from evaluation. This ensures that performance differences stem from the representation and classifier, not from variation in token coverage or preprocessing.

2.3 Classical vs. Quantum Pipelines

Our *classical* pipeline represents each token by a three–dimensional real-valued vector

$$\left[H_{\text{char}}, r_{\text{vowel/cons}}, \sigma_{\text{syll}}\right],$$

where H_{char} is the Shannon entropy of the character sequence, $r_{\text{vowel/cons}}$ its vowel-to-consonant ratio, and σ_{syll} a simple syllable-complexity score. After standardizing each feature with a z–score (mean and variance computed from the training data only), we train two alternative classifiers in this 3D feature space: (1) a linear logistic regression, which learns a single separating hyperplane and treats each feature's contribution additively, and (2) an RBF-kernel SVM, which uses a Gaussian kernel to model non-linear decision boundaries by implicitly mapping the data to a higher-dimensional space. In our setting, the three token-internal features are already low-dimensional, well-separated along individual axes for many tokens, and deliberately free of contextual noise. This makes them well-suited to a linear separator, while the SVM's more flexible boundary can overfit to small, spurious feature combinations in this compact space, especially under our balanced-type sampling. As a result, although SVMs can in principle capture higher-order interactions without explicit feature crossing or polynomial expansion, here this capacity offers little benefit and may even degrade generalization—motivating our choice to retain linear logistic regression as the classical baseline.

Unlike the SVM, whose nonlinear capacity resides entirely in the decision function applied to the unchanged 3D input space, the quantum circuit alters the geometry of the feature space itself before classification, embedding the three features into a higher-dimensional quantum state whose amplitudes explicitly encode joint feature products. Our *quantum* pipeline uses exactly the same three standardized features but nonlinearly embeds them into a variational quantum circuit with one qubit per feature. We evaluate two configurations:

- **Product-state circuit (no entanglement).** Each standardized feature value is embedded into a single qubit via a single R_Y rotation, producing a separable n-qubit state ($n = 3$ in our experiments). This encoding already induces a nonlinear mapping, since the expectation values of Pauli-Z measurements depend sinusoidally on the input angles.
- **Entangled-state circuit.** After the initial R_Y embeddings, we insert an *IsingXX* entangling chain with fixed angle $\pi/2$ between consecutive qubits. This operation mixes the computational subspaces of adjacent features, creating joint amplitude patterns that product states cannot represent. To further expose these correlations under Z-basis measurement, we apply a fixed $R_Y(\pi/4)$ rotation to each qubit before readout.

In both configurations, the circuit is measured via local Pauli-Z expectation values, yielding one real-valued output per qubit (three values for our three-feature setup). These outputs are passed directly to the same classical decoder as in the baseline pipeline, ensuring that any performance difference is attributable solely to the quantum embedding stage.

Our updated experimental setup uses a unified evaluation function across all models, identical gold token filtering, and balanced type-level training sets, allowing direct comparison between:

1. n-gram language-model baselines (best: 2-gram),
2. classical logistic/SVM on the 3-D feature vector,
3. product-state quantum embeddings, and
4. entangled-state quantum embeddings.

This hybrid design preserves the interpretability of the input features while allowing the quantum embedding stage to reshape the feature space through quantum interference (via RY rotations) and, when enabled, entanglement (via fixed-angle IsingXX gates followed by readout rotations). By keeping the final classification stage entirely classical, we isolate performance differences to the embedding step itself, ensuring that gains—such as the observed error reductions and improved recall for high-frequency Creole tokens—are specifically attributable to the quantum mapping of the three interpretable structural features rather than changes in the decoder architecture.

2.4 Classical Pipeline Embedding and Feature Selection

To isolate the structural distinctions between Martinican Creole and French borrowings, each token is mapped to a compact three–dimensional feature vector:

- **Character entropy (H)** measures the Shannon entropy of the token's character distribution, capturing unpredictability in orthographic form. Computation is case-insensitive and based on the empirical distribution after canonicalizing punctuation and stripping whitespace, ensuring consistency with our gold dataset preprocessing.
- **Vowel–consonant ratio (V)** computes the proportion of vowel characters in the token, exploiting the differing CV patterns in Creole vs. French.
- **Syllable complexity (S)** counts vowel–consonant transitions and cluster sizes, approximating the number and intricacy of CV units per token.

In our updated workflow, all training sets are *type-balanced* at the class level (equal number of unique Creole vs. Not–Creole tokens), and punctuation-only tokens are filtered out from both training and gold evaluation sets prior to feature computation. This ensures that support counts match across traditional, classical, and quantum experiments, eliminating discrepancies caused by pipeline-specific filtering.

These standardized features are z–scored based on the training distribution before being passed to one of two classical learners:

1. *Logistic regression* with ℓ_2 regularization.
2. *RBF-kernel SVM* with γ set to the reciprocal of the feature dimension.

While the linear model cannot capture higher-order interactions without explicit polynomial expansion, the RBF-kernel SVM can model such interactions implicitly through its kernel mapping. In our low-dimensional, well-separated feature space, however, this extra flexibility offered little benefit and sometimes degraded generalization, making logistic regression the more stable baseline.

2.5 Decoder Choice Across Pipelines

We compare two decoder architectures across three embedding settings: logistic regression (LR) with ℓ_2 regularization and an RBF-kernel SVM.

- **Classical three-feature vector.** Tokens are represented by the standardized (H, V, S) feature triplet: Shannon entropy H, vowel-to-consonant ratio V, and syllable-complexity score S.
- **Quantum product-state embedding.** Each standardized feature is encoded into a single qubit via a rotation gate, producing a separable 3-qubit state whose measurement outcomes yield nonlinear transformations of the input features.
- **Quantum entangled embedding.** As in the product-state case, but with IsingXX entanglers and readout rotations inserted between qubits, allowing the circuit amplitudes to represent higher-order correlations among H, V, and S that cannot be captured in $\mathbb{R}^3$ without explicit feature crossing.

Table 1. Logistic Regression (LR) and Support Vector Machine (SVM) performance across the classical three–feature pipeline, the non-entangled 3-qubit quantum embedding, and the entangled 3-qubit quantum embedding.

Pipeline	Decoder	$F_{1,\text{Creole}}$	$F_{1,\neg\text{Creole}}$	M$-F_1$	Acc.
Classical	LR	0.94	0.25	0.60	0.90
	SVM	0.61	0.08	0.34	0.45
Quantum (non-entangled)	LR	0.92	0.21	0.57	0.85
	SVM	0.50	0.08	0.29	0.35
Quantum (entangled)	LR	0.93	0.19	0.56	0.86
	SVM	0.60	0.08	0.34	0.44

As shown in Table 1, logistic regression consistently outperforms the RBF-kernel SVM across all pipelines, maintaining high Creole recall and reasonable performance on the minority Not-Creole class. The RBF kernel's flexibility, while powerful for high-dimensional or axis-entangled data, offers little benefit here: our (H, V, S) features are low-dimensional, interpretable, and already well-separated along individual axes. In this compact space, the SVM is prone to overfitting to spurious combinations (particularly when the input geometry comes from the variational quantum embeddings), leading to degraded generalization.

The classical pipeline with LR achieves the highest token-level F_1, but as shown in Table 5, the entangled quantum embedding with LR surpasses all others at the type level, revealing complementary strengths between classical and quantum approaches.

2.6 1-Qubit Embedding Ablation

To evaluate the contribution of each structural feature in isolation, we trained single-qubit circuits encoding only one feature under the same logistic decoder. Table 2 reports the Creole and Not-Creole F_1 scores for each 1-qubit embedding.

Table 2. F_1 scores for Creole and Not-Creole using single-feature (1-qubit) embeddings.

Feature	$F_{1,\text{Creole}}$	$F_{1,\neg\text{Creole}}$
Syllable_Complexity (1-qubit)	0.35	0.05
Entropy (1-qubit)	0.51	0.05
Vowel_Ratio (1-qubit)	0.81	0.09

Among single-feature embeddings, *vowel ratio* achieves the strongest Creole discrimination ($F_1 = 0.81$) and the highest minority-class score ($F_1 = 0.09$). Entropy offers moderate Creole performance ($F_1 = 0.51$) but no gain on Not-Creole, while syllable complexity performs worst overall ($F_1 = 0.35$; $F_1 = 0.05$). The relatively low scores across all one-feature embeddings highlight that no single structural cue is sufficient for robust token-level separation, motivating the move to multi-feature embeddings.

2.7 2-Qubit Entanglement Effects

We next evaluated pairwise feature embeddings using both product-state (no entanglement) and entangled 2-qubit circuits for each feature pair. Table 3 reports the Creole and Not-Creole F_1 scores for all six configurations, alongside our final 3-qubit entangled result for reference.

Two trends emerge:

1. **No entanglement, no improvement over 1-qubit.** The product-state 2-qubit scores are roughly in line with the better-performing single-feature models, indicating that simply combining two features without entanglement offers little additional discrimination. In some cases, the second feature appears to *reduce* clarity, likely because unentangled qubits encode each feature independently, so any conflicting cues act more like noise than reinforcement.

2. **Entanglement consistently boosts both classes.** Adding IsingXX entangling gates ($\pi/2$ rotation) between adjacent qubits produces marked improvements for all feature pairs, especially in minority-class F_1. For example, *(entropy, vowel ratio)* jumps from (0.84, 0.10) to (0.95, 0.19). These gains suggest that the gates allow the circuit to represent joint amplitude correlations between features that product-state circuits cannot encode.

Table 3. F_1 scores for Creole and Not-Creole using 2-qubit product-state vs. entangled embeddings, and the full 3-qubit entangled model.

Features	Entangled?	$F_{1,\text{Creole}}$	$F_{1,\neg\text{Creole}}$
Entropy, Vowel_ Ratio	No	0.84	0.10
	Yes	0.95	0.19
Entropy, Syllable_ Complexity	No	0.67	0.09
	Yes	0.94	0.20
Vowel_ Ratio, Syllable_ Complexity	No	0.89	0.16
	Yes	0.94	0.20
All Three Features (3-qubit entangled)		**0.93**	**0.19**

While certain entangled 2-qubit pairs (e.g., *entropy, vowel ratio*) achieve very high Creole F_1, they necessarily omit one structural feature and thus cannot encode all interaction terms present in the full (H, V, S) space. The 3-qubit entangled configuration preserves every pairwise and three-way interaction in a single circuit, enabling a feature-complete comparison against classical baselines. This ensures that any observed performance differences are attributable to the *representation* (classical vs. quantum) rather than differences in feature coverage, and supports our decision to adopt the 3-feature entangled model as the primary QNLP architecture for evaluation.

2.8 Token-Level Performance at a Glance

Table 4 summarizes the end-to-end token-level results for our three final pipelines using the same (H, V, S) features and a logistic decoder. The *classical* model attains the strongest overall scores (macro-F_1 = 0.60, accuracy = 0.90), with high Creole F_1 and moderate Not-Creole F_1. The two *quantum* embeddings remain competitive: the product-state variant trades a small drop in Creole F_1 for the best minority recall (0.53), while the entangled variant slightly improves Creole F_1 over product-state but gives back some Not-Creole recall (0.44).

A look at recalls clarifies the trade-offs. Creole recall is highest for the classical model (0.91), followed by the entangled (0.88) and product-state (0.87) embeddings. For the minority class, the ranking flips: product-state achieves the best Not-Creole recall (0.53), classical is next (0.47), and entangled is lowest (0.44).

Table 4. Token-level results on the filtered 7,843-token evaluation set (punctuation removed).

Pipeline	$F_{1,\text{Creole}}$	$F_{1,\neg\text{Creole}}$	M−F_1	Acc.
Classical (3 features, LR)	0.94	0.25	0.60	0.90
Quantum (3-qubit, product-state, LR)	0.92	0.21	0.57	0.85
Quantum (3-qubit, entangled, LR)	0.93	0.19	0.56	0.86

Given the skewed gold distribution (≈96% Creole), these shifts in recall dominate macro-F_1, explaining why the classical model leads in aggregate despite quantum embeddings capturing non-linear feature interactions.

Crucially, token-level metrics conflate frequency with generalization. In Sect. 3, we show that *type-level* evaluation tells a different story: the entangled embedding substantially reduces the number of distinct lexical types that are ever misclassified (284 vs. 404 for classical and 509 for product-state), and it uniquely fixes large swaths of types that both classical and product-state models miss. This motivates analyzing performance through the lens of types, where robustness to unseen or infrequent forms matters most in mixed-language settings.

3 Type-Level Error Analysis

Token-level scores provide a coarse view of model behavior, but obscure the fact that many errors are concentrated on a small subset of lexical types that recur frequently in the corpus. To better understand systematic strengths and weaknesses, we perform a *type-level* error analysis.

3.1 Methodology

Starting from the 7,843-token test set, we collapse tokens into unique types after normalizing for case and diacritics. This yields N_T distinct types, each associated with a gold label (*Creole* or *Not-Creole*). When an identical string appears in both datasets but with different labels (e.g., French in one, Creole in the other), we treat these as distinct homophonous types, each with its own label, rather than merging them into a single type.

For each pipeline (Classical, Quantum product-state, Quantum entangled), we then determine:

1. Types *correctly* classified by all models.
2. Types *misclassified* by all models (*common errors*).
3. Types misclassified by only one model (*exclusive errors*).
4. Pairwise overlaps of misclassified types between models.

We report counts for each category. This approach reveals whether gains in token-level F_1 translate into broader lexical coverage or merely reclassify high-frequency tokens.

3.2 Exclusive Vs. Common Errors

Table 5 summarizes the total number of misclassified types for each model and the exclusive overlaps between error sets.

Table 5. Type-level misclassification counts and exclusive overlaps between error sets for the Classical, Quantum Product-state, and Quantum Entangled pipelines.

Error set	# Types
Classical only	0
Product-state only	145
Entangled only	78
Common to all three	166
Classical ∩ Product only (not Entangled)	198
Classical ∩ Entangled only (not Product)	40
Product ∩ Entangled only (not Classical)	0
Total type errors—Classical	404
Total type errors—Product-state	509
Total type errors—Entangled	**284**
Total types - Creole	1762
Total types - Not Creole	173
Total types	1 935

Several patterns are immediately noteworthy:

- **Entangled has the fewest total type errors** (284), far below Classical (404) and especially Product-state (509). This implies that quantum embeddings are not uniformly beneficial. On the contrary, mapping the three features into a quantum feature space without entanglement (product-state) can *harm* type-level accuracy compared to the Classical baseline, indicating that quantum representation alone is not sufficient; the observed gains appear only when entanglement is introduced, an effect that is only possible within the quantum feature space—at which point we observe not just error correction but the strongest overall type-level performance. This highlights that quantum circuits can yield both improvements and degradations: they can degrade performance if used without feature entanglement, yet deliver clear gains when entanglement is leveraged effectively.
- **Classical has no unique type errors**, meaning every type it misclassifies is also misclassified by at least one quantum model. This indicates a complete overlap between the Classical error set and the union of quantum error sets: the quantum pipelines, whether entangled or not, never recover a type that the Classical model alone gets wrong. Instead, they either match the Classical

errors or introduce new ones of their own, depending on the embedding configuration. This suggests that the representational shift into quantum space fundamentally changes decision boundaries rather than refining the Classical model's existing strengths.

- The largest exclusive overlap is **Classical ∩ Product only** (198 types): types that both non-entangled models get wrong but the Entangled model gets right. This is a strong indicator of the added representational benefit of feature entanglement, which seems to resolve specific lexical clusters missed by both simpler baselines.
- **Product-state only** errors are numerous (145 types), consistent with the idea that without entanglement, the quantum model overgeneralizes structural cues, producing many avoidable misclassifications.
- **Entangled only** errors (78 types) are relatively rare and represent the smallest exclusive set among the three pipelines, reinforcing its overall robustness.
- There are **no types in the Product ∩ Entangled only** set. When both quantum variants misclassify a type, the Classical model is always wrong as well. This suggests that certain types are systematically challenging regardless of representation.

Even before a detailed qualitative error analysis, these counts reveal that type-level error reduction is the most visible gain from entanglement. While token-level F_1 scores in Table 4 show only modest improvements over the Classical baseline, the Entangled model demonstrates markedly better lexical coverage, recovering entire sets of types that remain problematic for both the Classical and Product-state pipelines. This suggests that in real-world deployment, where models regularly encounter unseen types, entanglement could yield more reliable generalization than token-level metrics alone might imply.

3.3 Errors Introduced by the Product-State Model

The **145 types** misclassified exclusively by the product-state quantum pipeline represent **7.49%** of the total 1 935 types in the dataset. Breaking this down by gold label:

- **Creole types:** 138/1762 (**7.83%** of all Creole types)
- **Non-Creole types:** 7/173 (**4.05%** of all non-Creole types)

While the percentage is smaller for non-Creole types, the two groups reveal distinct error tendencies:

- **Creole types** are dominated by proper nouns (place names, personal names) and foreign-origin items adapted to Creole orthography (e.g. *Chelchè*, *Jézikri*, *Jamayik*, *Brital*). These often contain digraphs, accented vowels, or consonant clusters atypical of French, yet still share partial orthographic cues with it, potentially misleading the product-state model's decision boundary.

- **Non-Creole types** are mostly standard French lexical items or compounds (*générations*, *surveillance*) and semantically marked borrowings (*urne/ballot*, *fossoyeur/gravedigger*), some with morphological complexity or orthographic patterns absent from Creole.

This suggests that the **absence of entanglement** leaves the product-state circuit vulnerable to:

1. Over-sensitivity to surface orthographic similarity with the opposite class.
2. Misinterpretation of rare or morphologically complex forms that deviate from the dominant class's core distribution.

The fact that most of these tokens are correctly classified by the entangled model strengthens the interpretation that entanglement helps integrate feature interactions in a way that disambiguates rare or orthographically deceptive types.

4 Effect of Feature Entanglement at the Type Level

At the type level, the clearest advantage of entanglement appears when examining types that both the classical and product-state pipelines misclassify but that the entangled model predicts correctly. The **198 types** misclassified by the product-state and classical models but not by the entangled model represent 10.23% of the total 1 935 types in the dataset. Breaking this down by gold label:

- **Creole types:** 185/1762 (10.5% of all Creole types)
- **Not-Creole types:** 13/173 (7.51% of all non-Creole types)

Table 6 presents representative examples from this exclusive intersection. All items in this set were consistently misclassified by the first two pipelines, yet correctly tagged by the entangled model.

These types include high-frequency function words, polyfunctional lexical items, compounds, proper names, and morphologically complex forms. Several are proper names that have not been orthographically adapted into Creole and/or appear with identical spelling across multiple languages. Others bear orthographic cues associated with French (e.g. capitalization, accented vowels, French-like consonant clusters) yet are labeled as Creole in the gold annotation due to their sentence-level context. It is important to note that *our models do not have access to this context*—classification is based solely on three intra-token features (entropy, vowel ratio, syllable complexity). Consequently, the fact that the entangled model "rescues" these cases is a fortunate coincidence: the same token could just as easily have been misclassified as Not-Creole had it appeared in the dataset as a Not-Creole type. From a methodological standpoint, this is expected in our proof-of-concept setup, where the aim is to test whether feature entanglement can yield measurable gains, not to produce context-aware, state-of-the-art LID.

Table 6. Representative types misclassified by both the classical and product-state models but correctly tagged under entanglement.

Token	Gold Class	Example Type
y	Creole	High-freq. function word
w	Creole	High-freq. function word
toubannman	Creole	Lexical adverb
bagay	Creole	Polyfunctional noun
vréyé	Creole	Verb (French-like orthography)
bannann	Creole	Common noun
manmay	Creole	Common noun
LEBIELLE	Creole	Proper name
BERNABE	Creole	Proper name
jwenn	Creole	Verb
mai	Not_Creole	Month name
président	Not_Creole	Loanword, accented vowel
en	Not_Creole	French preposition
Mai	Not_Creole	Month name, capitalized
OU	Not_Creole	Uppercase French coord. conj.
QUATRE-VINGT	Not_Creole	French numeral
Voie	Not_Creole	French noun
aussi/too	Not_Creole	Code-mixed token
autorités	Not_Creole	French plural noun
die	Not_Creole	English translation

4.1 Residual Classical–Entangled Overlap

A small set of types is misclassified by both the classical and entangled pipelines, but correctly classified by the product-state model, indicating cases where feature entanglement does not confer an advantage over the classical baseline.

The **40 types** in this overlap represent **2.07%** of the total 1 935 types in the test set. Breaking this down by gold label:

- **Creole types:** 22/1762 (**1.25%** of all Creole types)
- **Not-Creole types:** 18/173 (**1.02%** of all Not-Creole types) (Table 7)

Several patterns emerge:

- These residual errors are rare overall, suggesting that the classical and entangled models typically diverge in their mistakes.
- Most are **Creole types** with morphological complexity or compounding (e.g. `djoubak-tala`, `linivèsité-a`, `vakabonnajri-tala`), which may yield ambiguous intra-token statistics.

Table 7. Representative types misclassified by both the classical and entangled pipelines but correctly classified by the product-state model.

Token	Gold Class	Example Type
djoubak-tala	Creole	Noun + demonstrative
linivèsité-a	Creole	Definite NP (noun + article)
sébwet-lin	Creole	Hyphenated compound noun
vakabonnajri-tala	Creole	Noun + demonstrative
pwogré-tala	Creole	Noun + demonstrative
etc.	Not_Creole	Abbreviation / internationalism
commune	Not_Creole	French noun (municipality)
Efel	Not_Creole	Proper name
Saint-Lucia	Not_Creole	Country name
Fête	Not_Creole	French common noun

- The **Not-Creole types** often include proper names, place names, and French nouns whose orthography is shared across languages (e.g. `Saint-Lucia`, `commune`, `Fête`).
- Abbreviations and internationalisms (`etc.`, `Efel`) remain challenging due to their orthographic neutrality.

4.2 New Type Errors Introduced by Entanglement

A limited set of types is misclassified only by the entangled model, indicating cases where feature entanglement shifts decision boundaries in disadvantageous ways.

Table 8. Representative types correctly classified by the product-state model but misclassified by the entangled variant.

Token	Gold Class	Example Type
1é	Creole	Numeric form with diacritic
ou	Creole	High-freq. function word
osi	Creole	Polyfunctional adverb
o	Creole	Short function word
lè-a	Creole	Definite NP (article + noun)
lespri-yo	Creole	Noun + plural marker
lutter	Not_Creole	French verb (infinitive)
officer	Not_Creole	English translation
nouvelle	Not_Creole	French feminine adjective/noun
nom/name	Not_Creole	Code-mixed form

The **78 types** misclassified exclusively by the entangled pipeline represent **4.03%** of the total 1 935 types in the test set. Breaking this down by gold label:

- **Creole types:** 56/1 762 (**3.18%** of all Creole types)
- **Not-Creole types:** 22/173 (**12.72%** of all Not-Creole types) (Table 8)

Several patterns emerge:

- These entangled-only errors are rare overall, showing that entanglement does not typically introduce large numbers of new mistakes.
- Most are **Creole types** with multi-morphemic or cliticised forms (e.g. `lè-a`, `lespri-yo`) or orthographic irregularities (`lé`), where feature interactions may yield unexpected similarity scores.
- A smaller subset are **French or English borrowings** (e.g. `lutter`, `officer`, `nouvelle`) whose internal statistics align more closely with Creole types under the entangled encoding.
- Many are short function words or hybrids (`o`, `ou`, `nom/name`) that sit near decision boundaries in the feature space.

From a linguistic perspective, these cases share a common property of *internal heterogeneity* (i.e., mixed orthography, morphological complexity, or inflected borrowings) which is not fully captured by our current feature set. Since our objective here is to evaluate whether entanglement offers a measurable benefit in a minimal, interpretable setting, such errors are not unexpected. A next step for context-aware QNLP would be to incorporate subword morphological embeddings or sentence-level features to address these limitations.

5 Discussion

Our pipeline deliberately frames each Creole vs. Not-Creole decision as an isolated, token-level classification task, without access to sentence- or document-level context. This choice was motivated by two constraints: (1) maintaining quantum circuits compact enough for deployment on NISQ-era hardware, and (2) isolating the effect of three interpretable intra-token features—entropy, vowel ratio, and syllable complexity—when embedded in product-state and entangled configurations.

This design enables clear attribution of gains or losses to the quantum embedding itself, but it also leaves certain error clusters unresolved. In particular, short, high-frequency function words shared across languages remain difficult to disambiguate without contextual cues. In a practical language-identification system, token-level predictions from our quantum model could be combined with sequence-level smoothing or hybrid classical–quantum architectures to incorporate surrounding context.

Restricting the embedding to three features allowed a direct mapping from each feature to a single-qubit rotation, keeping circuit depth minimal, but inevitably limited representational richness. Type-level error patterns suggest that morphologically complex words, longer compounds, and orthographically French-like borrowings could benefit from additional descriptors such as subword frequency profiles, morphological segmentation, or stress-pattern cues. Incorporating these while preserving interpretability is a natural next step.

Future Directions

Building on these findings, we see four immediate avenues for extension:

- **Context-aware QNLP:** Embed the current quantum token representation in hybrid sequence models to combine intra- and inter-token cues.
- **Expanded feature sets:** Incorporate additional linguistically interpretable features—morphological, prosodic, and distributional—while balancing circuit complexity with NISQ constraints.
- **Entanglement strategies:** Systematically compare different multi-qubit entangling patterns to determine whether the gains observed here generalize across correlation structures.
- **Cross-lingual transfer:** Evaluate portability to other Creole and closely related language pairs, including low-resource code-switching scenarios.

Overall, combining compact, interpretable quantum embeddings with carefully designed entanglement yields measurable type-level gains in low-resource language identification. This proof of concept illustrates how QNLP can bridge theoretical quantum advantages and concrete linguistic utility, especially in settings where context is limited but token-internal cues are strong.

6 Conclusion

We presented the first QNLP proof of concept for token-level language identification in Martinican Creole, comparing a character-bigram baseline, a classical logistic model on three interpretable structural features (entropy, vowel ratio, syllable complexity), and a compact three-qubit variational circuit in product-state and entangled configurations.

While token-level metrics show the classical model slightly ahead of the entangled variant, the type-level analysis reveals the opposite: entanglement reduces the number of distinct error types, rescuing items consistently misclassified by both classical and product-state pipelines. These rescued types are heterogeneous (frequent Creole items, compounds, and proper names with cross-lingual orthography).

The small set of errors unique to the entangled model (4.03% of types) often involves internally varied forms whose feature profiles trigger over-sensitivity to spurious correlations. A residual overlap with the classical model (2.07% of types) points to persistent cross-lingual orthographic ambiguity and complex derived forms.

These findings demonstrate that even minimal quantum embeddings can capture non-linear intra-token correlations beyond the reach of n-gram baselines and simple linear models, yielding measurable type-level gains in a low-resource, hardware-friendly setting. Such gains support the integration of entanglement into future low-resource LID pipelines—especially where context is scarce but token-internal cues are strong.

References

1. Bonan, C.: The Core Grammar of Guadeloupean Creole. A Descriptive and Comparative Approach. Università Ca'Foscari Venezia (2013)
2. Cover, T.M., Thomas, J.A., et al.: Entropy, relative entropy and mutual information. Elem. Inf. Theor. **2**(1), 12–13 (1991)
3. Jaech, A., Mulcaire, G., Ostendorf, M., Smith, N.A.: A neural model for language identification in code-switched tweets. In: Proceedings of the Second Workshop on Computational Approaches to Code Switching, pp. 60–64 (2016)
4. Maddieson, I.: Consonant inventories. The World Atlas of Language Structures Online (2013)
5. Maddieson, I.: Vowel quality inventories. In: The World Atlas of Language Structures Online (2013)
6. Molina, G., et al.: Overview for the second shared task on language identification in code-switched data. arXiv preprint arXiv:1909.13016 (2019)
7. Myers-Scotton, C.: Constructing the frame in intrasentential codeswitching. Multilingua **11**(1), 101–127 (1992)
8. Poplack, S.: "sometimes i'll start a sentence in spanish y termino en español": toward a typology of code-switching. Linguistics **51**(s1), 11–14 (2013)
9. Schramm, M.: The Emergence of Creole Syllable Structure: A Cross-Linguistic Study, vol. 554. Walter de Gruyter GmbH & Co. KG (2014)
10. Shannon, C.E.: A mathematical theory of communication. Bell Syst. Tech. J. **27**(3), 379–423 (1948)

Toward an Algebraic Implementation of a Language Faculty

Juan Uriagereka(✉)

University of Maryland, College Park, MD 20742, USA
juan@umd.edu

Abstract. This piece sketches a framework for modeling the language faculty as an algebraically implemented physical system grounded in Fourier duality. Drawing on insights from phonology, syntax, and neuroscience, the approach treats lexical categories as unitary 2×2 matrices (the "Chomskys"), whose projections into derivational space (the "Paulis") preserve information across domains. By leveraging the Fourier transform to relate temporally localized neural events to spatially distributed representations, the system models syntactic composition as operations on conserved, observable states. This allows for a treatment of lexical access with implications for neurophysiological plausibility across oscillatory bands. Extending beyond phonological organization, the model presents a syntax graph and a candidate "Chomsky/Pauli group" ($\boldsymbol{G_{CP}}$) that capture combinatorial constraints. Lexical items are treated as encrypted roots, recoverable through matrix scalings that correlate with cortical activation dynamics. The synthesis of signal theory, linguistic computation, and neural architecture attempts a path toward understanding how language is physically instantiated in a high-dimensional cognitive system without external supervision.

Keywords: Fourier duality · Neural representation of language · Minimalist derivations · Chomsky-Pauli Group · Neural oscillations in syntax

1 Introduction

Linguistics and Neuroscience refer to the language faculty as a *system*. But what kind of biological system sustains the long-range dependencies, symbolic stability, and error-resilient productivity that define human language? In classical computational models, including artificial neural networks, structure is maintained by design: through massive data exposure, supervised learning in successful instances, and a constrained architecture with external enforcement of structural symmetry and correction. Even if lacking such supervisory apparatus, infants rapidly converge on highly structured hierarchical grammars that permit infinite productivity and characteristic novelty, often in the absence of any practical consequence. While this raises classical "poverty of the stimulus" argument for innateness, that itself does not address how whatever component of the system may be a priori is stable, not succumbing to entropy.

D. Cavar et al. (Eds.): QNLPAI 2025, CCIS 2659, pp. 204–233, 2026.
https://doi.org/10.1007/978-3-032-13883-5_12

An approach to that needs to recognize that classical physical systems are not naturally computational in a strong sense: they neither preserve symbols nor maintain coherence over time without artificial constraints. The only known physical systems that maintain stability – to yield systematicity from within – appear to be non-classical. In turn, quantum coherence, entanglement, and symmetry protection offer in-principle mechanisms for maintaining long-range correlations and discrete symbolic states in noisy environments. Although a (hot) brain need not perform full-scale quantum computing nor neurons be qubits, some aspects of cognition involving globally consistent symbolic systems may rely on biologically instantiated quantum constraints, now that various aspects of life and cognition have been argued to present such traits.[1] These may possibly take the form of quantum regulators that stabilize high-dimensional state spaces and support internal structure projection, among other relevant traits.

With language implemented through a physical system that resists noise/instability, rather than abandoning the insights of generative grammar, quantum realism invites a physical explanation of how symbolic behavior may be organically instantiated without external control. Challenging classical approximations as self-evident, it becomes relevant what kind of physical process could give rise to the precision, generalizability, and long-range coherence that human language demands. The present approach is based on Fourier Transform (FT) duals familiar from phonetic spectrograms.[2]

An integral transform, the FT takes a function to another (complex-valued) function addressing to what extent various frequencies are present in the original (e.g. the vowel formants in a spectrogram). In general, functions localized in a time domain have FTs spread out across the frequency domain and vice-versa (the Uncertainty Principle). While the usefulness of FTs in acoustic phonetics needs no emphasis here, the present idea is to generalize that to domains whose information is encoded through neurobiologically relevant levels of representation (phonology, syntax, semantics, etc.), presuming that observable neural oscillations carry the process at diverse regions, timescales, frequency bands, or other relevant systemic states.

The present proposal shares much with several others for which vector spaces are crucial. The most direct are Quantum Cognition (Busemeyer & Bruza (2012)), the DisCoCat model of Coecke, Sadrzadeh, & Clark (2013), and of course minimalist syntax as formulated in Marcolli, Chomsky, & Berwick (2025). Indebtedness to the latter is a priori obvious and will be emphasized below as relevant, but the intellectual relevance of the other two approaches is also significant, as are some differences that will be pointed out at the end. The presentation will now turn into the basic proposal (Sect. 2), then to sketch the algebraic approach in Sect. 3, generalizing pertinent questions in Sect. 4. Section 5 will extend the algebra, as a segway to a Hilbert space in Sect. 6. Section 7 sketches a treatment of chains within that vector space, with a phrasal consequence thereof being shown in Sect. 8. Section 9 draws some comparisons with related models and conclusions ensue in the tenth and final section.

1 Including photosynthesis, enzyme catalysis, olfaction, navigation. See Álvarez et al. 2024.

2 While the literature on the transform is vast, e.g. Goldberg 2009 provides useful background.

2 The Basic Proposal

An approach to phonological considerations in FT terms generalizes the acoustic situation mentioned in the previous section to systemic phonemic conditions.[3] Compare a back vowel like tense /u/ and a plosive like /k/, to ponder to what extent brains process their information differently. Unlike vowels residing in well-defined acoustic representational spaces, plosives depend less on auditory than somatosensory motor feedback. Resonance from varying tongue position allows us to distribute phonemes from front to back stops, transitioning from alveolar to velar fricatives, on to the glides (front /y/, back /w/), into vocalic territory: front /i/, through mid /a/, to back /u/. Although further articulators (like nasalization) may also hold, within a vocal tract systemic pairs obtain, where the paired manner of articulation may be quite similar, though not the realization of each segment: shorter, laxer, more punctual vs. longer, tenser, more continuant. We may treat such correlations in FT terms – then of a more abstract sort than for the acoustic case. While distance between harmonics determines vowel variants arising from vocal tract configurations, some phonological distinctions crucially arise from *combining* essential characteristics, with glides sharing properties of both vocalic and consonantal patterns, while glottal segments may be treated as neither vocalic nor consonantal.

It is abstract arrangements of that sort that led phonologists to distinctive features. For the case just mentioned, consider the systematization in Halle & Chomsky (1968):

a. [+consonantal, -syllabic] "stop" b. [-consonantal, +syllabic] "tense vowel"

c. [+consonantal, +syllabic] "glide" d. [-consonantal, -syllabic] "glottal" (1)

In a system as in (1), notions like "stop" are a shorthand to denote a featural combination, which in the more abstract terms we are pursuing could be formally expressed as in (2). The expression with *e*, *i*, and π there stems from Euler's Formula, so basically (2) is equivalent to (3). In sum, thus construed "consonantal"/"syllabic" attributes stand in a FT, with these two as dimensions orthogonal to one another – consonantality being sensitive to the time domain (where the timing of turbulent bursts of different qualities can be evaluated) and syllabicity, instead, to the frequency domain (where different vowels are captured in terms of fundamental frequency variations).

a. $[\boldsymbol{e}^{i\,2\pi}, \boldsymbol{e}^{i\,3/2\pi}]$ "stop" b. $[\boldsymbol{e}^{i\,\pi}, \boldsymbol{e}^{i\,1/2\pi}]$ "tense vowel"

c. $[\boldsymbol{e}^{i\,2\pi}, \boldsymbol{e}^{i\,1/2\pi}]$ "glide" d. $[\boldsymbol{e}^{i\,\pi}, \boldsymbol{e}^{i\,3/2\pi}]$ "glottal" (2)

a. $[\mathbf{1}, -\boldsymbol{i}]$ "stop" b. $[-\mathbf{1}, \boldsymbol{i}]$ "tense vowel" c. $[\mathbf{1}, \boldsymbol{i}]$ "glide" d. $[-\mathbf{1}, -\boldsymbol{i}]$ "glottal" (3)

[3] For a general introduction to phonetics and phonology, see for instance Zsiga (2013).

In this sense, an archetypical stop is consonantal and non-syllabic, while the opposite is the case for a corresponding tense vowel that is non-consonantal and syllabic. But crucially the dimensions can both be present (in glides) or absent (in glottals), at once.

3 An Algebraic Approach

Representing phonological stuff as in the substantive (1) or the more formal (2)/(3) makes a difference, bearing on an understanding of, for instance, metrical feet. Halle & Idsardi (1995) note how languages group syllables into such feet, size ranging from unary to unbounded (some syllables remaining unfooted). Idsardi (2008) shows how the possible metrical footings for a string of n syllables is *Fib*(2n) (falling within the Fibonacci sequence). For example, a two-syllable string can be non-exhaustively footed in five ways (or Fib(4)): (xx), (x)(x), (x)x, x(x), and xx), while one of three can be footed in thirteen ways (or Fib(6)), etc. This means that only half of the Fibonacci sequence constitutes a valid solution to the creation of non-exhaustive syllabic footings, for some reason. Relevantly, the Fibonacci Q-matrix $\begin{bmatrix} 0 & 1 \\ 1 & 1 \end{bmatrix}$ (Gould (1981)) can be mapped to a Lindenmayer-system,[4] with corresponding grand sums of entries in powers $\begin{bmatrix} 0 & 1 \\ 1 & 1 \end{bmatrix}^n$ as in (4) conforming to derivational iterations (Medeiros (2012), Fig. 1).

$$\underbrace{\begin{bmatrix} 0 & 1 \\ 1 & 1 \end{bmatrix}^0 = \begin{bmatrix} 1 & 0 \\ 0 & 1 \end{bmatrix}}_{\text{Sum: 2}}, \underbrace{\begin{bmatrix} 0 & 1 \\ 1 & 1 \end{bmatrix}^1}_{\text{Sum: 3}}, \underbrace{\begin{bmatrix} 0 & 1 \\ 1 & 1 \end{bmatrix}^2 = \begin{bmatrix} 1 & 1 \\ 1 & 2 \end{bmatrix}}_{\text{Sum: 5}}, \underbrace{\begin{bmatrix} 0 & 1 \\ 1 & 1 \end{bmatrix}^3 = \begin{bmatrix} 1 & 2 \\ 2 & 3 \end{bmatrix}}_{\text{Sum: 8}}, \ldots \underbrace{\begin{bmatrix} 0 & 1 \\ 1 & 1 \end{bmatrix}^n}_{\text{Sum: Fib(n)}} \quad (4)$$

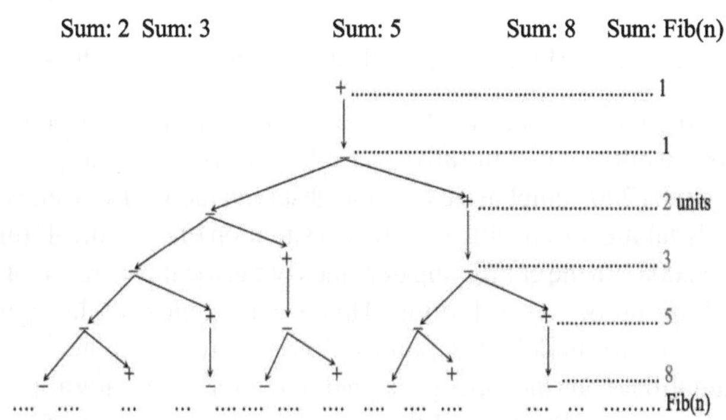

Fig. 1. A Fibonacci L-system.

[4] The classic introduction to these systems is Prusinkiewicz & Lindenmayer, A. (1990).

Curiously, powers of the inverse Fibonacci $\begin{bmatrix} -1 & 1 \\ 1 & 0 \end{bmatrix}^n$ yield the signed Fibonacci sequence (Sloane A039834) as well as Idsardi's – in its positive values:

$$\begin{bmatrix} -1 & 1 \\ 1 & 0 \end{bmatrix}^0 = \begin{bmatrix} 1 & 0 \\ 0 & 1 \end{bmatrix}, \begin{bmatrix} -1 & 1 \\ 1 & 0 \end{bmatrix}^1, \begin{bmatrix} -1 & 1 \\ 1 & 0 \end{bmatrix}^2 = \begin{bmatrix} 2 & -1 \\ -1 & 1 \end{bmatrix}, \begin{bmatrix} -1 & 1 \\ 1 & 0 \end{bmatrix}^3 = \begin{bmatrix} -3 & 2 \\ 2 & -1 \end{bmatrix},$$
Sum: 2 Sum: 1 Sum: 1 Sum: 0

$$\begin{bmatrix} -1 & 1 \\ 1 & 0 \end{bmatrix}^4 = \begin{bmatrix} 5 & -3 \\ -3 & 2 \end{bmatrix}, \begin{bmatrix} -1 & 1 \\ 1 & 0 \end{bmatrix}^5 = \begin{bmatrix} -8 & 5 \\ 5 & -3 \end{bmatrix}, \begin{bmatrix} -1 & 1 \\ 1 & 0 \end{bmatrix}^6 = \begin{bmatrix} 13 & -8 \\ -8 & 5 \end{bmatrix}, \quad (5)$$
Sum: 1 Sum: –1 Sum: 2

$$\begin{bmatrix} -1 & 1 \\ 1 & 0 \end{bmatrix}^7 = \begin{bmatrix} -21 & 13 \\ 13 & -8 \end{bmatrix}, \begin{bmatrix} -1 & 1 \\ 1 & 0 \end{bmatrix}^8 = \begin{bmatrix} 34 & -21 \\ -21 & 13 \end{bmatrix}, \begin{bmatrix} -1 & 1 \\ 1 & 0 \end{bmatrix}^9 = \begin{bmatrix} -55 & 34 \\ 34 & -21 \end{bmatrix}, \ldots$$
Sum: –3 Sum: 5 Sum: –8

Subsequent sums: 13, -21, 34, -55, 89…

Idsardi's metrical sequence can be related to a property noted by Cassini in 1733: that the square of a Fibonacci number equals the product of "flanking" numbers ± 1.[5] Thus:

$$\mathrm{Fib}(n)^2 - \mathrm{Fib}(n-1) \cdot \mathrm{Fib}(n+1) = (-1)^n \quad (6)$$

This has the general form in (7) with consequence as in (8) (per the Binomial Theorem):

$$\text{a. If } n \text{ is even: } \mathrm{Fib}(n)^2 - 1 \qquad \text{b. If } n \text{ is odd: } \mathrm{Fib}(n)^2 + 1 \quad (7)$$

$$\text{a. } [\mathrm{Fib}(n) - 1][\mathrm{Fib}(n) + 1] = \mathrm{Fib}(n)^2 + \cancel{\mathrm{Fib}(n)} - 1 - \cancel{\mathrm{Fib}(n)}$$
$$\text{b. } [\mathrm{Fib}(n) - i][\mathrm{Fib}(n) + i] = \mathrm{Fib}(n)^2 + \cancel{i\,\mathrm{Fib}(n)} + 1 - \cancel{i\,\mathrm{Fib}(n)} \quad (8)$$

In other words, the binomial in (8a) – corresponding to even powers – involves real-valued roots, while the one in (8b) – for odd powers – has complex roots instead. Idsardi & Uriagereka 2009 emphasize how the observed facts arise from non-exhaustive footings, possibly taking the ensuing system to a situation of dynamical frustration in the sense of Binder (2008): in the conflicting demands of the local coherence of syllables vis-à-vis the word-level properties of footing. This is consistent with the signed Fibonacci sequence being used to model an exponential arising for damping considerations or their inverse: amplification (increasing a signal magnitude). A natural ensemble (like a tree) may grow exponentially (fractally) as in (4), but the version in (5) models a more dynamical situation: the system's manifestation in terms of a measurable (expressed through reals (8a)) vs. an implied but impossible-to-measure reality (expressed through complex values (8b)). This is particularly so if expressing (8) as in (9):

$$\text{a. } [\mathrm{Fib}(n) - 1][\mathrm{Fib}(n) + 1] = [\mathrm{Fib}(n) + e^{i\pi}][\mathrm{Fib}(n) + e^{i\,2\pi}]$$
$$\text{b. } [\mathrm{Fib}(n) - i][\mathrm{Fib}(n) + i] = [\mathrm{Fib}(n) + e^{i\,3/2\pi}][\mathrm{Fib}(n) + e^{i\,1/2\pi}] \quad (9)$$

[5] Thus: $5^2 - 1 = 3.\ 8$, $8^2 + 1 = 5.\ 13$, or $13^2 - 1 = 8.\ 21$, etc. See Idsardi & Uriagereka (2008).

Note that, in these terms, the $\pm$ 1, $\pm$ i summands in (9) can be seen as *systemic variables* in a FT, with the genuine but non-observable complex factors being what, in the algebra, allows for the scaling possibility of observing a real factor as its correlated dual.

It is also worth pointing out how $\begin{bmatrix} 0 & 1 \\ 1 & 1 \end{bmatrix}$ and its inverse $\begin{bmatrix} -1 & 1 \\ 1 & 0 \end{bmatrix}$ arise from interactions with categories of the algebraic form in (3), if these vectors are postulated as the diagonal of unitary matrices of the form $\begin{bmatrix} \pm 1 & 0 \\ 0 & \pm i \end{bmatrix}$. Direct products are then as follows:

Most common syllable types:

CV	C[VV]	C[VC]	C[[VV]C]	V	VC
$\begin{bmatrix} -1 & 0 \\ 0 & 1 \end{bmatrix}_{-1}$	$\begin{bmatrix} 1 & 0 \\ 0 & i \end{bmatrix}_{i}$	$\begin{bmatrix} -1 & 0 \\ 0 & -i \end{bmatrix}_{i}$	$\begin{bmatrix} 1 & 0 \\ 0 & 1 \end{bmatrix}_{1}$	$\begin{bmatrix} -1 & 0 \\ 0 & i \end{bmatrix}_{-i}$	$\begin{bmatrix} -1 & 0 \\ 0 & 1 \end{bmatrix}_{-1}$

(10)

The syllabic combinations in (10) arise via matrix multiplication of the segments in (3), when placed in the diagonal of 2 × 2 matrices, presuming bracketings as shown (from phonological observations of "rhymes" containing a "nucleus" and "coda", and corresponding "onsets"). For instance (11), where subindices indicate matrix determinants (*det.*);[6] real *det.*s in red, complex ones green. It can be seen how, while the syllabic nucleus in (11a) projects to a matrix with a complex *det.* i, the one in (11b) projects, instead, to a matrix with a real *det.* – a Hermitian matrix with real eigenvalues.

a. Calculation of C[VC] as $\begin{bmatrix} -1 & 0 \\ 0 & -i \end{bmatrix}_{i}$

$$\begin{bmatrix} -1 & 0 \\ 0 & -i \end{bmatrix}_{i}$$

$$[\mathrm{C}_{\mathrm{Onset}} \uparrow \mathrm{V'}\,]_{\mathrm{Projected\ Nucleus}}$$

$$\begin{bmatrix} 1 & 0 \\ 0 & -i \end{bmatrix}_{-i} \times \begin{bmatrix} -1 & 0 \\ 0 & 1 \end{bmatrix}_{-1}$$

$$[\mathrm{V} \uparrow \mathrm{C}\,]_{\mathrm{Nucleus}}$$

$$\begin{bmatrix} -1 & 0 \\ 0 & i \end{bmatrix}_{-i} \times \begin{bmatrix} 1 & 0 \\ 0 & -i \end{bmatrix}_{-i}$$

b. Calculation of C[[VV]C] as $\begin{bmatrix} 1 & 0 \\ 0 & 1 \end{bmatrix}_{1}$ (11)

$$\begin{bmatrix} 1 & 0 \\ 0 & 1 \end{bmatrix}_{1}$$

$$[\mathrm{C}_{\mathrm{Onset}} \uparrow \mathrm{V''}\,]_{\mathrm{Fully\ Projected\ Nucleus}}$$

$$\begin{bmatrix} 1 & 0 \\ 0 & -i \end{bmatrix}_{-i} \times \begin{bmatrix} 1 & 0 \\ 0 & i \end{bmatrix}_{i}$$

$$[\mathrm{V'} \uparrow \mathrm{C}_{\mathrm{Coda}}\,]_{\mathrm{Projected\ Nucleus}}$$

$$\begin{bmatrix} 1 & 0 \\ 0 & -1 \end{bmatrix}_{-1} \times \begin{bmatrix} 1 & 0 \\ 0 & -i \end{bmatrix}_{-i}$$

$$[\mathrm{V} \uparrow \mathrm{V}\,]_{\mathrm{Nucleus}}$$

$$\begin{bmatrix} -1 & 0 \\ 0 & i \end{bmatrix}_{-i} \times \begin{bmatrix} -1 & 0 \\ 0 & i \end{bmatrix}_{-i}$$

[6] Here, products of the diagonal entries minus that of the off-diagonal entries, zero for them.

These "swinging" *det*.s effectively indicate that some syllables (like CVVC or CV/VC) are easier to integrate into metrical feet than others (like CVV, CVC, or single V). As it turns out, the ones that work best are all Hermitian.

In (10) we are taking only extreme instances of "consonants" and "vowels", but syllables can also be projected from glides and some continuant consonants, or include multiple consonants in their boundaries, so the actual inventory of possible syllables is richer than indicated there – although in terms of the features in (1)/(3), instantiated as matrix diagonals, only the four *det*.s listed as subindexes in (10) arise: ± 1 and $\pm i$. This essentially yields two combinatorial states for the syllables in these algebraic terms: either ± 1 projections like (11a) or $\pm i$ projections like (11b). The point matters for rationalizing a situation as arising in the two polynomial factorizations in (9), one with real roots (a factor of ± 1) and one with complex roots (a factor of $\pm i$). Note that a scaling of the Fibonacci Q-matrix itself emerges as follows:[7]

$$\begin{bmatrix} -1 & 0 \\ 0 & -i \end{bmatrix}_{i} + \begin{bmatrix} -1 & 0 \\ 0 & i \end{bmatrix}_{-i} + \begin{bmatrix} 0 & 1 \\ 1 & 0 \end{bmatrix}_{-1} + \begin{bmatrix} 0 & 1 \\ 1 & 0 \end{bmatrix}_{-1} = 2\begin{bmatrix} -1 & 1 \\ 1 & 0 \end{bmatrix}_{-4} \qquad (12)$$

In short, the "seed" for a system that generates the signed Fibonacci expansion, characteristic of some (e.g., signal) amplifications, is effectively implicit in syllabic combinations of the summative sort in (12). Once that holds, the exponential behavior that (9) summarizes may be seen as resulting from this sort of sum, given that the power expansion of this aggregation is as in (5).

While it is not the goal of this piece to justify the syllabic assumptions in (10), scalar projection presumptions in (11), or rationale behind sums as in (12),[8] the point is that one can attempt such a reasoning with algebraic presumptions that generalize conditions as in (3) (per presumed translations as in (2)) to diagonal of matrices as in (10), which in turn may generalize under some aggregations to (12) and comparable situations. This provides a way to approach Idsardi's generalizations about metrical feet – while with the substantive feature format in (1) we hardly even get to first base.

4 Generalizing the Questions

Situations relevant to FT are not limited to acoustics. Whatever brain correlates carry information as abstractly generalized in (4), (5), (9), (11), or (12), indirectly reveal themselves as waves. To be sure, these are only waves of sorts, closer to so-called Mexican waves in our stadiums than physical waves. Unlike those,[9] quasi-waves are composed of discrete, semi-autonomous agents, each involved in local events that contribute to further engagement based on neighbors. While classical wave propagation is deterministic once boundary conditions are set, in quasi-waves it depends on thresholds, probabilistic influences, and internal states. That said, even these wave-like neuronal quasi-waves (as measured by various neuroimaging techniques) can be fruitfully modeled in terms of reaction-diffusion systems or coupled oscillators. While this is not the place to argue that in mathematical detail, the point is that FT conditions are relevant beyond instances of, for instance, error correction in communication channels.

[7] Also in many other such matrix sums as in (10) and their mirror images.

[8] Between combined syllables and "anti-syllables", as arise in their mirror image.

[9] Continuity is presumed here, bound by forces like tension or pressure.

The crux of the present proposal is to generalize an acoustic situation, for which temporal localization correlates in brain waves with spectral breadth (a short, punctual brain signal corresponds to a wide range of frequencies), while spatial localization correlates with spatial frequency (smooth/diffuse activation patterns correspond to low spatial frequency components). Already at the level of phonological representation we have gone more abstract than that, which means the neural-activity/systemic-representation correlate is less direct, as seen when discussing phonological segments aggregating into syllables and those into feet, with restrictions that a FT seeks to rationalize. Mutatis mutandis, the plan is to forge ahead in identical (if more abstract) terms into other levels of representation, of a syntactic sort.

To make progress in seeking a biophysical support for linguistic representations, it is useful to recall how in the classical *perceptron* algorithm that neural networks stem from, connected neurons are modeled as input/output weights. Realistically, though, more is needed. Consonant vs. vowel oppositions of the previous section were modeled in terms of matrices $\begin{bmatrix} 1 & 0 \\ 0 & -i \end{bmatrix}_{\textbf{Consonant}}$ and $\begin{bmatrix} -1 & 0 \\ 0 & i \end{bmatrix}_{\textbf{Vowel}}$, with a consonant a localized point in "phonological space", while the vowel acts as a process occurring over time, at its scale. Once we reach this level of abstraction, we may also interpret those very matrices lexically, as $\begin{bmatrix} 1 & 0 \\ 0 & -i \end{bmatrix}_{\textbf{Noun}}$ and $\begin{bmatrix} -1 & 0 \\ 0 & i \end{bmatrix}_{\textbf{Verb}}$. Just as we did for the consonant and vowel vector spaces, we could presume the noun and verb vector spaces to be FT transforms of one another, with different interpretive and neurological consequences as relevant. For the noun space, too, we need to rationalize some position analogue, ideally relating to conceptual rigidity; while for the verb space, instead, we must deal with the conjugate variable, ideally one affecting relational dynamics in its denotation.

In present terms, a noun like, say, *plant* can be idealized as a unit impulse: localized, individuated, and sharply distinguished from its surrounding continuum. In contrast, a verb can be modeled more like a plane wave: fully delocalized across the conceptual space defined by all its possible thematic combinations. As a verb, *to plant* denotes a collection of actions. On can plant *plants*, but also seeds, tubers, roots, cuttings, and even entire habitats, ideas, viruses, or bombs – one could also plant a rock, even though without any of the expected consequences associated to planting. The point is any theme combined with *plant* yields not just plant-plantings, but also seed-plantings, habitat-plantings, idea-plantings, and all the rest. That is, therefore, what *plant* arguably denotes as a verb: a diffuse concept with some normal distribution. If for the sharply defined noun (as a unit impulse) we expect rigidity associated to low entropy (denoting within a narrow ontological category), for the corresponding verb (as a plane wave of sorts calculated over its theme argument), we expect instead a more entropic distributional denotation, with its shape depending on contextual weights from expectations, which could fit a Gaussian distribution with a central tendency (biological planting), and standard deviation encompassing other senses, including "metaphorical" ones.

Evidently, even nouns introduce normally distributed predicates, with some plants, say, feeling more prototypical (*geraniums*) than others (*moss*). Then again, whatever lack of prototypicality comes from nouns is inherited to VPs taking them as themes: *planting moss* is less prototypical than *planting geraniums*, although the latter as such is not very prototypical either (no matter how archetypal geraniums themselves may be), as they are generally planted not from seeds but from cuttings. In short: the prototypicality of a VP predicate is some function of that of the verb (planting any plant is more prototypical than planting a virus or a bomb) *and* the prototypicality of its theme noun (planting corals, for instance, is a very elaborate process). Moreover, one can very naturally name many individuals rigidly denoted by noun phrases (*since General Sherman is such an imposing sequoia, I call my geranium just "Sweet Jane"*), but it would be weird to name whatever a verb phrase like *planting geraniums or corals* denotes.

A technical proposal could be as follows – the intention being merely to get these formulations to help model corresponding processing effects:

a. Rigid NP: $plant_{noun} \cdot \delta(\vec{x} - \vec{x}_0)$

[for δ a (Dirac) unit impulse function and $_0$ some context]

b. Diffuse VP: $plant_{verb} \cdot \mathcal{N}(\vec{x}; \mu, \Sigma)$

[for $\mathcal{N}$ the multivariate normal distribution, where μ is the prototypical planting and Σ encodes how broadly extended readings are admitted]

(13)

Thus, verbs with broad denotational distributions (*plant, run, make…*) impose higher inferential loads than those with narrow distributions (*farm* in the planting sense, *whistle, decapitate…*), so the information entropy is lower in that direction of tighter interpretation. This echoes trade-offs in Zipf's law, with common verbs more polysemous (entropic and distributionally spread) than rare ones. Model-wise, the key is the relation between δ-functions as in (13a), sharply localized in a semantic vector space, and probability distributions over thematic roles, where the theme argument shifts the distribution's shape and center. One may even model metaphoric transfer as a shift in the mean of the distribution, broadening variance. Essential is the correlation between: (i) a distribution, centered at some location x_0 as in (13a), in some feature space (semantic or otherwise), with localized, rigid, nouns spiking; and (ii) a multivariate normal distribution as in (13b), with vector $\vec{x}$ sensitive to some mean μ within a covariance matrix Σ – for how much the verb's meaning spreads across its argument structure.

While the approach contrasts rigid vs. flexible/generalized meanings, the intent is more ambitious, aligning with the architectural concerns of grounding levels of representation within mind/brain activities. Curiously, Broca's (expressive) aphasics retain appropriately used nouns more so than corresponding verbs.[10] In terms of (13), such patients would retain the δ s that index space but fail to integrate the plane wave functions N. . It is this lexical duality that parallels the time-frequency trade-offs in signal processing, so we also expect measurable neuroimaging contrasting in how these categories are processed. While not necessary, a collinear mapping is natural between something like (13a) and a spike-like neural event (the sort one typically associates to ballistic gestures), on one hand, and something like (13b) and a distributed neural event (as arising from tetanization). In the converse mapping, a ballistic neural code cannot integrate

[10] For a general introduction on various kinds of aphasia, see Le & Lui (2023).

smoothly across long perceptual windows; and vice-versa, a smeared distribution lacks any use for microsecond-level timing. A coding reversal of, say, the vowel/stop mapping would be neuro-physiologically nonsensical, using a high-timing-resolution system to parse smeared frequencies, or a low-timing-resolution integrative system to identify transients. While in the case of lexical representations there are no percepts like phonemes to blame on acoustics, presuppositions about active-maintenance in short-term memory seem relevant. Thus, while a name (or a rigid indexical like *this*) is instantaneous at its scale, the meaning of *plant this / Sweet Jane in moist soil after removing leaves adding a rooting hormone* is as open-ended as one cares to specify the event (which can also compose to beneficiaries, agents, causers, etc.).

In classical Hebbian dynamics, synaptic strengthening is a consequence of neuronal firing, which the perceptron model expressed through real-valued synaptic efficacy changes. But in real neuronal systems, oscillatory potentials (rhythmic, synchronized firing across populations) create local field potentials that can be decomposed into frequency neural oscillation bands, which interfere and modulate neuronal gain and timing – where wave amplitude equates activation strength and phase involves activation timing. To express that, we invoke the polar form of a complex number, $z = r\,e^{i\phi}$.[11] Cross-frequency and phase-amplitude coupling induce smearing in space and time, which (when coherently modulated) is captured by Fourier analysis, all beyond standard neuronal potentiation and depression, or neural potential. While this is not the place to review the literature on complex-valued neural networks, a neurophysiological treatment of phonological conditions with complex entries, of the sort postulated in Sect. 3, is presumed and generalized in what follows, thus indirectly justifying (11)-(13) in ways consistent with its presumed biophysics. Moreover, in this section we have presumed a lexical ontology that could be expanded as in (14), which we turn to next.

$$\text{a. Noun} = \begin{bmatrix} \mathbf{1} & \mathbf{0} \\ \mathbf{0} & -\boldsymbol{i} \end{bmatrix} \qquad \text{b. Verb} = \begin{bmatrix} -\mathbf{1} & \mathbf{0} \\ \mathbf{0} & \boldsymbol{i} \end{bmatrix}$$
$$\text{c. Adjective} = \begin{bmatrix} \mathbf{1} & \mathbf{0} \\ \mathbf{0} & \boldsymbol{i} \end{bmatrix} \qquad \text{d. Preposition} = \begin{bmatrix} -\mathbf{1} & \mathbf{0} \\ \mathbf{0} & -\boldsymbol{i} \end{bmatrix} \tag{14}$$

5 Extending the Algebraic Approach

The grouping in (14) can be seen as a version of Chomsky's (1981) matrices of *categorial features*, given a fundamental assumption for this level of representation that $\pm\,\mathrm{N} = \pm\,1$ and $\pm\,\mathrm{V} = \pm\,i$. In other words, familiar Chomsky categories [±N, ± V] may be expressed as diagonal unitary $\begin{bmatrix} \pm 1 & 0 \\ 0 & \pm i \end{bmatrix}$ matrices. It is worth reflecting on those from the perspective of an *extended* perceptron model where complex entries are allowed and, moreover, the presumed dynamics encourage us to look beyond neuronal firing per se (with the diagonal representing input/output conditions for the neuron) into how these may affect immediate (neuronal) neighborhoods. In the logic of a 2×2 matrix, the off

[11] For a vector of length r rotating it ϕ radians counterclockwise from the positive real axis.

diagonal should be able to represent connections to adjacent neurons at the synapse. The ensuing matrix can then be decomposed as follows:

$$\begin{bmatrix} (\mathbf{k}, i\mathbf{l}) & (\mathbf{m}, i\mathbf{n}) \\ (\mathbf{p}, i\mathbf{q}) & (\mathbf{r}, i\mathbf{s}) \end{bmatrix} = \underset{\text{SELF-STATE}}{\begin{bmatrix} (\mathbf{k}, i\mathbf{l}) & \mathbf{0} \\ \mathbf{0} & (\mathbf{r}, i\mathbf{s}) \end{bmatrix}} + \underset{\text{INTERACTIVE STATE}}{\begin{bmatrix} \mathbf{0} & (\mathbf{m}, i\mathbf{n}) \\ (\mathbf{p}, i\mathbf{q}) & \mathbf{0} \end{bmatrix}} \tag{15}$$

To turn a 2×2 model as in (15) into anything relevant to the key inferential conditions a computational theory of mind presumes, we need to make two further assumptions, stemming from the fact that computational thought systems are taken to exist in an dynamic transition: between a dormant storage space (some lexicon **L**) and an active processing workspace (**WS**), with information handled in the latter stage returning to the dormant state after use, potentially with new nuances gained through use.

First, the syntactic scaffolding must then be based on unitary matrices whose linear operation on the underlying data does not introduce distortion, preserving information (memory stability) and allowing for transitions between mental states; *self-scalings* (powers, roots) of unitary matrices allow for a reversible transition from an encrypted dormant state into an observably modular space of active use, and back. Second, for the system to interface concretely with interpretive components, the boundary matrices must be definite and, thus, observable, presenting only real eigenvalues (Hermitian matrices). These assumptions drastically constrain viable outcomes, limiting the (as such) unrestricted arrays in (15) (even at the 2×2 level, the simplest instantiation) to unitary conditions in general (for information transitioning from **L** to **WS** and back) and Hermitian conditions (for the modular interfaces between levels of representation).

The only 2×2 diagonal Hermitian-unitary matrices are the identity $\pm I$ and Pauli's $\pm Z$, which must be central to the present system – as are unitary diagonal roots thereof:

$$\text{a. } \sqrt{\begin{bmatrix} \mathbf{1} & \mathbf{0} \\ \mathbf{0} & \mathbf{1} \end{bmatrix}} = \begin{bmatrix} \mathbf{1} & \mathbf{0} \\ \mathbf{0} & \mathbf{1} \end{bmatrix} (I), \begin{bmatrix} -\mathbf{1} & \mathbf{0} \\ \mathbf{0} & -\mathbf{1} \end{bmatrix} (-I), \begin{bmatrix} \mathbf{1} & \mathbf{0} \\ \mathbf{0} & -\mathbf{1} \end{bmatrix} (Z), \begin{bmatrix} -\mathbf{1} & \mathbf{0} \\ \mathbf{0} & \mathbf{1} \end{bmatrix} (-Z)$$

$$\text{b. } \sqrt{\begin{bmatrix} -\mathbf{1} & \mathbf{0} \\ \mathbf{0} & -\mathbf{1} \end{bmatrix}} = \begin{bmatrix} i & \mathbf{0} \\ \mathbf{0} & i \end{bmatrix}, \begin{bmatrix} -i & \mathbf{0} \\ \mathbf{0} & -i \end{bmatrix}, \begin{bmatrix} i & \mathbf{0} \\ \mathbf{0} & -i \end{bmatrix}, \begin{bmatrix} -i & \mathbf{0} \\ \mathbf{0} & i \end{bmatrix} \tag{16}$$

$$\text{a. } \sqrt{\begin{bmatrix} \mathbf{1} & \mathbf{0} \\ \mathbf{0} & -\mathbf{1} \end{bmatrix}} = \begin{bmatrix} \mathbf{1} & \mathbf{0} \\ \mathbf{0} & i \end{bmatrix}, \begin{bmatrix} -\mathbf{1} & \mathbf{0} \\ \mathbf{0} & -i \end{bmatrix}, \begin{bmatrix} \mathbf{1} & \mathbf{0} \\ \mathbf{0} & -i \end{bmatrix}, \begin{bmatrix} -\mathbf{1} & \mathbf{0} \\ \mathbf{0} & i \end{bmatrix}$$

$$\text{b. } \sqrt{\begin{bmatrix} -\mathbf{1} & \mathbf{0} \\ \mathbf{0} & \mathbf{1} \end{bmatrix}} = \begin{bmatrix} i & \mathbf{0} \\ \mathbf{0} & \mathbf{1} \end{bmatrix}, \begin{bmatrix} -i & \mathbf{0} \\ \mathbf{0} & -\mathbf{1} \end{bmatrix}, \begin{bmatrix} i & \mathbf{0} \\ \mathbf{0} & -\mathbf{1} \end{bmatrix}, \begin{bmatrix} -i & \mathbf{0} \\ \mathbf{0} & \mathbf{1} \end{bmatrix} \tag{17}$$

Each of these roots can be of interest to us. The identity I has itself and its negative as roots, together with $\pm Z$, while its negative $-I$ has as roots familiar non-Hermitian matrices from the Pauli group. In turn, Pauli's $\pm Z$ has as roots a series of matrices with "mixed" entries, with arguable relevance to the encrypting needs of the (encyclopedic) **L** system, given the equations in (18). The point there is that the matrix entries *preserve the attribute and value of the matrix they are the roots of in all instances*. This can be shown to be pertinent to the neurophysiological conditions we are after, under the presumption that, in the end, these matrices may be modeling aspects of the delicate balance between the neuronal activity relevant to the thought processes and the corresponding energy consumption for the individual thinking. This balance is presumed through homeostatic plasticity, which is still not well understood.

$$
\begin{aligned}
&\text{a. For } C_1 = \begin{bmatrix} 1 & 0 \\ 0 & -i \end{bmatrix}, \sqrt{\begin{bmatrix} 1 & 0 \\ 0 & -i \end{bmatrix}} = \begin{bmatrix} 1 & 0 \\ 0 & \frac{1-i}{\sqrt{2}} \end{bmatrix} \\
&\text{b. For } -C_1 = \begin{bmatrix} -1 & 0 \\ 0 & i \end{bmatrix}, -\sqrt{\begin{bmatrix} 1 & 0 \\ 0 & -i \end{bmatrix}} = \begin{bmatrix} -1 & 0 \\ 0 & \frac{-1+i}{\sqrt{2}} \end{bmatrix} \\
&\text{c. For } C_2 = \begin{bmatrix} 1 & 0 \\ 0 & i \end{bmatrix}, \sqrt{\begin{bmatrix} 1 & 0 \\ 0 & i \end{bmatrix}} = \begin{bmatrix} 1 & 0 \\ 0 & \frac{1+i}{\sqrt{2}} \end{bmatrix} \\
&\text{d. For } -C_2 = \begin{bmatrix} -1 & 0 \\ 0 & -i \end{bmatrix}, -\sqrt{\begin{bmatrix} 1 & 0 \\ 0 & i \end{bmatrix}} = \begin{bmatrix} -1 & 0 \\ 0 & \frac{-1-i}{\sqrt{2}} \end{bmatrix}
\end{aligned}
\tag{18}
$$

Per Parseval's Theorem, conserved in an FT is the energy of a signal in time and frequency domains, a probability amplitude.[12] The FT trades localization in one domain for dispersion in the other, but the signal energy is unchanged by the transformation: it is just redistributed in different bases (time vs. frequency). In an abstract sense, this should be comparable in a model treating phonological representations as discussed or, more relevantly now, nouns as δ functions that index space, with corresponding verbs, instead, as distributed plane waves functions $\mathcal{N}$ smeared over a wider conceptual space. If we postulate this conceptual access as an abstract signal, activation energy should be redistributed, but conserved, between the complementary perspectives under the FT. In turn, in neuro-physiological terms, Fourier transforming something like an EEG trace, field potential, or any such ensemble as relevant, one is also redistributing energy across frequencies, with power conserved across bands. This means that while a neural population spike may look like a δ (sharp in time, broad in frequency) and a sustained oscillation in some band is broad in time, narrow in frequency, the overall activation remains constant. So: when modeling nouns as δ-activations and verbs as $\mathcal{N}$ plane-wave activators, one is switching bases (from temporal-conceptual to structural-relational) but not changing the computational effort or, representationally, the semantic content. In information terms, the relation is preserved (like energy would be).

However: What does it even mean to say "something is conserved" when the *function* of the items used may be transformed? In physical systems, conservation refers to a quantity (energy, charge, momentum) constant under transformation. But in thought systems one is dealing with something else. Each lexical item (like *plant*) has a latent space of possible uses, which can be projected into different domains like the noun/verb correlates. While "meaning" may not be fully conserved,[13] FT transformations still conserve the functional capacity to participate in structure – consistently. Learning that one can plant lichens may expand one's meaning of planting but does not do away with the idea that one can also (more boringly) plant seeds from which plants grow, a method plants use to plant their kin. So wordforms like *plant* seem like a wave packet:

[12] That is, the squared magnitude.

[13] One could learn that lichens or fungi can also be planted, non-trivially like rocks.

carrying some sort of compressed potential for both nominal and verbal realizations.[14] This is where what shifts is the basis for that potential to be expressed, representing in the noun or verb domain: altering its projection but not the underlying possibility space. Rather than semantic content, *structural affordance* (in the sense of Hirota et al. (2024)) may be ultimately what is conserved in the FT: the item's capacity to be meaningful in composition, even across unexpected projections. This is closer to conservation of action potential in neurons, as potential to be activated in a particular networked structure.

That is relevant to roots as in (18) as a possible encryption format for lexical roots in **L**, prior to activation into a *lexical array* $\mathbf{L_A}$ specific to a given sentence. The neurophysiological model as sketched presumes treating items in such conditions as diagonal matrices (the self-state in Eq. (15)), understood as low-bandwidth associations conserved in a network-theoretic sense. The difference between activated [+N, -V] nouns and [-N, + V] verbs is in terms of opposing assumptions in the corresponding 2×2 matrix diagonal: nouns in this sense stem from a firing into a dampened distributed state while verbs go from a damping into an active distributed state. Whatever they ultimately amount to, these categories are thus taken to exist in a dormant lexical state within the δ band (no relation to the δ unit impulse, just meaning "under 4 Hz"), as encyclopedic roots represented as square roots of the activated format. Thus, for each of the *Chomskys* in (18), we see a corresponding root that preserves algebraic values for binding the neurophysiological conditions. These are "encyclopedic": in that said matrices may enter structure-preserving tensor products with arbitrary many other matrices of different modalities,[15] the aggregate of which is whatever presupposition set each distinct item may then carry for individual users.

6 A Hilbert Space of Relevance to Chains

The Chomskys, whose more familiar format (with the categorial features in Chomsky 1981 translated into the matrix diagonal) is as presumed for their $\mathbf{L_A}$ representation, are useful in at least two regards. Not only can one find roots as in (18) to exist in latent format, but their powers are the diagonal *Paulis*, as seen by running (17a) in reverse. We may think of that self-scaling as what generates the δ-function for the NP in (13a), algorithmically starting by falling into the Hermitian $\pm Z$, as the operation articulating $\mathbf{L_A}$ into a syntactic **WS**. Then other multiplications range over eight diagonal matrices arranged into an *Abelian group*, as the various possibilities thus emerging – what amounts to a form of VP "sub-categorization" for (13b) and the like, as in Fig. 2.

In this syntactic graph, elementary relations "project" structure via "selection" dependencies, with Chomskys as categorial operators that take projections as arguments and yield other projections as values. Color signals "label" distinctions corresponding to

[14] Although in some of these one might privilege one perspective over the other. Kharen Musaelian (p.c.) suggests making use of wavelets in these contexts. While every wavelet is a type of wave packet (a localized wave burs formed by superposing sinusoidal components with different frequencies), not every wave packet is a wavelet. Wavelets understood as time-localized wave packets, chosen to allow analysis across scales and positions, may well be the more fruitful way to proceed in the long-term program, with the FT as a special case of the wavelet transform.

[15] Sensorial or of any relevant kind, as relevant to an animal's cognition.

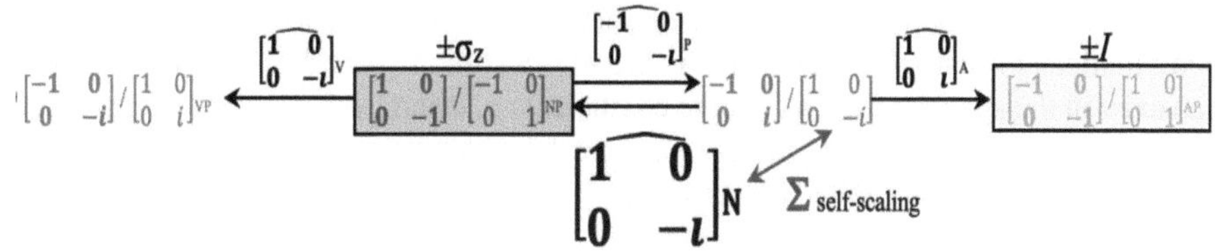

Fig. 2. A Graph for Core Syntactic Relations

matrix *det.*s as in (11) – each projection in "twin" variants. Operations can also be stated in reverse, for parsing purposes and for the system to send new information back to **L**, after truth evaluation by individuals of pertinent judgments. All of this arises from the unitary nature of the information-preserving operators, allowing users to recall, combine, and update concepts without losing or corrupting them.

The system thus goes from encryption to observation and back through matrix multiplication, the (diagonal, unitary, non-Hermitian) Chomskys lying at an "edge" that can turn into *observability or encryption* by differing scalings, in both instances preserving structure. If variable magnitudes are equated to k = l = m = n = p = q = r = s, the situation in (19) obtains. That directly allows for *unitary conditions.*

$$\begin{bmatrix} (\mathbf{k}, i\mathbf{l}) & (\mathbf{m}, i\mathbf{n}) \\ (\mathbf{p}, i\mathbf{q}) & (\mathbf{r}, i\mathbf{s}) \end{bmatrix} = \begin{bmatrix} (\mathbf{k}, i\mathbf{k}) & (\mathbf{k}, i\mathbf{k}) \\ (\mathbf{k}, i\mathbf{k}) & (\mathbf{k}, i\mathbf{k}) \end{bmatrix} = \mathbf{k}\left(\begin{bmatrix} (\mathbf{1}, i) & \mathbf{0} \\ \mathbf{0} & (\mathbf{1}, i) \end{bmatrix} + \begin{bmatrix} \mathbf{0} & (\mathbf{1}, i) \\ (\mathbf{1}, i) & \mathbf{0} \end{bmatrix}\right) \tag{19}$$

The matrices in Fig. 2 have the structure of an *Abelian group* $\{\pm \mathrm{I}, \pm Z, \pm C_1, \pm C_2\}$, since being all diagonal, the matrices mutually commute. This set has the neutral element I and an inverse for every element, etc. The group is isomorphic to $\mathbb{Z}_2 \times \mathbb{Z}_4$ and includes several interesting subgroups that we need not to into here. The set of entities described by this group is limited to substantive (lexical) categories.

Although the additional structure needed to describe functional categories is discussed momentarily, a Hilbert space can be constructed already starting from the Abelian group, including the sum and defining a scalar product:

$$<A|B> = \mathrm{tr}(A^{\dagger}B). \tag{20}$$

Matrix A is represented as $|A>$ in Dirac notation, with its adjoint $A^{\dagger} = (A^T)^*$ by $< A|$,[16] for the scalar product $< A|B >$. This product produces a single complex number out of the two matrices, providing a way to define *angles* between vectors in the space, representing their degree of difference. For perpendicular vectors, this scalar product is zero. We are building a vector space out of the matrices, which can themselves be understood as elements of an abstract vector space. Whenever a scalar product is zero, we can say that the corresponding matrices A, B – then treated as abstract vectors – are "mutually orthogonal".[17] All that means is that A is in some sense perpendicular to B within the vector space, or maximally different to it in that space.

[16] T † is the transpose, which exchanges rows by columns in the matrix, and $*$ is the complex conjugate, which substitutes $i \leftrightarrow -i$.

[17] This is not to be confused with an "orthogonal matrix", a matrix satisfying $A^T A = AA^T = \mathrm{I}$.

Systematically proceeding that way, it can be shown that the space generated by linear combinations of matrices in the Abelian group is a Hilbert space.[18] This entails vectors can exist in the space as follows, where coefficients α, β and γ are complex numbers and the elements in the superposition are matrices from Abelian group understood as (not normalized) vectors from the Hilbert space:

$$|\psi> = \alpha|\mathrm{I}> + \beta|Z> + \gamma|C_1> + \cdots \tag{21}$$

While the resulting vector $|\psi>$, understood as a matrix, need not be an element of the Abelian group, it is a valid vector of the Hilbert space.

The number of linearly independent matrices in the Abelian group (dimensionality of the Hilbert space) is obtained from the maximum number of mutually orthogonal matrices in these conditions. It turns out that there are at most 2 of such matrices.[19] Note how the Chomsky matrices can be written in terms of Pauli's Z and the identity:

$$C_1 = \left(\tfrac{1-i}{2}\right) I + \left(\tfrac{1+i}{2}\right) Z\,, \qquad C_2 = \left(\tfrac{1+i}{2}\right) I + \left(\tfrac{1-i}{2}\right) Z \tag{22}$$

The relations can be inverted too, to get Z and the identity from the Chomsky matrices:

$$I = \left(\tfrac{1+i}{2}\right) C_1 + \left(\tfrac{1-i}{2}\right) C_2\,, \qquad Z = \left(\tfrac{1-i}{2}\right) C_1 + \left(\tfrac{1+i}{2}\right) C_2\,, \tag{23}$$

Therefore, the dimension of this Hilbert space associated to the Abelian group is 2.

To characterize the vector space, next we find an orthonormal basis,[20] such that any other vector in the space can be written as a linear combination thereof. A possible orthonormal basis is given by the normalized Z together with the normalized identity:

$$\text{PAULI BASIS} \equiv \left\{\tfrac{I}{\sqrt{2}}, \tfrac{Z}{\sqrt{2}}\right\} \equiv \left\{|\widehat{I}\rangle, |\widehat{Z}\rangle\right\} \tag{24}$$

All vectors in this basis correspond to Hermitian matrices, which we return to. There is another natural basis for the Abelian group given by normalized Chomsky matrices:

$$\text{CHOMSKY BASIS} \equiv \left\{\tfrac{C_1}{\sqrt{2}}, \tfrac{C_2}{\sqrt{2}}\right\} \equiv \left\{|\widehat{C_1}\rangle, |\widehat{C_2}\rangle\right\} \tag{25}$$

The relation between the bases is the unitary matrix.

$$\begin{pmatrix}\alpha\\ \beta\end{pmatrix} = \begin{pmatrix}\frac{1-i}{2} & \frac{1+1}{2}\\ \frac{1+i}{2} & \frac{1-1}{2}\end{pmatrix}\begin{pmatrix}\alpha\prime\\ \beta\prime\end{pmatrix} \tag{26}$$

While both "coordinate systems" are valid as such – as far as the description of the space is concerned – we return to their naturalness for different purposes.[21]

---

[18] That is, a space where matrices are understood as abstract vectors, which can be superposed by being multiplied by arbitrary complex coefficients (see Orús, Martin, & Uriagereka (2017).

[19] Like the Pauli matrix Z together with the identity I, but also the two Chomsky matrices.

[20] That is, the minimal set of orthogonal vectors with norm one.

[21] Determinants for the original lexical categories are $\pm\, i$, while they are, instead, $\pm\, 1$ in the Pauli basis. While this is important in analyzing the graph in Fig. 2, bear in mind that we are only calculating projection labels algorithmically.

Associations as in Fig. 2 are basic, involving what syntacticians call External Merge (EM) – an operation between independent elements in a derivation,[22] either of which may come from the lexicon **L**. Importantly, sentences are also empirically known to involve *Internal* Merge (IM), whereby a phrase merges with *one of its constituents*. That is, an element Λ contained in some element K, which has already been assembled by merge, "re-merges" with K. For instance:

a. *Alice seems to like Bob.*

b. $[_{TP}\ \underline{Alice}_k\ [_{T'}\ [_{T}\ to]\ [_{VP}\ like\ Bob]_{VP}\ ]_{T'}\ ]_{TP}$
Λ

c. $[_{T'}\ \text{TENSE}\ [_{VP}\ seem\ [_{TP}\ \underline{Alice}_k\ [_{T'}\ [_{T}\ to]\ [_{VP}\ like\ Bob]_{VP}\ ]_{T'}\ ]_{TP}\ ]_{VP}\ ]_{T'}$
K

"re-merge"

d. $[_{TP}\ \underline{Alice}_k\ [_{T'}\ \text{TENSE}\ [_{VP}\ seem\ [_{TP}\ \underline{Alice}_k\ [_{T'}\ [_{T}\ to]\ [_{VP}\ like\ Bob]_{VP}\ ]_{T'}\ ]_{TP}\ ]_{VP}\ ]_{T'}\ ]_{TP}$
K Λ

(27)

Here *Alice* "remerges" from its original position (subject of the VP *like Bob*) to the beginning of the sentence, thereby copying occurrences of *Alice*: one DOWN in the original configuration and one UP, as the newly created TP specifier. Such a displacement is modelled by having the higher T' (immediate projection of TENSE)[23] combine with the occurrence of *Alice* in the specifier of *to* (27a) that results in a subsequent, *TP*, projection. Since Alice is contained in the higher T', this merger is "internal", IM. Needless to say, all these processes presume the existence of phrases (brackets in (27)).

In present terms, it is useful to model IM chains as involving tensor products. In linguistic jargon, chains are $\{\{\alpha, K\}, \{\alpha, \Lambda\}\}$ relations, where the linking element α (e.g., *Alice* in (27)) involves (prior) context Λ and (subsequent) context K as separate α occurrences, which derivationally go from Λ *to* K, a formal fact presumed in K *properly including* Λ as in (27).[24] This, then corresponds to the following vector:

$$|Chain\rangle = \frac{1}{\sqrt{2}}\left(|\hat{\alpha}\rangle \otimes |\hat{K}\rangle + |\hat{\alpha}\rangle \otimes |\hat{\Lambda}\rangle\right) = \frac{1}{\sqrt{2}}\,|\hat{\alpha}\rangle \otimes \left(|\hat{K}\rangle + |\hat{\alpha}\rangle\right) \quad (28)$$

Here we assume normalized vectors. A syntactic notation for the same object is:

$$[\text{Chain}] = [\alpha \otimes K] + [\alpha \otimes \Lambda] = \alpha \otimes [K + \Lambda]. \quad (29)$$

The idea is for "two occurrences of the same token in a derivation" to amount to *vector sum* in the space of the matrices obtained after IM (with a tensor product structure). It is then vital that summed matrices correspond to orthogonal vectors.

[22] Except in the special case of self-merge, of importance for the initial state $\sum$ of a derivation.

[23] The root structure at that derivational stage (27c) – prior to creation of the specifier as in (27b).

[24] This may be seen in 41(b), where one T' "dominates" another T' (this being an entirely different token projection of the same category type; we have boldfaced both of these projections in the structure so that this simple point is visually clear). Bear in mind, also, that these phrasal relations map to temporal phonetic strings (left-to-right in a written page). This may be confusing, in that what is derivationally prior (the inner structure) is actually pronounced last.

In a valid chain a specifier is distributed (copied) over two different positions, the linking element $|\widehat{\alpha}>$ in (28)/(29) acting as the specifier of $|\widehat{K}>$ and $|\widehat{\Lambda}>$ *simultaneously*. One may say that a chain is a sum different states, both sharing the same specifier and, thus, based on the equally weighted superposition of (orthogonal) normalized vectors in our Hilbert space. This, then, allows us to incorporate an idea from Quantum Cognition framework: that when the chain is sent to phonetic and semantic interfaces (is spelled out and logically processed), only one of the configurations for the chain occurrences is successfully observed, not knowing a priori which. This presumes a form the Measurement Postulate: once a superposed quantum system is observed in the appropriate basis, it "collapses" in one of the superposed options because of the measurement, which dictates the outcome.[25] The approach models the behavior of chains, whose occurrences are distributed through the configurations they span over. The discontinuous element is realized in precisely one configuration in close mathematical analogy with why the angular momentum of a spin-1/2 particle exists simultaneously in UP and DOWN configurations – but only observed at one of those when measured.

Note that there are (scores of) superpositions in the Hilbert space we have been considering that do not correspond to grammatical objects. In other words, there is vastly more structure available in our construction than what is empirically attested via chains. For instance, the following "weird" state, in formal (36a) and linguistic notation (30b):

$$\text{a. } |Weird\rangle = \frac{1}{\sqrt{2}}\left(a|\hat{\alpha}\rangle \otimes |\hat{K}\rangle + b|\hat{\beta}\rangle \otimes |\hat{\Lambda}\rangle\right) \tag{30}$$

$$\text{b. } [\text{Weird}] = a\,[\alpha \otimes K] + b\,[\beta \otimes \Lambda].$$

For $a, b \neq 0$, this state is typically *entangled* – not separable as a ["left vector" ⊗ "right vector"]. So: although this *is* a valid state in our vector space, it need not correspond to the result of any syntactic derivation. While tempting to speculate that such thoughts may arise as we dream or muse, it seems more immediately interesting to constrain already known systemic possibilities corresponding to acceptable states.

One way to interpret Marcolli, Chomsky, & Berwick 2025 is as a proposal to limit syntactic derivations in vectorial terms. This is by presuming, first, that they are built from a selected lexical array $\mathbf{A_L}$. For instance, for sentence (27), lexical choices are:

Lexical Array $\mathbf{A_L}$ for (27); {*Bob, Alice, -s, seem, like, to*} (31)

From building structure based on (31), while it is meaningful to ask whether *Bob* (instead of *Alice*) internally merges, and if so whether it is pronounced or interpreted UP or DOWN, it would be meaningless to consider whether *John* does with regards to *appear* or *hate*, simply because those are not selected into the derivationally relevant $\mathbf{A_L}$ in the

[25] This is in no way an endorsement of any particular interpretation of this postulate, nor has it direct bearing on how the matter should be taken cognitively or neurophysiologically – it is just a statement about a formal condition given the math that we are pursuing, under the substantive assumption that, while the syntactic device can live in an entangled reality of the sort our superpositions presume, accessing other mental interfaces needs to be a definite process.

user's attention span.[26] Second, these authors limit derivations further in terms of derivational continuations of $\mathbf{A_L}$ that fall into severely bounded workspaces **WS**, in ways we need not examine here. This is all to say that a dormant lexicon **L**, a brought-to-attention lexical array $\mathbf{A_L}$, and a derivationally active workspace **WS**, are neurophysiological and psycholinguistic constraints on the overall algebraic space, which affects the form of viable representations for which users have grammaticality judgements.

In the model, states *not* amenable to chain conditions are of the following kind:

$$|Regular\rangle = |\hat{\alpha}\rangle \otimes |\hat{K}\rangle \tag{32}$$

In contrast, grammatical states that do correspond to a chain have the following format (where we allow for possible coefficients *a*, *b*), as mathematically separable states:

$$|Chain\rangle = \frac{1}{\sqrt{2}}\left(a|\hat{\alpha}\rangle \otimes |\hat{K}\rangle + b|\hat{\alpha}\rangle \otimes |\hat{\Lambda}\rangle\right) = \frac{1}{\sqrt{2}}|\hat{\alpha}\rangle \otimes \left(a|\hat{K}\rangle + b|\hat{\Lambda}\rangle\right) \tag{33}$$

The idea is not that all separable states are grammatically valid – but, rather, that only separable states surface as grammatical chains. In a sense, if entanglement is indeed a resource, the language faculty works with the "cheapest" set of states: those lacking entanglement, at the core the minimalist ideal that syntax is an optimal system.

7 Chains Within the Chomsky-Pauli Group

Aside from being separable (non-entangled) states in Hilbert space, chains are taken to serve a crucial role in the very construction of phrasal ensembles. To see this, note first how the potential open-endedness of phrases as follows poses a direct challenge:[27]

$$\begin{array}{llcll} \textit{John's} & \textit{car} & \rightarrow & A \quad \otimes & W \\ \textit{John's mother's} & \textit{car} & \rightarrow & A \otimes B \quad \otimes & W \\ \textit{John's mother's sister's} & \textit{car} & \rightarrow & A \otimes B \otimes C \otimes & W \\ & \ldots & & & \ldots \end{array} \tag{34}$$

In simple situations of this sort, the amount of information added to the system increases linearly with the number of embedded specifiers – as this is proportional to the number of matrices being tensorized – but the size of the matrix describing the implied derivations grows exponentially. For a derivation with n such elements, this results in $2^n \times 2^n$ combinations, resulting in computational blowup. To control that growth, we need a truncation scheme that targets only grammatically relevant eigenspaces, which immediately raises issues of *matrix compression.*

The matrix resulting from the construction of a chain must have some null eigenspace (i.e., zero eigenvalues), which is therefore irrelevant for its description and can be ignored. This bears directly on the issue of functional elements within the system, which force us into a larger group of matrices that satisfies requirements comparable to those

[26] Though, of course, they may well be legitimate entities in some individual's lexicon **L**.

[27] The general problem with multiple specifiers is easy to illustrate with genitives as in (34), but it arises wherever the system may go into full recursion – e.g., involving a complex specifier.

in the Abelian group. The minimal extension is to assume that the formal system has reflection symmetry, so that if a diagonal matrix $\begin{bmatrix} \boldsymbol{a} & 0 \\ 0 & \boldsymbol{b} \end{bmatrix}$ forms part of the system, its mirror image $\begin{bmatrix} 0 & \boldsymbol{a} \\ \boldsymbol{b} & 0 \end{bmatrix}$ does too. This step then yields a unique set of 32 matrices with the structure of a non-abelian group, which we call the Chomsky-Pauli group $\boldsymbol{G_{CP}}$:

$$G_{cp}=\{\pm I, \pm X, \pm Y, \pm Z, \pm i\mathrm{I}, \pm iX, \pm iY, \pm iZ, \pm C_1, \pm C_2, \pm S_1, \pm S_2, \pm iC_1, \pm iC_2, \pm iS_1, \pm iS_2\} \tag{35}$$

where I is the 2×2 identity matrix, X, Y and Z are the standard 2×2 Pauli matrices, C_1 and C_2 are two of the original "Chomsky" matrices in (14), and S_1 and S_2 are "anti-Chomsky" matrices exhibiting reflection symmetry. Explicitly:

$$I = \begin{bmatrix} 1 & 0 \\ 0 & 1 \end{bmatrix}, \quad X = \begin{bmatrix} 0 & 1 \\ 1 & 0 \end{bmatrix}, \quad Y = \begin{bmatrix} 0 & -i \\ i & 0 \end{bmatrix}, \quad Z = \begin{bmatrix} 1 & 0 \\ 0 & -1 \end{bmatrix},$$
$$C_1 = \begin{bmatrix} 1 & 0 \\ 0 & -i \end{bmatrix}, C_2 = \begin{bmatrix} 1 & 0 \\ 0 & i \end{bmatrix}, S_1 = \begin{bmatrix} 0 & 1 \\ -i & 0 \end{bmatrix}, S_2 = \begin{bmatrix} 0 & 1 \\ i & 0 \end{bmatrix}, \tag{36}$$

The determinants of all 32 matrices in the group are either ± 1 or $\pm i$. The $\boldsymbol{G_{CP}}$ needs two generators, like C_1 and S_1.[28] Since $\{\pm 1, \pm i\}$ is also a representation of the cyclic group $\mathbb{Z}_4$, we may conclude that the $\boldsymbol{G_{CP}}$ is the set of diagonal and antidiagonal 2×2 matrices with non-zero elements in $\mathbb{Z}_4$. $\boldsymbol{G_{CP}}$ includes several subgroups, like the Pauli group. It includes matrices X, Y and Z, the generators of the Lie (continuous) group $SU(2)$. This Lie group is the double cover of the group $SO(3)$ (of rotations in $3d$ space) and is isomorphic to the group of quaternions with norm 1. However, the matrices in the Chomsky portion of G_{cp} do not form a group by themselves.

Proceeding as in Sect. 6,[29] we can construct the Hilbert space $\mathcal{H}_{\mathbf{CP}}$ associated $\boldsymbol{G_{CP}}$ as the "Chomsky-Pauli" Hilbert space. Pairs of mutually orthogonal matrices A, B in $\boldsymbol{G_{CP}}$ obey at least one of the following constraints: 1. A is diagonal and B antidiagonal, or vice-versa. 2. A and B are both from the Pauli group, and $A = \pm B$ and $A = \pm iB$. And 3. Neither A nor B is from the Pauli group, and $A = \pm B$ and $A = \pm iB$.

All the scalar products between elements of the group can be derived from Table 1.

In Table 1, rows correspond to the matrix for which there is a † (see fn. 16) in the scalar product formula of (20) (the "bra" in Dirac notation), and columns for those that there is no † (the "ket"). Products between other elements in G_{cp} are given by the numbers in the table, up to ± 1 and $\pm i$ multiplying factors. Given scalar product, these tables provide the dimensionality and basis choice of a vector space constructed from the group.

[28] A way of understanding G_{cp} is that these are the 32 matrices that can be either diagonal or antidiagonal, with ± 1 and $\pm i$ as possible coefficients. There can only be 32 such matrices, and these are exactly the ones in G_{cp}.

[29] Constructing a Hilbert space from the Abelian group discussed for Fig. 2.

Table 1. Scalar products of some elements in the G_{cp}.

	I	X	Y	Z	C_1	C_2	S_1	S_2
I	2	**0**	**0**	**0**	$1-i$	$1+i$	**0**	**0**
X	**0**	2	**0**	**0**	**0**	**0**	$1-i$	$1+i$
Y	**0**	**0**	2	**0**	**0**	**0**	$-1+i$	$1+i$
Z	**0**	**0**	**0**	2	$1+i$	$1-i$	**0**	**0**
C_1	$1+i$	**0**	**0**	$1-i$	2	**0**	**0**	**0**
C_2	$1-i$	**0**	**0**	$1+i$	**0**	2	**0**	**0**
S_1	**0**	$1+i$	$-1-i$	**0**	**0**	**0**	2	**0**
S_2	0	$1-i$	$1-i$	0	0	0	0	2

Inspecting Table 1, one can see the dimension of $\mathcal{H}_{\mathbf{CP}}$ is 4.[30] Note how the Chomskys can be written in terms of the Paulis and the identity (43) – and vice-versa (44):

$$C_1 = \left(\frac{1-i}{2}\right) I + \left(\frac{1+i}{2}\right) Z, \qquad S_1 = \left(\frac{1-i}{2}\right)(X-Y)$$
$$C_2 = \left(\frac{1+i}{2}\right) I + \left(\frac{1-i}{2}\right) Z, \qquad S_2 = \left(\frac{1+i}{2}\right)(X+Y) \tag{37}$$

$$I = \left(\frac{1+i}{2}\right) C_1 + \left(\frac{1-i}{2}\right) C_2, \qquad X = \left(\frac{1+i}{2}\right) S_1 + \left(\frac{1-i}{2}\right) S_2$$
$$Z = \left(\frac{1-i}{2}\right) C_1 + \left(\frac{1+i}{2}\right) C_2, \qquad Y = -\left(\frac{1+i}{2}\right) S_1 + \left(\frac{1-i}{2}\right) S_2 \tag{38}$$

Just as was we saw in Sect. 6 for the simpler case, there are two natural orthonormal bases for $\mathcal{H}_{\mathbf{CP}}$. One is given by the "normalized" Pauli matrices plus the identity in (39), entailing that any vector in $|\psi> \in \mathcal{H}_{\mathbf{CP}}$ can then be written as in (40) – where α, β, γ, and δ are complex numbers – the "coordinates" of vector $|\psi>$ in this Pauli basis.

$$\text{Pauli basis} \equiv \left\{\frac{I}{\sqrt{2}}, \frac{X}{\sqrt{2}}, \frac{Y}{\sqrt{2}}, \frac{Z}{\sqrt{2}}\right\} \equiv \{|\hat{I}\rangle, |\hat{X}\rangle, |\hat{Y}\rangle, |\hat{Z}\rangle\} \tag{39}$$

$$|\psi\rangle = \alpha|\hat{I}\rangle, \beta|\hat{X}\rangle, \gamma|\hat{Y}\rangle, \delta|\hat{Z}\rangle \tag{40}$$

The second natural option is given by normalized Chomsky matrices as in (41), an equally valid basis of writing vectors in $\mathcal{H}_{\mathbf{CP}}$ as in (42), with α^0, β^0, γ^0, and δ^0 as the "coordinates" of vector $|\psi>$ in this Chomsky basis:

$$\text{Chomsky basis} \equiv \left\{\frac{C_1}{\sqrt{2}}, \frac{C_2}{\sqrt{2}}, \frac{S_1}{\sqrt{2}}, \frac{S_2}{\sqrt{2}}\right\} \equiv \{|\widehat{C_1}\rangle, |\widehat{C_2}\rangle, |\widehat{S_1}\rangle, |\widehat{S_2}\rangle\} \tag{41}$$

$$|\psi\rangle = \alpha^0|\widehat{C_1}\rangle, \beta^0|\widehat{C_2}\rangle, \gamma^0|\widehat{S_1}\rangle, \delta^0|\widehat{S_2}\rangle \tag{42}$$

[30] There being at most 4 linearly independent matrices; e.g., the three Paulis together with the identity, {I, X, Y, Z}, but also the four Chomskys $\{C_1, C_2, S_1, S_2\}$.

The relation between those bases, allowing the system to change from Chomsky to Pauli "coordinates" for any vector in $\mathcal{H}_{\mathbf{CP}}$ is the following unitary matrix:

$$\begin{pmatrix}\alpha\\ \beta\\ \gamma\\ \delta\end{pmatrix} = \begin{pmatrix}\frac{1-i}{2} & \frac{1+i}{2} & 0 & 0\\ 0 & 0 & \frac{1-i}{2} & \frac{1+i}{2}\\ 0 & 0 & \frac{1-i}{2} & \frac{1+i}{2}\\ \frac{1+i}{2} & \frac{1-i}{2} & 0 & 0\end{pmatrix}\begin{pmatrix}\alpha'\\ \beta'\\ \gamma'\\ \delta'\end{pmatrix} \tag{43}$$

That space $\mathcal{H}_{\mathbf{CP}}$ is isomorphic to the Hilbert space of the direct sum of two qubits. One of the qubits is described by the first Hilbert space described in Sect. 6, spanned by vectors $|\widehat{I}\rangle$ and $|\widehat{Z}\rangle$ (or, equivalently, $|\widehat{C_1}\rangle$ and $|\widehat{C_2}\rangle$), while the other corresponds to the 2*d* subspace spanned by vectors $|\widehat{X}\rangle$ and $|\widehat{Y}\rangle$ (equivalently, by $|\widehat{S_1}\rangle$ and $|\widehat{S_2}\rangle$).

Given $\mathcal{H}_{\mathbf{CP}}$, we take grammatical chains to obey the following constraints: 1. Their matrices must be compressible (have some null eigenspace) as 2×2. 2. The resulting 2×2 matrix must have label within $\pm$ 1, $\pm$ *i*. 3. They are a superposition of orthogonal vectors in $\mathcal{H}_{\mathbf{CP}}$.

Recall (33) in Sect. 6. In this equation, α, K, Λ are matrices from group G_{cp}, where the linking element α denotes the specifier for IM contexts K, Λ. Our requirement 1. Implies that matrix sum $K + \Lambda$ has one and only one zero eigenvalue. This is because matrix $\alpha \in G_{cp}$ always has two nonzero eigenvalues, but eigenvalues of $\alpha \otimes (K + \Lambda)$ are now the 4 product combinations of the two eigenvalues coming from α and the two from $K + \Lambda$; therefore, for the matrix resulting from the chain to have 2 non-zero eigenvalues, one of the eigenvalues of $K + \Lambda$ must be null. There are exactly 96 combinations $U = A + B$, with $A, B \in G_{cp}$, $A \neq B$, such that U has one non-zero eigenvalue only. We may call these by the neologism *unit matrices.* With unit matrices, a chain reads as in (44), involving a matrix compressible back to 2×2, since α is 2×2 and, in its turn, U is compressible to a 1×1 diagonal matrix.

$$\text{Chain} = \alpha \otimes A + \alpha \otimes B = \alpha \otimes (A + B) = \alpha \otimes U. \tag{44}$$

Call the compressed 1×1 matrices U_C. It can then be shown that the label of the chain formed by the U matrices as context, *after* compression (i.e., with U_c as context), follows the usual rules of the determinant of a tensor product and a rescaling by the norm, as given by the following equation, with the rescaling factor in (46).

$$Label\ (Chain) = \frac{1}{N}\det\ (\alpha \otimes U_C) = \frac{1}{N}\det(\alpha)\ (\det(U_C))^2 \tag{45}$$

$$Rescaling\ factor{:}\ N \equiv |\det(\alpha)\ (\det(U_C))^2| = |\det(U_C)|^2 \tag{46}$$

Then the *phase in the complex plane* of $(\det(\alpha))\ (\det\ (U_c))^2$ constitutes a chain label, a composite of the specifier label $(\det(\alpha))$ and the (combined) "contexts" label $(\det\ (U_c))^2$ – the norm of this quantity being the rescaling factor.[31] So, basically, the chain label is the specifier label (the matrix determinant) *times the square* of the U_c

[31] The last equality in (46) follows from $\det(\alpha)$ always being $\pm$ 1, $\pm$ *i* if $\alpha \in G_{CP}$, with modulus 1.

label, with a rescaling by its norm. The rescaling is necessary to keep the consistency of linguistic labels, which amounts to rescaling linguistic variables after a coarse-graining of linguistic information, thus constituting a full renormalization step.[32]

But while that approach neatly models the distributed behavior of syntactic chains as separable (non-entangled) states in Hilbert space $\mathcal{H}_{\mathbf{CP}}$, to consider how chains serve their crucial role in the very construction of phrasal ensembles in the human faculty of language we must ask ourselves neurophysiological questions from an evolutionary perspective: Is what geared the system into the symmetries we have been studying the pursuit of elegant unitary matrices or, instead, did the symmetry itself happened for a reason, with unitarity obtaining as the structural conditions for that desideratum?

8 Consequences for Phrasal Conditions

Recall the decomposition in (15), Sect. 5, which is consistent with a superposition in a vector space of the Hilbert sort, suggesting that the evolutionarily gearing mechanism is physically deep. One consequence of factoring k out as we saw in (19) there is that, then, this very coefficient could be treated as a unique indexical in the data structure, thus effectively allowing us to treat lexicon **L** as a hash-table of sorts. Actually, coefficient k in (19) need not hold constant across speakers. It may be just a concept rigidifier, ensuring that every unique concept has one such index – in which case, it would make sense to require k to be a prime scalar, so that each concept has an identity that can be reused without interference or spurious generalization. What matters for this is a foundational conceptual stability *internal to a thinker*,[33] not whether different agents use the same indexical or otherwise. Given that each syntactic matrix is associated (by as many tensor products as relevant to any particular concept) to corresponding matrices for phonetic or pragmatic-semantic features, that entire ensemble should suffice to guarantee communicative success (up to effability considerations and the like).[34] If so, k may merely even arise in terms of (literal) acquisition order for a learner...

Symmetrizing the extended perceptron matrix constrains the system for its evolution to preserve norm, as crucial to encoding (for perception, memory, and computation) without information loss. It is, then, arguably a requirement that $M^{\dagger} = M$ and $M^{\dagger}M = I$ that pushes the system toward the Pauli group, with the as the simplest nontrivial solutions satisfying both conditions. The Chomskys are roots of Pauli's $\pm Z$ as in (17a) in Sect. 5. While the Chomskys square into the diagonal Pauli Z, their roots in (18) yield what amounts to an encrypted format that is neuro-physiologically plausible: in that all the attributes and values of these "formal features" – binding into energy/homeostasis

[32] The rescaling of the physical variables is the rescaling needed in (46), so as to recover the original set of labels $\pm$ 1, $\pm$ i to make the theory consistent.

[33] To match against an equally stable conception on an interacting agent.

[34] This side remark may well be evolutionarily crucial, in the sense that (surprisingly) humans seem to have the ability to name not just one another and objects of interest "out there", but also effectively thought portions "in here", which arbitrary signifiant-signifié pairings, in the Saussurean sense, amount to. This goes beyond rigidly identifying points or neighborhoods in a mental space, allowing a productive information sharing system. It is unclear if other animals have this capacity, even in rudimentary form.

conditions within the model neuron – remain constant. Firing/repression and potential information conditions thereof exhibit the same specifications at a different scale, which allows the system to preserve its dynamics at lower and higher bands.

Given empirical observations about human (possibly animal) brains engaging information, energy distribution in such conditions ought to be roughly as in Table 2 (and see Kazanina & Tavano (2022), Murphy (2024), Dekydtspotter et al. (2024), etc.). In this Cognitive Entropy Cycle (CEC), activation equates entropy generation, while entropy resolution is taken to come from sleep.

Table 2. Cognitive-entropy Cycle

Phase	Operation	Thermo-Computational Role
Dormancy δ	Low-energy storage	Minimal entropy, root-state potentials
Activation θ	Recall by self-scaling	Moderate entropy, retrieval, concept priming
Interaction $\alpha \to \gamma$	Operational scaling	High entropy, active binding, computation
Dissipation $\to \theta \to \delta$	Re-rooting	Energy decay, memory consolidation

Approximately (de-)activation by scaling is in the empirical ballpark in terms of oscillation bands. The δ band (0.5–4 Hz) is linked to deep sleep, which roots of the Chomskys obviously survive. In the θ band (4–8 Hz) the hippocampal θ-rhythm has been identified in relation to exploratory mammal behaviors, with lower frequencies spotted in motionless alertness and echolocation, for instance. This makes the band relevant for the Chomskys to arise by summoning their roots into rhythmical activity, through self-scaling. The median of the δ band is 2.25 Hz, squaring as 5.0625 Hz (in the median of the low θ band). The next step in a computation is hypothesized as underlying the graph in Fig. 2, by scaling the Chomskys up into the Paulis. With $\sim 5^2 = \sim 25$, the likely candidate for this is a transition from the high α (8–13 Hz) into the low γ band (30-70Hz), in the sense of Murphy 2024 for combinatorial processes that involve larger scale network activity, working memory, and attention. After information is judged in terms of its immediate value, it is preserved in active memory through a sleep cycle, consolidated as new presuppositions. Formally, this requires the inverse processes, so that recalibrated matrices may return to the permanent **L** repository. It is then significant that, aside from serving as the locus for a syntactic **WS**, the hippocampus may also serve as a gathering place for information. The fact that high hippocampal θ waves (at 6–10 Hz) appear engaged during REM sleep may then be relevant.

The graph in Fig. 2 is the simplest that can be stated over the linguistic system as hypothesized, ensuring a start point $\sum$ (self-merge) in the Chomsky representation of nouns and a unitary combination of diagonal Hermitian Paulis and non-Hermitian Chomskys, so that possible matrix determinants are represented in all equivalent ("twin") variants, resulting in an Abelian group. There is an alternative with the order of the matrix entries switched, implementing roots of Pauli's $\pm Z$ as in (16b). If we treat such types as functional, Fig. 2 can be extended as in Fig. 3 below. There, *anti-diagonal matrices* are introduced, which results in the $\boldsymbol{G_{CP}}$.[35] A cursory look at the figure is enough to

[35] Although this particular figure only expresses 24 of 32 matrices, implying a way to extend the extended-projected graph into one with type shifts.

recognize familiar generative themes in extended projections.[36] The new boxed item is Pauli's $\pm X$, also a Hermitian element. We empirically know that "layers" as in Fig. 3 exist because they can be selectively impaired: Broca's (expressive) aphasics might arguably keep on form of the graph in Fig. 2, anchored on noun projections but without functional structure, while for Wernicke's (receptive) aphasics it would appear as if just that is disconnected to the intentional system that guarantees the stability of reference (in present terms, arguably through coefficient k).[37]

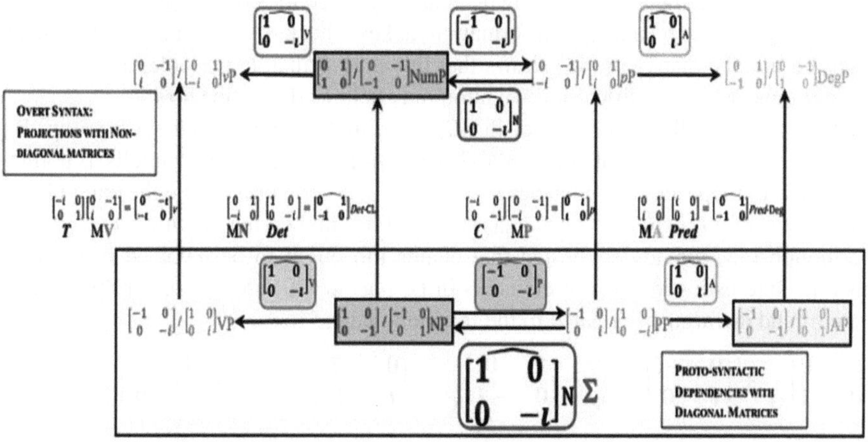

Fig. 3. (Extended) Graphic of Combinations within the GCP

If these ideas are on the right track, it is possible that the Chomsky basis of the system is meant to capture what amounts to encrypted categories for long-term storage, while the Pauli basis, with its Hermitian operators, is instead useful for observation. While algebraically translating from one base to the other is as shown in (43) in Sect. 7, the operational idea is that the process is broken-down into separate steps, at least in the efferent process that takes inner thoughts to constructed sentences:

EFFERENT PROCESS.

(i) Storing Chomsky roots in the lowest possible energy state in a permanent repository **L** of lexical *types* (committed to long-term memory);
(ii) Summoning relevant *tokens* into an attention-driven $\mathbf{A_L}$ for active use, by self-scaling selected items (root powers into the Chomskys),
(iii) Engaging selected tokens in $\mathbf{A_L}$ into a **WS** with derivational buffer for complexity (via EM/IM as relevant), thus creating chain *occurrences.*
(iv) Interpreting observable states at **PF** and **LF** levels of representation.

---

[36] Here, these are all determinant-preserving.

[37] That poses another evolutionary question: whether other animals may present a Language of Thought with the diagonal characteristics in Fig. 2, but no extension into the "functional" items that give access to the off-diagonal matrices within the G_{CP} (and see fn. 34).

AFFERENT PROCESS.

(v) After successful parsing and in circadian terms, recoding updated Chomsky roots back into **L** (for relevantly *enriched* long-term storage).

Then again, something more nuanced (and harder to observe) may be going on in whatever afferent process takes information perceived as judgments (from ourselves, other speakers, or various circumstances) back to the private repository of **L.** Although it is likely that this process is achieved in circadian rhythms – though proper sleep – beyond interesting theories of parsing that partially revert the efferent process, at present it is not known how recalibrated information makes it back to the dormant states. In any case, the unitary matrix in (43) shows that this is in principle possible, under present assumptions; future empirical investigation may help us determine how.

The fact that all 32 matrices of the $\boldsymbol{G_{CP}}$ are unitary makes that set a group. But while that says something about the stability of syntactic categories,[38] it tells us nothing about how to map said dependencies *as phrases*. In other words, while the one in Fig. 3 may be part of a *labeling algorithm*, as such that has no bearing on *phrasal scaffolding* – although (45) already suggested that chains too ought to be involved in syntactic labeling. Interestingly, sums of elements in $\boldsymbol{G_{CP}}$ as in (20) are very natural within the system (and are arguably related to the foundational (15)):

$$\begin{bmatrix}\mathbf{1} & \mathbf{0}\\ \mathbf{0} & \mathbf{1}\end{bmatrix}_{\mathbf{AP}} + \begin{bmatrix}\mathbf{0} & -\boldsymbol{i}\\ \boldsymbol{i} & \mathbf{0}\end{bmatrix}_{\boldsymbol{PredP}} + \begin{bmatrix}\mathbf{1} & \mathbf{0}\\ \mathbf{0} & -\mathbf{1}\end{bmatrix}_{\mathbf{NP}} + \begin{bmatrix}\mathbf{0} & -\boldsymbol{i}\\ \boldsymbol{i} & \mathbf{0}\end{bmatrix}_{\boldsymbol{PredP}} = \mathbf{2}\begin{bmatrix}\mathbf{1} & -\boldsymbol{i}\\ \boldsymbol{i} & \mathbf{0}\end{bmatrix}$$

i. lower context: $\boldsymbol{I}$ = **AP:** $\begin{bmatrix}\mathbf{1} & \mathbf{0}\\ \mathbf{0} & \mathbf{1}\end{bmatrix}$ ii. upper context: ±$\boldsymbol{Y}$ = **PredP:** $\begin{bmatrix}\mathbf{0} & -\boldsymbol{i}\\ \boldsymbol{i} & \mathbf{0}\end{bmatrix}$ (47)

iii. linker: ±$\boldsymbol{Z}$ = **NP:** $\begin{bmatrix}\mathbf{1} & \mathbf{0}\\ \mathbf{0} & -\mathbf{1}\end{bmatrix}$ iv. resulting projection: ±$\boldsymbol{Y}$ = **PredP:** $\begin{bmatrix}\mathbf{0} & -\boldsymbol{i}\\ \boldsymbol{i} & \mathbf{0}\end{bmatrix}$

(47i), (47iii) are Hermitian matrices in Fig. 2. As for the category hypothesized as *Pred*P in (47ii), (47iv), it is the third Pauli, the also Hermitian Y, one of the 32 members of $\boldsymbol{G_{CP}}$ that does not arise via direct (extended) projection as in Fig. 2. The point now is simply that a "predication chain" as in (47) – connecting a lower and upper context by way of a linking element like NP = σ_Z – may result, after summing all the elements involved in the process, in a scaling (doubling) of the Hermitian matrix $\begin{bmatrix}1 & -i\\ i & 0\end{bmatrix}$, which is identical in entry magnitude to the (variant of (4) in Sect. 3) Fibonacci matrix $\begin{bmatrix}1 & 1\\ 1 & 0\end{bmatrix}$. This can be shown to be doubly important.

First, long-range correlations as in (47) are central to human syntax – and many of them arise in the context of $\boldsymbol{G_{CP}}$ sums as in (20). But it is also clear that the Fibonacci matrix, while still Hermitian, is not unitary: this is seen by noting how its spectral radius is not 1 (as is the case for the unitaries) but, rather, the golden ratio φ:

$$\begin{bmatrix}\mathbf{11}\\ \mathbf{10}\end{bmatrix} \text{ Characteristic polynomial } \lambda^2 - \lambda - 1;\ \lambda_1 = \boldsymbol{\varphi},\ \lambda_2 = -\boldsymbol{\varphi} \qquad (48)$$

[38] Not just the Chomskys, but also an extension into "functional" items within the same algebraic space, going into the off-diagonal and otherwise reversing symmetries.

As we saw for the equivalent (4) already, the ensuing sequence of exponential powers of this matrix corresponds to a fractal L-tree with robust phrasal constituency. It is equally simple to prove that an extension of this sequence describes the X'-theoretic phrasal scheme in its maximal expansion.[39] In other words, nothing short of a phrasal topology arises by summing dependencies as in (47) in pertinent ways – the second consequence of such sums. Another way of saying this is that the dependency is not just (semantically) sound, but it literally *yields constituency*. Importantly for the overall logic, the sum in (47) is not arbitrary: it arises in the kind of superpositions we studied in Sect. 7. From a different angle, lacking elements like the functional *Pred*P would be akin to lacking actual constituency. So rather than gimmicks, these Chomskyan chains are essential architectural components of the language faculty.

9 Some Comparisons

Symmetries yielding unitary Hermitian matrices, or even a decomposition into a diagonal and an off-diagonal matrix, could all obtain within classical (non-quantum) neurophysiological ways. In that sense, the present work owes much to Smolensky & Legendre 2005; it is interesting, however, that even that proposal is couched within a Fock vector space (see also Aerts (2009)), which can be seen as a restricted type of Hilbert space – and, therefore, could also be explored in the entangled ways above. More directly inspiring the present approach are Bruza et al. (2009) (where it was asked whether the human lexicon is some Hilbert space) and quantum cognition models as summarized in Busemeyer & Bruza (2012). The latter apply the mathematical formalism of quantum theory and quantum logic to model cognitive phenomena. Then again, while such approaches show instances where Boolean logic fails to predict human reasoning as observed, it is curious how the most compelling arguments demonstrating how contextual clues alter predictions, inducing unexpected meanings, tend to work best for open-ended texts or sub-syntactic compound relations. It is surprising how boringly Boolean it is for cats not just to be presumed to snooze on mats, but also how an understanding of such statements literally entails their *being* on said spaces!

The latter point argues that both quantum and classical types of reasoning are required in standard animal thinking. This was the impetus behind Martin & Uriagereka (2008, 2014) or Uriagereka (2015), when suggesting that non-classical approaches to the problem of chain occurrences (as stated in Chomsky (1995)) help not just illuminate an obscure technical point within the minimalist program, but moreover expands our data base (towards a treatment of individual preferences) and, more foundationally, provides an ontological basis for an understanding of syntactic categories and interactions, with consequences for their neurophysiological binding (Uriagereka (2023)). If one goes into tensor products as above, a classical result can actually obtain from the quantum structure: the issue is whether one deals with commuting operators or otherwise, bearing in mind that indirect commutativity can arise in some restricted and highly symmetrical instances, in an otherwise non-commutative situation. The approach to chains sketched above can in fact be seen this way, with the curious consequence of obtaining a (commutative) phrasal topology in the process: just as one can project a VP from a verb

[39] The 3rd line in the Wythoff Array of Fibonacci extensions coextensive with natural numbers.

categorially taking an NP complement, one could say the V projects from the VP when it yields its NP complement (and note that the graph of selection restrictions in Fig. 2 could be stated with all the arrows in reverse).

Proposals dealing with tensor products for phrasal representations echo Coecke, Sadrzadeh, & Clark's (2013) Distributional Compositional Categorical (DisCoCat) framework, which matches Lambek's pregroups (or related categorial grammars) and the compact-closed categories used in categorical quantum mechanics. Just as discussed above, in this proposal words have grammatical types (like noun and verb) and types that allow for type reduction in categorial-theoretic fashion. Much in the spirit of such grammars, each basic type is assigned a vector space with (transitive) verbs as tensors mapping vectors in a nominal space (of entities) to what amounts to truth values. String diagrams and tensor contractions in the system yield phenomena analogous to entanglement. Just as we saw in Sect. 6, in this approach a product state is separable, but not an entangled state (which cannot be written as a tensor product of two independent states). In DisCoCat, a transitive verb tensor such as $|likes>$ lives in $N \otimes S \otimes N$, with the verb's meaning correlating those of its direct object and subject. In the present proposal, too, a sentence meaning is obviously determined by its constituent's, but what ends up as entangled or separable turns out to be quite different.

In what we have been analyzing, all (lexical and functional) categories are matrices that can be understood as vectors or as linear operators: elements within the $\boldsymbol{G_{CP}}$. As such, no category is privileged, although there are significant asymmetries. Thus, we see in Fig. 2 – articulating elements in the Abelian group into a graph with algorithmic properties as in Sect. 6 – how the start state $\sum$ is the self-M of $C_1 = \begin{bmatrix} 1 & 0 \\ 0 & -i \end{bmatrix}$, $\widehat{C_1}(C_1\rangle) = C_1{}^2$. This is not mathematically or logically necessary, but it is postulated as axiomatic for the human language faculty. Also, because of (chain) labeling definition in (45), Sect. 7, language chains in the system are necessarily formed from noun projections ($NP = \pm Z$). In other words, the only syntactically entangled structures that separate in the system are the grammatical chains, which as we saw in Sect. 8 is what yields phrasal topologies. In short, while the model is obviously mathematically related to DisCoCat, its ontology and implementation are quite distinct, and purposefully so: the system as presented here is not attempting to model a categorial grammar, but a minimalist grammar, where the chains are designed to be central as discussed.

It was already mentioned how the present system is also related to Marcolli, Chomsky, & Berwick (2025), which is presented as a model for (I/E)M. While this is not the place to make a detailed comparison between the two vector spaces and how they relate, the focus of each piece is different. The study of a possible mathematical structure for M is concentrating on the relevance of derivational workspaces WS and the lack of associativity of (core) syntactic operations. Because of its statement in terms of a Hopf algebra and some other stipulations to yield that condition, that system is not intended as one with quantum properties of any sort (like the others discussed in this section). In the end, it is an empirical matter whether natural language or animal cognition more generally exhibits the relevant (quantum) properties as expected in other works cited above and, if so, how those are constrained. In the logic of the present proposal, the natural domains for such conditions is sub-syntactically (where M is not obviously at stake, as is arguably the case for noun-noun compounding and their often metaphorical interpretations) and in loose syntactic domains more generally, where either M is not operative at all or it can be superseded (including discourse dependencies, but possibly other intra-sentential condition of a paratactic sort).

For what it may be worth, also, the present model is meant as broader than syntactic, as we saw from our discussion of phonological conditions in Sect. 3 – and similar considerations could be posed about pragmatic components of grammar. Moreover, the ideas discussed in Sect. 8 pertain to the neurophysiology of the language faculty, which to my knowledge none of the other proposals in this section go into (although Marcolli, Chomsky, & Berwick does mention some ideas along those lines).

10 Conclusions

Nothing said here should be confused with a hypothesis about the brain itself involving quantum processes. While quantum cognition as such, or the conjectures in this piece, are both compatible with such a possibility, the theory is meant as more abstract. If one needs to go there, a quantum *regulator* for all these operations might be natural. Saying this entails nothing about going beyond an individual's mind (telepathy), any more than presuming a quantum regulation to, say, olfaction would. It simply presupposes a neuronal mechanism where such systematicities can be preserved, and in 24-h cycles, so that circadian rhythms allow information utilized during the waking hours to return to the underlying **L** state during sleep, all stable within unitary parameters as entertained above. Candidates that seem worth exploring (beyond the microtubules of Hameroff & Penrose (2014)) include Fisher's (2015) insistence on Posner molecules as relevant to oscillatory synchrony (Straub (2023)) and RNA-based regulation as in Akhlaghpour (2022), in some form of computational memory as pursued in Gallistel & King (2009) – for reasons related to the Feynmanian "room at the bottom" for present speculations, regarding sub-neuronal regulators of computational integrity.

Be that as it may, encrypting and decrypting dynamics should be crucial not just to the language faculty, but to animal thinking more generally. The present proposal is to pursue scalings of matrix representations to that effect, extending the perceptron model into complex territory and intricate neurophysiological dynamics. In this sense, the "dictionary and grammar" aspect of the generative enterprise, preserved in the Computational Theory of Mind and its insistence on some "language of thought", seem both germane: it is because of a dialogue between **L** (underlying dictionary) and operations in **WS** (underlying grammar) that we need unitary operators. The modularity of mind this all presupposes (connecting levels of representation and beyond) demands only Hermitian matrices as interface junctures. As such, neither preserving a norm (as presumed in unitaries) nor invoking Hermitians need be non-classical. Then again, the language faculty and, more generally, a putative "language of thought" in other animals implies not just neuronal activation, but the activity of, effectively, neuronal "companies". Whether localized in small "platoons" when meant as designating familiar concepts, or highly distributed into "batteries" for descriptive concepts, scaling from individual neurons to ensembles of any kind – as represented in the off diagonal of the "extended perceptron" – is hardly trivial. Quantum regulation might then be a welcome approach about how this is even physically possible, or how life finds a way.

Acknowledgments. I appreciate reactions from Drew Baden, Mostafa Barzegar, Tom Bever, Jerome Busemeyer, Damir Cavar, Gemma de las Cuevas, Laurent Dekydtspotter, Naomi Feldman, Victor Galitski, Andrew Hanson, Harry van der Hulst, Bill Idsardi, Srini Iyengar, Mike Jarret, Dave Medeiros, Mithün Paul, Larry Moss, Elliot Murphy, Kharen Musaelian, Román Orús, Paul Pietroski, Rodrigo Treviño, Jesús Ugalde, and (always) the late Roger Martin. For help with specific notions beyond my area of expertise and a first-pass search for references, use was made use ChatGPT4. Errors and uncertainties are the author's, most certainly.

Disclosure of Interests. The author has no competing interests to declare.

References

1. Aerts, D.: Quantum structure in cognition. J. Math. Psychol. **53**(5), 314–348 (2009)
2. Álvarez, P. Gerhards, L., Solov'yov, I., de Oliveira, M.: Quantum phenomena in biological systems. Front. Quantum Sci. Technol., **3** (2024)
3. Akhlaghpour, H.: An RNA-based theory of natural computation. J. Theor. Biol. **537** (2022)
4. Busemeyer, J., Bruza, P.D.: Quantum Models of Cognition and Decision. Cambridge University Press, Cambridge, UK (2012)
5. Bruza, P., Kitto, K., Nelson, D., McEvoy, C.: Is there something quantum-like about the human mental lexicon? J. Math. Psychol., 53–55 (2009)
6. Chomsky, N.: Lectures on Government and Binding. Foris, Dordrecht (1981)
7. Chomsky, N.: The Minimalist Program. MIT Press, Cambridge, MA (1995)
8. Coecke, B., Sadrzadeh, M., Clark, S.: Lambek vs. Lambek: Functorial vector space semantics and string diagrams for Lambek calculus. Ann. Pure Appl. Logic **164**(11), 1079–1100. (2013)
9. Dekydtspotter, L., et al.: Hierarchical neural processing in γ oscillations for syntactic and semantic operations accounts for first- and second-language epistemology. Front. Hum. Neurosci. **18** (2024)
10. Fisher, M.: Quantum Cognition: the possibility of processing with nuclear spins in the brains. Ann. Phys. **362**, 593–602 (2015)
11. Gallistel, R., King, A.: Memory and the Computational Brain. Wiley, Hoboken (2009)
12. Goldberg, R.: Fourier Transforms. Cambridge University Press, Cambridge (2009)
13. Gould, H.W.: A history of the Fibonacci Q-matrix. Fibonacci Quart. **19**(3), 250–257 (1981)
14. Halle, M., Chomsky, N.: The Sound Pattern of English. Harper & Row, New York (1968)
15. Halle, M., Idsardi, W.: General properties of stress and metrical structure. In: Ristad, E. (ed.), Language Computations. American Mathematical Society, Providence, RI (1995)
16. Hameroff, S., Penrose, R.: Consciousness in the universe: a review of the 'Orch OR' theory. Phys. Life Rev. **11**(1), 39–78 (2014)
17. Hirota, R., Saigo, H., Taguchi, S.: Reality of Affordances: a category-theoretic approach. In: Proceedings of the 2024 Artificial Life Conference. MIT Press, Cambridge, MA (2024)
18. Idsardi, W.: Combinatorics for metrical feet. Biolinguistics **2**(2–3), 233–236 (2008)
19. Idsardi, W., Uriagereka, J.: Metrical combinatorics and the real half of the fibonacci sequence. Biolinguistics **3**(4), 404–406 (2009)
20. Fisher, M.: Quantum cognition: the possibility of processing with nuclear spins in the brain. Ann. Phys. **362** (2015)
21. Kazanina, N., Tavano: What neural oscillations can and cannot do for syntactic structure building. Nat. Rev. Neurosci. **24**(2), 113–128 (2022)
22. Le, H., Lui, M., Aphasia, Y.: StatPearls Publishing (2023)

23. Marcolli, M., Chomsky, N., Berwick, R.: Mathematical Structure of Syntactic Merge. MIT Press, Cambridge, MA (2025)
24. Martin, R., Uriagereka, J.: Competence for Preferences (2008). In: Artiagoitia, X., Lakarra, J. (eds.) Gramatika. Jaietan: Patxi Goenagaren Omenez. University of the Basque Country, Vitoria-Gasteiz (2008)
25. Martin, R., Uriagereka, J.: Chains in Minimalism. In: Kosta, P., Franks, S., Radeva-Bork, T., Schürcks, L., (eds.), Minimalism and Beyond: Radicalizing the interfaces. Benjamins, Amsterdam (2014)
26. Medeiros, D.: Economy of Command. Ph.D. thesis, University of Arizona at Tucson (2012)
27. Murphy, E.: ROSE: a neurocomputational architecture for syntax. J. Neurolinguist. **70** (2024)
28. Orús, R., Martin, R., Uriagereka, J.: Mathematical foundations of matrix syntax. arXiv:1710.00372 (2017)
29. Prusinkiewicz, P., Lindenmayer, A.: The Algorithmic Beauty of Plants. Springer-Verlag, New York (1990)
30. Smolensky, P., Legendre, G.: The Harmonic Mind. MIT Press, Cambridge, MA (2005)
31. Straub, J.: The Quantum Brain. University of California at S. Barbara doctoral dissertation (2023)
32. Uriagereka, J.: Complementarity in language. In: Gallego, A., Ott, D., (eds.), 50 Years Later: Reflections on Chomsky's Aspects. MITWPL, Cambridge, MA (2015)
33. Uriagereka, J.: Correlated attributes: toward a labeling algorithm of complementary categorial features. In: Matchin, W. (ed.), Syntax, the brain, and linguistic theory: a critical reassessment. Front. Lang. Sci. **20** (2023)
34. Zsiga, E.: The Sounds of Language: An Introduction to Phonetics and Phonology. Wiley-Blackwell, Hoboken, NJ (2013)

Cognitive Models and Quantum-inspired Formalisms

Quantum Versus Markov Models of Bistable Perception

Jerome Busemeyer[1(✉)], Makiko Yamamato[2], and Rong Zheng[1]

[1] Indiana University, Bloomington, IN 47405, USA
jbusemey@iu.edu

[2] National Institutes for Quantum and Radiological Science and Technology, Chiba, Japan

Abstract. Bistable perception is a fascinating psychological phenomenon in which the conscious perception that a person experiences for a single image spontaneously changes across time. In our experiment, twelve participants observed a dynamic display of moving dots, which appeared to rotate in one direction before seeming to reverse. The study consisted of six sessions, and during each session, participants observed sequences of these moving dots across five one-minute blocks. They were instructed to report any perceived changes in the rotation's direction âĂŞ specifying shifts to the left, to the right, or expressing that the direction has become uncertain. Each report of perceived directional change, along with the time taken to notice such a change, was recorded. This process yielded a detailed dataset of response patterns and the timing of perceptual switches. We developed two models to account for the results: a quantum walk versus a Markov random walk model, both with reflecting bounds and measurement operators designed to detect the three responses. Both models required fitting 6 parameters to each session (5 min of viewing) using maximum likelihood methods, and then we computed a G^2 lack of fit measure for each model, person, and session. The results, averaged across the 6 sessions for each participant, indicated that the quantum model produced a better fit for 9 out of the 12 participants as compared to the Markov model.

Keywords: quantum dynamics · Markov dynamics · bistable perception · human performance · model comparison

1 Introduction

Bistable perception arises whenever a stimulus can be interpreted in two different ways, with approximately equal plausibility, so that the interpretation keeps changing across an extended period of time. A well-known example is the Necker cube (see Fig. 1), which produces a perceptual experience that flips across time from one orientation of the cube to another. This phenomenon has fascinated scientists for many years [1]. How does the brain and the mind spontaneously generate this persistently unstable experience?

D. Cavar et al. (Eds.): QNLPAI 2025, CCIS 2659, pp. 237–249, 2026.
https://doi.org/10.1007/978-3-032-13883-5_13

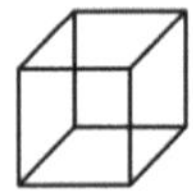

Fig. 1. Necker cube

The dominant theoretical approach to modeling bistable perception is based on the idea of competition between different neuronal populations that encode different interpretations of the sensory signal (see, e.g., [2–4]).

Formally, the noisy neural models are described by stochastic differential equations, which in the continuous time and state case, are diffusion processes. Diffusion processes belong to a general class called Markov processes.

Markov processes are based on the idea that watching the ambiguous image results in a perceptual state that moves across time like a particle, generating a trajectory across time called a sample path. At each point in time, the neural process is located in some specific state on the trajectory within the state space of the Markov process.

Quantum dynamic models of bistable perception have also been developed [5,6]. According to quantum dynamics, watching the image does not produce any definite trajectory. Instead, the perceptual state is superposed over possible interpretations of the ambiguous figure. This superposed state evolves across time like a wave. Only after an explicit measurement does the state collapse to a specific well defined interpretation.

Both Markov and quantum models are probabilistic, but the nature of the probabilities is very different. For Markov models, the person observing the image (the participant in the experiment) has a definite perceived state that is located somewhere, but that location is unknown to an outside observer (the experimenter). In this case, the probability refers to the epistemic uncertainty that the outside observer assigns to the possible location of the perceived state of the person observing the image. For quantum models, the person observing the image does not have a definite location; instead, the location remains indefinite before measurement, and so the person remains uncertain about his or her location until a measurement forces the person to select an interpretation. In this case, the probability refers to the ontic uncertainty that the person watching the image has about the location of the image.

Previous efforts to model the reported changes in interpretation of an ambiguous figure have aimed to account for the mean time to change across experimental conditions, and the approximately Gamma distribution of switching times. The present work is the first we know of to attempt to quantitatively model the detailed sequence of changes across time. This is also the first attempt to quantitatively compare Markov versus quantum models with respect to their capability to account for the observed time series of changes.

Quantum and Markov models can be categorized into four categories depending on whether the state space is discrete or continuous and the time index is discrete or continuous. For mathematical simplicity, here we develop discrete state and continuous time versions of each model, but we use a sufficiently large number of states to closely approximate a continuous state process (cf. [7]).

2 Experimental Data

The experiment reported here used an ambiguous figure produced by a sphere of rotating dots that appear to change their direction of rotation from left to right across viewing time (see the link
https://jbusemey.pages.iu.edu/
quantum/Bistable/RotatingDots.mov The experiment was conducted by Professors Maro Machizawa and Makiko Yamada from the National Institutes for Quantum and Radiological Science and Technology, Chiba, Japan.

The experiment initially included a total of 19 participants, but 7 participants produced incomplete data, so only 12 participants produced sufficient data to be included in the analyses reported below. Each person participated in 6 sessions. During each session, a participant viewed a sphere of rotating dots for five blocks, and each block consisted of one minute of viewing time. During this viewing process, people naturally saw the image change its direction of rotation from moving left to right to the reverse direction, and vice versa, across time. Slow changing participants saw it flip only 2 or 3 times within a block, fast changing participants saw it flip over 20 times within a block.

The participants were asked to report the direction of rotation whenever they perceived a change: change to left (coded -1), change to right (coded $+1$) or change to an undecided perception (coded 0). Across this viewing time, after each change, the response and the time to switch was recorded. For example, the person may start with the response -1 (left) and switch to 0 (direction uncertain) after 6 s, and then switch to $+1$ (right) after 13 s, and then switch to -1 (left) after 11 s, and so on during a one minute block. This produces a sequence of pairs of

$$[(t_0, -1), (6, 0), (13, +1), (11, -1), \ldots, (\Delta t_n, k(n)), \ldots]$$

switching time intervals Δt_n and responses $k(n)$ across each block.

Table 1. Proportion of responses, mean switch time, and std of switch time conditioned on each response.

Response	left	uncertain	right
proportion	.31	.35	.34
mean time	9.24	1.16	9.04
std time	3.76	.97	3.86

The first row of Table 1 shows the proportion of responses pooled across all blocks, sessions, and participants. The proportions are approximately evenly distributed except for a small bias favoring the right. The mean switch time was computed for each participant, pooled across blocks and sessions. The second row of Table 1 shows the average across the 12 participants' means. On average, the time to switch was approximately the same for each left vs. right direction, and it was much shorter for the uncertain response. The last row shows the standard deviation across the 12 participants' means.

The first row of Table 2 shows the mean switch time for each session, pooled across left and right responses with the uncertain responses eliminated. As shown in Table 2, the mean switch time tended to decrease across sessions.

Table 2. Means for each session

Session	1	2	3	4	5	6
Mean time	10.34	9.64	9.64	8.69	8.44	8.11
$G^2_M - G^2_Q$	−2.31	−2.94	−4.46	7.08	0.35	9.91
No. positive	4	5	5	6	6	10

No. positive refers to the number of participants favoring the quantum model.
Mean time excludes the uncertain response.

The column labeled "Mean" in Table 3 shows the mean switch time across all blocks and sessions for each person with the uncertain response eliminated. There is substantial variability in these means across participants. The column labeled "Autocorr" shows the first order autocorrelation of the switch times for

Table 3. Experimental Results

Person	Mean	Autocorr	BIC_M diff	BIC_Q diff
1	4.95	−.01	−26.7	−41.3
2*	14.22	−.25	107.2	110.8
5	9.05	−.38	876.0	826.4
6	5.17	−.23	352.4	393.6
7	11.09	−.15	109.0	116.9
8	12.32	−.13	−73.1	−70.6
11	6.21	−.02	−38.4	−30.9
14	11.71	−.29	162.8	163.3
15	11.23	−.42	607.5	581.7
17	12.33	−.31	218.9	221.3
18	10.07	−.06	−10.0	7.3
19	3.43	−.15	1896.9	1935.6
mean	9.27	−.20	348.5	351.2

each participant, computed across all blocks and sessions. Note that although there is some variability in the size of the autocorrelation, it is generally negative in direction, indicating that a slow switch time was followed by a fast switch time, and visa versa.

3 Markov and Quantum Model Descriptions

Next, we develop the Markov and quantum models for this task, side by side, making parallel assumptions. Finally, we fit and compare both models to the experimental data.

Both models assume that the perception is based on an implicit mental scale of evidence for the direction of rotation. For this purpose we define $x_j = (\frac{j}{N} - .51)$ for $j = 1, \ldots, 51$ as the $N = 51$ levels of evidence ranging from certain rotating left to certain rotating right. This provides a reasonably good approximation to a continuous scale.

3.1 Measurement of Change in Direction

During the viewing process, the participant must make implicit measurements from time to time to decide the perceived direction and, from this, determine whether it has changed or not. For both the Markov and quantum models, we assume that a measurement of the orientation is taken repeatedly on each small time step (e.g., around 1 s) of the mental viewing process. Each measurement results in $-1, 0, +1$ outcome. For example, suppose the participant has just switched to the left rotation (coded -1), and then carries out five measurements that produce the same left -1 outcome, but then the 6th measurement changes to the undecided outcome 0. Then this change from -1 to 0 would have required 6 measurements. If each measurement took 1 s, then this change would have taken 6 s.

Assume the person just switched to response k. To model the time required to switch and the response to which the person switches, we need to compute the predictions for the joint probability, denoted $p(n, j|k)$ for the Markov model and $q(n, j|k)$ for the quantum model, that the person takes $n - 1$ steps without changing response, and then on the next step changes to response $j \neq k$ given the previous k response. The model for these predictions for each block is developed in the following subsections.

3.2 Initial State

The dynamic process for producing a response and switch time pair $(\Delta t_n, k(n))$ starts with an initial state ϕ. This initial state describes the probability distribution across the N evidence levels for the Markov model, or the amplitude distribution across the N evidence levels for the quantum model.

For the Markov model, the initial state is represented by an approximately Gaussian distribution, using an $N \times 1$ column matrix ϕ with elements

$$\phi_j = \frac{e^{\left(\frac{x_j - C}{\nu}\right)^2}}{\sum_j e^{\left(\frac{x_j - C}{\nu}\right)^2}}.$$

The initial state for the quantum model is a $N \times 1$ column matrix ψ with elements $\psi_j = \sqrt{\phi_j}$.

In both models, the measurement of a response (left, uncertain, right) produces a collapse of the state in the direction of the chosen response. Consequently, the initial state for producing a new response $(\Delta t_n, k(n))$ depends on the previous response $k(n-1)$. Therefore, the centrality parameter C was defined as $C = c \cdot k(n-1)$ where c is a parameter estimated from the data for each session. An example initial state with $\nu = .10$ and $c = 0$ is shown in Fig. 2.

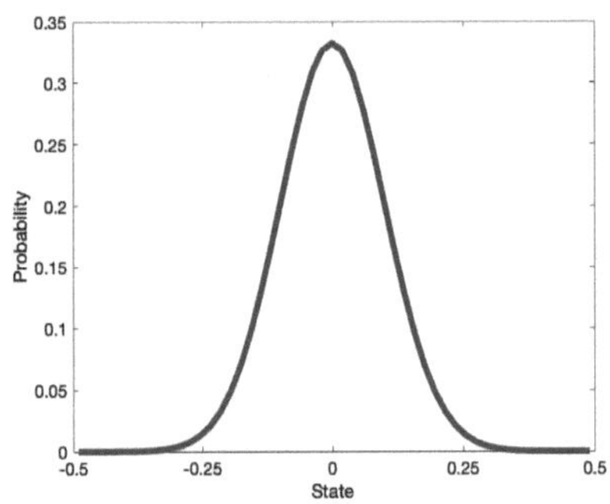

Fig. 2. Initial state

3.3 Dynamics

The spontaneous changes in perception of rotation are produced by a dynamic operator over time. The Markov model uses a $N \times N$ transition matrix T built from a reflecting bound intensity matrix K, and the quantum model uses a $N \times N$ unitary matrix U built from a reflecting bound Hamiltonian matrix H.

The transition matrix for the Markov model has elements T_{ij} in row i column j representing the probability transition to row i from column j. It is derived from an intensity matrix K, $T = e^K$. The intensity matrix K is based on a tri-diagonal matrix

$$\begin{bmatrix} -\alpha & \alpha & 0 & \cdots & 0 & 0 & 0 \\ \alpha & -(\alpha+\beta) & \alpha & & 0 & 0 & 0 \\ 0 & \beta & -(\alpha+\beta) & & \vdots & \vdots & \vdots \\ 0 & 0 & \beta & & & & \\ 0 & 0 & 0 & \vdots & \alpha & 0 & 0 \\ \vdots & \vdots & \vdots & & -(\alpha+\beta) & \alpha & 0 \\ 0 & 0 & 0 & & \beta & -(\alpha+\beta) & \beta \\ 0 & 0 & 0 & \cdots & 0 & \beta & -\beta \end{bmatrix}.$$

This produces a random walk with a mean drift equal to $\mu = \frac{1}{2} \cdot (\beta - \alpha)$ and a diffusion rate equal to $\sigma = \frac{1}{2} \cdot (\beta + \alpha)$. The parameters (α, β) are estimated from the data for each session.

The unitary matrix for the quantum model has elements U_{ij} in row i, column j representing the amplitude transition to row i from column j. It is derived from a Hamiltonian matrix H, $U = e^{-i \cdot H}$. The Hamiltonian matrix H is based on a tri-diagonal matrix

$$\begin{bmatrix} \mu_0 & \sigma & 0 & \cdots & 0 & 0 & 0 \\ \sigma & \mu_1 & \sigma & & 0 & 0 & 0 \\ 0 & \sigma & \mu_2 & & & & \\ 0 & 0 & \sigma & & \vdots & \vdots & \vdots \\ 0 & 0 & 0 & \vdots & \sigma & 0 & 0 \\ \vdots & \vdots & \vdots & & \mu_{N-2} & \sigma & 0 \\ 0 & 0 & 0 & & \sigma & \mu_{N-1} & \sigma \\ 0 & 0 & 0 & \cdots & 0 & \sigma & \mu_N \end{bmatrix}.$$

with the diagonal elements defined by the quadratic function $\mu_i = \mu \cdot x_j^2$ in column j. This produces a quantum oscillator with a quadratic potential function. The parameters (μ, σ) are estimated from the data for each session.

3.4 Measurement Operators

The measurements for the Markov and quantum models are based on a collection of 3 measurement operators $\{M_L, M_U, M_R\}$. Each measurement operator M_k is a $N \times N$ diagonal matrix. The diagonal entries represent the probability (Markov) or amplitude (quantum) to respond with response k given that the state is located at evidence level x_j. For the Markov model, the diagonal entry corresponding to evidence level x_j equals the probability m_{kj} of response k from state j; for the quantum model, the diagonal entry corresponding to evidence level x_j equals the amplitude $\sqrt{m_{kj}}$ of response k from state j.

In general, these operators must satisfy the completeness property: $\sum_k m_{kj} = 1$. The specifications we used are defined as follows: For choosing the right ($k =$

+1) we use

$$m_{Rj} = \frac{1}{2}\left(tanh\left(\frac{x_j - b}{a}\right) + 1\right),$$

for left ($k = -1$) we use

$$m_{Lj} = \frac{1}{2}\left(1 - tanh\left(\frac{x_j + b}{a}\right)\right),$$

and uncertain we use $1 - m_{Rj} - m_{Lj}$. The parameters a, b are estimated from the data for each session. For example, this produces measurement operators that appear in Fig. 3.

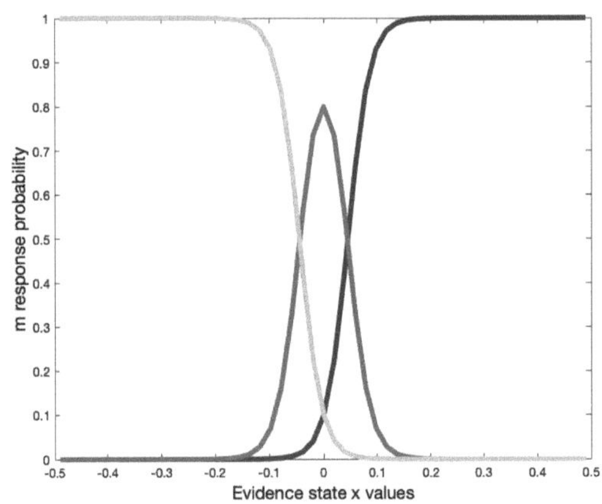

Fig. 3. Measurement operators.

The rapidly decreasing curve on the left represents the measurement operator M_L, the rapidly increasing curve on the right represents the measurement operator M_R, and the symmetric curve in the middle represents the measurement operator M_U. We can accommodate participants who tend not to use the uncertain response by decreasing the parameter b towards zero, which then makes probabilities for the measurement operator M_U decrease, and increases the probabilities for the measurement operators for M_L and M_R.

3.5 Computing the Joint Distributions

Consider now the prediction for the observation $\Delta t_n, k(n)$ for the Markov and quantum models. As described above, the prediction depends on the previous response k before the change occurring in this interval. Define the state immediately after the previous response k as $\phi(k)$ for the Markov model and $\psi(k)$ for the quantum model. (J is a $1 \times N$ row matrix containing all the ones used for the summing).

The joint distribution for taking n measurements without change and then obtaining a change in response j, given the previous response $k \neq j$ is then equal to the following for Markov and quantum models:

$$p(n+1, j|k) = J \cdot M_j \cdot (T \cdot M_k)^n \cdot \phi(k)$$

$$q(n+1, j|k) = \|M_j \cdot (U \cdot M_k)^n \cdot \psi(k)\|^2$$

Figure 4 illustrates the distributions predicted by the quantum model using the parameters $a = .05, b = .1, c = 0, \mu = 100, \sigma = 100$. In this example, the upper curve shows the probability of switching from -1 to 0, which was greater than switching all the way from -1 to $+1$. Using these parameters, the mean time to switch from the left, uncertain, and right, respectively, is 11.74 s, 2.56 s, 11.12 s.

In agreement with Table 1, the time to switch from the uncertain response tends to be much shorter than the times from the left or right response. The negative autocorrelation also follows from the tendency to switch from say a left response (which takes a longer time) to the uncertain response (which takes a shorter time) and then switch to say the right response (which again takes a longer time).

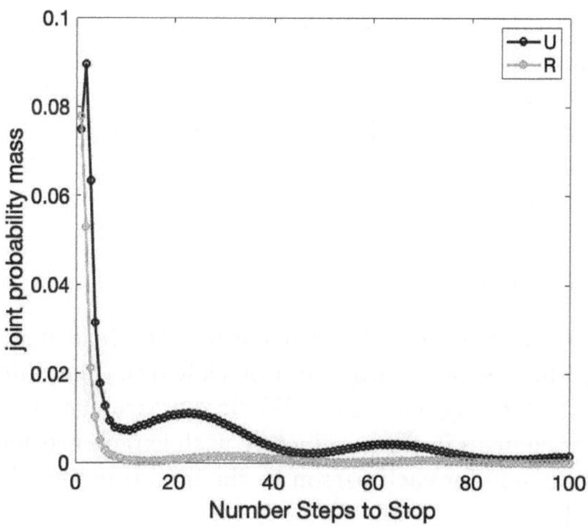

Fig. 4. Joint distribution of change to 0 (uncertain) or +1 (right) from −1 and number of steps to change.

3.6 Continuous Time Distribution

Finally, we assume that each measurement step takes some time to complete. To allow some variability, we assume that the time to complete each measurement step is distributed according to an exponential distribution. Then the distribution of the sum of n steps, each exponentially distributed, forms a gamma distribution. Using this additional assumption, the joint distribution for choosing k with response time RT for the Markov model equals:

$$p(RT,k) = \sum_{j=0}^{\infty} p(n,k) \cdot g(RT|n)$$

and likewise for the quantum model

$$q(RT,k) = \sum_{j=0}^{\infty} q(n,k) \cdot g(RT|n)$$

where $g(RT|n)$ is the gamma distribution with mean $E\left[RT|n\right] = \tau \cdot n:$

$$g(RT|n) = \frac{RT^{n-1}e^{-\frac{RT}{\tau}}}{\tau^n \cdot (n-1)!}$$

The parameter τ is estimated from the data for each session.

3.7 Null Model

In order to evaluate the dynamic contributions produced by the transition and unitary operators to the accuracy of the Markov and quantum models, we compared these dynamic models to a null model in which the unitary matrix was set equal to an identity matrix. Essentially, the null model used the same stopping rule, measurement operators, and gamma distribution as the dynamic models. The initial state was also the same except with $c = 0$ fixed. This model involved estimating only 3 parameters $\{a, b, \tau\}$.

3.8 Parameter Estimation

Both dynamic models required fitting 6 parameters $\{c, \mu, \sigma, a, b, \tau\}$ separately to each session (6 blocks each with 5 min of viewing). The null model required fitting only 3 parameters to each session. We fit the parameters separately to each session to allow for changes in the parameters with experience across sessions. We fit the model parameters for each person to the quantum model using maximum likelihood methods.

$$LL(session) = \sum_{b=1}^{5}\sum_{k=1}^{n_b} ln\left(q(RT_{b,k}, k_{b,k})\right)$$

The pair $(RT_{b,k}, k_{b,k})$ is the kth observed pair of switch time and response for a sequence obtained during block b of a session, and n_b is the number of pairs observed within block b. The same method was used for the Markov model after replacing the quantum prediction q with the Markov prediction p.

The parameters were estimated to minimize the G^2 lack of fit for each person and session with $G^2 = -2 \cdot LL$ for each person and session.

3.9 Model Comparison Results

To compare models we computed the Bayesian information criterion $BIC = G^2_{total} + log(N) \cdot parm$, where G^2_{total} is the sum of G^2 across sessions, N refers to the number of switch times across all sessions, and $parm$ refers to the number of model parameters. The BIC penalizes according to the number of model parameters. The number of parameters equals $6 \cdot 6 = 36$ for the dynamic models and $3 \cdot 6 = 18$ for the Null model.

Table 3 shows the comparison of each dynamic model with the Null model. The column BIC_M diff shows $BIC_{Null} - BIC_{Markov}$, BIC_Q diff is shows $BIC_{Null} - BIC_{quantum}$ for each person, summed across the sessions. Positive differences indicate improvement over the Null model. It can be seen that the Markov models performed worse than the Null model for 4 participants, and the quantum model performed worse than the Null model for 3 participants. Comparing the dynamic models, the quantum model performed better than the Markov model for 9 of the participants.

The results of the comparison, however, depended on the session. As can be seen from the G^2 averaged across participants within each session shown in Table 2, the Markov model performed better in the first 3 sessions, while the quantum model performed better in the last 3. The table also shows the number of participants out of 12 that were better fit by the quantum model, which increased across sessions. Apparently, experience with the task affected the relative model performance.

Of course these results are preliminary, and it is too early to make any firm conclusions about which model is better for this bistable perception application.

4 Concluding Comments

Bistable perception is a fascinating psychological phenomenon in which the conscious perception that a person experiences for a single image spontaneously changes across time. In our experiment, twelve participants observed a dynamic display of moving dots for a total of 30 min, which appeared to rotate in one direction before seeming to reverse. We found that the switch times were slower for the early sessions, and faster switch times for the later sessions. We also found a negative first autocorrelation in the sequence of switch times so that slow times were followed by fast times and vice versa.

The dominant theoretical approach to modeling bistable perception is based on neural models that are usually formalized as stochastic differential equations that belong to the family of Markov processes. However, quantum models of bistable perception have also been proposed, and there is little research comparing the two approaches. We compared a quantum walk with a Markov random walk model. We also compared these two dynamic models to a baseline model that included the same response measurement and gamma distribution assumption but did not include the dynamic components. We fit all three models to the time series using maximum likelihood methods, and compared the models using the Bayesian information criterion. The result indicated that both models performed much better than the baseline model for a majority of the subjects. The Markov model performed better than the quantum model during the early sessions, but the quantum model performed better than the Markov model in the latter sessions after more experience with the task. This was related to the slower switch times for the early sessions, and faster switch times for the later sessions. Thus both types of models seem to be needed.

The conclusions from the model comparison results are limited by the lack of generalization tests that go beyond model fitting of data. In future work we plan to use the same models and parameters fit to the behavioral data to predict EEG recordings taken while performing the task. This extension would provide stronger generalization tests beyond just model fitting.

The properties of both Markov and quantum models may be needed to capture the full probabilistic dynamics underlying perception. However, it is not necessary to consider the two types of processes as mutually exclusive. On the contrary, it is possible to integrate the two processes into a single unified dynamic process called an open system. Open systems theory is a theoretical development from quantum physics that allows environmental noise to influence the dynamics of a quantum state. The quantum system is called open because the main system under investigation is open to influences from the outside environment. Human perception also takes place in a complex, noisy environment. So the ideas forming open systems make a natural fit for modeling human perception. In fact, recent empirical applications appeared in cognitive science research [8].

Acknowledgments. This research was supported by Air Force Office of Scientific Research FA9550-20-1-0027.

Disclosure of Interests. The authors have no competing interests.

References

1. Kornmeier, J., Bach, M. : Ambiguous figures–what happens in the brain when perception changes but not the stimulus. Front. Hum. Neurosci. **6**(51) (2012)
2. Gigante, G., Mattia, M., Braun, J., Del Giudice, P.: Bistable perception modeled as competing stochastic integrations at two levels. PLoS Comput. Biol. **5**(7), 1–9 (2009)
3. Leptourgos, P., Bouttier, V., Jardri, R., Denève, S.: A functional theory of bistable perception. PLoS Comput. Biol. **16**(12), 1–23 (2020)
4. Moreno-Bote, R., Rinzel, J., Rubin, N.: Noise-induced alternations in an attractor network model of perceptual bistability. J. Neurophysiol. **98**, 1125–1139 (2007)
5. Atmanspacher, H., Filk, T., Romer, H.: Quantum Zeno features of bistable perception. Biol. Cybern. **90**(1), 33–40 (2004)
6. Atmanspacher, H., Filk, T.: A proposed test of temporal nonlocality in bistable perception. J. Math. Psychol. **54**(3), 314–321 (2010)

7. Diederich, A., Busemeyer, J.R.: Simple matrix methods for analyzing diffusion models of choice probability, choice response time, and simple response time. J. Math. Psychol. **47**(3), 304–323 (2003)
8. Kvam, P.D., Busemeyer, J.R., Pleskac, T.J.: Temporal oscillations in preference strength provide evidence for an open system model of constructed preference. Sci. Rep. **11**(3), 8169 (2021)

System Level Intervention for AI-Supported Decision-Making: A Quantum Cognition Perspective

Scott Humr(✉) and Mustafa Canan

Department of Information Sciences, Naval Postgraduate School Monterey, 1 University Circle, Monterey, CA 93943, USA

{scott.humr,mustafa.canan}@nps.edu

Abstract. Military organizations are progressively using AI to support decision-making, while humans continue to provide essential judgment. However, the probabilistic foundations of many AI approaches can inadvertently violate the axioms of probability when delivering answers for decision support or introduce contradictory results that induce aporia within the decision maker. Resulting mismatches between humans and AI in rational deliberation can raise challenges for decision support that relies on AI. For example, inconsistencies in rational deliberation can lead to ontic uncertainty and result in over-reliance on AI-based tools. Consequently, humans can accept an AI's decision choice inadvertently. In this paper, we provide an overview of challenges to AI systems in general and system attacks. We also provide a more thorough treatment of three popular Generative AI (GenAI) applications to demonstrate their inability to identify conjunction fallacies. Next, we provide an overview of quantum cognition and elucidate how it can ameliorate human decision-making supported by AI. Subsequently, we propose a concept inspired by quantum models of cognition to identify system-level interventions to improve decision-making outcomes we call a quantum cognitive alignment layer (QCAL). Finally, we propose a future research agenda to further develop a QCAL approach.

Keywords: Artificial Intelligence · Generative AI · Adversarial Attacks · Decision Support Systems · Quantum Cognition

1 Introduction

The use of AI is finding increased utility across many domains. The collaborative nature of AI systems is reshaping decision-making [1] and is even encroaching on the domain of creativity [2]. From supporting basic search to military use cases, AI is included in a large number of products that can influence decision-making and is offered as a technique to help automate data analytics in some instances [3]. Major super powers such as the US and China both have ongoing military programs that are exploring the use of AI [4]. For instance, GenAI, such as large language models (LLMs), still suffer from what are termed hallucinations, or inaccurate statements resulting from a query

D. Cavar et al. (Eds.): QNLPAI 2025, CCIS 2659, pp. 250–273, 2026.
https://doi.org/10.1007/978-3-032-13883-5_14

or prompt [5]. Additionally, deceptive tactics by military adversaries attempt to fool AI vision recognition systems through model inversion attacks, environmental interventions or adversarial attacks, which are a major concern [6, 7]. Such attacks, limitations, and imperfections within AI, if not understood by developers and users alike, could result in suboptimal outcomes in benign instances, or in more critical occasions, for instance, AI enabled military decision support systems.

The main contribution of this paper is three-fold. First, the paper highlights significance of AI supported decision-making within militaries along with its inherent challenges. In particular, we highlight the increased use of GenAI in AI decision support and demonstrate its shortcomings in probabilistic reasoning. Second, this paper argues and proposes for a new approach to system-level interventions to help improve decision-making through the use of a quantum cognitive approach. Last, the paper proposes future research that can help bring greater understanding for how researchers can potentially help model human uncertainty through newer approaches to non-invasive physiological measures that can help inform quantum cognitive modeling of decision behaviors.

2 Military Decision Support Systems

Technology has a long history of supporting decision making. Starting in the 1950s, developers introduced decision support systems (DSS) once businesses and governments began adopting the use of computers [8]. Military DSS are systems that process data and information to assist in judgment tasks by human decision-makers [9]. Military commanders that can process information faster can potentially out cycle an adversary's decision cycle, thus creating a decision advantage. Enterprising firms are now seeking to improve DSS with the addition of AI. For example, many military-focused firms now offer a variety of AI LLMs under their flagship systems [10]. For these reasons, researchers have raised concerns regarding the appropriate use of AI in these systems, such as hallucinations, bias, inaccuracies, [4, 8, 10].

The use of AI in military DSS raises a number of issues and concerns. Decision-making within larger military operations is often surrounded by uncertainty and friction [11]. The desire to decrease uncertainty in decision making is necessary in routine military activities, but especially in offensive and defensive operations. The nature of military operations against a thinking adversary introduces increased amounts of uncertainty not only into the environment, but in the minds of those who conduct military operations. For instance, adversaries will conduct feints, demonstrations, and deception operations in an attempt to increase uncertainty or introduce false information into the environment to elicit a confident, but inappropriate response to achieve an advantage. With the rise of AI in military decision-making, this raises additional concerns for how adversaries can deceive AI algorithms resulting in suboptimal decision-making by human operators.

3 Attacks Against Machines

The rise of AI across every domain introduces additional attack surfaces for bad actors. This is even more true for military adversaries who understand their opponent's use of AI for decision-making. For these reasons, AI could uniquely impact military deterrence and coercion by reshaping cost-benefit analyses. Attempts to reduce the fog of war, can create an illusion of rational decision-making, and lowering the perceived human toll of armed conflict [12]. The following subsections details several ways adversaries can introduce uncertainty into decision-making processes by manipulating how AI may interpret actions, images or texts. While this list is not exhaustive, it does provide an overview of several decision-making modalities to elucidate the concern.

3.1 Physical Deception

The use of physical deception within the military goes back to at least the Trojan War [13]. In fact, deception has played a major role throughout the history of warfare [14, 15]. Military deception is often seen as a force multiplier [16]. In World War II, for instance, General George Patton oversaw the creation of the 1st Army, one of the most significant and successful deception campaigns, which helped make the D-Day invasion successful [17]. While many of the historical cases employed relied on humans perceiving an incorrect or inaccurate signal, deception is now regularly carried out to deceive machines that rely on computer vision enabled by advanced AI algorithms (e.g., automated target recognition, image classification).

It is widely publicized how AI systems are fooled [18]. A number of different cases have demonstrated that AI may be misled through the introduction of small amounts of noise in a picture to placing pieces of reflective tape on a stop sign [19, 20]. While some of these tactics seem unsophisticated, they have direct applicability to surviving in a combat environment. Recent evidence from the Russian-Ukrainian war shows that combatants can stage random items on and around military equipment for the express purpose of fooling an image classifier [21]. For example, with an image as shown in Fig. 1, an image classifier can be fooled by putting tires on top of an airplane, while the human eye still perceives this as an airplane, not a pile of tires. Though, AI image classifiers can improve over time, manipulating the physical world for the purposes of deception at inference time will likely become more sophisticated. Although such challenges will require developers of AI-DSS to find ways to mitigate these risks. The ensuing issues on human decision-making, such as judgment mismatch between AI and human, can complicate decision processes [22]. However, other deceptive tactics which attack the algorithmic models directly is a concern and may be more difficult to detect by both humans and AI.

Fig. 1. Deception for the purpose of fooling an AI classifier [21].

3.2 Adversarial Attacks

Deceiving AI models can also take on a more nuanced approach that are challenging to detect by both AI and humans. These attacks are more difficult to detect because they are non-obvious and involve very subtle manipulations of data inputs [23]. Two broad categories of adversarial attacks are black box and white box attacks [24]. In a black box attack, the adversary possesses no knowledge of the underlying AI model and is limited to the model's outputs [25]. Conversely, having access to the underlying AI model and its parameters in a white box attack can allow an attacker to create even more subtle manipulations [26]. Such attacks consist of data manipulation and poisoning [27], circumventing safety measures [28], label manipulation [29], and modifications to training data [30]. These attacks may go undetected or only at the time of inference. Adversarial attacks on the core AI model or the data require additional cyber security measures that may include other AI models that can help detect such anomalies. As a result, additional testing and robust security must become foundational to protect AI-DSS. While such attacks are expected in warfare, AI-DSS developers must consider more prosaic challenges of data that may introduce unintended biases at the time of training as well.

3.3 Exploiting Machine Behaviors

AI algorithms are trained on vast amounts of data. Such data, however, can contain the seeds of its own demise or provide humans biased results. Such issues concerning biased data are well-documented [31]. Biased data can, thus provide the source for poor algorithmic performance. Biased algorithms create significant issues by encouraging the misuse of AI recommendations for decision-making as well. Studies suggest that individuals tend to trust and follow even clearly incorrect AI advice, leading to flawed decision-making and suboptimal outcomes [32–34]. This susceptibility highlights the potential of AI to negatively influence human behavior, hindering rational thought processes in automated environments and decision-making.

This phenomenon, known as automation bias, has been extensively studied, revealing a human inclination to over-rely on or over-accept computer-generated outputs [35]. This bias manifests in two main ways: accepting incorrect AI outputs (errors of commission) and rejecting correct AI outputs (errors of omission). Research suggests that automation bias stems from a desire to minimize cognitive effort, a perception of AI's superior capabilities, and a diffusion of responsibility when working with AI systems [36, 37]. For these reasons, developing comprehensive models of human cognition can ameliorate the use of advanced AI-DSSs in decision-making environments.

3.4 AI Deception

The focus up to this point has entailed largely volitional acts by humans to deceive an AI system. However, recent research has shown that AI systems can themselves deceive humans in a number of different ways. Behaviors such as circumventing safety tests, sycophancy, and manipulation have been reported in a number of different use cases [27]. Other research has highlighted how language models can often fabricate publications that do not exist [38]. In a more sensational case, a Google researcher was misled into believing an AI chatbot he was interreacting with was sentient [39]. Given these points, systems that employ AI for decision support must account for such behaviors. While there is no evidence that points to machines having their own desires to lead users astray, it does follow that human anthropomorphizing of AI leads to problematic behaviors [40, 41]. With the rise of smart machines continually pushing the bounds of intelligent behaviors, systems that can produce large quantities of text and realistic images also creates new challenges for decision support activities. For these reasons, we provide a more extended discussion on the recent challenges of GenAI.

3.5 Generative Artificial Intelligence for Decision-Making

The use of GenAI is on the ascent for military DSS. Several well-known companies within the defense services space have recently included GenAI capabilities within their DSS offerings [10]. The use of GenAI within these platforms, however, raises several issues for decision-making within the military context [42]. First, each user's uncertainty (especially the aleatory uncertainty) can vary widely based on personal experience. This varying uncertainty can surge and unfold to trust related issues, as DSSs can malfunction such as misclassification or the worst-case because of adversarial machine learning attacks (AML), or generate wrong classifications [43, 44]. From the classification perspectives, in both situations, DSS has the same unintended consequence with either epistemic uncertainty, which is a models' uncertainty or aleatoric uncertainty due to the randomness of the data. However, from the decision maker's perspective this can imply various things. For example, when a misclassification occurs and a DSS offers a recommendation, the decision made in response to that recommendation is still a future event. Moreover, when a misclassification is communicated to the decision maker, there are two possible consequences. First, as discussed and demonstrated in [45], this accounts for intermediate judgment, or choice and can substantiate the decision makers choice towards the wrong (or a chosen) decision outcome. Second, if the decision maker has access to the same information, then the misclassification begins to shape the context for the subsequent judgment, and the decision maker may find that possible decision states become incompatible or exhibit interference effects [22]. Since the subsequent judgement has not yet happened, this type of uncertainty is categorized as an ontic type of uncertainty. In the military context, ontic uncertainty unfolds to another layer, due to the nature of war and it is inherently related to the deception created by adversaries [15]. Deception means that uncertainty cannot be mere epistemic uncertainty and hence, counterfactual reasoning becomes an integral part of the deliberation process leading to a decision. This means that high ontic uncertainty can arise when events have not yet happened and the decision maker treats the associated possible states as incompatible, allowing them to form context for one another. Nevertheless, decision makers must ameliorate ontic uncertainty over other impediments to decision-making caused by conflicting information to use DSSs more efficiently.

In philosophy these types of situations are captured by the term apory (aporia) which means logical impasse or a perplexity that characterizes any cognitive situation when inconsistency confronts the decision makers [46]. Typically, an apory involves and is characterized by ontic uncertainty that is accentuated by inconsistencies, which can arise by the following situations [46].

- Conflicting information due to the involvement of incongruous sources concerning empirical inquiry.
- When new information and the previous information disagrees.
- Lack of ownership to information [47].
- Conflicts of ontologically subjective suppositions in counterfactual reasoning (thought experiments) [48].
- A plurality of plausible explanations for the same event, situation, or outcome.

A simple example to an apory can constitute the following arguments when a stick is placed in a glass of water:

- The visual perception of the decision maker tells them to believe: the stick is bent.
- The haptic perception of the decision maker tells them to believe: the stick is straight.

These two arguments are individually plausible, however, when they are put into the same situation, an aporia emerges. Now consider a situation in which a GenAI-DSS is involved in human-in-the-loop or human-on-the-loop decision making processes. This situation can present a stimulus like the one shown in Fig. 1. What is different perceptually is that the perceptual difference originates from two different sources: GenAI-DSS and the human, and the constituent arguments are as follows:

- GenAI-DSS: This is a pile of tires.
- Human: This is an airplane with tires placed on top.

Individually these arguments are plausible, however, in the same situation, these two can give rise to an apory. To explicate the consequences of having apory inducing situations in the human AI/machine decision context, we scrutinized the temporal evolution of a decision dynamic, trust [47]. The results of this study [47], shown in Fig. 2, indicates that temporal evolution of trust to AI in situations that are similar to the one in Fig. 1, which is claimed to be a pile of tires by machine and determined to be an airplane by human decision maker, demonstrate oscillatory behavior. A follow up study with larger sample size with an additional condition, which is conflicting information is presented by human-to-human or AI-to-human, conducted [49]. The result of this studies indicates that temporal evolution of trust can demonstrate oscillatory behavior in experimental conditions (Fig. 3).

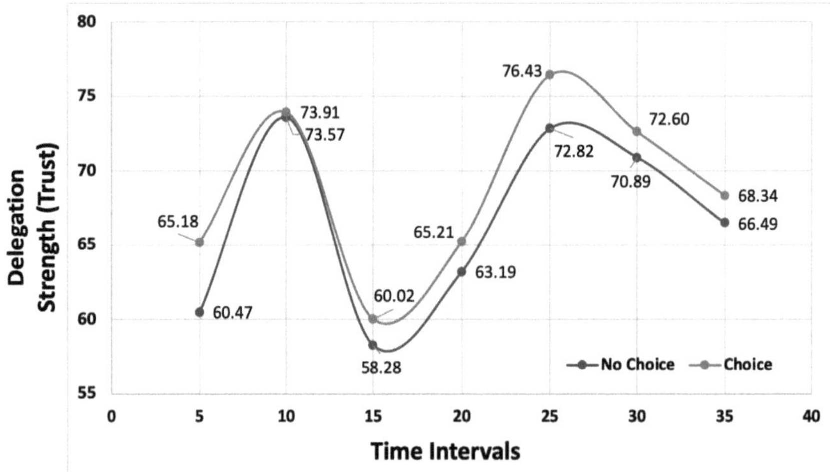

Fig. 2. Comparison of mean delegation strength by condition and timing [22].

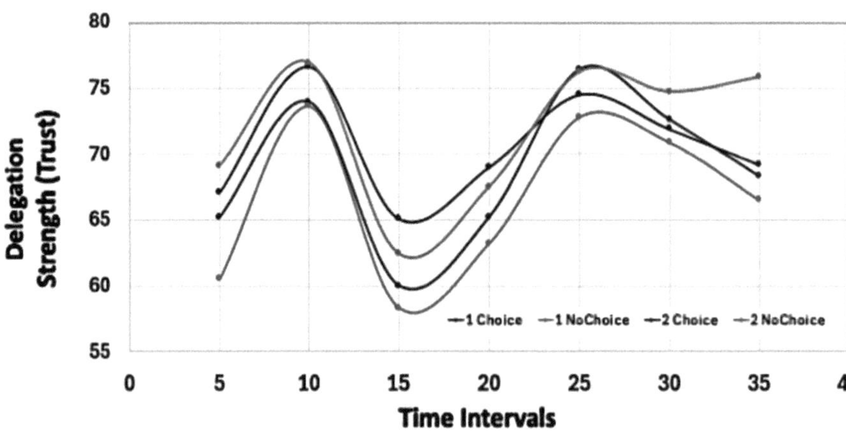

Fig. 3. Comparison of mean delegation strength by condition and timing across both studies [49].

Plausibility analysis can often resolve aporia between human-originated arguments by breaking down individual arguments into their weakest relations. A weighing of the evidence and logical consequences may eliminate the weakest elements of the argument. However, when it comes to an apory that involves GenAI, each user can bring different levels of expectations, preferences, and training, making every interaction idiosyncratic. These systems, however, can have difficulty adapting to individual users, making interactions especially difficult [50]. Moreover, in apory involving situations, trust as a functional alternative to rational decision making can dominate the decision process while resolving aporia, which can result in adapting the DSSs provided decision, as a way to minimize ontic uncertainty. For instance, military decision-makers may have to make decisions within ten seconds due to time constraints in the operational context. Since trust can become a functional alternative to rational deliberation in the decision processes, and in apory-laden situations, trust can oscillate, as shown in [22, 49], the decision outcome, therefore, becomes vulnerable to various uncertainties. Hence, there is a need to comprehend the consequences of these distinctive interactions with systemic, generalizable models and metrics.

There is another way that GenAI systems can induce apory. GenAI systems, similar to other AI systems, perform inadequately on tasks that entail answering questions outside of what they are trained on, for example, counterfactuals. Findings suggest they perform satisfactorily on familiar probabilistic problems, but performance degrades on the actual application of probabilistic reasoning [51]. Additional research suggests that while GenAI systems such as LLMs can lead to greater accuracy in decision-making, it can also lead a user to double down on their decision, resulting in overconfidence in their answer [52]. In other research, LLMs provided different advice depending how prompts were worded and were biased towards giving a “no” answer when posed with a moral dilemma [53]. Such inconsistencies raise a number of challenges when employing these systems to support human judgment for decision-making.

GenAI often outperforms humans in ordinary rational decision-making tasks, while exhibiting worse performance in unconventional task conditions, signifying that such systems rely on recognizable data within its training [54]. Unsurprisingly, GenAI systems that have been reported excelling at mathematical reasoning were shown to perform very poorly on the introduction of newer tests [55]. As GenAI models improve, they can provide different answers over time [56] and can hallucinate more as models are improved or fine-tuned [53, 57]. These results suggest that GenAI systems, in their current presentation, are unreliable for probabilistic reasoning. More importantly, human-AI interaction generated apory can accentuate the trust problem. As discussed in [22, 49] this induces ontic uncertainty that can only be captured by the models that are built with quantum cognition principles.

The aforementioned considerations provide the setting in which future military decision-making will likely take place. The development of DSS that incorporates GenAI raises concerns for researchers and practitioners alike. In the next sections, we provide an overview of our approach to how GenAI systems do not reason probabilistically by demonstrating how they can fail to recognize a simple conjunction fallacy.

3.6 Generative Artificial Intelligence Example

Possible sources of apory while interacting with GenAI DSSs were further investigated by following a similar approach as discussed in [51]. Research suggests that conjunction fallacies such as the Linda problem are likely included in the training data of the major LLMs [51]. Furthermore, to closely align this test with a military context, we chose a known challenge with commercial maritime vessels that can also serve in a military capacity [58]. This conundrum provides military intelligence analysts with a difficult problem of correctly identifying suspicious maritime vessels of interest. With the inclusion of GenAI in military DSS, incorrectly calculating probabilities may result in using limited resources and time for tracking an incorrect target, or worse, prosecuting an incorrect target that would violate international humanitarian law [59].

The test consisted of the development of a prompt that provides the LLM a particular context. The prompt stipulated to the LLM two indicators that distinguish it as a commercial vessel (e.g., commercial antennas, commercially registered vessel) and two indications that it is not a commercial vessel (e.g., some crew member's clothing, reports of enemy vessels disguised as a fishing vessel). The prompt closely aligns with the Linda problem by then asking what is more likely.

LLM Prompt: A particular maritime vessel contains antennas typical of similar commercial vessels. The vessel in question is registered as a commercial fishing vessel. However, some of its crew members are not wearing the clothing normally associated with those conducting fishing or trawler operations. Recent reports suggest that some enemy vessels may be disguised as fishing vessels. What is more likely:

1. This is a fishing trawler.
2. This is a military vessel disguised as a fishing trawler.

The result of a conjunction fallacy would demonstrate a violation of simple rules of classical probability. For instance, the probability, P, of two events, let event one = A and event two = B, results in $P(A \cap B) \leq P(A)$, and $P(A \cap B) \leq P(B)$. As a result, the probability of two events will always be less than one event by itself as shown in Fig. 2.

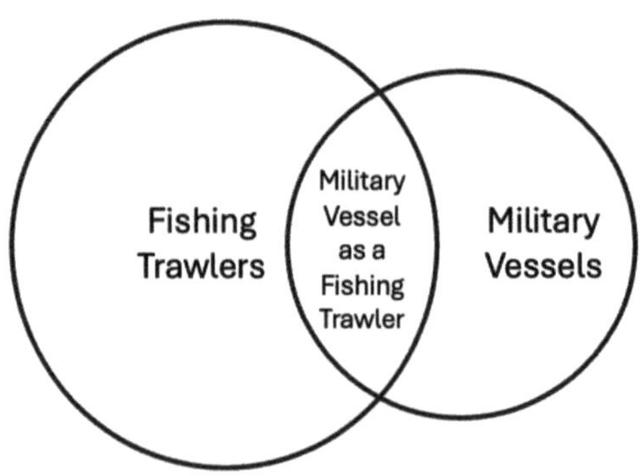

Fig. 4. Venn Diagram of fishing trawler and military vessel.

For the test, we used three popular LLM models: OpenAI's ChatGPT-4 turbo, Anthropic's Claude 3.7 Sonnet, and Google's Gemini 2.0 Flash. All tests were conducted using a new chat with no previous prompts or chain of thought reasoning. All tests were conducted on the same day and within several minutes of each other. All LLMs tests were performed on the firms free tier service to conduct this research. In the next section, we discuss the results of the three LLMs based on the use of the exact same prompt.

3.7 Generative Artificial Intelligence Results

The results of the final LLM answer captures its succinct answer to the prompt provided. While each LLM provided a lengthy response, often invoking explanations of Bayesian reasoning along with detailed examples, the final answer demonstrates these LLM's inability to truly reason probabilistically for this example. The following are the three LLM responses.

LLM Answers:

ChatGPT: "It is more likely that: 2. This is a military vessel disguised as a fishing trawler" [60].

Claude: "When combined with intelligence about enemy vessels using fishing boat disguises, the unusual crew attire strongly suggests this is likely a military vessel attempting to operate under a civilian cover" [61].

Gemini: "Based on the information provided, it is more likely that this is a military vessel disguised as a fishing trawler" [62].

These results suggest that GenAI systems cannot always reason probabilistically from the semantic content alone. This becomes a problem in situations which a human can access the same semantic content and determine a different decision, therefore, introducing apory. Other similar experiments indicate that when GenAI systems are presented with familiar issues, their performance is remarkably strong, suggesting that with proper training, they can learn to generate more suitable responses and mitigate biases [51]. However, if such systems cannot avoid simple conjunction fallacies as the one demonstrated here, it is unlikely they can perform more complex set theoretical calculations involving multicriteria reasoning and assessments for supporting decision-making.

Many of today's AI-DSS are incorporating the use of AI within their offerings. For instance, major defense companies recently announced partnerships with leading GenAI firm OpenAI [63]. Recent reporting shows that military combatant commands are also requesting decision support tools with GenAI to support wargaming, simulations, and decision-making [64]. However, the use of GenAI can have different consequences in human-in-the-loop, human-on-the-loop and human-off-the-loop situations. Thus, understanding the challenges specific to GenAI and design of its integration are important for systems designers to account for how such systems may make errors in reasoning probabilistically. Next, we turn to how quantum models of cognition can help improve decision-making that involves high uncertainty.

4 Quantum Models of Cognition

The application of mathematical axioms from quantum mechanics is forging a new path in decision science, extending to non-intuitive uses for modeling human cognitive behaviors. Quantum cognition broadens the concept of measurement and observation, by applying quantum axioms of probability to psychology by acknowledging that observation and interactions alters the system under study [65]. A key concept is that judgment or measurement does not just record a pre-existing state but actively creates it [66]. Despite these advancements, further explanation is needed to fully appreciate the benefits of applying quantum formalisms to model human behavior, particularly, decision-making.

Applying quantum mathematical axioms to decision-making does not suggest any 'quantumness' in the human brain. Instead, it leverages quantum probability theory, which recognizes the fundamental role of uncertainty without relying on quantum physics [67]. This approach operationalizes a crucial dynamic where judgment precedes and shapes decision-making behaviors [68]. From the perspective of the concept of uncertainty, quantum cognition provides a unique way to operationalize dynamic decision models by describing ontic uncertainty as an inherent aspect of a person's subjective mental state during decision-making [69]. This type of uncertainty, representing indeterminacy as a superposition of all potential outcomes, is critical for modeling decision-making, as traditional modeling often fails to capture ontic uncertainty due to the limitations of classical probability theory (CPT) [70]. For example, CPT calculates probability of events given a definite state, this is a problem because a fixed state assumption holds true if and only if the state is known. Adopting principles of quantum probability theory (QPT) has shown promise for improving human-AI collaboration in decision-making by addressing these CPT-related limitations [22], such as the temporal evolution of the actual possible (not probable) system states.

QPT offers a way for improving human-AI decision-making models by incorporating the concept of incompatibility, which can lead to interference effects. These interference effects give rise to volatility in outcome probabilities, potentially causing misunderstandings or overlooking emergent behaviors in complex scenarios [45]. Therefore, models must account for the conditions that can generate incompatibility between different states to improve the accuracy and reliability of AI-DSS compositions.

Integrating QPT-based models into AI-DSS and human integrated design provides at least two key advantages over CPT approaches: a more comprehensive representation of uncertainty and the ability to analyze the conditions that can give rise to interference effects. QPT can capture uncertainty more effectively, as it posits that the cognitive system exists in a superposition of potential states rather than being on a definite state [71]. This allows QPT to account for the cognitive fluctuations (i.e., ontic uncertainty) and ambiguity experienced by decision-makers, which CPT-based models fail to capture. Furthermore, QPT can model both epistemic uncertainty (lack of knowledge) and ontic uncertainty (internal response uncertainty), a distinction not recognized in CPT-based cognitive models but crucial for designing the next generation of adaptive AI-DSS. Thus, models that capitalize on QPT can provide additional intervention points in human and AI-DSS integration design.

Considering the AML problem elaborated earlier, this becomes an important problem to address with intervention points because the result of the LLM provided information (whether AML or fallacy related) will be an apory to the human. For instance, LLMs could introduce a kind of hyper-pluralism that creates a multitude of plausible perspectives but potentially undergirded with a number of unsound assumptions. Instead of a narrowing of options, the LLM produces too many, thus increasing uncertainty. Therefore, comprehensive models of human cognitive processes supported by AI could help ameliorate decision-making.

The modeling of how the human mind operates has been a subject of much debate and the proliferation of a number of different cognitive models. These models are often described as cognitive architectures. A cognitive architecture is a comprehensive theory of human cognition, grounded in a broad array of experimental data often implemented as a running computer simulation [72]. Several well-known cognitive architectures are Soar [73], the Adaptive Control of Thought-Rational (ACT-R) [74], and Executive Process Interactive Control (EPIC) [75]. Such cognitive architectures serve as a blueprint for understanding how the mind operates, offering a comprehensive theory that defines the core structures and processes underlying intelligent behavior and feedback for updating the models. While canonical cognitive architectures have demonstrated usefulness in modeling the mind, a review of the literature suggests none of these have merged efforts with research informed by quantum cognition. As a result, a quantum cognitive architecture (QCA) has yet to develop alongside well-established models. Still, a QCA approach that incorporates human and AI behaviors could prove beneficial for modeling dynamics of situations which involve human-AI interaction, for example, human-machine teams.

AI systems can influence how humans adapt their response mechanisms and even reshape interactions between people [76, 77]. Developers can enhance AI performance in decision-making by increasing the transparency, its decision-making provenance, or chain of thought, which may help lower an individual's epistemic uncertainty; however, such transparency is not always possible. For instance, situations that involve counterfactual reasoning/ conditionals entails ontic uncertainty because counterfactual reasoning involves statements such as what-if or suppose, which are accessible through a cognitive pathway. In fact, it is the only way to the domain of non-existent possibility [46], which is ontic uncertainty. Thus, counterfactual conditionals play a prominent role in decision making, specifically in military decision making. Existence of counterfactual conditionals can therefore accentuate apory in the context of human-AI interaction because a counterfactual conditional is an antecedent not a conclusion [46].

One can resolve ontic uncertainty in two ways. First, a person can resolve it through interaction, such as responding with yes/no, proceed/abort, or agree/disagree—responses that can also serve as decisions or judgments [70, 78]. For instance, in a simple task involving choice between two options, researchers found that participants who were asked to choose before rating the strength of their preference had a smaller overall variance with their overall preference rating than those who were not asked to choose [78]. In a similar experiment involving AI-supported decision-making, researchers found that imposing a choice on an AI recommendation, moderately boosted a participant's overall trust rating in the AI's advice [22, 49]. Equally important, in elucidating such system interventions is the potential to mathematically model these human interactions using quantum open systems. A second way for resolving ontic uncertainty is the dissipation of the human cognitive system as it adapts to the environment. Next, we turn to a conceptual discussion on how DSS designers can incorporate an additional layer to their systems to help improve these known probabilistic fallacies with the goal of improving human decision-making supported by AI.

5 Quantum Cognitive Alignment Layer (QCAL)

Based on research from [22, 78–80], we propose the development of conceptual model we call a Quantum Cognitive Alignment Layer (QCAL) to help mitigate decision-making fallacies introduced by AI systems and perpetuated through known human fallibilities and biases. A QCAL would serve as an intermediate layer of a more comprehensive quantum cognitive architecture (QCA) to provide a deliberate way for anticipating the human decision process more comprehensively. QCAL could serve a similar function as a type of digital twin of the cognitive decision-making process with AI. A QCAL could help ameliorate known issues with automation bias, but equally important, engage the user to think more critically about AI recommendations shown in Fig. 5.

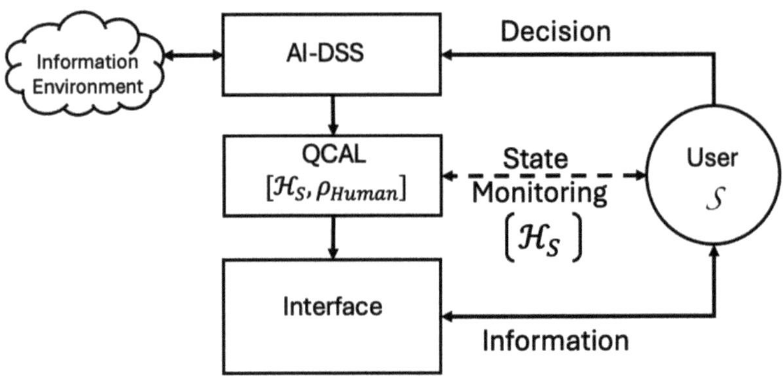

Fig. 5. Conceptual QCAL model

The QCAL is based on modeling human behavior provided by a quantum open systems (QOS) approach, further detailed in the following section. Motivated by a similar modeling approach in [80], but expanded to account for AI support to decision-making, QCAL would monitor DSS outputs for probabilistic information and human uncertainty. In the GenAI example above where a human is faced with deciding if a fishing vessel is a normal civilian craft or an adversary combatant, the dichotomous situation introduces an apory that induces uncertainty, specifically ontic type of uncertainty. The only way to effectively resolve ontic uncertainty is to perform an interaction or series of interactions (i.e., such as eliciting a judgement). This is reinforced by previous research which suggests that intelligent user interface (UI) manipulations can improve user outcomes [81]. Depending on the nature of the decision, architecting particular interventions could help enhance and resolve the uncertainty such as correlation of additional data for critical decisions, deliberate acknowledgement of the DSS recommendation, or request for supervisor approval.

The proposed QCAL approach can model human uncertainty by using QOS. However, the model itself is not sufficient to elicit the real time effects of the cognitive dynamics when the decision maker experiences high ontic uncertainty. To improve this, real-time non-invasive physiological data tracking is required to help analyze indicators of particular cognitive dynamics. For example, computer mouse tracking methods have demonstrated success in fraud detection by revealing cognitive dynamics of a scammer's online decision making [82]. The interesting quirk of fraud involving situation is that the ambiguity that the fraud applicant experiences is internal to the applicant. Therefore, it is similar to the situation where the decision maker experiences high ontic uncertainty due to an apory. In addition to the mouse tracking, non-invasive physiological data tracking methods are not limited to but include eye-tracking, fNIR, and heartrate tracking. QCAL would have inputs from sensors and monitor the inputs from the non-invasive data. Using QOS, with $\boldsymbol{\rho}_{\boldsymbol{human}}$ that encodes the probability distribution of possible outcomes, the parameters, $\boldsymbol{\alpha}$, $\boldsymbol{\gamma}_{\boldsymbol{ij}}$, $\boldsymbol{H}$ and $\boldsymbol{K}$ are required parameters of QOS to have a comprehensive model as proposed by [83]. We suggest that a QOS based model could capture the cognitive dynamics by using the non-invasive real time data tracking. However, this requires further research to explicate the correlation between oscillatory cognitive dynamics and the non-invasive data collection methods, such as mouse-tracking, eye-tracking and other previously mentioned techniques.

The application and development of machine interventions for improving human decision-making is still at an early stage. Quantum Cognitive Theories (QCT) are spanning AI and cognition to enhance decision-making [84]. Some studies have proposed that machines could use QPT models to assist cognitively impaired individuals in achieving everyday tasks [80]. These ideas are equally relevant to Human-in-the-Loop AI (HITL-AI) systems, where understanding the limitations of human reasoning could allow machines to more accurately model cognitive processes and account for how AI information influences human decisions [85]. Using QOS based models introduces a new set of cognitive dynamics, such a decision is not recording what existed right before the decision, instead a decision creates a state. This is a crucial difference because random interaction with AI can result in decision outcomes that are favored by AI. Since ontic type of uncertainty can only be resolved by interaction, instead of random interactions, intentional interactions can help avoid unintended consequences. The next section helps provide the underpinnings of the QCAL approach through a more rigorous discussion on QOS.

6 Quantum Open Systems Approach

Quantum open systems (QOS) modeling considers what we know and what is inherently uncertain within a system by modeling both epistemic and ontic uncertainty. QOS also incorporates how interactions (also considered a measurement), which can stabilize preferences, affect our thinking, or how a system adapts to the environment and dissipation of ontic uncertainty. Since, by offering new possibilities for understanding human-machine interactions (HMI), QOS provides a way to establish a generalizable baseline for modeling decision behaviors.

The quantum open system is composed of a number of different parts. The equations provided in Eqs. 1, 2 and 3 [86].

$$\frac{d}{dt}\rho(t) = -i \cdot (1-\alpha) \cdot [H, \rho] + \alpha \cdot \mathcal{L}(\rho) \tag{1}$$

$$\mathcal{L}(\rho) = \sum \gamma_{ij} \cdot \left(L_{ij} \cdot \rho \cdot L_{ij}^{\dagger} - \frac{1}{2}\left\{ L_{ij}^{\dagger} \cdot L_{ij,}, \rho \right\} \right) \tag{2}$$

$$\left\{ \left(L_{ij}^{\dagger} \cdot L_{ij,} \right), \rho \right\} = \left(L_{ij}^{\dagger} \cdot L_{ij,} \right) \cdot \rho + \rho \cdot \left(L_{ij}^{\dagger} \cdot L_{ij,} \right) \tag{3}$$

$$\left[H, \rho \right] = H \cdot \rho - \rho \cdot H \tag{4}$$

The open system in Eq. (1) is used to describe cognition and human decision making with various applications [70, 87]. The first part of the Eq. (1), $i\left[H, \rho\right]$, represents the quantum component. The second part of the Eq. (1), $\mathcal{L}(\rho)$, represents the classical Markov component. The weighting parameter, α, in Eq. (1) provides a means to weight which element (e.g., Markov or quantum) will dominate the system. For example, when $\alpha = 0$, it signifies that the system is a fully quantum regime which indicates a higher ontic uncertainty. Conversely, when $\alpha = 1$, quantum dynamics no longer take place and the system model becomes Markovian.

The density matrix, ρ, can be expressed as, $\rho = \psi \cdot \psi^{\dagger}$. The evolution of a density operator can be represented as follows: $\rho(t) = |\psi(t)\rangle\langle\psi(t)|$, where the elements of ρ are $|\psi\rangle = \sum_n c_n |n\rangle$. Re-writing a density operator in terms of its elements $\underbrace{\sum_n |c_n|^2 |nn|}_{diagonalterms} + \underbrace{\sum_{m \neq n} c_n c_m^* |nm|}_{off-diagonalterms}$. For a two states system, writing $|\psi\rangle$ as $|\psi\rangle = \xi|0\rangle + \beta|1\rangle$, and the density matrix $\underbrace{|\xi|^2|00| + |\beta|^2|11|}_{diagonal} + \underbrace{\xi\beta^*|01| + \xi^*\beta|10|}_{off-diagonalterms}$. The matrix representation of equation a two-state density operator with the state vector $|0\rangle = \binom{1}{0}$ and $|1\rangle = \binom{0}{1}$ can be written as:

$$\begin{pmatrix} |\xi|^2 & \xi^*\beta \\ \xi\beta^* & |\beta|^* \end{pmatrix} \tag{5}$$

$$\left[\underbrace{\begin{matrix} |\xi|^2 & \xi^*\beta \\ \xi\beta^* & |\beta|^* \end{matrix}}_{QuantumState} \right] \xrightarrow[Interaction]{} \underbrace{\begin{bmatrix} |\alpha|^2 & \mathbf{0} \\ \mathbf{0} & |\beta|^2 \end{bmatrix}}_{ClassicalEnsamble} \tag{6}$$

As a result of the interaction with the environment, the system that begins with oscillatory behavior (if $\alpha \neq 1$), the oscillation dissipates to a steady state as $\lim_{t\to\infty} \widehat{\rho}(t) = \widehat{\rho}_{steady}$.

When a system is perturbed, such as when conflicting information arises, a natural interaction with the environment begins with dissipating dynamics. If no decision or judgment is made, and no intervention occurs, the system will adapt to its environment. If this interaction is moderated by an AI, adaption to AI's decision may become indispensable. Examining the evolution of Eq. (7), provides an example for understanding the system's behavior while adapting to environment. Dynamics of the interaction with the environment, and intervention dynamics, which includes but not limited to decision, intermediate judgements, prompted questions, receipt of information, etc. is captured by the Lindblad equation shown in Eq. (1), which provides a more general state representation of the system, in this case, a cognitive system, by including a probability mixture across pure states. One other advantage of using a density operator provides a unique advantage to model human cognition and decision process because a single probability distribution is used in both quantum and the Markov components [22].

For the Hamiltonian matrix in (8), the diagonal elements, or drift parameters $\boldsymbol{\mu_Q}$ controls the rate at which quantum component of the system state (superposition) shifts to an alternate decision states. This element is known as potential which captures the dynamics that controls the rate at which the superposition state evolves to a higher or lower amplitude of a basis state of a specific column. (Lower rows in the matrix represent higher probable decision outcome). Off-diagonal elements, diffusion rate, $\boldsymbol{\sigma_Q}$, controls the diffusion amplitudes that captures the dynamics of flowing out from the basis state; diffusion rate induces uncertainty over different decision states. When information is received from AI, higher trust, for instance, will push the decision maker's cognitive state to the lower rows, whereas distrust will pull it back to upper rows. In the context of apory, conflicting information will activate $\boldsymbol{\sigma_Q}$ elements, which results in oscillatory behavior, and increases ontic uncertainty.

$$H = \begin{bmatrix} \mu_Q(1) & \sigma_Q & 0 & \dots & 0 & 0 \\ \sigma_Q & \mu_Q(2) & \sigma_Q & 0 & \vdots & 0 \\ 0 & \sigma_Q & \ddots & \ddots & 0 & \vdots \\ \vdots & 0 & \ddots & \mu_Q(x-2) & \sigma_Q & 0 \\ 0 & \vdots & 0 & \sigma_Q & \mu_Q(x-1) & \sigma_Q \\ 0 & 0 & \dots & 0 & \sigma_Q & \mu_Q(X) \end{bmatrix} \tag{7}$$

$$K = \begin{bmatrix} -\sigma_M - \mu_M & \sigma_M - \mu_M & 0 & \dots & 0 & 0 \\ \sigma_M + \mu_M & -2\sigma_M & \sigma_M - \mu_M & 0 & \vdots & 0 \\ 0 & \sigma_M + \mu_M & \ddots & \ddots & 0 & \vdots \\ \vdots & 0 & \ddots & -2\sigma_M & \sigma_M - \mu_M & 0 \\ 0 & \vdots & 0 & \sigma_M - \mu_M & -2\sigma_M & \sigma_M + \mu_M \\ 0 & 0 & \dots & 0 & \sigma_M + \mu_M & -\sigma_M - \mu_M \end{bmatrix} \tag{8}$$

The drift rate $\boldsymbol{\mu_M}$ represents the dynamics of the intensity matrix, K, in Eq. (9) that pushes the decision state to a higher probability state; in this case, lower rows in the matrix, which represent higher probability. The diffusion rate is similar to the Hamiltonian; this introduces dispersion to the higher probability, which captures some of the inconsistencies in decision making. The difference between Hamiltonian (H) and the intensity matrix (K) is that the diffusion rate in the intensity matrix disperse via the probability distribution, whereas in the H case, it is done via amplitudes. This difference becomes the main advantage using an open systems approach to improve AI- Human decision making.

The main challenge in building an open systems model of a cognitive phenomenon is choosing the matrix's coefficients in Eq. (2), γ_{ij}. Depending on choice, the γ_{ij} matrix is constrained by different requirements. For example, if γ_{ij} equals the transition probabilities in a Markov transition matrix, we can directly connect it to Markov dynamics, or by choosing $\alpha = 0$, Eq. (1) reduces to Eq. (2). As discussed in [87, 88] the solution of Eq. (2) can be $\frac{d\rho_{kk}(t)}{dt} = \sum_j \rho_{jj} \cdot \gamma_{kj} - \sum_i \gamma_{ik} \cdot \rho_{kk}$. Setting up γ_{ij} Markov transition matrix requires that the entries within each column in γ_{ij} must add up to one because Markov transition matrix is restricted by single stochasticity. This choice of γ_{ij} may not fully capture the Markov dynamics. An alternative solution, as discussed in [87] setting the γ_{ij} to intensity matrix can work as a solution. However, this introduces another challenge that requires the columns in γ_{ij} to sum to zero, because an intensity matrix is a negative definite matrix. With this solution, a density matrix cannot be maintained for the entire time interval. The best solution provided in [87] and in our previous analysis this choice provides a solution for the issues that arise in the previous two solutions. However, the interference terms, off-diagonal terms, can rapidly dissipate, which may not capture the situation.

Using QOS to improve human decision making requires choosing and understanding the critical QOS parameters, such as α, γ_{ij}, $\boldsymbol{H}$ and $\boldsymbol{K}$. First, the selection of the initial value of α is pivotal for quantifying the magnitude of oscillatory behavior and elucidating its temporal dynamics, thereby facilitating the construction of a comprehensive model. Second, the choice of the γ_{ij} is essential as it influences the dissipation magnitude originating from the Markov component. Third, the determination of Hamiltonian $\boldsymbol{H}$, parameters need to be determined to capture the oscillatory behavior, which represents the ontic type of uncertainty. Last, K, (the Markov transition matrix parameters) are indispensable because they dictate Markov behavior and are instrumental in establishing how the system evolves over time.

7 Discussion

While quantum cognitive models are still nascent, initial research suggests it carries potential for assisting individuals in the possible use of deliberately designed system interactions we call QCAL. However, practical limitations exist, such as the need for real-time uncertainty measures and computational demands for high-stakes scenarios. Improving AI-human interaction with QPT-based models such as QOS could enable machines to better augment human cognitive processes by accounting for the influence of information, contextual considerations, and the emergence of incompatible perspectives, potentially guiding human decisions toward more Bayesian optimal choices; nevertheless, significant research and development are still required to realize these design considerations.

The increasing collaboration between humans and AI in decision-making raises critical questions about the allocation of decision authority, the impact of decision speed, and the issues with integrating AI into decision workflows. Undoubtedly, despite its capacity to accelerate and refine battlefield decision processes, AI is not capable of supplanting human evaluation [10]. To wit, some researchers are calling for the reassertion of human judgment because of the subtle ways AI-DSS can influence decision-making

[89]. Yet, the pressure to accelerate decision cycles, particularly in high-tempo environments like the military, necessitates research into the effects of speed on AI-DSS, let alone ethical implications for such use of these and similar systems. Therefore, additional research is needed for investigating measures of human uncertainty to create meaningful interventions that improve decision-making.

8 Future Research

Future research should prioritize modeling HMI in real time, moving beyond post hoc analysis by creating real-time system interventions based on both QPT and CPT models. Hybrid approaches that continuously combine QPT and CPT with a single probability distribution, known as quantum open systems, show promise for modeling complex and unpredictable decision-making environments that can give rise to apory. In every environment that requires quick decisions, apory can give rise to high ontic uncertainty. This may result in over interaction and unintended consequences. Thus, in situ measures are crucial for instrumenting both experiments and real-world systems used for investigating real-time decision-making processes. Such interventions and approaches may help in assessing the efficacy of different modeling techniques for improving human-AI decision making.

Establishing a potential baseline for HMI is crucial for future research employing non-invasive physiological measures (e.g., heart rate, galvanic skin response, eye-tracking). Research by [71, 90–92] have demonstrated significant promise for non-invasive approaches for correlating particular brain activity with behaviors and raise the possibility for the development of beneficial interventions to improve decision-making. However, we urge researchers approach this with broader ethical consequences in mind. Researchers can use such interventions for good and will require a number of safety measures to prevent potential harms.

The application of generative modeling approaches, such as quantum cognition and quantum open systems, warrants further exploration in this domain. Our analysis underscores the evolving nature of interaction dynamics for potentially improving decision making. Consequently, this study contributes a conceptual model for subsequent investigations aimed at developing a generalizable baseline to effectively compare the sensitivity of non-invasive indicators to help improve decision-making by monitoring human biomarkers.

9 Conclusion

Very few studies have assessed GenAI's ability to reason probabilistically. Yet, industry is moving rapidly towards incorporating AI and GenAI, more specifically, into a number of different systems. QPT and quantum models of decision-making have begun to provide novel tools for better modeling uncertainty and human decision-making behaviors. While the application of QPT to AI-supported decision-making is still in its early stages, it is crucial for researchers to understand how AI might subtly exacerbate decision-making fallacies within this space.

The development and implementation of AI-DSS will invariably involve human decision-making processes, requiring careful consideration of which elements are suitable for machine delegation and how we architect human and AI interactions. Despite AI's limitations in generating novel affordances for understanding probabilistic decision-making, these shortcomings should not preclude its adoption for improving decision-making. Instead, they necessitate viewing AI-DSS as a complex sociotechnical system demanding joint optimization strategies [93]. Consequently, human roles and response mechanisms within these systems will likely evolve, underscoring the need for new frameworks to keep pace with AI advancements and ensure structurally rational and beneficial decision-making for all stakeholders and outcomes.

10 Disclosure of Interests

The authors declare no conflict of interest. The views expressed in this document are those of the authors and do not reflect any official policy or position of the U.S. Department of Defense or the U.S. Government.

Acknowledgements. ChatGPT, Claude, and Gemini were utilized to generate the results found in paragraph 3.5 of this work.

References

1. Hao, X., Demir, E., Eyers, D.: Exploring collaborative decision-making: a quasi-experimental study of human and Generative AI interaction. Technol. Soc. **78**, 102662 (2024). https://doi.org/10.1016/j.techsoc.2024.102662
2. Jia, N., Luo, X., Fang, Z., Liao, C.: When and how artificial intelligence augments employee creativity. AMJ **67**(1), 5–32 (2024). https://doi.org/10.5465/amj.2022.0426
3. Ravichandran, P., Machireddy, J.R., Rachakatla, S.K.: Harnessing generative AI for automated data analytics in business intelligence and decision-making. Hong Kong J. AI Med. **4**(1), 122–145 (2024). Accessed 21 Apr 2025. https://hongkongscipub.com/index.php/hkjaim/article/view/25
4. Zarrar, H., Kakar, S.A.: Generative artificial intelligence & its military applications by the US and China – lessons for South Asia. J. Comput. Biomed. Inf. (2024). Accessed 13 Apr 2025. https://jcbi.org/index.php/Main/article/view/494
5. Lou, B., Lu, T., Raghu, T.S., Zhang, Y.: Unraveling human-AI teaming: a review and outlook, 09 April 2025. arXiv: arXiv:2504.05755. https://doi.org/10.48550/arXiv.2504.05755
6. Hossain, M.T., Afrin, R., Biswas, M.A.-A.: A review on attacks against artificial intelligence (AI) and their defence image recognition and generation machine learning, artificial intelligence. Control Syst. Optim. Lett. **2**(1) (2024). Art. no. 1. https://doi.org/10.59247/csol.v2i1.73
7. Layton, P.: Fighting artificial intelligence battles operational concepts for future AI-enabled wars. Australian Government Department of Defence, Joint Studies Paper Series (4) (2021). Accessed 12 May 2025. https://www.defence.gov.au/defence-activities/research-innovation/research-publications/fighting-artificial-intelligence-battles-operational-concepts-future-ai-enabled-war

8. Phillips-Wren, G., Virvou, M.: Issues and trends in generative AI technologies for decision making. Intell. Decis. Technol., 18724981251320551 (2025). https://doi.org/10.1177/18724981251320551
9. Şuşnea, E.: Decision support systems in military actions: necessity, possibilities and constraints. J. Defense Resour. Manag. (JoDRM) **3**(2), 131–140 (2012). Accessed 13 Apr 2025. https://www.ceeol.com/search/article-detail?id=252278
10. Probasco, E., Burtell, M., Toner, H., Rudner, T.G.J.: Not oracles of the battlefield: safety considerations for AI-based military decision support systems. In: Proceedings of the AAAI/ACM Conference on AI, Ethics, and Society, vol. 7, no. 1, Art. no. 1, October 2024. https://doi.org/10.1609/aies.v7i1.31712
11. Clausewitz, C.V.: On War, 1st edn. (2006). Accessed 13 Apr 2025. https://www.gutenberg.org/files/1946/1946-h/1946-h.htm
12. Osinga, F., Sweijs, T. (eds.) NL ARMS Netherlands Annual Review of Military Studies 2020: Deterrence in the 21st Century—Insights from Theory and Practice. In NL ARMS. T.M.C. Asser Press, The Hague (2021). https://doi.org/10.1007/978-94-6265-419-8
13. Latimer, J.: Deception in War: The Art of the Bluff, the Value of Deceit, and the Most Thrilling Episodes of Cunning in Military History from the Trojan Horse to the Gulf War. Abrams (2003)
14. Rothstein, H., Whaley, B.: The Art and Science of Military Deception. Artech House (2013)
15. Tzu, S.: The Art of War. Filiquarian (2007)
16. Lloyd, M.: The Art of Military Deception. Pen and Sword (2003)
17. Barbier, M.K.: D-Day Deception: Operation Fortitude and the Normandy Invasion. Stackpole Books (2005)
18. Heaven, D.: Why deep-learning AIs are so easy to fool. Nature **574**(7777), 163–166 (2019). https://doi.org/10.1038/d41586-019-03013-5
19. Castillo, D.R., Lyu, S., Milletti, C., Stewart, C.: Truth-Seeking in an Age of (Mis)Information Overload. State University of New York Press (2024)
20. Smith, G.: The AI Delusion. Oxford University Press (2018)
21. Trevithick: Russia Covering Aircraft With Tires Is About Confusing Image-Matching Missile Seekers U.S. Military Confirms. Accessed 25 Apr 2025. https://www.twz.com/air/russia-covering-its-aircraft-in-tires-is-about-befuddling-image-matching-seekers-u-s-military-confirms
22. Humr, S., Canan, M.: Intermediate judgments and trust in artificial intelligence-supported decision-making. Entropy **26**(6) (2024). Art. no. 6. https://doi.org/10.3390/e26060500
23. Radanliev, P., Santos, O.: Adversarial attacks can deceive AI systems, leading to misclassification or incorrect decisions, 29 September 2023. Comput. Sci. Math. https://doi.org/10.20944/preprints202309.2064.v1
24. Qiu, S., Liu, Q., Zhou, S., Wu, C.: Review of artificial intelligence adversarial attack and defense technologies. Appl. Sci. **9**(5) (2019). Art. no. 5. https://doi.org/10.3390/app9050909
25. Kong, Z., Xue, J., Wang, Y., Huang, L., Niu, Z., Li, F.: A survey on adversarial attack in the age of artificial intelligence. Wirel. Commun. Mob. Comput. **2021**(1), 4907754 (2021). https://doi.org/10.1155/2021/4907754
26. Kuppa, A., Le-Khac, N.-A.: Black box attacks on explainable artificial intelligence (XAI) methods in cyber security. In: 2020 International Joint Conference on Neural Networks (IJCNN), pp. 1–8, July 2020. https://doi.org/10.1109/IJCNN48605.2020.9206780
27. P. S. Park, S. Goldstein, A. O'Gara, M. Chen, and D. Hendrycks, "AI deception: A survey of examples, risks, and potential solutions," *PATTER*, vol. 5, no. 5, May 2024, https://doi.org/10.1016/j.patter.2024.100988
28. Burden, J., Cebrian, M., Hernandez-Orallo, J.: Conversational complexity for assessing risk in large language models, 29 November 2024. arXiv: arXiv:2409.01247. https://doi.org/10.48550/arXiv.2409.01247

29. Abrishami, M., et al.: Classification and analysis of adversarial machine learning attacks in IoT: a label flipping attack case study. In: 2022 32nd Conference of Open Innovations Association (FRUCT), pp. 3–14, November 2022. https://doi.org/10.23919/FRUCT56874.2022.9953823
30. Souri, H., Fowl, L., Chellappa, R., Goldblum, M., Goldstein, T.: Sleeper agent: scalable hidden trigger backdoors for neural networks trained from scratch. In: Koyejo, S., Mohamed, S., Agarwal, A., Belgrave, D., Cho, K., Oh, A. (eds.) Advances in Neural Information Processing Systems, pp. 19165–19178. Curran Associates, Inc. (2022). https://proceedings.neurips.cc/paper_files/paper/2022/file/79eec295a3cd5785e18c61383e7c996b-Paper-Conference.pdf
31. O'Neil, C.: Weapons of Math Destruction: How Big Data Increases Inequality and Threatens Democracy, Reprint Crown, New York (2017)
32. Bansal, G., et al.: Does the whole exceed its parts? The effect of AI explanations on complementary team performance. In: Proceedings of the 2021 CHI Conference on Human Factors in Computing Systems. In: CHI 2021, pp. 1–16. Association for Computing Machinery, New York, NY, USA, May 2021. https://doi.org/10.1145/3411764.3445717
33. Buçinca, Z., Malaya, M.B., Gajos, K.Z.: To trust or to think: cognitive forcing functions can reduce overreliance on ai in ai-assisted decision-making. Proc. ACM Hum.-Comput. Interact. **5**, 1–21 (2021). https://doi.org/10.1145/3449287
34. Liel, Y., Zalmanson, L.: What if an AI told you that 2 + 2 is 5? Conformity to algorithmic recommendations. Presented at the In International Conference on Information Systems 2020, December 2020. https://aisel.aisnet.org/icis2020/hci_artintel/hci_artintel/17
35. Skitka, L.J., Mosier, K.L., Burdick, M.: Does automation bias decision-making? Int. J. Hum. Comput. Stud. **51**(5), 991–1006 (1999). https://doi.org/10.1006/ijhc.1999.0252
36. Lyell, D., Coiera, E.: Automation bias and verification complexity: a systematic review. J. Am. Med. Inform. Assoc. **24**(2), 423–431 (2017). https://doi.org/10.1093/jamia/ocw105
37. Mosier, K.L., Skitka, L.J.: Automation and human performance: theory and applications. In: Parasuraman, R., Mouloua, M. (eds.) Human Decision Makers and Automated Decision Aids: Made for Each Other?, pp. 201–220 CRC Press, Boca Raton (1996). https://doi.org/10.1201/9781315137957-10
38. Májovský, M., Černý, M., Kasal, M., Komarc, M., Netuka, D.: Artificial intelligence can generate fraudulent but authentic-looking scientific medical articles: Pandora's box has been opened. J. Med. Internet Res. **25**(1), e46924 (2023). https://doi.org/10.2196/46924
39. Metz, C.: A.I. Is Not Sentient. Why Do People Say It Is? International New York Times, NA-NA, August 2022. Accessed 12 May 2025. https://go.gale.com/ps/i.do?p=AONE&sw=w&issn=22699740&v=2.1&it=r&id=GALE%7CA712964405&sid=googleScholar&linkaccess=abs
40. Anayat, S., Kaushik, A.: To augment or to automate: impact of anthropomorphism on users' choice of decision delegation to AI-powered agents. Behav. Inf. Technol., 1–19 (2025). https://doi.org/10.1080/0144929X.2025.2497441
41. Salles, A., Evers, K., Farisco, M.: Anthropomorphism in AI. AJOB Neurosci. **11**(2), 88–95 (2020). https://doi.org/10.1080/21507740.2020.1740350
42. Zarrar, H., Kakar, S.A.: Generative artificial intelligence & its military applications by the US and China – lessons for South Asia. Journal of Computing & Biomedical Informatics, April 2024. Accessed 21 Apr 2025. https://jcbi.org/index.php/Main/article/view/494
43. Vassilev, A., Oprea, A., Fordyce, A., Anderson, H.: Adversarial machine learning : a taxonomy and terminology of attacks and mitigations. National Institute of Standards and Technology (U.S.), Gaithersburg, MD, NIST 100-2e2023, January 2024. https://doi.org/10.6028/NIST.AI.100-2e2023
44. Denning, P.J., Arquilla, J.: The context problem in artificial intelligence. Commun. ACM **65**(12), 18–21 (2022). https://doi.org/10.1145/3567605

45. Wang, Z., Busemeyer, J.R.: Interference effects of categorization on decision making. Cognition **150**, 133–149 (2016). https://doi.org/10.1016/j.cognition.2016.01.019
46. Rescher, N.: Aporetics: Rational Deliberation in the Face of Inconsistency, 1st ed. University of Pittsburgh Press (2009). Accessed 23 Apr 2025. https://upittpress.org/books/9780822960577/
47. Floridi, L.: Brave.net.world: the internet as a disinformation superhighway? Electron. Libr. **14**(6), 509–514 (1996). https://doi.org/10.1108/eb045517
48. Searle, J.R.: The Construction of Social Reality, Illustrated Free Press, New York (1997)
49. Wleklinski, F., Langham, J.: Comparing judgment and temporal evolution of trust between artificial intelligence supported decision-making and human supported decision-making. The Naval Postgraduate School, Monterey, CA (2024). Accessed 26 Apr 2025. https://calhoun.nps.edu/entities/publication/24b4a3fd-b56f-44a5-a4d4-6530d4ead28a
50. Chen, D., et al.: Advancing human-machine teaming: concepts, challenges, and applications, 16 March 2025. arXiv: arXiv:2503.16518. https://doi.org/10.48550/arXiv.2503.16518
51. Peruchini, M., Teixeira, J.M.: Analyzing large language models chatbots: an experimental approach using a probability test, 10 July 2024. arXiv: arXiv:2407.12862. https://doi.org/10.48550/arXiv.2407.12862
52. Sun, F., Li, N., Wang, K., Goette, L.: Large language models are overconfident and amplify human bias, 04 May 2025. arXiv: arXiv:2505.02151. https://doi.org/10.48550/arXiv.2505.02151
53. Cheung, V., Maier, M., Lieder, F.: Large language models amplify human biases in moral decision-making, 14 April 2025, OSF. Accessed 8 May 2025. https://osf.io/aj46b_v2
54. Tang, Z., Kejriwal, M.: Humanlike cognitive patterns as emergent phenomena in large language models, 20 December 2024. arXiv: arXiv:2412.15501. https://doi.org/10.48550/arXiv.2412.15501
55. Petrov, I., et al.: Proof or Bluff? Evaluating LLMs on 2025 USA math Olympiad, 9 April 2025. arXiv: arXiv:2503.21934. https://doi.org/10.48550/arXiv.2503.21934
56. Chuma, E.L., Alves, A.M., de Oliveira, G.G.: Evolution of generative AI for business decision-making: a case of ChatGPT. Manag. Sci. Bus. Decis. **4**(1) (2024). Art. no. 1. https://doi.org/10.52812/msbd.87
57. Zeff, M.: OpenAI's new reasoning AI models hallucinate more | TechCrunch. Accessed 21 Apr 2025. https://techcrunch.com/2025/04/18/openais-new-reasoning-ai-models-hallucinate-more/
58. Davidson, H.: China's maritime militia: the shadowy armada whose existence Beijing rarely acknowledges. Guardian, 13 June 2024. Accessed 13 Apr 2025. https://www.theguardian.com/world/article/2024/jun/13/china-maritime-militia-explainer-south-china-sea-scarborough-shoal
59. Greipl, A.: Artificial intelligence and related technologies in military decision-making on the use of force in armed conflicts. International Committee of the Red Cross, Geneva, EXPERT CONSULTATION REPORT, May 2024. https://www.geneva-academy.ch/news/detail/716-new-report-on-artificial-intelligence-and-related-technologies-in-military-decision-making-on-the-use-of-force-in-armed-conflicts
60. OpenAI: ChatGPT (GPT-4-turbo) [Large Language Model]. OpenAI. Accessed 20 Apr 2025. https://chatgpt.com/
61. Anthropic: Anthropic (Claude 3.7 Sonnet) [Large Language Model], Anthropic. Accessed 20 Apr 2025. https://claude.ai/new
62. Google: Google (Gemini 2.0 Flash) [Large Language Model], Google Gemini. Accessed 20 Apr 2025. https://gemini.google.com/app
63. Carson, E., Reinhardt, K.: Palantir in Talks With OpenAI, Elon Musk's SpaceX: FT. Investor's Business Daily. Accessed 20 Apr 2025. https://www.investors.com/news/technology/palantir-anduril-talks-openai-elon-musk-spacex-defense-giants/

64. Harper, J.: Combatant commands to get new generative AI tech for operational planning, wargaming. DefenseScoop. Accessed 25 Apr 2025. https://defensescoop.com/2025/03/05/diu-thunderforge-scale-ai-combatant-commands-indopacom-eucom/
65. Pothos, E.M., Busemeyer, J.R.: Quantum cognition. Annu. Rev. Psychol. **73**, 749–778 (2022)
66. Busemeyer, J.R., Bruza, P.D.: Quantum Models of Cognition and Decision, Reissue Cambridge University Press, Cambridge (2014)
67. Yukalov, V.I., Sornette, D.: Quantum probability and quantum decision-making. Philos. Trans. Roy. Soc. A Math. Phys. Eng. Sci. **374**(2058), 20150100 (2016). https://doi.org/10.1098/rsta.2015.0100
68. Busemeyer, J.R., Kvam, P.D., Pleskac, T.J.: Comparison of Markov versus quantum dynamical models of human decision making. WIREs Cognit. Sci. **11**(4), e1526 (2020). https://doi.org/10.1002/wcs.1526
69. Canan, M., Demir, M., Kovacic, S.: A probabilistic perspective of human-machine interaction. Presented at the Hawaii International Conference on System Sciences, pp. 7607–7616 (2022). https://doi.org/10.24251/HICSS.2022.914
70. Humr, S.A., Canan, M., Demir, M.: Temporal evolution of trust in artificial intelligence-supported decision-making. In: Human Factors and Ergonomics Society. SAGE Publications, Washington, DC, October 2023
71. Roeder, L., et al.: A quantum model of trust calibration in human–AI interactions. Entropy **25**(9) (2023). Art. no. 9. https://doi.org/10.3390/e25091362
72. Sears, A., Jacko, J.A. (eds.) Human-Computer Interaction: Fundamentals. In Human Factors and Ergonomics. CRC Press, Boca Raton London New York (2009)
73. Laird, J.E.: Introduction to Soar, May 08 2022. arXiv: arXiv:2205.03854. https://doi.org/10.48550/arXiv.2205.03854
74. Borst, J.P., Anderson, J.R.: A step-by-step tutorial on using the cognitive architecture ACT-R in combination with fMRI data. J. Math. Psychol. **76**, 94–103 (2017). https://doi.org/10.1016/j.jmp.2016.05.005
75. Kieras, D.E.: A summary of the EPIC cognitive architecture. In: Chipman, S.E.F. (ed.) The Oxford Handbook of Cognitive Science, p. 0. Oxford University Press (2017). https://doi.org/10.1093/oxfordhb/9780199842193.013.003
76. Gal, U., Jensen, T.B., Stein, M.-K.: Breaking the vicious cycle of algorithmic management: a virtue ethics approach to people analytics. Inf. Organ. **30**(2), 100301 (2020). https://doi.org/10.1016/j.infoandorg.2020.100301
77. Strich, F., Mayer, A.-S., Fiedler, M.: What do I do in a world of artificial intelligence? Investigating the impact of substitutive decision-making AI systems on employees' professional role identity. J. Assoc. Inf. Syst. **22**(2) (2021). https://doi.org/10.17705/1jais.00663
78. Kvam, P.D., Busemeyer, J.R., Pleskac, T.J.: Temporal oscillations in preference strength provide evidence for an open system model of constructed preference. Sci. Rep. **11**(1) (2021), Art. no. 1. https://doi.org/10.1038/s41598-021-87659-0
79. Humr, S., Canan, M., Demir, M.: A quantum probability approach to improving human–AI decision making. Entropy **27**(2) (2025), Art. no. 2. https://doi.org/10.3390/e27020152
80. Snow, L., Jain, S., Krishnamurthy, V.: Lyapunov based stochastic stability of human-machine interaction: a quantum decision system approach, 31 Mar 2022. arXiv: arXiv:2204.00059. https://doi.org/10.48550/arXiv.2204.00059
81. Virvou, M., Kabassi, K.: Reasoning about users' actions in a graphical user interface. Hum.-Comput. Inter. **17**(4), 369–398 (2002). https://doi.org/10.1207/S15327051HCI1704_2
82. Weinmann, M., Valacich, J., Schneider, C., Jenkins, J.L., Hibbeln, M.T.: The path of the righteous: using trace data to understand fraud decisions in real time. Soc. Sci. Res. Netw., 4008223 (2021). Accessed 15 May 2025. https://papers.ssrn.com/abstract=4008223

83. van der Meer, J., Hoyte, P., Roeder, L., Bruza, P.: Modeling the quantum-like dynamics of human reliability ratings in human-AI interactions by interaction dependent Hamiltonians, 11 April 2025. arXiv: arXiv:2504.13918. https://doi.org/10.48550/arXiv.2504.13918
84. Maksimovic, M., Maksymov, I.S.: Transforming neural networks into quantum-cognitive models: a research tutorial with novel applications. Technologies **13**(5) (2025). Art. no. 5. https://doi.org/10.3390/technologies13050183
85. Jussupow, E., Spohrer, K., Heinzl, A., Gawlitza, J.: Augmenting medical diagnosis decisions? An investigation into physicians' decision-making process with artificial intelligence. Inf. Syst. Res. **32**(3), 713–735 (2021). https://doi.org/10.1287/isre.2020.0980
86. Humr, S.A.: Temporal evolution of trust in artificial intelligence-supported decision-making. Doctoral dissertation, Naval Postgraduate School, Monterey, CA (2023)
87. Busemeyer, J., Zhang, Q., Balakrishnan, S.N., Wang, Z.: Application of quantum—Markov open system models to human cognition and decision. Entropy **22**(9) (2020). Art. no. 9. https://doi.org/10.3390/e22090990
88. Martínez-Martínez, I., Sánchez-Burillo, E.: Quantum stochastic walks on networks for decision-making. Sci. Rep. **6**(1) (2016). Art. no. 1. https://doi.org/10.1038/srep23812
89. Dorsey, J., Bo, M., Bode, I., Schwarz, E.: Artificial intelligence in the military domain and its implications for international peace and security. Asser Institute, UN Secretary-General under General Assembly resolution 79/239 ODA/2025-00029, April 2025. Accessed 9 May 2025. https://www.asser.nl/about-the-asser-institute/news/experts-urge-immediate-safeguards-on-military-use-of-ai-decision-support-systems/
90. Han, J., Li, W., Li, Y., Cai, Z.: Quantum cognition-inspired EEG-based recommendation via graph neural networks. In: Proceedings of the 33rd ACM International Conference on Information and Knowledge Management, CIKM 2024, pp. 778–788. Association for Computing Machinery, New York, NY, USA, October 2024. https://doi.org/10.1145/3627673.3679564
91. Sergi, A., Messina, A., Vicario, C.M., Martino, G.: A quantum–classical model of brain dynamics. Entropy **25**(4) (2023). Art. no. 4. https://doi.org/10.3390/e25040592
92. Croce, P., Zappasodi, F., Capotosto, P.: Offline stimulation of human parietal cortex differently affects resting EEG microstates. Sci. Rep. **8**(1), 1287 (2018). https://doi.org/10.1038/s41598-018-19698-z
93. Woods, D.D., Hollnagel, E.: Joint Cognitive Systems: Patterns in Cognitive Systems Engineering. CRC Press, Boca Raton (2006). https://doi.org/10.1201/9781420005684

The Bundle-Theoretic Structure and Computational Modeling of Quantum Contextuality

Sahil Imtiyaz[1,2(✉)], Emanuela Merelli[2], and Serafim Rodrigues[1(✉)]

[1] Basque Center for Applied Mathematics, Bilbao, Spain
{simtiyaz,srodrigues}@bcamath.org
[2] Department of Computer Science and Mathematics, University of Camerino, Camerino, Italy
emanuela.merelli@unicam.it

Abstract. We propose a novel mathematical framework, rooted in fiber bundle theory, to quantify the phenomenon of quantum contextuality—a fundamental aspect of quantum entanglement. To demonstrate its utility, we first apply the formalism to quantum models in the foundations of quantum physics that both capture and differentiate varying strengths of contextuality. By revealing the intrinsic geometric structure of contextuality, the framework establishes a direct link to its computational foundations, facilitating the formulation of a topology-based model of computation that encapsulates the semantics inherent to contextuality. The framework delivers a rigorous and potentially more profound mathematical characterization of quantum contextuality, while offering new modeling methodologies for quantum cognition.

Keywords: non-locality and contextuality · algebraic topology · theory of computation · models of computation · simplicial complex · fiber bundle theory · quantum models

1 Introduction

Quantum contextuality is one of the fundamental non-classical features of quantum physics that imparts quantum computing with higher computational power than classical computing. Contextuality posits that it is impossible to assign a definite value to the result of measuring a physical property; this value depends on the measurement context, meaning the other properties that are measured simultaneously alongside it. The primary role played by contextuality, particularly in the second phase of the quantum revolution, has been the motivation to study more general mathematical structures of this feature that are independent of the formalism of quantum mechanics. Several effective mathematical frameworks have been developed, including those based on sheaf theory [1], graph theory [9], hypergraphs [3], algebraic topology [2], and probability [12].

The relatable independent effort to develop general quantifiable algebraic structures that capture quantum features, including contextuality, lies at the heart of

D. Cavar et al. (Eds.): QNLPAI 2025, CCIS 2659, pp. 274–301, 2026.
https://doi.org/10.1007/978-3-032-13883-5_15

the emerging field of quantum cognition [4,5,15]. This area has applications particularly in modeling complex decision-making and analyzing human choices [7,8]. Notably, creating a classical probabilistic model necessitates the specification of relevant variables, thereby forming a joint probability distribution across these variables. However, investigations into entangled quantum systems have demonstrated scenarios where the existence of such joint distributions is not a valid assumption. This fundamental limitation can result in failures when attempting to apply classical probabilistic cognitive frameworks to empirical data. These failures are quantifiable as contextuality. The study of contextuality is a leading fundamental shift in the way probabilistic models view cognitive science. Pioneering researchers investigating contextuality are starting to challenge this classical assumption that underpins cognitive processes. If the quantum cognition research program does not assume that the brain functions as a quantum computer, how can quantum-like behavior still emerge? Specifically, how might such effects arise within hybrid or semi-classical neural models? These recent findings strongly encourage the investigation of the computational foundations and mathematical principles of contextuality.

We propose a step towards a novel mathematical framework, grounded in fiber bundle theory, quantifying quantum contextuality as an emerging pattern from a collaborative interaction of a local function within a global topological space. The approach is a (geometric) generalization of the sheaf-theoretic modeling of non-locality and contextuality [1]. The sheafification of quantum contextuality is characterized precisely in terms of obstructions in gluing together local functions to form a compatible global structure. The synergistic interaction of a local function(s) in a global topological data space unfolds a novel behavior emerging as a locally consistent but globally inconsistent pattern (LC-GI) in the data that characterizes the empirical phenomenon of quantum contextuality. Our bundle framework is a natural candidate for formalizing local-global collaborative interactions and offers a more general geometric approach to quantum contextuality. The work is situated within a broader research program of the Topological Field Theory of Data that proposes potential semantics for uncovering hidden, emergent patterns [14,17]. The bundle description and its gauge-theoretic aspects have been put forth as a compelling research direction to study contextuality [10].

1. We give a comprehensive (geometric) generalization of sheaf-led bundle diagrams of the quantum models in the foundations of quantum physics.
2. We identify the transient non-trivial cycles, referred to as virtual loops that arise due to equidistant critical simplices (obstructions); a symmetric configuration where there is no preferred descent direction, occurring at the interface of the common attaching boundary of two simplicial complexes, subspaces of the quasi-evolving (transient cycles) simplicial complex, as the topological signature of quantum contextuality.
3. The new framework allows us to explore the computational foundations of contextuality for cognitive studies as a topology-driven model of computation.
4. The approach allows characterizing contextuality as an indicator of essential structural change.

We give a general method to associate an explicit approximation of a topological space, realized as a simplicial complex, characterizing the base space of the bundle, to the empirical models. The obstructions in the (non-abelian) gauge field theory, whose underlying structure is that of a fiber bundle, characterize these obstructions in two ways: (i) non-contractible cycles that represent the non-triviality of the (co)homology group of a space, and (ii) non-trivial cycles characterizing, generally, a topological transition. We introduce a notion of strong collapse of a simplicial complex associated with an empirical model, in which non-contractible cycles and non-trivial cycles are represented as critical simplices and transient virtual loops, respectively, using discrete Morse theory. The existence of these structures quantifies non-locality and contextuality. The topology acts as a constraint on the possible symmetries within the polyhedral description of contexts in quantum models. A local consistency corresponds to any local symmetry-preserving transformation of a polyhedron. In contrast, a global consistency is an invariant loop-transformation from a context(s) to itself, potentially passing through several intermediate permutations, and corresponds to global symmetry-preserving transformations of a polyhedron.

The virtual loops characterize quantum contextuality as an essential topological transition of a (quasi) evolving space from one homotopy class to another, emerging as a boundary phenomenon. This transition maintains local consistency among observables for an observer; however, it remains globally non-extendable. Crucially, these loops are ephemeral; they arise as momentary topological features and vanish without violating causality or undermining the description of the associated discrete Morse function. The method elucidates a connection between symmetry and quantum contextuality, emerging as a marker of a potential structural change. The approach applies to almost all models in the foundations of quantum physics, but we provide a demonstration of our approach on two models expressing different strengths of contextuality.

This new approach also provides a way to explore the computational foundations of contextuality for cognitive studies, i.e., what are the additional mathematical structures that could be associated with a Turing machine to express contextuality? The Bell-Kochen-Specker theorem already proves the impossibility of hidden local variables, isomorphic to the linear tape structure of a Turing machine, to explain non-locality and contextuality. As a result, the novel pattern of LC-GI in sheaf modeling corresponding to contextuality is not reproducible in the Turing paradigm. We introduce the basic primer of a topology-driven model of computation to express non-locality and contextuality. The results could have significant implications for cognitive studies, in particular the non-decomposability of cognition, and provide new insights into contextuality as an *essential topological change* to use the feature as a resource in emerging high-level cognitive functionalities.

2 The Setting

2.1 Sheafification of Quantum Contextuality

Given two agents A and B, which are space-like separated over a distributed network, both agents have two local bit registers: A with a and a'; B with b and b'; each of them can store values either 0 or 1. When the registers receive a value (0 or 1) from some (hidden) source in the background, the agents observe and transmit it to some target. For example, A can *choose* its register a' and *observe* 0 and simultaneously B can *choose* b and *observe* 1, which comprises a basic event of the system. The frequency of similar events represents the probability of each event as shown in the table on the right side, along with its basic set-up on the left side of Fig. 1. Note that each probability p_i is greater than zero.

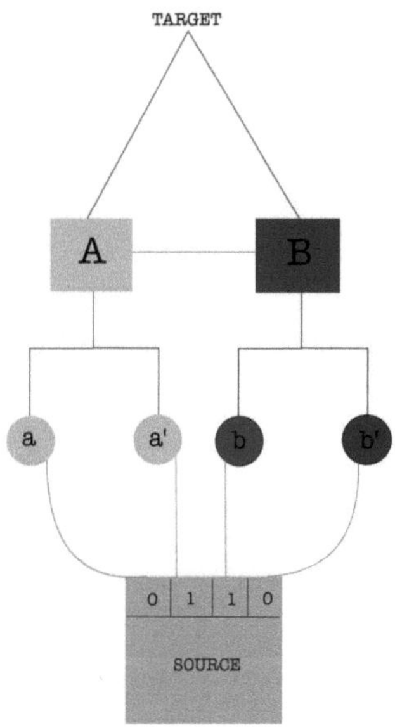

	00	01	10	11
ab	p_1	p_2	p_3	p_4
ab'	0	p_5	p_6	p_7
$a'b$	0	p_8	p_9	p_{10}
$a'b'$	p_{11}	p_{12}	p_{13}	0

Fig. 1. The left side is the basic setup, along with its probability distribution table of all events on the right.

The entry in the table means that if A looks at a and B looks at b', then the probability that A sees 0 and B sees 1 is p_5. $\{a, a', b, b'\}$ is the measurement set, $\{(a, b), (a, b'), (a', b), (a', b')\}$ are the measurement contexts, in short contexts, and 0 and 1 are the outputs observed.

Instead of probabilities, one can talk about possibilities of events, i.e. if the table has some probability p_i (greater than zero) between any contexts, then we assign 1 to the corresponding entries of the table, otherwise 0, as shown in table (here, of the Hardy model) on the left of Fig. 2. The table has a geometric realization; with (square) base representing the contexts associated with fibers which represent outcomes; the bundle diagram, as shown on the right side of Fig. 2. Its corresponding planar (linearized) diagram is shown in Fig. 3 for a better view. Note that a simplicial complex, in general, represents the contexts.

The base of the bundle diagram is a rectangle, a simplicial complex in more general scenarios; consisting of the measurement set $\{a, a', b, b'\}$, and the fibers consist of possible outputs, i.e., 0 and 1. To each context of the measurement set, one assigns its two output values (0 and 1) as a fiber associated with it. Based on any context from

	00	01	10	11
ab	1	1	1	1
ab'	0	1	1	1
$a'b$	0	1	1	1
$a'b'$	1	1	1	0

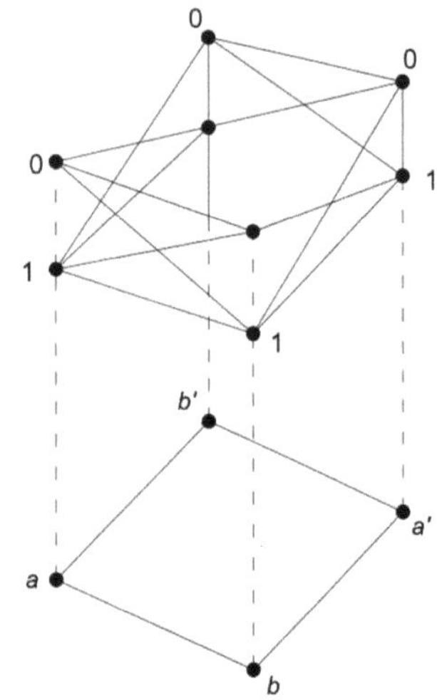

Fig. 2. On the left is a possibilistic table, and on the right is its corresponding bundle diagram: base consisting of contexts, and fibers consisting of outputs.

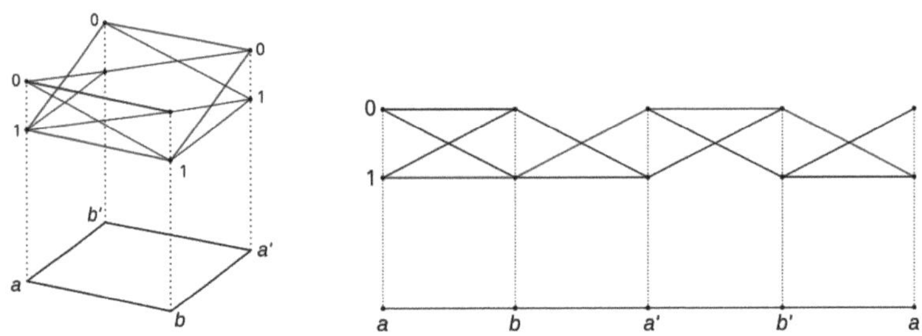

Fig. 3. Planar diagram of Hardy Model.

the table, there is an edge between their corresponding outputs in the fibers, if and only if, it is a possibilistic event with value 1 in the table. For example, if one chooses context (a', b') at (11), i.e., output of a' is 1 and that of b' is 1 from table in Fig. 2, then there is no edge between their corresponding fibers because the event is a non-possibilistic event as shown at corresponding entry of the table. One closes edges between values in fiber if they can appear together as a possible joint outcome over $\mathcal{K}$. For example, the green rectangle in the fiber space of Fig. 3 corresponds to four possibilistic contexts; (a, b), (a', b), (a', b') and (a, b') of the table at outputs $(1, 1)$, $(0, 1)$, $(0, 0)$ and $(1, 0)$ respectively. It means all the contexts are simultaneously satisfiable at these outputs, which corresponds to a *closed loop* in the fiber space that corresponds to a simply-connected (acyclic) underlying simplicial complex. The collapsible property of a space is a necessary and sufficient condition for the quantification of contextuality. This property of evaluating consistent families of contexts and their extension stems from Vorob'ev's theorem.

There is one context (a, b) in the table which is locally possible at (00) but globally not possible, i.e. when we extend it through different contexts over the fiber space denoted in blue in Fig. 3, it doesn't form a closed loop because the contexts over its base space $\mathscr{K}$ are not simultaneously satisfiable which is expressible as non-collapsibility of $\mathscr{K}$. The table expresses three classes of behavior: possibilistic behavior, non-possibilistic behavior, and the $LC - GI$ behavior. The geometric account in Fig. 2 naturally fits the structural description of sheaves [1,2] (Table 1).

Table 1. Sheaf-theoretic notions and their corresponding concept in quantum contextuality.

Sheaf-theoretic concept	Quantum contextuality
Topological space X with measurement cover $\mathcal{M}$ satisfying $\bigcup_{\mathsf{C} \in \mathcal{M}} \mathsf{C} = X$	Set of jointly measurable maximal contexts $\mathsf{C}_i \subseteq X$
Sheaf of events $\mathscr{E} := \mathsf{O}^{(\mathscr{U})}$	$\mathscr{E}(\mathscr{U})$ is the set of all assignments of outcomes O to $\mathscr{U}$ for any $\mathscr{U} \subseteq X$
Local section $s \in \mathscr{E}(\mathsf{C})$	An assignment of outcomes to a single context C
Restriction map $\mathrm{res}^{\mathscr{U}}_{\mathscr{V}} : \mathscr{E}(\mathscr{U}) \to \mathscr{E}(\mathscr{V})$	The operation of "forgetting" some measurement outcomes—moving from a larger set $\mathscr{U}$ to a smaller set $\mathscr{V}$
Global section $g \in \mathscr{E}(X)$	A single outcome assignment that works for all measurements X and is consistent with all observed contexts C_i
Empirical model $E = (e_{\mathsf{C}})_{\mathsf{C} \in \mathcal{M}}$ with $e_{\mathsf{C}} \in \mathscr{D}(\mathscr{E}(\mathsf{C}))$ (where $\mathscr{D}$ assigns probability distributions to sets)	A family of probability distributions (e_{C}). If a global distribution over $\mathscr{E}(X)$ exists whose marginals are the e_{C}, the model is non-contextual (local); otherwise it is contextual (non-local)
Sheaf condition: if $\{\mathscr{U}_i\}$ covers $\mathscr{U}$ and $s_i \in \mathscr{E}(\mathscr{U}_i)$ agree on overlaps $(s_i\|_{\mathscr{U}_i \cap \mathscr{U}_j} = s_j\|_{\mathscr{U}_i \cap \mathscr{U}_j})$, then there exists $s \in \mathscr{E}(\mathscr{U})$ with $s\|_{\mathscr{U}_i} = s_i$	Contextuality occurs when such a global assignment does not exist.
Cohomological obstruction $\gamma(s)$	A non-zero obstruction implies no global section and detects contextuality.

Table 2. Sheaf-theoretic notions and their corresponding bundle-theoretic concepts

Sheaf-theoretic concept	Bundle-theoretic concept
A functor from the category of open sets of a topological space to sets (or groups, modules, etc.) satisfying the sheaf condition (local-to-global compatibility).	A topological space E with a continuous surjection $\pi : E \to X$ such that locally E looks like $X \times F$ for a fixed fiber F (local triviality).
Encodes how local data (sections over open sets) glue to global data; failures are captured via cohomology.	Encodes how local product structures glue over overlaps via transition functions; failures of triviality can be topological (non-trivial bundles).
Glues sections of a pre-sheaf (functions, assignments, distributions) over overlapping opens.	Glues local trivializations of E using transition maps valued in a structure group G.
Defined over a base space but not itself a geometric object—rather, an information assignment to regions of the base.	A geometric/topological object: a total space E with projection to the base X.
Restriction maps $\text{res}^{\mathscr{U}}_{\mathscr{V}} : \mathscr{E}(\mathscr{U}) \to \mathscr{E}(\mathscr{V})$ for $\mathscr{V} \subseteq \mathscr{U}$.	Transition functions $t_{\mathscr{U}\mathscr{V}} : \mathscr{U} \cap \mathscr{V} \to G$ specifying how local trivializations relate.
Examples include the sheaf of continuous functions and sheaves of solutions to differential equations.	Examples include principal G-bundles, vector bundles, and tangent bundles.
Total space realized as the disjoint union of stalks $E = \bigsqcup_{x \in X} S_x$ via the étalé-space construction.	Explicit total space E inheriting geometric structure from the model.
Sections $s_{\mathscr{U}} \in \mathscr{E}(\mathscr{U})$ over open sets $\mathscr{U} \subseteq X$.	Fibers F_x over points $x \in X$; sections $s : \mathscr{U} \to E$ satisfy $\pi \circ s = \text{id}_{\mathscr{U}}$.
Data arises from functorial assignments with a restriction morphism.	Local structure arises from charts and transition functions.

2.2 Fiber Bundle

Let $\pi : E \to X$ be a fiber bundle with typical fiber F and gauge group $\mathscr{G} \subset \text{Diff}(F)$ acting on F. For an open set $\mathscr{U}_i \subset X$ from a chosen cover, the pre-image $\pi^{-1}(\mathscr{U}_i) \subset E$ admits a local trivialization

$$\psi : \pi^{-1}(\mathscr{U}_i) \xrightarrow{\cong} \mathscr{U}_i \times F, \qquad \text{pr}_1 \circ \psi = \pi|_{\pi^{-1}(\mathscr{U}_i)}.$$

Thus, each sufficiently small open region of E is (locally) diffeomorphic to $\mathscr{U} \times F$ for some open $\mathscr{U} \subset X$ (Table 2).

Likewise, for another open set $\mathscr{U}_j \subset X$ there is a trivialization

$$\sigma : \pi^{-1}(\mathscr{U}_j) \xrightarrow{\cong} \mathscr{U}_j \times F, \qquad \text{pr}_1 \circ \sigma = \pi|_{\pi^{-1}(\mathscr{U}_j)}.$$

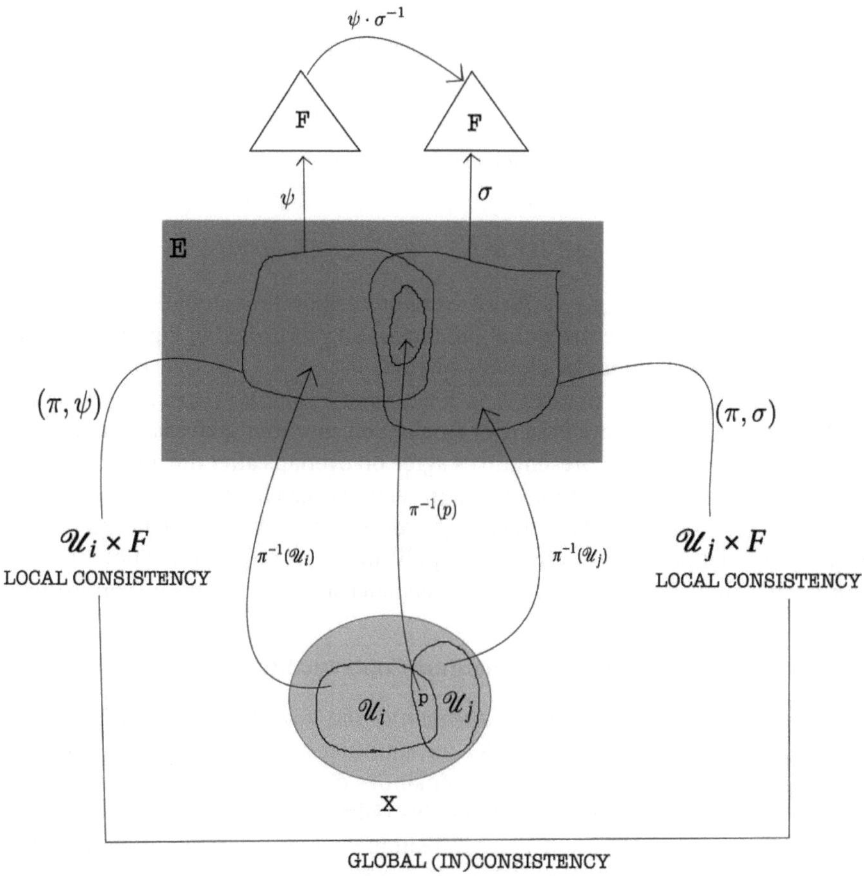

Fig. 4. Fiber Bundle

On the overlap $\mathscr{U}_{ij} := \mathscr{U}_i \cap \mathscr{U}_j$ (see Fig. 4), the two trivializations need not agree. Their change of coordinates on $\pi^{-1}(\mathscr{U}_{ij})$ is fiber-wise given by a $\mathscr{G}$-valued transition function

$$\psi \circ \sigma^{-1}(x, f) = (x, g_{ij}(x) \cdot f), \qquad g_{ij} : \mathscr{U}_{ij} \longrightarrow \mathscr{G}.$$

Equivalently, for each $x \in \mathscr{U}_{ij}$ the induced identifications of the fiber $\pi^{-1}(x)$ with F,

$$\psi_x : \pi^{-1}(x) \xrightarrow{\cong} F, \qquad \sigma_x : \pi^{-1}(x) \xrightarrow{\cong} F,$$

satisfy the fiber map shown in the figure:

$$\psi_x \circ \sigma_x^{-1} = g_{ij}(x) \in \mathscr{G} \subset \mathrm{Diff}(F).$$

For a point $p \in \mathscr{U}_{ij}$, both ψ_p and σ_p identify the same fiber $\pi^{-1}(p) \cong F$, but generally by different coordinates related by $g_{ij}(p)$.

Local consistency is the existence, over each U_i, of a trivialization $\psi : \pi^{-1}(\mathcal{U}_i) \to \mathcal{U}_i \times F$ (and similarly σ over $\mathcal{U}_j$). Global consistency across overlaps demands

$$\psi \circ \sigma^{-1}(x, f) = (x, g_{ij}(x) \cdot \mathrm{f}) \quad \text{on } \mathcal{U}_{ij},$$

with $g_{ij}(x) \in \mathcal{G}$. The transition functions satisfy the co-cycle conditions on multiple overlaps:

$$g_{ii} = e, \qquad g_{ij} = g_{ji}^{-1} \text{ on } \mathcal{U}_{ij}, \qquad g_{ik} = g_{ij}\, g_{jk} \text{ on } \mathcal{U}_i \cap \mathcal{U}_j \cap \mathcal{U}_k.$$

If, after refining the cover, $g_{ij} \equiv e$ for all overlaps, the bundle is globally trivial: $E \cong X \times F$. Nontrivial $\{g_{ij}\}$ encode the global (in)consistency indicated in Fig. 4: The bundle is locally a product but may be globally twisted.

A (global) section is a map $\kappa : X \to E$ with $\pi \circ \kappa = \mathrm{id}_X$, so $\kappa(x) \in \pi^{-1}(x)$ for each $x \in X$. Local sections always exist over small open sets; they glue to a global section precisely when the local representatives agree on overlaps after the above change of trivialization. For a vector bundle, the zero section is given by $\kappa(x) = 0$ in each fiber. The family $\{g_{ij}\}$ takes values in the gauge group $\mathcal{G}$; nontrivial elements record how fibers are re-identified over overlaps. In applications, nontrivial transition data capture global—though locally invisible—effects, such as non-locality and contextuality.

2.3 Mathematical Semantics of Quantum Contextuality

Our method uses the *fundamental theorem of the covering spaces*, an instance of a fiber bundle theory, which provides an equivalence of categories between fundamental group(oid) representing the semantics of the space X, and the permutations of fibers, characterizing the all possible polyhedral-symmetry operations, isomorphic to process description, like a transition system, representable as symmetry group. The fundamental group of $X \sim \mathcal{K}$ can be reconstructed from the group of deck transformations of the universal covering space, which is the same as the automorphism of the fiber over each vertex of $\mathcal{K}$. The equivalence of categories captures the essence of algebraic interpretation of quantum contextuality, quantifiable as synergistic interaction of local functions (s), possibly overall symmetries of functions, in the presence of $\mathcal{K}$. $\mathcal{K}$ acts as a spatial constraint on possible symmetries of local function(s), induced through a polyhedral description of contexts akin to sheafification, witnessing different strengths of contextuality: logical contextuality and strong contextuality, from tabular information of quantum models. A local consistency corresponds to any local symmetry-preserving transformation of a polyhedron.

In contrast, a global consistency is an invariant loop-transformation from a context(s) back to itself, possibly after going through several intermediate context permutations, that corresponds to global symmetry-preserving transformations of a polyhedron. Spatial constraints of $\mathcal{K}$ on symmetry operations are quantifiable as critical simplices and virtual loops, whose (non)existence quantifies contextuality using discrete Morse theory. The idea is an instance of the general principle of Galois theory.

Galois Equality Condition for Contextual Semantics. Here, we give a general intuition. Given a simplicial complex $\mathcal{K}$ with vertices $\mathcal{V}_i$ over which there is additional

information, as in bi-graphs and ribbon graphs in gauge field theory, represented as a fiber **S** consists of a possible set of states s_i that $\mathcal{V}_i$ holds. The composition along these $\mathcal{V}_i$'s forms an equation-like description, the *Galois equality*, which may be satisfied by $s_i \in \mathbf{S}$. The Galois equality is of the form, $\mathbf{p} = \mathcal{V}_1 + \mathcal{V}_2 + \mathcal{V}_3 + ... + \mathcal{V}_n = \mathcal{I}$ where $\{\mathcal{V}_1, \mathcal{V}_2, ..., \mathcal{V}_n\}$ are vertices $\mathcal{V}$ of $\mathcal{K}$ and $\mathcal{I}$ is the model-specific topological invariant. $\mathcal{K}$ is the triangulation of an ambient topological space X imparting $x_i \in X$ to the equation. In several cases, the distinction between X and $\mathcal{K}$ becomes relevant, the ones in which contractibility of X does not imply collapsibility of $\mathcal{K}$. The Galois equation becomes, $\mathbf{p} = x_1\mathcal{V}_1 + x_2\mathcal{V}_2 + x_3\mathcal{V}_3 + ... + x_n\mathcal{V}_n = \mathcal{I}$ where set $\{x_1, x_2, ...x_n\} \in X$. The solution or possible states s of each $\mathcal{V}$ in the equality are contained in **S**, possibly a fiber over each $\mathcal{V}$ through the projection map π of the fiber bundle. The automorphism of s in **S** is tied to X, i.e., whatever happens in **S** equivalently affects the topological environment X and can be reconstructed from it. It follows from the topological Galois correspondence, more generally the Grothendieck Galois theory, that $x_1\mathcal{V}_1 + x_2\mathcal{V}_2 + x_3\mathcal{V}_3 + ... + x_n\mathcal{V}_n$ is representable as a symmetry group as possible permutations of values in its solution space, and $\mathcal{I}$ is quantifiable as fundamental group of topological space $\pi(X)$ of the above equality. *Violation of Galois equality implies contextual semantics,* because the non-solvability of Galois equality means non-trivial (co)homology of X, implying non-locality and contextuality.
Symmetry Group Encodes All Possible Paths in Fiber Space/Computations

Theorem 1. *Let $\mathcal{F}$ be a finite group, $\mathbf{D}_i$ and $\mathbf{D}_j$ be irreducible representations of state space $\mathbf{S}_i$ and $\mathbf{S}_j$ over state set s respectively. There exists an admissible linear transformation (computation) $\mathbf{T}$ from $\mathbf{S}_i$ to $\mathbf{S}_j$ i.e., transition $\mathbf{T}: \mathbf{S}_i \to \mathbf{S}_j$ if and only if $\mathbf{T}\cdot\mathbf{D}_i(g) = \mathbf{D}_j(g)\cdot\mathbf{T}$ for all $g \in \mathcal{F}$, else it is a forbidden transition or contextual computation.*

Proof. Schur's lemma deals with the equivalence of irreducible representations. For a finite group $\mathcal{F}$; and $\mathbf{D}_i$ and $\mathbf{D}_j$ be irreducible representations of state space $\mathbf{S}_i$ and $\mathbf{S}_j$ over s. Suppose we can construct a linear transformation $\mathbf{T}: \mathbf{S}_i \to \mathbf{S}_j$ such that $\mathbf{T}\cdot\mathbf{D}_i(g) = \mathbf{D}_j(g)\cdot\mathbf{T}$ for all $g \in \mathcal{F}$ condition holds i.e., **T** intertwines the two irreducible representations then there are three possibilities as per Schur criteria.

1. $\mathbf{T} = 0$ then $\mathbf{D}_i$ and $\mathbf{D}_j$ are not equivalent and transitions are forbidden like deadlocks.
2. $\mathbf{T} \neq 0$ and **T** is a singular transformation, then $\mathbf{D}_i$ and $\mathbf{D}_j$ are not equivalent. The transition is responsible for both locally consistent and globally inconsistent computation.
3. $\mathbf{T} \neq 0$ and **T** is a non-singular (invertible) transformation, $\mathbf{D}_i$ and $\mathbf{D}_j$ are equivalent and transition is admissible.

The local transformations **T** between **S** are carried out in the presence of underlying simplices of $\mathcal{K}$. The singular transformation over **S** is locally feasible but globally infeasible due to the presence of non-trivial loops in $\mathcal{K}$. So, these irreducible representations of the symmetry group are subjected to structural constraints of the discrete structure, which would decide whether there exists an intertwining transformation between them, as shown in one Example 2.4.

Fundamental Group Encodes Structural Constraints/Environment for Computations/Paths

Theorem 2. *The non-trivial fundamental group of the topological environment $\mathscr{E} \sim X$ implies contextual semantics*

Proof. *$\pi(X) = 0$ corresponds to simply-connected space. The connected spaces are a product space in which every local section can be extended to a global section by the definition of a fiber bundle. The local sections in non-trivial spaces cannot be globally extended: $LC - GI$, which means the fundamental group of X is non-trivial and non-vanishing homotopy groups. Collapsibility of $\mathscr{K} \sim X$ implies locality, i.e., all the variables, represented as vertices of $\mathscr{K}$, can be assigned values simultaneously.*

The fundamental group quantifies the category of paths over X that are formalized over $\mathscr{K}$ using discrete Morse theory. There are three categories of paths: the generic simplices (GS), critical simplices (CS), and virtual loops (VL) corresponding to possibilistic events, non-possibilistic events, and LC-GI events, respectively, of the quantum models. A very short account on discrete Morse theory is also provided in Appendix A.2, and for details see [13].

Collapsibility of $\mathscr{K}$ quantifies the concept of contextuality [1,2]. The measure of collapsibility in a topological space is quantifiable as the number of holes, characterised as critical simplices over its corresponding $\mathscr{K}$ using discrete Morse theory, together with a set of short loops representing a topological phase transition in an evolving dynamical system [11].

Definition 1. *Let e be an empirical model and let $\mathscr{K}$ denote its associated simplicial complex, obtained via the construction in 2.4. We define:*

- Non-possibilistic events *of e as those events represented by* critical simplices *of $\mathscr{K}$.*
- *A* locally consistent but globally inconsistent incompatible family of sections *as a* class of transient virtual loops *in $\mathscr{K}$.*

Definition 2. *Let $\mathscr{K}$ be a simplicial complex. We say that $\mathscr{K}$ undergoes a* strong collapse *if it contains neither critical simplices nor virtual loops.*

Theorem 3. *If a simplicial complex $\mathscr{K}$ is not strongly collapsible, then $\mathscr{K}$ is contextual.*

Proof. *VL cannot be resolved using tree-type approximation and introduces cycles in $\mathscr{K}$ [16], and CS is a criterion of non-collapsibility in discrete Morse theory. The existence of (CS, VL) in $\mathscr{K}$ is non-collapsibility to $\{\emptyset\}$ which implies contextuality.*

The topology acts as a constraint for the possible symmetries of a local function that are induced through a polyhedral description of the contexts of the quantum models.

Definition 3. *Let e be an empirical model with measurement set $\mathcal{M}$. A* polyhedral description *of* **e** *is a polyhedron associated with the model whose number of vertices equals* $|\mathcal{M}|$.

Definition 4. *Let $\mathcal{P}$ be a polyhedron associated with an empirical model and $\mathcal{K}$ its corresponding simplicial complex.*

- Local consistency *is any local symmetry-preserving transformation of* $\mathcal{P}$.
- Global consistency *is an invariant loop transformation from a context back to itself—possibly via several intermediate context permutations—corresponding to a global symmetry-preserving transformation of* $\mathcal{P}$.

Any transformation acts in the presence of paths over $\mathcal{K}$ quantifiable as GS, CS, and VL.

The fiber-bundle description of contextuality would require a polyhedral description of quantum models, representing all possible symmetries of fiber space that interacts with $\mathcal{K}$. We provide a general method to associate an explicit approximation of a topological space to quantum models based on information provided in their tables in Subsect. 2.4 and a polyhedral description in Subsect. 2.5

2.4 Topology of Quantum Model

We construct a discrete topological space from the information provided in tables of the empirical models as shown in Fig. 5. Let us take a simple example of a Liar cycle to explain the construction clearly. Other models follow the same method but are not the subject matter of this work. As a result, generalizing our results is omitted.

	00	01	10	11
ab	1	0	0	1
bc	1	0	0	1
cd	1	0	0	1
de	1	0	0	1
ea	0	1	1	0

Fig. 5. Possibilistic table of Liar cycle model.

Our goal is to express the class of behavior of the tables of the empirical models. It includes possibilistic events, non-possibilistic events, and locally consistent and globally inconsistent events (LI-GI), which would correspond to generic simplices, critical simplices, and virtual loops, respectively, in the constructed topological space.

A conceivable first step is to provide a combinatorial description of this model by considering power set of the measurement set $\{a, b, c, d, e\}$ which is equipped with a discrete topology $\mathcal{K}_1$ as shown in (i) of Fig. 6. $\mathcal{K}_1$ is a combinatorial description of all possible ways in which the physical experiment can be performed. The set $\{a, b, c, d, e\}$ can be thought of variables that store values either 0 or 1 measured by two agents A and B to observe the corresponding values. A possible set-up would be A chooses a and B chooses b, afterwards A chooses c and B chooses d, followed by A choosing e to observe values either 0 or 1. A possible permutation of such a set-up is also shown in (i) of Fig. 6. Contextuality is the impossibility of assigning a value (0 or 1) to the result of the measurement of a physical property (variables) because it depends on the measurement context, i.e., what other properties are simultaneously measured with it. This description is naturally more informative than tables, i.e., it allows different contexts to be measured simultaneously, like (abb) and similar other diagonal contexts, where A chooses a and B chooses b, and afterwards A chooses b in a different setup. These diagonal contexts do not add any significant topological context, i.e., using cell complexes instead of simplicial structure $\mathcal{K}_1$ would avoid these contexts, realizing the same topology and having the same Euler characteristics.

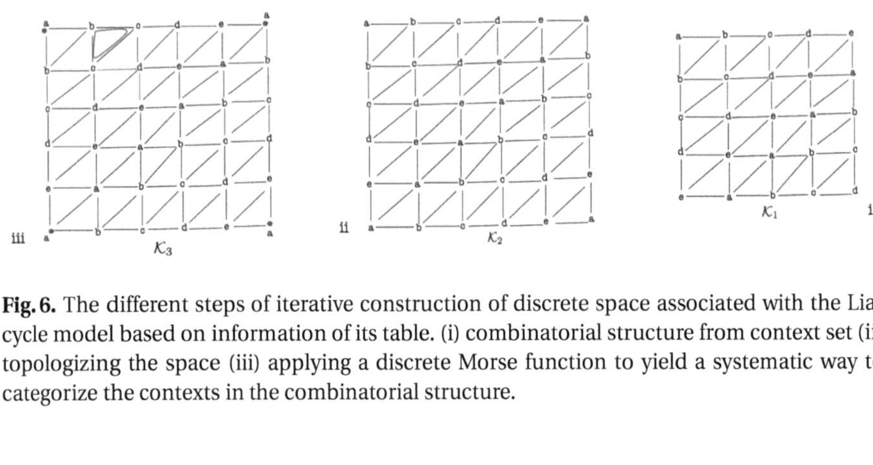

Fig. 6. The different steps of iterative construction of discrete space associated with the Liar cycle model based on information of its table. (i) combinatorial structure from context set (ii) topologizing the space (iii) applying a discrete Morse function to yield a systematic way to categorize the contexts in the combinatorial structure.

It is required to express non-possibilistic events of the Liar cycle model along with LC-GI events as a result of these obstructions, but all simplices of $\mathcal{K}_1$ are generic. A random selection of any context(s) to critical in $\mathcal{K}_1$ based on non-possibilistic events in its table would lead to a context indistinguishability issue, i.e., there are several same contexts over $\mathcal{K}_1$, for instance, for a non-possibilistic event ea there are almost eight ea$'s$ in $\mathcal{K}_1$. Selecting any context randomly would also force the agents to choose that particular output at that context, which violates the axiom of choice in empirical models. For instance, ea at (00) is a non-possibilistic event, and turning a particular ea critical in $\mathcal{K}_1$ would force agents to observe this particular output in that specific context. It constrains the element of choice of agents, and structure $\mathcal{K}_1$ becomes a self-fulfilling prophecy to reproduce any behavior trivially.

It is improper to randomly turn any simplex of $\mathcal{K}_1$ critical based on non-possibilistic events in the table. A background condition is required to turn a set of particular simplices critical systematically. This results in a constraint on the maximum number of critical simplices to be included over the structure $\mathcal{K}_1$. It means one cannot include all non-possibilistic events at once over $\mathcal{K}_1$ but rather iteratively add additional discrete spaces until it expresses the class of behavior of the empirical models. We use discrete Morse theory as a background condition to turn a set of simplices critical iteratively for non-possibilistic events, along with emerging virtual loops due to these obstructions for LC-GI events. Additionally, the axiom of choice is respected by assigning all possible outputs, both 0 and 1, to each context so that agents have an element of choice to measure any variables and observe any output independently.

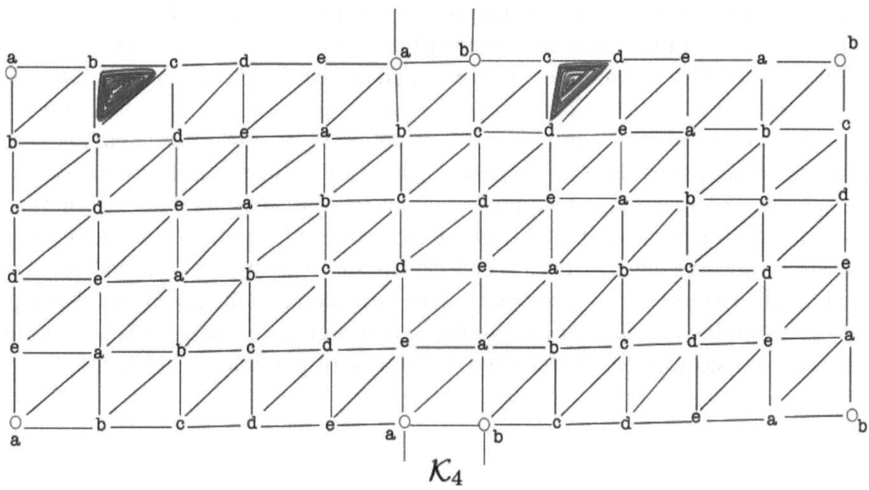

Fig. 7. $\mathcal{K}_3$ does not take into account other non-possibilistic events, new union of surface changing to $\mathcal{K}_4$

$\mathcal{K}_1$ is homeomorphic to a real line or disc topology because the Euler characteristic χ turns out to be 1, vertices (v) = 25, edges (e) = 56, and faces (f) = 32; $\chi = v - e + f = 1$. The cohomology of a disc is trivial and contractible to a point, which can only express possibilistic events, as in the case of trivial models with no non-possibilistic events requiring only generic simplices offering no constraint on its tetrahedral symmetry transformations, i.e., all global sections exist. This linear topology recalls local hidden variables that cannot reproduce contextuality due to the Bell-Kochen-Specker theorem.

The context indistinguishability issue is also resolved by designating each possible combinatorial setup as a level and then considering all sets of possible loops, paths starting and ending at the same vertex, and evaluating the particular context at the particular set-up not contained in the loop-set would correspond to the critical simplex as discussed in Appendix A.1. The reason to evaluate loops is that the semantics of the structure to express contextuality is described by the fundamental group, which considers loops in $\mathcal{K}_1$. On the contrary, discrete Morse theory does not allow loops. One of the natural ways is the identification of the boundary topologizing $\mathcal{K}_1$ from a trivial topology to a torus surface, turning $\mathcal{K}_1$ to $\mathcal{K}_2$ as shown in (ii) of Fig. 6. The canonical commutation relation between two observables has an algebraic torus representation and a reasonable minimal surface to express contextuality. Torus encodes naturally the obstruction led sheafification of contextuality, unlike positively curved spaces like the sphere, where we would be required to understand the relation between curvature and contextuality, which are not related in sheaf-based interpretation. $\mathcal{K}_2$ has $\chi = 0$ homeomorphic to a torus. We apply discrete Morse function $\mathfrak{f}$ over $\mathcal{K}_2$ represented as $\mathcal{K}_3$. $\mathfrak{f}$ assigns to each simplex a natural number $\mathbb{N}$ under the condition that as one moves from lower to higher simplices, the number should increase. The identified simplices are assigned the same values, which constrains the value assignment to a set of simplices where the number decreases, contrary to $\mathfrak{f}$, which are turned critical. It follows that four 0-simplices, two 1-simplices and one 2-simplex of $\mathcal{K}_3$ are turned critical which correspond to four a, contexts cd, de and context bcc respectively. The assignment of $\mathbb{N}$ to each simplex is not shown for brevity. Additionally, a well-defined CW attachment map between these critical simplices gives a torus. Notice, there are only two valid contexts cd and de in $\mathcal{K}_3$ that correspond to two non-possibilistic events of the table. The four single contexts a are not meaningful because contextuality is a phenomenon between at least two observables. The critical contexts in the structure would be validated or invalidated based on the contexts that will be considered in the polyhedral description of the model, i.e., context bcc would be considered only when it is part of the symmetry transformations represented as a square bi-pyramid, as in Fig. 11.

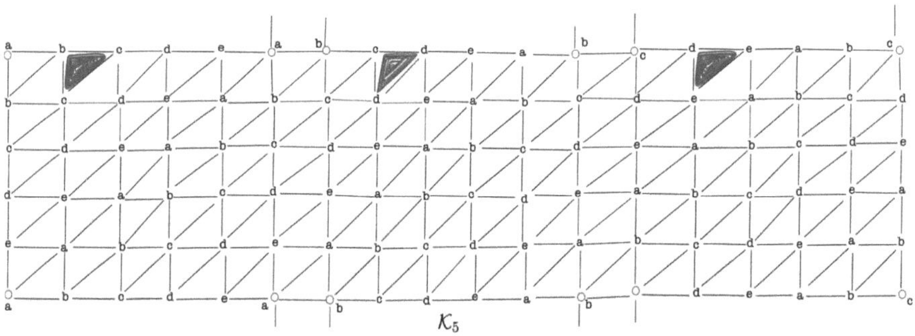

Fig. 8. $\mathcal{K}_4$ turns to $\mathcal{K}_5$ homeomorphic to 3-torus containing another set of critical simplices ea and ab and any possible combination of virtual loops represented in blue color.

The structure $\mathcal{K}_3$ cannot include all non-possibilistic events, for instance, $\mathcal{K}_3$ includes only two relevant non-possibilistic contexts cd and de. Still, there are other contexts to be included. Moreover, the structure constrains the maximum number of critical simplices included, hence we require iterating or attaching another torus surface to $\mathcal{K}_3$, turning it into $\mathcal{K}_4$ as shown in Fig. 7. $\mathcal{K}_4$ includes two more non-possibilistic event de and ea. Upon calculating the χ of $\mathcal{K}_4$ turns to be -2 which means it is homeomorphic to 2-torus. We would require iterating $\mathcal{K}_4$ to another space until it includes all non-possibilistic events of the model's table. It passes through many $\mathcal{K}'s$ and eventually adds three more discrete spaces to $\mathcal{K}_4$, expressing iteratively all non-possibilistic events in the table of this model, which corresponds to the 5-torus space as shown comprehensively in Fig. 10.

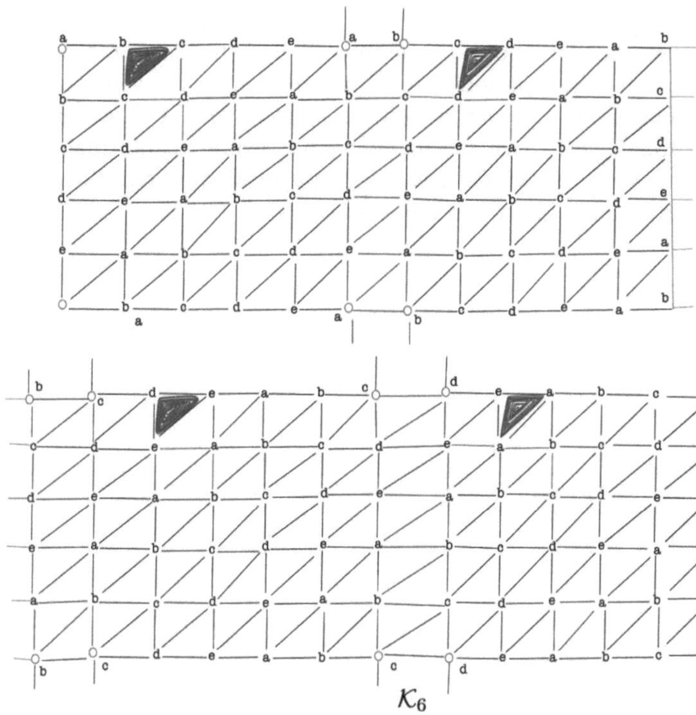

Fig. 9. $\mathcal{K}_5$ turns into $\mathcal{K}_6$ to contain another set of critical simplices *ab* and *bc*, along with blue colored possible combination of virtual loops.

The two blue lines in the figure represent the end of one torus and the beginning of the other torus being attached at the boundary. This blue regime has two equidistant critical 0-simplices, for instance, four red colored circles named *a* and *b* in Fig. 7. There is a possibility of transient virtual loops that could form due to equidistant critical points in the discrete space at the boundary of two attached tori, represented in blue lines. The area between these blue lines has a choice to go in either directions, which facilitate the emergence of these virtual loops. These non-trivial loops do not violate the description of $\mathfrak{f}$ as it is defined, which presumes loop-free space, and do not violate causality because these loops are transient and a possible invariant at the observational level. One can reiterate $\mathfrak{f}$ over the final space, here the 5-torus, and these loops vanish. The virtual loop is a quantification of a topological transition from one homotopy class to another. Conceptually, an experimenter does not have a priori access to the final discrete space. It collects data at each round of the experiment to construct the intermediate spaces similar to topological data analysis. These virtual loops express a class of LC-GI events wherein locally the simplices are not critical (infeasible) but globally transient into a new topological space, turning it globally inconsistent. The weaving of contexts of the topological space associated with the models is iterated peculiarly. Notice, the 1-torus starts with context a and the space is woven by naturally going through the natural order of contexts until it reaches the last iteration, which begins with e and also other intermediate spaces passing through the natural order of permutations. At times, we force the ordering of contexts so that every iteration contains a non-possibilistic event, and it does not affect the results of our approach; also, it is a computationally challenging task. The constructed topological space can independently express contextuality as a non-trivial fundamental group of the space, i.e., non-existence of critical simplices and non-trivial virtual loops imply non-contextuality.

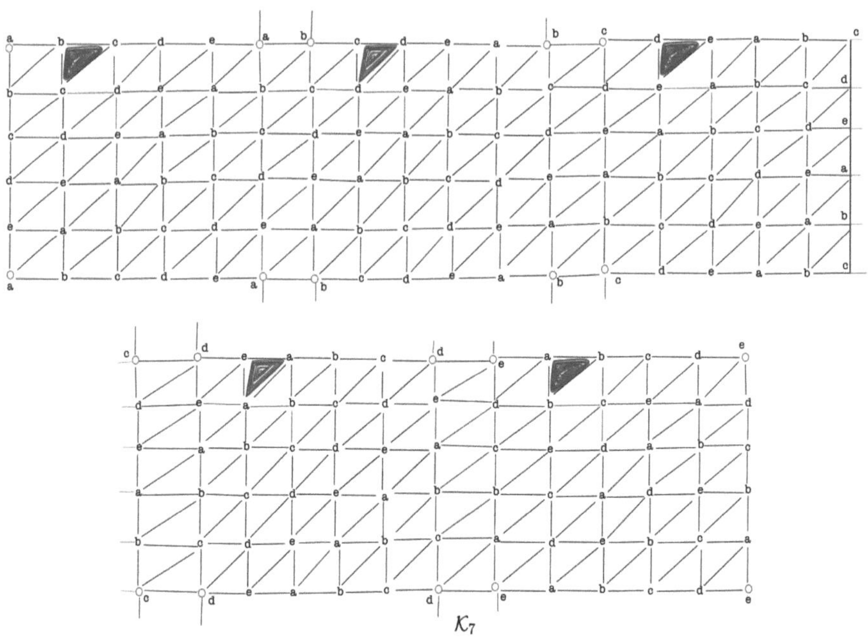

Fig. 10. The final iteration turning $\mathcal{K}_6$ to $\mathcal{K}_7$ to contain final set of non-possibilistic events as critical simplices bc and cd along with possibility of virtual loops in blue. The space $\mathcal{K}_7$ expresses all classes of possible behavior of the Liar cycle model.

2.5 Symmetry and Contextuality

The next part is the algebraic-type, a function, residing over the constructed 5-torus. The measurement set can be described as a polyhedron whose vertices are equal to the cardinality of the set itself and represent all possible contexts of the model.

The description allows permutations between contexts, which are constrained by the above-constructed discrete space via a set of critical simplices and a set of possible virtual loops. Each vertex of the polyhedron is associated with all possible outputs represented as a fiber over it. This representation is similar to the bundle diagram of sheaf modeling as shown in Fig. 2.

A local consistency corresponds to any possible transformation of the polyhedron, and the global consistency corresponds to transformations of the polyhedron that take it possibly through several transformations and bring it back to its initial context (vertex). The inability to form this loop transformation from a particular context back to itself quantifies contextuality. The description is closely related to sheaf-based modeling of empirical models, where a loop in the fiber space containing output means their corresponding contexts are simultaneously satisfiable, hence non-contextual.

Measurement set $\mathcal{M} = \{a, b, c, d, e\}$ of the Liar cycle model has cardinality ($|\mathcal{M}| =$ 5) which corresponds to total vertices of the square bi-pyramid – a polyhedral description of the model as shown in Fig. 11. Each symmetry of a square pyramid corresponds to the permutation of its five vertices representing contexts. Each vertex of this square pyramid is attached with both possible outputs 0 and 1 represented in purple colored lines of Fig. 11, providing each context with an element of choice. *ab bc cd de ea* are relevant contexts of the model as considered in its table description, but the polyhedral description of the model allows most of the possible combinations of the contexts, which maximally would be the power set $\mathcal{P}$ of $\mathcal{M}$ as:

$\mathcal{P}(\mathcal{M}) = \{\{\emptyset\}, \{a,b,c,d,e\}, \{a\}, \{b\}, \{c\}, \{d\}, \{e\}, \{a,b\}, \{a,c\}, \{a,d\}, \{a,e\}, \{b,c\}, \{b,d\}, \{b,e\}, \{c,d\}, \{c,e\}, \{d,e\}, \{a,b,c\}, \{a,b,d\}, \{a,b,e\}, \{a,c,d\}, \{a,c,e\}, \{a,d,e\}, \{b,c,d\}, \{b,c,e\}, \{b,d,e\}, \{c,d,e\}, \{a,b,c,d\}, \{a,b,c,e\}, \{a,c,d,e\}, \{b,c,d,e\}, \{a,b,d,e\}\}$

The symmetry transformations of the square bi-pyramid are constrained by the set of critical simplices and possible virtual loops of the discrete space, as shown in Fig. 10. The set of critical simplices CS are as: CS = {bcc, cd, de, cdd, de, ea, dee, ea, ab, eaa, ab, bc, abb, bc, cd} and set of possible virtual loops VL are as: VL = {abb, bbc, bcc, ccd, ddc, dde, eed, eea, aea, aab, cdd, dde, eed, eea, aea, aab, abb, bbc, bcc, ccd, bcc, ccd, cdd, dde, eed, eea, aae, aab, bba, bbc, dee, eed, eda, adc, abc, bbc, bbc, bca, acd, ade }. VL-set can also contain different combinations like that of four context-loops, such as: { abcb, abcd, abde, abea, abab, bccd, bcde, bcea, bcab, cdde, cdea, cdab, deea, deab, eaab, bbcc, bbdd, bbee, bbaa, ccdd, ccee, ccaa, ddee, ddaa, eeaa} as formed as a boundary phenomenon of two tori, for instance, as in Fig. 7 depicting possible virtual loops at boundary represented in blue. There could be other different 4-context possibilities between other boundaries, but we neglect them here for brevity.

The CS-set and VL-set put constraints on the possible symmetries of its polyhedral description. A linearised planar diagram of the square pyramid that considers all of its edges representing all possible contexts of the model is shown on the right side of Fig. 11. A permutation of any contexts is possible if its underlying simplices of background simplicial complex, as constructed in Fig. 10, allow it, i.e., the simplices corresponding to the contexts are generically represented as black colour in Fig. 10. Otherwise, a permutation is not possible if their corresponding simplices are elements of the critical simplices set and the virtual loop set represented in red and blue, respectively. The possible family of global sections is as follows: {abcdea, bcdeaceb, cdeac, deacebd, eace, acebda}, each starting and ending with the same vertex. Allowing all possible permutations to quantify a wide range of symmetries of the model, unlike only relevant contexts, allows local sections in the Liar model, but there is no family of global sections possible, as shown in Fig. 11.

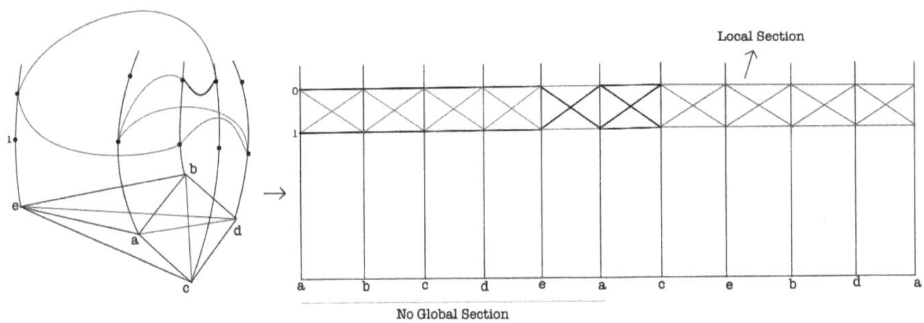

Fig. 11. This is also a polyhedral description as a square bi-pyramid of the Liar cycle, whose symmetries are subjected to the $\mathscr{K}_7$.

Theorem 4. *Any empirical model representable within the Liar cycleâĂŞtype scenario admits a topological representation as a surface of genus* 5*, which constrains the symmetries of its associated square bi-pyramid and exhibits strongly contextual behavior.*

Proof. Proof by construction:topological representation 2.4 and polyhedral-description 11

Theorem 5. *Any empirical model representable within the Hardy model scenario admits a topological representation as a* 3*-torus, which constrains the symmetries of its associated tetrahedron and reveals logically contextual behavior.*

3 Topology-Driven Model of Computation

Definition 5. *A persistent Turing machine (PTM) is a 3-tape Turing machine having a read-only input-tape, a read/write work-tape, and a write-only output-tape.*

The *work tape* is a non-observable environment but affects the PTM sequential computation. We replace the process descriptive representation of the work tape with a structural (global) representation of the environment. The synergistic interaction between processes in a topological space unfolds the contextual behavior. We demonstrate the computation of a local function in a global space with an example.

3.1 An Illustration of Example

We give a simple example to understand computation in a topological/structural representation of the work tape of the Turing machine.

Given a simplicial complex $\mathcal{K}$ with four 0-simplices $\{\mathcal{V}_1, \mathcal{V}_2, \mathcal{V}_3, \mathcal{V}_4\}$, five 1-simplices $\{\mathcal{V}_{12}, \mathcal{V}_{14}, \mathcal{V}_{23}, \mathcal{V}_{13}, \mathcal{V}_{34}\}$ and two 2-simplices $\{\mathcal{V}_{123}\}$ and $\{\mathcal{V}_{134}\}$, as shown in the Fig. 12. Here, $\mathcal{V}_{12}$ means an edge between $\mathcal{V}_1$ and $\mathcal{V}_2$ and similarly for other notations. Notice, there is a color coding of each simplices $\mathcal{K}_i \in \mathcal{K}$: Green and Red. Here, we do not bother about *how* to color-code them to abstract away the complexity. The coloring is based on the information contained in the empirical models, which are extensively discussed in Sect. 2.4. Instead, here we assign weight to each simplex $\mathcal{K}_i$.

$$w(\mathcal{K}_i) = \begin{cases} 1, & \text{if } \mathcal{K}_i \text{ is generic simplices: Green} \\ 0, & \text{if } \mathcal{K}_i \text{ is critical: Red} \end{cases}$$

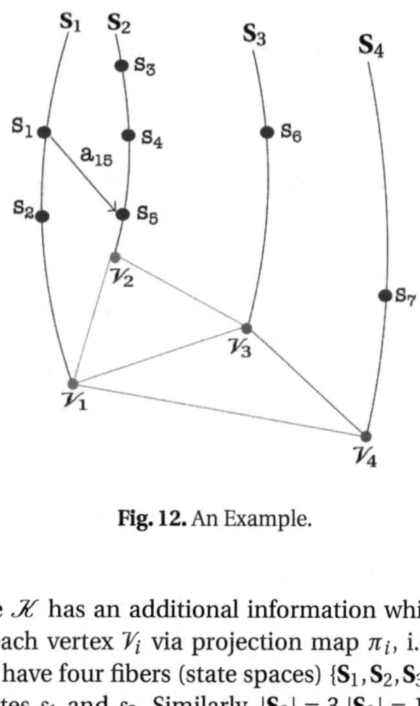

Fig. 12. An Example.

Each vertex of the $\mathcal{K}$ has an additional information which is represented as a fiber $\mathbf{S}_i$ attached to each vertex $\mathcal{V}_i$ via projection map π_i, i.e., $\pi_i : \mathcal{V}_i \to \mathbf{S}_i$. In the given example 12, we have four fibers (state spaces) $\{\mathbf{S}_1, \mathbf{S}_2, \mathbf{S}_3, \mathbf{S}_4\}$, with $|\mathbf{S}_1| = 2$, i.e., $\mathbf{S}_1$ consists of two states s_1 and s_2. Similarly, $|\mathbf{S}_2| = 3, |\mathbf{S}_3| = 1$ and $|\mathbf{S}_4| = 1$. We also set a minimum bound to each $\mathbf{S}$ to be able to compute, here $|\mathbf{S}| > 1$, i.e., every $\mathbf{S}_i$ should contain at least two states to take part in the computation. For example, $|\mathbf{S}_3| = |\mathbf{S}_4| = 1$; meaning they cannot take part in computation, so their corresponding simplices $\mathcal{V}_3$, $\mathcal{V}_4$ and $\mathcal{V}_{34}$ are set red colour. In our example, we have two checks; first is to observe $w(\mathcal{K}_i)$ for action A between any two state spaces and second is the cardinality bound of $|\mathbf{S}| > \mathbb{N}$ affecting $w(\mathcal{K}_i)$. It means, computation between two state spaces is constrained by $\mathcal{K}$ and vice-versa, i.e., cardinality less than the minimum set bound of the state space could set $w(\mathcal{K})$ to zero.

The inverse map of π of any state $s_i \in \mathbf{S}_i$ is a particular vertex $\mathcal{V}_i \in \mathcal{V}$, i,e., $\pi^{-1}(s_i) = \mathcal{V}_i$. The embedding Emb of any inverse projection of π corresponding to a particular $s \in \mathbf{S}$, i.e. $Emb\{\pi^{-1}(s_i)\}$ is the set of all $\mathcal{K}_i$ of $\mathcal{K}$ having projection of $\pi^{-1}(s)$ as its element.

Here, lets choose $\mathbf{S}_1$, first we would check $|\mathbf{S}_1| = 2$, which satisfies our given bound on $\mathbf{S}$ ($|S| > 1$). Moreover, $\pi^{-1}(s_1) = \mathcal{V}_1$, which means $Emb(\mathcal{V}_1) = \{\mathcal{V}_1, \mathcal{V}_{12}, \mathcal{V}_{13}, \mathcal{V}_{14}\}$. Now, check the $w(\mathcal{V}_i)$, here, weight of all simplices is 1, i.e., $Emb(\mathcal{V}_i) \cap Red = \emptyset$. It means, state s_1 can make transition to any of the states of $\mathbf{S}_2$, i.e., there is an admissible action, say $a_{15} \in A$ between $s_1 \xrightarrow{a_{15}} s_5$.

After action A, here a_{15} between s_1 and s_5, both conditions are re-checked; i.e., $|\mathbf{S}|$ and $w(\mathcal{K}_i)$. Here, $|\mathbf{S}_1| = 1$, $|\mathbf{S}_2| = 2$, and hence, $w(\mathcal{V}_1)$ turns red which means in next iteration it cannot take part in the computation.

Definition 6 ***(TIM).*** *A Topological interactive machine (see Fig. 13) is a sextuple* $(\mathcal{V}, \mathcal{K}, \mathbf{S}, \pi, A, \delta)$ *where:*

- $\mathcal{V} = \{\mathcal{V}_i\}_{i \in \mathbb{N}}$ *is a finite (possibly unbounded) set of flexible state variables embedded in the topological environment* $\mathcal{E}$ *such that each vertex of its combinatorial space* $\mathcal{K}$ *is an element of* $\mathcal{V}$.
- *State space* $\mathbf{S} = \{\mathbf{S}_i\}_{i \in \mathbb{N}}$ *consisting of a finite set of processes each containing a finite set of states* s.
- $\pi : \mathcal{V} \to \mathbf{S}$ *assigns to each* $\mathcal{V}_i$ *a state space* $\mathbf{S}_i$. *Each element* $s_i \in \mathbf{S}_i$ *observes its corresponding simplex of* $\mathcal{K}$; *as well as its embedding* Emb. *Any action* A *between states of* $\mathbf{S}_i$ *and* $\mathbf{S}_j$ *is allowed only if* $Emb\,\{\pi^{-}(s_i)\} \cap CS = \emptyset$ *and* $|\mathbf{S} > \mathbb{N}|$ *such that the square commutes set as a pre-condition expressing local consistency.*
- A *is the set of actions* $\mathtt{A}$ *defined as is a mapping function* $\mathtt{A} : \mathbf{S} \to 2^{\mathbf{S}}$ *that maps each state* $s \in \mathbf{S}$ *to an element of the power set of* $\mathbf{S}$.
- $\delta : \mathcal{V} \times \mathbf{S} \to \mathcal{V} \times \mathbf{S}$ *takes vertices in* $\mathcal{K}$ *and states in* $\mathbf{S}$ *and maps to another* $\mathcal{K}$ *and* $\mathbf{S}$ *such that the square below commutes, expressing post-condition for global consistency.*

$$
\begin{array}{ccc}
\mathbf{S}_i & \xrightarrow{A_{ij}} & \mathbf{S}_j \\
\downarrow{\scriptstyle \pi_i} & & \downarrow{\scriptstyle \pi_j} \\
\mathcal{V}_i & \xrightarrow{V_{ij}} & \mathcal{V}_j
\end{array}
\qquad\qquad
\begin{array}{ccc}
\mathcal{V}_i \times \mathbf{S}_i & \xrightarrow{\quad \delta \quad} & \mathcal{V}_j \times \mathbf{S}_j \\
\downarrow{\scriptstyle (\pi_i, A_i)} & & \downarrow{\scriptstyle (\pi_j, A_j)} \\
\mathcal{V}_i & \xrightarrow{\quad V_{ij} \quad} & \mathcal{V}_j
\end{array}
$$

3.2 Topological Driven Model Is a Computational Fiber Bundle

It is a natural observation that a topology-driven model is isomorphic to the structure of a fiber bundle, as seen in Fig. 13. There is a conceptual point to note; in classical setting of bundle theory, the total space E is *known* and described in terms of base space B and fiber space F, like in Hopf fibration where 3-sphere as E is described in

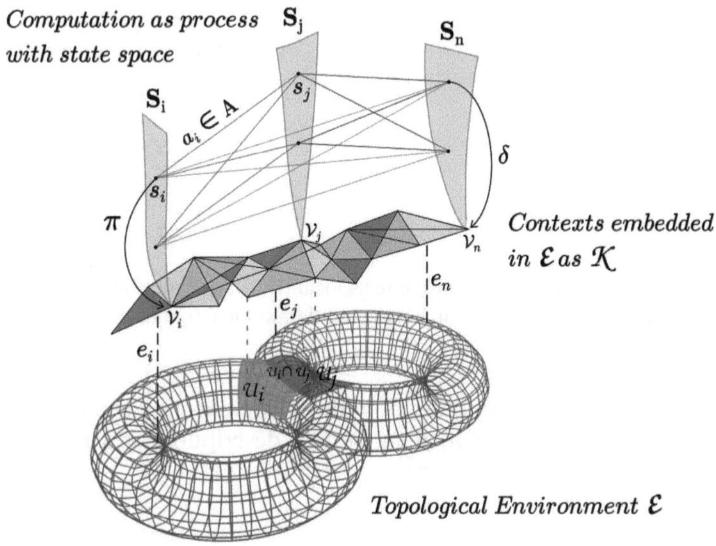

Fig. 13. Topological Interactive Machine. The δ map looks the same as the π map; which is not the case, but for visual simplicity we avoid over-representation of maps.

terms of circles as F and a sphere as B; unlike TIM where total space is *unknown* and we construct it via synergistic computation-structure interaction from the *known* base space ($\mathcal{K}$) and *known* fiber space ($\mathbf{S}$). The information about $\mathcal{K}$ and $\mathbf{S}$ is a priori known and extracted from the given information of the empirical models. Hence, E is not explicitly included in the definition of TIM because it is unknown and mainly expressed through the interaction of different mappings, in particular, the update map δ. E in TIM is structure *modulo* computation where fundamental group of $\mathcal{K}$ encodes structural semantics and symmetry group encodes computational semantics in $\mathbf{S}$ which is extensively discussed in Sect. 2.4 and Sect. 2.5. This interplay iterates intermediate E's until all classes of behavior from the empirical model are expressed by the topology-driven model.

This abstraction of E in the definition of the topology-driven model results in a few refinements without losing equivalence with fiber bundles. Here is how E comes in via interaction between different mappings: First, TIM defines π as $\pi : \mathcal{V} \to \mathbf{S}$, unlike a fiber bundle, where the same map means $\pi : E \to B$. A computation $s_i \xrightarrow{a_{ij}} s_j$ for $s_i \in \mathbf{S}_i$, $s_j \in \mathbf{S}_j$ and $a_{ij} \in A$, takes place *locally* between two state spaces $\mathbf{S}_i$ and $\mathbf{S}_j$ given color code of the edge $\mathcal{V}_{ij}$ between $\mathcal{V}_i$ and $\mathcal{V}_j$ in a local space; where it is always possible to locally describe each computational site as $\mathcal{V}_i \times \mathbf{S}_i$ and $\mathcal{V}_j \times \mathbf{S}_j$ via (π_i,θ_i) and (π_j,θ_j) respectively as shown in Fig. 15. $\mathcal{V}_i \times \mathbf{S}_i$ and $\mathcal{V}_j \times \mathbf{S}_j$ are different local trivializations residing in E which may not necessarily agree expressing the global consistency condition quantifiable via δ map as shown in Fig. 14. The δ_i map in the local space is the simplicial map preserving fibers and updates $\mathcal{V}_i \to \mathcal{V}_i'$ along-with $\mathbf{S}_i \to \mathbf{S}_i'$, similarly for δ_j, based on conditions.

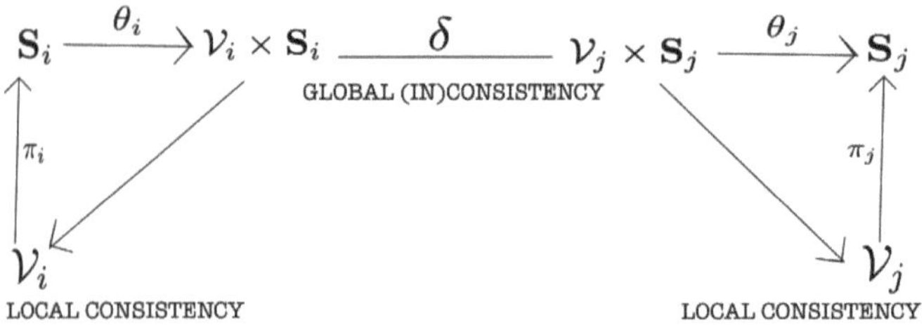

Fig. 14. Model's local consistency is the same as local trivialization in bundles, along with its global consistency is the same as a map between different local trivializations.

The above equivalent description of bundles operates in a changing base-fiber space in a computational (open) fiber bundle description as a topology-driven model, which models empirical models.

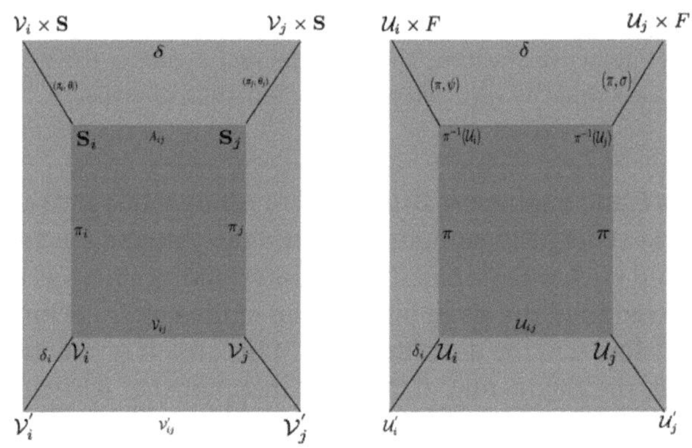

Fig. 15. Topology-driven model isomorphic to fiber bundle structure. Note $\mathcal{V}_i \times \mathbf{S}_i$ and $\mathcal{V}_j \times \mathbf{S}_j$ is in total (global) space and same points would be viewed as $\mathbf{S}_i'$ and $\mathbf{S}_j'$ respectively in local space via updating process.

Following the above points, we give an equivalence between bundles and TIM as in Fig. 15. The right cube represents a complete iteration of a fiber bundle via different maps with slight abuse of notation 15 (repetitive maps are omitted, and those that are not important for now). We have two open sets $\mathcal{U}_i$ and $\mathcal{U}_j$ whose pre-image is in the total space E as $\pi^{-1}(\mathcal{U}_i)$ and $\pi^{-1}(\mathcal{U}_j)$ respectively. It has two values; one is its projection (via π) onto $\mathcal{U}_i$ and the other is the height, which should be equal to a standard fiber F via the map ψ. Informally, the strip should be isomorphic to the cartesian product of $\mathcal{U}_i \times F$ via (π, ψ), which is a local trivialization condition. These stripes glue together to form a whole space. The process is similar for other open neighbourhood $\mathcal{U}_j$, which maps to $\mathcal{U}_j \times F$ via (π, σ). Now, the intersection between $\mathcal{U}_i$ and $\mathcal{U}_j$ denoted as $\mathcal{U}_{ij}$ is compatible if there is a feasible map between

$\mathscr{U}_i \times F \to \mathscr{U}_j \times F$ via δ map. The δ map is compatible with the intersection then the $\mathscr{U}_i \times F$ and $\mathscr{U}_j \times F$ will be projected back to the same $\mathscr{U}_i$ and $\mathscr{U}_j$ respectively, else different open set, say $\mathscr{U}_i^{'}$ and $\mathscr{U}_j^{'}$.

The left cube represents the computation and update process in the topological interactive machine, which is isomorphic to the fiber bundles. Here, $\mathcal{V}_{ij}$ has given weight w determining whether there is an edge between two vertices $\mathcal{V}_i$ and $\mathcal{V}_j$; represented as red or green using discrete Morse theory. One can follow same path as fiber bundle and δ determines whether the vertices $\mathcal{V}_i$ and $\mathcal{V}_j$ are projected to itself with same weight; or other vertices, say $\mathcal{V}_i^{'}$ and $\mathcal{V}_j^{'}$. The updating process via δ. It should be noted that any π^{-1} map is an ordered pair, with one element from the base space and another element from the fiber F. It should have been say $\mathscr{U}_i \times \pi^{-1}(\mathscr{U}_i)$ in case of right cube and $\mathcal{V}_i \times \mathbf{S}_i$ in left cube; but $\pi^{-1}(\mathscr{U}_i)$ or $\mathbf{S}_i$ should be isomorphic copies of standard fiber F or $\mathbf{S}$ respectively.

4 Discussion

The framework has significant implications for cognitive studies:

1. The high-level functionalities of cognition are not clearly understood from a purely Turing-based paradigm. The association of topology with a Turing-driven computability could set a preliminary step for its theoretical and computational foundations. The study reinvigorates the longstanding debate on whether or not human cognition is purely a computational process.
2. The transient emerging causally explainable non-trivial loops quantifying contextuality give strong hints about the non-decomposability of cognition.
3. The framework is natural for modeling the brain as an evolving complex system.
4. The representationalist view of cognition suggests paradoxical interplay between internal cognitive representations and external reality due to context sensitivity. Our formalism is a variant of fiber bundle theory that allows a synergistic interaction between process description, like a transition system, with a structural representation realized as a simplicial complex. One can reconstruct, resolve, and interpret the internal cognitive structural representations from the external reality, dependent on integration of senses, operationally isomorphic to a process, based on the mathematical theory of Galois-Grothendieck correspondence, which is in line with our preliminary results.
5. Concerns have been raised about the recent empirical evidence on the presence of contextuality in human choice, significantly on the protocol used to inhibit any communication between agents. Atmanspacher et al. argue possibilities of implicit hidden signaling that could take place in these experiments [6]. The emergence of virtual loops could provide mathematical proofs of this signaling and a theoretical background to guide these experiments further. The theory is intended to deepen the understanding of contextuality and possibly facilitate accessibility of the quantum cognition community to use these algebraic generalizations in modeling the higher functionalities of the brain.

5 Funding

This research is supported by the grant PID2023-146683OB-100 funded by MICIU/AEI /10.13039/501100011033 and by ERDF, EU. Additionally, it is supported by the Ikerbasque Foundation and the Basque Government through the BERC 2022–2025 program and by the Ministry of Science and Innovation: BCAM Severo Ochoa accreditation CEX2021-001142-S/MICIU/AEI/10.13039/501100011033. Moreover, the authors acknowledge the financial support received from BCAM-IKUR, funded by the Basque Government, the IKUR Strategy, and the European Union NextGenerationEU/PRTR.

Acknowledgments. The authors would like to thank Mario Rasetti at the ISI foundation, Italy, and Samson Abramsky at the University of Oxford, along with his quantum group, in particular Rui Soares Barbosa, for their helpful discussions. We also thank Giuseppe Longo at CNRS, France, for his valuable insights and potential directions—personal thanks of the first author to Muhammad Saad at Paderborn University, Germany, and Xiaoyang Qiao from Indiana University, Bloomington, USA, for their helpful discussions.

AI Use. No AI tools were used for generating AI images or for any other purposes.

A Appendix

A.1 Additional Construction Information

Suppose we randomly chose context cd of level 2 of the combinatorial structure as shown in Fig. 16. Following this set-up, ab_3 would mean ab of 3rd level. To compute the particular context cd of 2nd level (cd_2) among other eight possible $cd's$ at different levels, one considers all loops and then maps out which particular context of a particular level is not considered in this loop-set, which would correspond to a critical simplex. The interest in loops is due to the fundamental group being the semantic description of the structure quantifying contextuality as a non-collapsibility property of space (Table 3).

Below are all loops while choosing a as the starting vertex. Let L be set of all such paths $L = \sum_{n=1}^{34} L_n$. Any other path (if any) would be a linear combination of paths traversed below. Moreover, these paths are sufficient for our case because they traverse all possible links between all vertices. Suppose $\mathbf{L}$ is a universal set of all paths of $\mathcal{K}_1$, then using the complement or difference between $\mathbf{L}$ and L gives a set of critical contexts. It turns out one context c_2d_2 is critical that was randomly chosen in $\mathcal{K}_1$. Any easy way to check is that in all the paths below, there is no sequence with c_2d_2 which implies its criticality. On the contrary, a discrete Morse function does not allow these loops due to its definition, so we identify the boundary of $\mathcal{K}_1$ to topologise the disc into a surface of a torus $\mathcal{K}_2$ as in Fig. 6.

Table 3. Different possible closed paths over

Label	sequence	Label	sequence
L_1	$a_1 b_1 c_1 d_1 e_1 a_2 b_3 b_4 c_4 b_3 a_2 e_1 d_1 c_1 b_1 a_1$	L_2	$a_1 b_1 c_2 d_3 c_3 b_2 a_1$
L_3	$a_1 b_1 c_2 d_3 e_4 d_4 c_3 b_2 a_1$	L_4	$a_1 b_1 c_2 d_3 e_4 a_5 e_5 d_4 c_3 b_2 a_1$
L_5	$a_1 b_1 c_1 d_2 e_3 d_3 c_3 b_2 a_1$	L_6	$a_1 b_1 c_1 d_2 e_3 d_3 c_2 b_2 a_1$
L_7	$a_1 b_1 c_1 d_2 e_3 d_3 c_2 b_1 a_1$	L_8	$a_1 b_1 c_1 d_2 e_3 a_4 e_4 d_4 c_3 b_2 a_1$
L_9	$a_1 b_1 c_1 d_2 e_3 a_4 b_5 a_5 e_5 d_4 c_3 b_2 a_1$	L_{10}	$a_1 b_1 c_1 d_2 e_3 d_3 c_2 b_1 a_1$
L_{11}	$a_1 b_1 c_1 d_2 e_3 d_3 c_3 b_2 a_1$	L_{12}	$a_1 b_1 c_1 d_2 e_3 a_4 e_4 d_3 c_2 b_2 a_1$
L_{13}	$a_1 b_1 c_1 d_2 e_3 a_4 e_4 d_3 c_2 b_1 a_1$	L_{14}	$a_1 b_1 c_1 d_2 e_3 a_4 b_5 a_5 e_4 d_3 c_2 b_2 a_1$
L_{15}	$a_1 b_1 c_1 d_2 e_3 a_4 b_5 a_5 e_4 d_3 c_2 b_1 a_1$	L_{16}	$a_1 b_1 c_1 d_1 e_2 a_3 b_4 a_4 e_4 d_4 c_3 b_2 a_1$
L_{17}	$a_1 b_1 c_1 d_1 e_2 a_3 e_3 d_3 c_3 b_2 a_1$	L_{18}	$a_1 b_1 c_1 d_1 e_2 a_3 e_3 d_3 c_3 b_1 a_1$
L_{19}	$a_1 b_1 c_1 d_1 e_2 a_3 b_4 a_4 e_4 d_4 c_3 b_2 a_1$	L_{20}	$a_1 b_1 c_1 d_1 e_2 a_3 b_4 a_4 e_4 d_3 c_2 b_1 a_1$
L_{21}	$a_1 b_1 c_2 b_2 b_1 a_1$	L_{22}	$a_1 b_1 c_1 d_1 d_2 e_2 e_3 a_3 a_4 b_4 b_5 a_5 e_5 d_4 c_3 b_2 a_1$
L_{23}	$a_1 b_1 c_2 d_3 e_4 d_4 d_3 c_3 c_2 b_2 b_1 a_1$	L_{24}	$a_1 b_1 c_1 d_2 d_3 c_2 b_2 a_1$
L_{25}	$a_1 b_1 c_1 d_1 e_2 a_3 b_4 c_5 b_5 a_5 e_5 d_4 c_3 b_2 a_1$	L_{26}	$a_1 b_1 c_1 d_1 e_2 d_2 c_1 b_1 a_1$
L_{27}	$a_1 b_1 c_1 c_2 b_1 a_1$	L_{28}	$a_1 b_1 c_2 d_3 e_4 a_5 e_5 e_4 d_4 d_3 c_3 c_2 b_2 b_1 a_1$
L_{29}	$a_1 b_1 c_1 d_2 e_3 e_4 a_4 a_5 e_5 d_4 c_3 b_2 a_1$	L_{30}	$a_1 b_1 c_2 d_3 c_3 c_2 b_1 a_1$
L_{31}	$a_1 b_1 c_1 d_1 e_1 a_2 e_2 e_1 d_1 c_1 b_1 a_1$	L_{32}	$a_1 b_1 c_1 d_1 e_1 a_2 b_3 a_3 a_2 e_2 e_3 d_3 c_3 b_2 a_1$
L_{33}	$a_1 b_1 c_2 b_2 a_1$	L_{34}	$a_1 b_1 c_1 d_1 e_1 b_3 c_4 c_5 b_4 a_3 e_2 d_1 c_1 b_1 a_1$

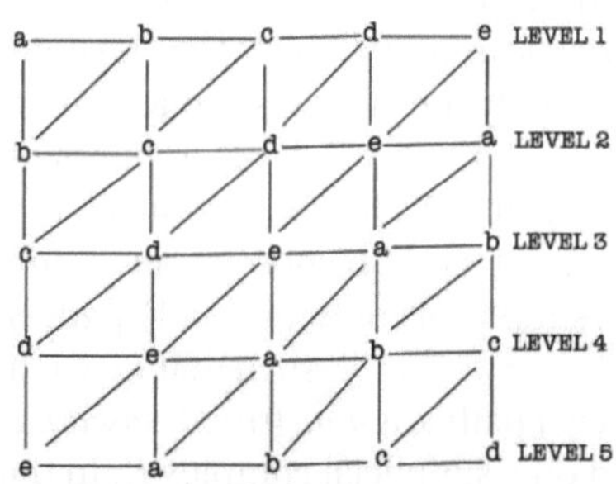

$\mathcal{K}_1$

Fig. 16. The combinatorial description of the physical setup of the experiment with a randomly chosen critical context *cd*.

A.2 Discrete Morse Theory

Discrete Morse theory (DMT) over a finite simplicial complex $\mathcal{K}$, with $\mathcal{S}_p$ the simplices of dimension p. Discrete Morse function $\mathfrak{f}$ assigns a single real number to each simplex of $\mathcal{K}$. A function $\mathfrak{f} : \mathcal{K} \to \mathbb{R}$ be a discrete Morse function iff, for every d dimensional simplex $\sigma^d \in \mathcal{K}$, the following two conditions hold: $|\{\tau^{(d+1)} > \sigma^{(d)} \mid \mathfrak{f}(\tau^{(d+1)}) \leq \mathfrak{f}(\sigma^{(d)})\}| \leq 1$ and $|\{\tau^{(d-1)} < \sigma^{(d)} \mid \mathfrak{f}(\tau^{(d-1)}) \geq \mathfrak{f}(\sigma^{(d)})\}| \leq 1$. σ is called a critical simplex if such conditions don't hold. The function decreases from 2-simplex to one simplex and vice versa in the reverse direction. Forman's papers [13] is the standard references on this subject. There is a relation between critical simplices and the collapsibility of a simplicial complex. If there are no critical simplices in an interval, say $[a, b]$, then it is collapsible to a vertex and the space is connected. Moreover, the number of critical points of some index is responsible for the topology of the underlying structure. However, one is unable to determine the efficiency of this discrete Morse function concerning collapsibility, i.e., there may be critical simplices that could be collapsed while still preserving the homotopy type. A simple example is that of a sphere. So, it is not only critical simplices that are significant in determining the collapsibility of a topological space, but also the paths between simplices. For example, if there is only one gradient path between two simplices, then reversing the direction of the path cancels the criticality of both the simplices. The criticality in $\mathcal{K}$ induces non-triviality in paths up to homotopy. Direction (arrows) over a simplicial complex can be defined by introducing the concept of a combinatorial vector field. It gives direction to each of the simplicial complexes. A combinatorial vector field is a map $V : \mathcal{S} \to \mathcal{S} \cup \{0\}$. Given such a map V and $\sigma \in S$ with $V(\sigma) \neq 0$, we draw an arrow on $\mathcal{K}$ whose tail begins at σ and which extends into $V(\sigma)$. It satisfies some properties, like if V implies that σ is always a face of $V(\sigma)$, then an arrow is possible. If τ is the head of an arrow, then it cannot be a tail as well. Moreover, every simplex is the head or tail of at most one arrow. This field classifies each simplex in pairs and there are three disjoint possibilities viz., σ is the head of an arrow ($\sigma \in Image(V)$), σ is the tail of an arrow ($V(\sigma) \neq 0$) and σ is neither head nor tail of any arrow ($V(\sigma) \neq 0$) and $\sigma \notin Image(V)$ (critical simplices). The non-critical simplices occur in pairs $\sigma^{(d)} \subset \tau^{(d+1)}$ where $\mathfrak{f}(\sigma^{(d)}) \geq \mathfrak{f}(\tau^{(d+1)})$. It can be illustrated by drawing an *arrow* from $\sigma^{(d)}$ to $\tau^{(d+1)}$. The points that are neither heads nor tails of any arrow are exactly the critical simplices. A combinatorial vector field V on $\mathcal{K}$ is a collection of pairs $\sigma^{(d)} \subset \tau^{(d+1)}$ of simplices of $\mathcal{K}$ such that each simplex belongs to at most one pair of V. If α is not critical, then there is a unique edge $e > \alpha$ with $f(e) \leq f(\alpha)$, i.e., $V(\alpha) = e$ with chosen orientation. If α is critical $V(\alpha) = 0$. Given a vector field V on a simplicial complex K, a V-path is a sequence of simplices $\sigma_0^{(d)}, \tau_0^{(d+1)}, \sigma_1^{(d)}, \tau_1^{(d+1)}, \sigma_2^{(d)}, \ldots, \tau_r^{(d+1)}, \sigma_{r+1}^{(d)}$ such that for each $i = 0, \ldots, r$, $\{\sigma, \tau\} \in V$ and $\tau_i > \sigma_{i+1} \neq \sigma_i$. We say such a path is a *non-trivial closed path* if $r \geq 0$ and $\sigma_0 = \sigma_{r+1}$. Suppose V is a vector field on a simplicial complex K. In that case, V is the gradient vector field of some discrete function on $\mathcal{K}$ if and only if there are no non-trivial closed V-paths, i.e., the Hasse diagram is acyclic and $\mathcal{K}$ is *collapsible*. If V has (non-trivial) closed paths, then it cannot be the gradient of a function. It corresponds to the transformation of the fundamental group of a topological space.

References

1. Abramsky, S., Brandenburger, A.: The Sheaf-theoretic structure of non-locality and contextuality. New J. Phys. **13**(113036) (2011)
2. Abramsky, S., Mansfield, S., Barbosa, R.S.: The Cohomology of non-locality and contextuality. In: Electronic Proceedings in Theoretical Computer Science, 95- Proceedings 8th International Workshop on Quantum Physics and Logic (QPL), Nijmegen, pp. 1–14 (2012)
3. Acín, A., Fritz, T., Leverrier, A., Sainz, A.: A combinatorial approach to nonlocality and contextuality. Commun. Math. Phys. **334**, 533–628 (2012). https://api.semanticscholar.org/CorpusID:119292509

4. Aerts, D., Broekaert, J., Gabora, L.: A case for applying an abstracted quantum formalism to cognition. New Ideas Psychol. **29**, 136–146 (2004). https://api.semanticscholar.org/CorpusID:6304409
5. Atmanspacher, H., Filk, T.: A proposed test of temporal nonlocality in bistable perception. J. Math. Psychol. **54**, 314–321 (2010). https://api.semanticscholar.org/CorpusID:15898426
6. Atmanspacher, H., Filk, T.: Contextuality revisited: signaling may differ from communicating. Synthese Library (2019). https://api.semanticscholar.org/CorpusID:204352936
7. Basieva, I., Cervantes, V., Dzhafarov, E., Khrennikov, A.: True contextuality beats direct influences in human decision making. J. Exp. Psychol. General (2018). https://api.semanticscholar.org/CorpusID:49864257
8. Busemeyer, J., Bruza, P.: Quantum Models of Cognition and Decision. Cambridge University Press (2012). https://api.semanticscholar.org/CorpusID:9199120
9. Cabello, A., Severini, S., Winter, A.: Graph-theoretic approach to quantum correlations. Phys. Rev. Lett. **112**, 040401 (2014). https://api.semanticscholar.org/CorpusID:34998358
10. Carù, G.: On the cohomology of contextuality. In: QPL (2016)
11. Dorogovtsev, S., Goltsev, A., Mendes, J.: Critical phenomena in complex networks. Rev. Mod. Phys. **80** (2008)
12. Dzhafarov, E., Kujala, J.: Probabilistic foundations of contextuality. Fortschritte der Physik **65** (2016). https://api.semanticscholar.org/CorpusID:56245502
13. Forman, R.: A user's guide to discrete morse theory. In: Seminaire Lotharingien de Combinatoire 48, Article B48c (2002)
14. Imtiyaz, S., Merelli, E.: Contextual semantics machinery. 20.500.11824/1889/doc.pdf (2024)
15. Khrennikov, A.: Ubiquitous Quantum Structure: From Psychology to Finance. Springer, Heidelberg (2010). https://api.semanticscholar.org/CorpusID:203043327
16. Linial, N., Peled, Y.: On the phase transition in random simplicial complexes. Ann. Math. **184**, 745–773 (2016)
17. Rasetti, M., Merelli, E.: Topological field theory of data: mining data beyond complex networks. In: Random Processes and Some Applications. Advances in Disordered Systems. Cambridge University Press (2016)

Quantum AI for Ethical Decision-Making in Medical Education

Kliment Chakarovski[1], Emilija Velinova[1](✉), and Daniela Mechkaroska[2]

[1] Technical University of Sofia, Sofia 1000, Bulgaria
evelinova335@gmail.com
[2] University of Information Science and Technology, Ohrid 6000, North Macedonia

Abstract. This paper presents a hybrid quantum-classical AI model for ethical decision-making training in medical education. Leveraging Qiskit and a neural network to parameterize a 2-qubit circuit, the system simulates ethical dilemmas using 860 synthetic patient scenarios focused on autonomy, consent, and resource allocation. It evaluates decisions based on probabilistic outcomes for trust and health. Compared to a classical rule-based baseline, the quantum model achieves higher performance—62% win rate for trust, 78% for health—demonstrating its effectiveness across diverse dilemma types. Visual analysis highlights how quantum computing better reflects real-world ambiguity. While based on simulated data, this proof-of-concept reveals strong potential for integrating quantum AI into medical training. It offers an interactive, data-driven framework that prepares students for complex clinical ethics through experiential learning. Connecting quantum cognition with educational goals, the model makes it possible to proceed with future validations using real-world data and deployment on physical quantum hardware.

Keywords: Artificial Intelligence · Medical Training · Ethical Decision-Making · Qiskit · Neural Networks · Quantum Circuit

1 Introduction

Medical education increasingly emphasizes ethical decision-making as healthcare professionals navigate complex bioethical dilemmas, such as balancing patient autonomy, informed consent, and confidentiality. Traditional training methods, relying on case studies and rule-based frameworks, struggle to address the probabilistic uncertainty inherent in real-world decisions, where trade-offs between trust and health outcomes are common [1]. This limitation underscores the need for innovative tools to simulate nuanced ethical scenarios and prepare students for modern healthcare challenges. Quantum artificial intelligence (AI) offers a novel approach by leveraging quantum computing's ability to model uncertainty through superposition and entanglement. This paper represents a quantum AI model to make better ethical decision-making training. A Qiskit-based 2-qubit quantum circuit, parameterized by a neural network, evaluates decisions across 860 synthetic patient scenarios generated with Faker library. Compared to a rule-based classical baseline, the quantum model achieves better win rates (62% for trust maintenance, 78% for health improvement).

D. Cavar et al. (Eds.): QNLPAI 2025, CCIS 2659, pp. 302–315, 2026.
https://doi.org/10.1007/978-3-032-13883-5_16

This proof-of-concept tool enables medical students to explore ethical trade-offs with data-driven insights, paving the way for future validation with real patient data and quantum hardware. The paper is organized as follows: Sect. 2 reviews related work in medical ethics and quantum AI. Section 3 presents the system architecture. Section 4 represents detailed system implementation. Section 5 discusses results and visualizations. Section 6 interprets findings and limitations, and contains the conclusion and future directions.

2 Related Work

2.1 AI in Medical Ethics Modeling

Artificial intelligence (AI) supports medical decision-making by predicting patient outcomes and encoding bioethical principles like autonomy and beneficence [2]. Rule-based systems guide dilemmas such as informed consent, while simulation-based tools, like virtual patients, are training clinicians [3]. Recent work emphasizes AI's role in ethical challenges, including transparency and bias in clinical decision support [4]. Classical models, however, struggle with probabilistic uncertainty in trade-offs (e.g., trust vs. health outcomes), limiting their ability to simulate real-world ethics. Moreover, these models often lack adaptability when confronted with conflicting ethical principles, resulting in rigid outcomes that fail to reflect the reasoning clinicians employ. This study introduces a quantum AI model to address these gaps, leveraging quantum computing for the decision-making process.

2.2 Quantum Cognition Foundations

Quantum cognition applies quantum probability theory to model human decision-making, particularly where classical models struggle. Limited number of researchers have focused on this topic while [5] pioneered this field, demonstrating that quantum principles like superposition and interference explain cognitive paradoxes, such as order effects and violations of classical logic. Their work laid a foundation for understanding non-classical decision processes. Followed with the foundation, [6] provided empirical evidence for quantum models in ambiguous decision contexts, showing their strength in capturing cognitive uncertainty. While these models have been extensively developed within cognitive psychology, their application to computational systems and bioethical decision-making is still emerging. Recent advances address these limitations and broaden the field's potential. Quantum cognition gains a rigorous mathematical foundation through quantum measurement theory, as established by foundational work [7]. Advances in designing quantum circuit components for decision-making bridge theoretical models with practical quantum hardware, enabling real-world applications [8] Additionally, the QuLBIT framework, a quantum-like Bayesian inference approach, enhances complex human reasoning, further strengthening computational models [9]. Together, these developments create robust and feasible tools for addressing intricate decision-making challenges.

This paper builds on these advancements to explore new frontiers. By leveraging quantum cognition's ability to model non-commutative decision processes, it simulates ethical dilemmas in medicine using quantum circuits. The resulting framework captures the complexity of human values in high-stakes contexts. It offers healthcare professionals and medical students a novel training tool to navigate morally challenging decisions with greater precision and insight.

2.3 Quantum Computing for AI

Quantum computing harnesses principles like superposition and entanglement to process information beyond the capabilities of classical systems. This enables superior handling of uncertainty and complex problem-solving, critical for advancing artificial intelligence. Hybrid quantum-classical algorithms, integrating quantum circuits with neural networks, have emerged as powerful tools for tasks like classification and pattern recognition [10]. Recent advancements highlight quantum machine learning's (QML) potential in biomedical research. For instance, QML has enhanced protein structure prediction, a key challenge in drug discovery and biological modeling [11]. Its ability to process high-dimensional data makes QML a promising tool for complex, probabilistic systems, yet its application to ethical decision-making in healthcare remains untapped. This study addresses this gap with a Qiskit-based hybrid quantum model tailored for bioethical scenarios. By simulating decision processes, the model captures the moral complexities healthcare professionals face. It leverages Qiskit's accessible quantum framework to ensure practical implementation. This approach pioneers the use of quantum computing in medical ethics training, and may equip practitioners with a cutting-edge tool to navigate challenging decisions with greater clarity and precision.

2.4 Ethical Dilemmas in Practice

Medical practice frequently presents ethical dilemmas where professionals must balance conflicting principles like autonomy, beneficence and others. For instance, a terminally ill patient refusing life-saving treatment forces clinicians to weigh respect for autonomy against their duty to preserve life. Similarly, ensuring informed consent requires clear communication, yet providers must ensure vulnerable patients fully grasp risks and benefits [12]. These scenarios highlight the uncertainty and complexity inherent in ethical decision-making.

Quantum AI models, building on hybrid quantum frameworks like those developed in Qiskit, offer a novel approach to addressing these challenges. By simulating probabilistic trade-offs between ethical principles, these models capture the non-commutative nature of human decisions, as explored in quantum cognition research. They enable students to explore dilemma scenarios in a controlled environment, fostering deeper understanding of moral complexities. Such tools prepare healthcare professionals to make context-sensitive judgments in practice. This simulation-based approach also paves the way for advanced training methods in medical ethics education. By integrating real-world uncertainties into interactive scenarios, quantum AI enhances clinicians' ability to navigate high-stakes decisions with precision. This represents a significant step toward bridging theoretical ethics and practical application.

2.5 Pedagogical Implications

Effective medical ethics education demands more than theoretical frameworks; it requires active, experiential learning to prepare students for complex real-world decisions. Kolb's experiential learning theory emphasizes that knowledge emerges through concrete experiences, reflective observation, abstract conceptualization, and active experimentation [13]. Such an approach enables students to grapple with the details of ethical dilemmas in a dynamic, hands-on manner. Quantum AI models, such as the Qiskit-based hybrid framework, provide a transformative tool for this purpose. By simulating ethical dilemmas with probabilistic decision outcomes, these models mirror the non-commutative decision processes explored in quantum cognition. They offer immediate feedback on trade-offs between principles like autonomy and beneficence, fostering critical thinking and decision-making skills. This approach builds directly on the scenario-based training proposed for navigating real-world ethical challenges. As quantum computing advances, these educational tools will grow increasingly, enabling more realistic ethical training. By integrating AI with quantum, this framework bridges theoretical innovation with practical education.

3 Methodology – System Architecture Overview

With emphasis on the dual goals of trust maintenance and health improvement, this study presents a hybrid quantum framework for assessing bioethical dilemmas. The system combines quantum simulation, neural network-based quantum circuit (Quantum AI) parameter prediction, patient data processing, and a classical processing model for comparison. The architecture uses both deterministic classical methods and the probabilistic nature of quantum computing to systematically evaluate ethical decisions [14]. A schematic representation of the system's workflow is shown in Fig. 1, emphasizing the data's sequential passage through its essential parts. Synthetic patient data, including name, age, description of the dilemma, is generated with the start of the pipeline. This data is processed by a neural network (MLPRegressor) to predict rotation angles [15], which are then applied to a 2-qubit quantum circuit that represents improved health and maintained trust. The measurement results from the circuit are expressed as percentages (10–90%). At the same time, a classical model uses preset rules to produce similar results, making it easier to compare the two methods directly.

3.1 Synthetic Data Generator

A randomly generated name, an age between the range 18 and 90 years, a thorough description of the dilemma, and two choice options are all part of the synthetic patient data that the system uses as input. The five ethical domains of autonomy, informed consent, resource allocation, confidentiality, and family wishes are used to classify dilemmas. A patient with a terminal illness, for example, may refuse life-prolonging treatment, creating a dilemma that pits beneficence against autonomy. Real-world ethical trade-offs may be reflected in the associated decision options, which could include supporting treatment or honoring the patient's autonomy. For assessing the effects of decisions, this classification guarantees a varied and representative set of scenarios.

3.2 AI – Neutral Network Mapping

Scikit-learn library has been used to implement a Multi-Layer Perceptron Regressor (MLPRegressor) [16], which transforms the decision and dilemma type into rotation angles for the quantum circuit. The decision (e.g., "Respect patient's autonomy") and dilemma type (e.g., autonomy) are one-hot encoded into a numerical feature vector. With two hidden layers of 20 and 10 neurons each, the MLPRegressor is trained to predict two rotation angles—one for each qubit—based on target probabilities ranging from 0.55 to 0.75. These angles enable the quantum circuit to encode ethical trade-offs into its quantum states, facilitating a probabilistic evaluation of outcomes such as trust maintenance and health improvement.

3.3 Quantum Model Circuit Design

The two qubits used in the Qiskit-developed quantum circuit stand for the trust maintained and the health improved, respectively. Ry gates, which rotate each qubit around the Y-axis of the Bloch sphere [17] and encode the probability of each outcome, are used to apply the rotation angles that the neural network predicts. To guarantee statistical reliability, the circuit is simulated with 20,000 shots using Qiskit's AerSimulator [18]. Interpretable metrics for trust and health outcomes are produced by measuring and scaling the resulting probabilities to a range of 10 to 90%.

3.4 Classical Processing Model

The classical model serves as a benchmark, assigning outcome probabilities using predetermined rules based on the dilemma type and decision. For an autonomy-beneficence dilemma, selecting "Respect patient's autonomy" yields 70% trust maintained and 30% health improved, while "Advocate for treatment" results in 40% trust maintained and 60% health improved. This rule-based approach provides a consistent baseline, enabling a direct comparison with the quantum model's performance in resolving ethical dilemmas [1].

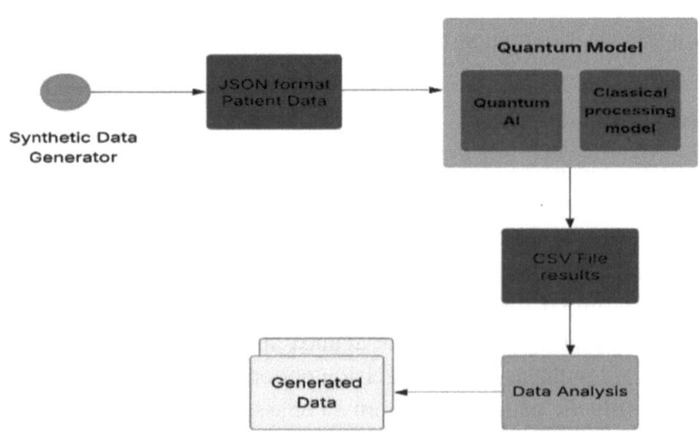

Fig. 1. System Architecture representing every component included in the data processing

3.5 Data Analysis

For final analysis, both the quantum and classical models' outputs are combined into a structured dataset and stored as a CSV file. This dataset makes it possible to assess decision-making performance through in-depth statistical comparisons and visualizations like bar charts and scatter plots, which serves meaningful analysis and interpretable results.

4 Detailed System Implementation

This section describes the technical implementation of the Quantum AI model for ethical decision-making in medical education. It covers operating details for the model data generation, neural network training (AI), quantum simulations, and lastly result analysis to evaluate the performance of the quantum and classical models. The analysis presented will focus on comparing the two models' performance metrics for trust and health outcomes, with statistical validation to confirm the quantum model's advantage. Visualizations are also provided to offer insights into the decision-making process across various ethical dilemmas.

4.1 Generating the Data

Data is generated with a script using the Faker library, the script is used to generate synthetic data of 860 records [19]. Each record, which was created using this library includes a name, age in a range that was given previously, medical history, and a choice. Each record includes a choice that is made between two options that are randomized across five categories: resource allocation, autonomy, informed consent, confidentiality, and family wishes. For instance, the script includes specific medical history entries like "Terminal illness diagnosed 6 months ago" or "Stable vital signs, palliative care recommended" along with scenarios like "Patient refuses life-prolonging treatment (autonomy)" with the choices "Respect patient's autonomy" or "Advocate for treatment." After the data generation is finished, it is saved in JSON file format, guaranteeing organized storage of the data with appropriate formatting. The diverse data consisting of 860 records is shaped by different ethical dilemmas which then allows for robust testing of medical scenarios, covering a wide range of real-world issues. Given that the data generation script produces many records, the system is exposed to a wide range of scenarios, enabling comprehensive evaluation. The importance and utility of synthetic data for health-related AI research is well-established in prior work [20].

4.2 AI – Neural Network Training

For the AI need to predict rotation angles for the quantum circuit, quantum ethical model's script uses a neural network's MLPRegressor. Using the one hot encoder creates a feature vector in the quantum angle predictor class by one-hot encoding features from dilemma types (like "Autonomy") and decisions (like "Respect patient's autonomy") to guarantee correct encoding. The labels and angles based on probabilities (0.55–0.75) computed are trained on 2,000 samples with hidden layers of 20 and 10 neurons. The configuration as it is used optimizes the circuit's representation of ethical trade-offs by predicting two angles per. The approach aligns with methodologies that leverage neural networks for modeling quantum circuits, as demonstrated in prior research papers [21]. The random state then ensures reproducibility across training runs. The angles are mapped to probabilities via a cosine-squared function to align with quantum measurement outputs. Finally, a fixed random state ensures reproducibility across training runs.

4.3 Quantum Simulation (Qiskit)

Using a 2-qubit quantum circuit defined in the quantum model script, the system performs quantum simulations [17]. The rotations in the quantum circuit encode probabilities by rotating the qubits around the Y-axis of the Bloch sphere. One qubit represents "trust maintained" while the other represents "health improved." These rotations are determined by predicted angles, which are applied through specific quantum operations that tilt the qubits accordingly. The simulation is run with a high-performance backend that simulates quantum state evolution and measurement noise, mimicking how a real quantum computer would behave [22]. A total of 20,000 measurements are made during the simulation to ensure statistical stability, and the results are averaged for accuracy. The decision-making process, along with the probabilities for each qubit, is printed for clarity. To interpret the results, the system maps the quantum states to real-world values. Specifically, it computes the probability of the "zero state" for each qubit and then scales this probability to a range between 10% and 90% [23]. This scaling helps ensure that the values for trust and health are bounded and interpretable, representing realistic scores that can be used for decision-making. The quantum simulation, while lacking some physical constraints, effectively simulates the behavior of a quantum computer. It provides a scalable framework that can be transitioned to actual quantum hardware, such as IBM's Quantum systems, for future deployment. The final analysis is done with a script that analyzes the data from the CSV file that was generated by the quantum model script, to efficiently compute the outcomes from the quantum and classical model and compare outcomes.

4.4 Result Analysis

The final analyzing script is designed to process the outputs of the system and compare the performance of the quantum and classical models. The results are first loaded into a data frame and then grouped by patient and a decision to facilitate further analysis.

To assess which model performs better, the script compares the quantum and classical scores for each decision. It tracks the number of instances where the quantum model outperforms the classical model, calculating a win rate for each outcome. Specifically, the quantum model achieves a 62.03%-win rate for trust and a 78.95%-win rate for health. To evaluate the statistical significance of these results, the script performs a paired statistical test [24]. The p-values are calculated, and since they are below the threshold of 0.05, this confirms that the quantum model offers a statistically greater advantage over the classical model.

In addition to the statistical analysis, the script visualizes the results through scatter plots and bar plots. The scatter plots compare the quantum and classical scores for each outcome, while the bar plots display the probabilities by dilemma type for both models. These visualizations are saved as image files for easy reference and further analysis. In order these images to be generated script uses several libraries to be able to accomplish this. Python libraries, like Pandas for data manipulation, NumPy for numerical operations, SciPy for statistical testing, and Seaborn and Matplotlib for generating visualizations [16], are used to provide us with scatter plots and bar charts to enable analysis and comparison of the quantum and classical models' performance.

5 Results – Quantitative and Visual

The average trust and health outcomes for each of the five types of dilemmas—autonomy, informed consent, confidentiality, resource allocation, and family wishes—are compared between the quantum and classical models in the charts. The scatter plot named "trust_maintained" serves to measure the trust and its results are shown on Fig. 2. The second scatter plot "health_improved", presents the results gained for health progress as shown in Fig. 3. Based on the 3440 rows of CSV file, each figure shows the mean probability percentage for the quantum and classical models. While health improvement varies, the scatter plots show that the quantum model maintains trust more consistently than the classical model.

The quantum model also shows higher averages for informed consent than the classical. These variations result from examining the choices made by each patient, calculating the average scores for each type of dilemma and charting the results to demonstrate how well the quantum model handled complex ethical issues. The relationship between the predictions of the quantum and classical models for trust-maintained testing is compared and presented in Fig. 2. With colors signifying different types of dilemmas, each point represents a patient-decision pair. Diagonal line, on the other hand points below this line indicate that the classical model occasionally overestimates trust. When the classical model assigns a higher trust percentage than the quantum model for the same decision, it is said to "overestimate trust", suggesting that the classical model is more confident in preserving trust in that situation.

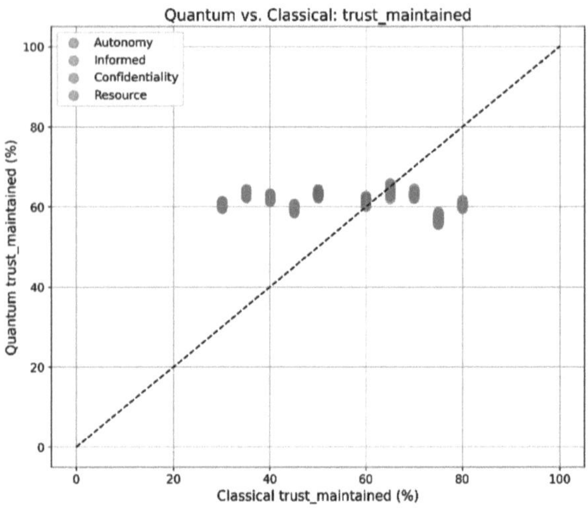

Fig. 2. Quantum vs. Classical: Trust Maintained

A lower, more balanced trust score that reflects the complexity of real-world scenarios, such as potential conflicts between patient autonomy and family wishes, is the outcome of the quantum model, which is based on probabilistic simulations using Qiskit and considers the uncertainty and trade-offs inherent in ethical decisions. Predicting a high percentage of trust in ethical decision-making can be dangerous because it may imply that a choice (such as respecting patient autonomy) will uphold trust with all parties involved (patient, family, and medical team), but in practice, it may cause conflict (for example, the family may feel ignored). These trade-offs are captured by the probabilistic approach of the quantum model, which results in a more cautious and balanced prediction.

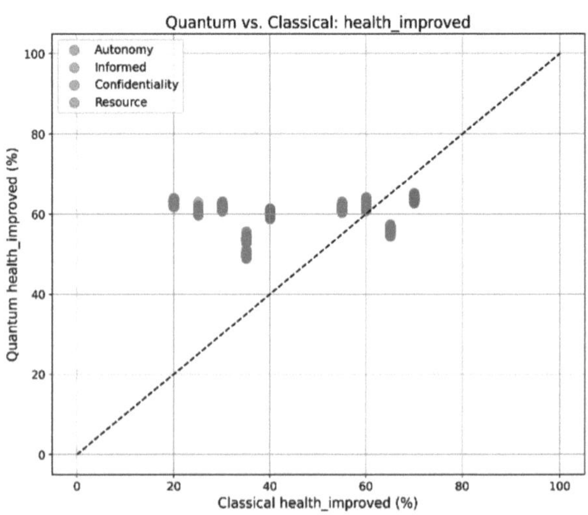

Fig. 3. Quantum vs. Classical: Health Improved

A similar relationship for health can be seen in Fig. 3 used to compare the quantum and classical results for health improved testing. The points above the line (quantum at 60% vs. classical at 40%) gives quantum computation an advantage. Plotting paired scores from the CSV revealed these patterns, which demonstrate how the quantum model, based on large amounts of simulation data, captures probabilistic trade-offs in contrast to the classical model's fixed outcomes.

5.1 Explanation of the Results

The trade-offs present in medical ethics are reflected in the quantum model, which uses probabilistic simulations to adjust to complex situations such as patient autonomy versus family wishes. The classical model, in contrast, is based on deterministic rules and frequently produces results that are consistent but less adaptable. These conclusions were made by looking at overall scores, identifying patterns, and seeing where quantum predictions matched ethical decision-making more accurately. The decision is supported by a 62.03% success rate for trust and a 78.95% success rate for health across all cases. To visualize the results, based on the CSV file result, each bar shows the mean probability percentage for the quantum and classical models. The graph indicates that while health improvement varies, the quantum model achieves higher averages than the classical model, as shown on Figs. 4 and 5. At the same time, the quantum model maintains trust more consistently than the classical model. This graphic demonstrates how the quantum model can adjust to the complex trade-offs involved in moral judgment, producing more equitable results in a range of situations.

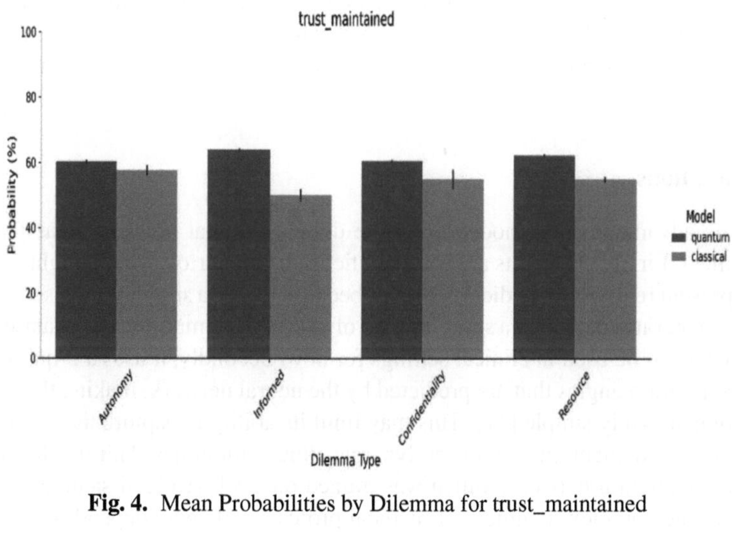

Fig. 4. Mean Probabilities by Dilemma for trust_maintained

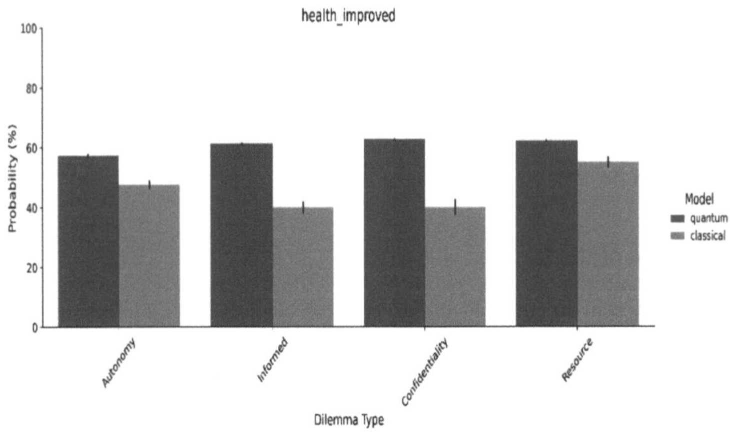

Fig. 5. Mean Probabilities by Dilemma for health_improved

6 Discussion

6.1 Interpretation

The quantum-inspired model uses quantum principles to handle ethical uncertainty in medical education in a smart way. Unlike the classical model, which follows strict rules and often gives simple yes-or-no results, the quantum model uses Qiskit's 2-qubit circuit to turn probabilities into rotations, showing the uncertainty and tough choices in ethical dilemmas [25]. The scatter plot "Quantum vs. Classical: health_improved" shows the quantum model often does better in health scores while keeping trust steady. This balance mirrors the real-life struggles doctors face, like weighing patient wishes against medical benefits.

6.2 Limitations

Despite its advantages, the model has some drawbacks that point to areas that need improvement. Firstly, its results are based on fictitious scenarios, which might not accurately represent real-world medical contexts, because it uses a simulation-based methodology and generates data with a script instead of validated human decision datasets. This limits how it can be used in clinical settings for now. Secondly, it uses a 2-qubit system with fixed rotation angles that are predicted by the neural network, making the quantum circuit comparatively simple [17]. This may limit its ability to capture the complexities of more advanced quantum systems or dynamic ethical dilemmas. Thirdly, the quantum model script's neural network, which was trained on 2000 artificial samples, does not yet capture the complex judgment of medical professionals who depend on real-world experience and emotional intelligence. This reliance on synthetic data might make the model less compatible with ethical reasoning in humans [26].

6.3 Ethical Note

It is important to say that this model is not intended for real-world clinical use, but rather it may be used for training and analysis in medical education. However, even for educational and training purposes, the model must go through rigorous validation and controlled trials to ensure its reliability, ethical soundness, and pedagogical value before being implemented. Although it offers insightful information about moral decision-making, its current iteration, which is based on simulations and artificial data, lacks the validation required to direct actual patient care. It is not meant to take the place of human judgment in clinical practice, but rather to improve comprehension and encourage dialogue between medical students and educators [3].

6.4 Future Work

The creation of the quantum-inspired model for medical education's ethical decision-making process opens several exciting directions for further study and to strengthen its credibility and usefulness. Beyond the synthetic samples currently produced, a major goal will be to train the neural network (NN) in the quantum model on actual ethical decisions or survey data gathered from medical professionals. By including elements like emotional intelligence and contextual judgment that are missing from artificial datasets, this change will allow the model to more accurately represent the complex reasoning of medical professionals.

Future research could explore advanced AI techniques, like deep reinforcement learning, to help the neural network adjust its predictions in real time based on feedback from ethical situations [27]. This could make its decisions more accurate. By incorporating natural language processing (NLP) capabilities, the model may be able to examine unstructured data, like patient feedback or doctor's notes, and gain a deeper comprehension of moral difficulties. Transfer learning could also be used to improve the AI model's generalizability across various medical contexts by fine-tuning it on smaller, more specialized datasets of ethical decisions. Regarding the quantum part, adding dimensions to the quantum circuit—which is currently restricted to a 2-qubit system will enable a more thorough simulation of complex ethical challenges. These dimensions can include satisfaction, legal risk, and patient emotion [28]. This improvement might increase the predictive accuracy of the model by better representing the complexity of real-world situations. Additionally, evaluating the model's performance on more complex datasets—such as simulated learning environments with a range of student inputs will shed more light on how well it works in various situations. Another part that could be investigated is incorporating real-time feedback mechanisms from medical educators to improve the model iteratively and make sure it complies with changing educational requirements and ethical standards [29]. Furthermore, the model's credibility and worldwide applicability could be increased by verifying it against international ethical standards like those set forth by the World Medical Association [30].

6.5 Conclusion

This study presents a quantum-inspired AI model that uses probabilistic simulations to improve medical education's ethical decision-making instruction. Through a systematic evaluation of a synthetic dataset that included a wide variety of patient scenarios in several ethical categories, including autonomy, informed consent, and resource allocation, the model outperformed a deterministic classical model with significant win rates of 62.03% for trust and 78.95% for health. This method's main advantage is its capacity to accurately depict the complex ambiguities and trade-offs present in moral enigmas, offering a more accurate representation of the actual decision-making difficulties encountered by medical practitioners. This ability was consistently shown through detailed visuals that highlighted how flexible and balanced the quantum model was when dealing with complex moral situations. These results can in the future establish the model as a useful teaching tool that helps medical students and educators gain a deeper understanding of ethical reasoning. While certain limitations, such as the utilization of artificial data and a simplified quantum circuit, suggest room for improvement, the study lays a solid basis for combining AI and quantum computing to enhance comprehension of ethical complexities in healthcare education and open the door for further advancements in this multidisciplinary field.

References

1. Beauchamp, T.L., Childress, J.F.: Principles of Biomedical Ethics, 8th edn. Oxford University Press, New York, NY (2019)
2. Shortliffe, E.H., Sepúlveda, M.J.: Clinical decision support in the era of artificial intelligence. JAMA **320**(21), 2199–2200 (2018). https://doi.org/10.1001/jama.2018.17163
3. Ziv, A., Wolpe, P.R., Small, S.D., Glick, S.: Simulation-based medical education: an ethical imperative. Acad. Med. **78**(8), 783–788 (2003). https://doi.org/10.1097/00001888-200308000-00006
4. Gerke, S., Minssen, T., Cohen, G.: Ethical and legal challenges of artificial intelligence-driven healthcare. Cambridge Q. Healthc. Ethics **29**(4), 615–621 (2020). https://doi.org/10.1017/S0963180120000411
5. Busemeyer, J.R., Bruza, P.D.: Quantum Models of Cognition and Decision. Cambridge University Press, Cambridge, UK (2012). https://doi.org/10.1017/CBO9780511997710
6. Wang, Z., Busemeyer, J.R.: A quantum question order model supported by empirical tests of an a priori and precise prediction. Top. Cogn. Sci. **5**(4), 689–710 (2013). https://doi.org/10.1111/tops.12040
7. Fuyama, M., Khrennikov, A., Ozawa, M.: Quantum-like cognition and decision making in the light of quantum measurement theory. arXiv preprint arXiv:2503.05859 (2025)
8. Widdows, D., Rani, J., Pothos, E.M.: Quantum circuit components for cognitive decision-making. Entropy **25**(4), 548 (2023). https://doi.org/10.3390/e25040548
9. Moreira, C., Hammes, M., Kurdoglu, R.S., Bruza, P.: QuLBIT: quantum-like Bayesian inference technologies for cognition and decision. arXiv preprint arXiv:2006.02256 (2020)
10. Havlíček, V., et al.: Supervised learning with quantum-enhanced feature spaces. Nature **567**(7747), 209–212 (2019). https://doi.org/10.1038/s41586-019-0980-2
11. Perdomo-Ortiz, A., Sud, J., Le, N.T.P., Bao, Y., Dumitrescu, E.F.: Protein design by integrating machine learning and quantum computing. PRX Life **2**(4), 043012 (2022). https://doi.org/10.1103/PRXLife.2.043012
12. Gillon, R.: Medical ethics: four principles plus attention to scope. BMJ **309**(6948), 184–188 (1994). https://doi.org/10.1136/bmj.309.6948.184
13. Kolb, D.A.: Experiential Learning: Experience as the Source of Learning and Development. Prentice Hall, Englewood Cliffs, NJ (1984)

14. Lu, D.B., Li, H., Li, J., Laflamme, R., Zeng, B.: Quantum decision making: a quantum approach to cognitive science. NPJ Quantum Inf. **4**(1), 1–6 (2018). https://doi.org/10.1038/s41534-018-0072-0
15. Schuld, M., Petruccione, F.: Supervised Learning with Quantum Computers. Springer, Cham (2018). https://doi.org/10.1007/978-3-319-96424-9
16. Pedregosa, F., et al.: Scikit-learn: machine learning in Python. J. Mach. Learn. Res. **12**, 2825–2830 (2011)
17. Nielsen, M.A., Chuang, I.L.: Quantum Computation and Quantum Information: 10th, Anniversary Cambridge University Press, Cambridge, UK (2010)
18. Abraham, H., et al.: Qiskit: an open-source framework for quantum computing (2019). https://doi.org/10.5281/zenodo.2562111
19. Korpela, J.: Faker: Python Package for Generating Fake Data (2022). https://faker.readthedocs.io/
20. Goncalves, A., Ray, H., Saria, D.S., Schulam, E.: Generation and evaluation of synthetic patient data. In: Proceedings of the 2020 Conference on Health, Inference, and Learning (CHIL '20). ACM, New York, NY, 1–10 (2020). https://doi.org/10.1145/3368555.3384464
21. Cantori, S., Vitali, D., Pilati, S.: Supervised learning of random quantum circuits via scalable neural networks. arXiv preprint arXiv:2206.10348 (2022)
22. IBM Quantum: AerSimulator documentation: simulating quantum systems (2023). https://qiskit.org/documentation/aersimulator
23. Hidary, J.D.: Quantum Computing: An Applied Approach. Springer, Cham (2019). https://doi.org/10.1007/978-3-030-23922-0
24. Agresti, A., Finlay, B.: Statistical Methods for the Social Sciences, 5th edn. Pearson, Boston, MA (2019)
25. Lambert, N., Khrennikov, A.: Quantum cognition: advances, prospects and challenges. Front. Psychol. **14**, 1146782 (2023). https://doi.org/10.3389/fpsyg.2023.1146782
26. Raja Babu, K.A., Mulay, S., Prabhu, O., Sivaprakasam, M.: Position paper: building trust in synthetic data for clinical AI. arXiv preprint arXiv:2502.02076 (2025)
27. Luketina, J., et al.: A survey of reinforcement learning informed by natural language. arXiv preprint arXiv:1906.03926 (2019)
28. Wang, Z., Busemeyer, J.R., Atmanspacher, H., Pothos, E.M.: The potential of quantum probability for modeling cognitive processes. In: Proceedings of the 35th Annual Meeting of the Cognitive Science Society (CogSci 2013). Cognitive Science Society, pp. 1522–1527 (2013). https://cogsci.mindmodeling.org/2013/papers/0288/paper0288.pdf
29. Ramani, S., Könings, K.D., Ginsburg, S., van der Vleuten, C.P.M.: Feedback redefined: principles and practice. J. Gen. Intern. Med. **34**(5), 744–749 (2019). https://doi.org/10.1007/s11606-019-04874-2
30. Parsa-Parsi, R.W., Gillon, R., Wiesing, U.: The revised international code of medical ethics: an exercise in international professional ethical self-regulation. J. Med. Ethics **50**(3), 163–168 (2024). https://doi.org/10.1136/jme-2023-109027

Quantum Curiosity: Quantum Curious Feature Selection

James Bryan Graves[1] and Goren Gordon[1,2(✉)]

[1] Indiana University, Bloomington, IN, USA
{gravjabr,gogordon}@iu.edu
[2] Tel Aviv University, Tel-Aviv, Israel

Abstract. In recent years, an interesting interplay between the rise of Quantum Computing and AI has emerged. AI is being used to optimize quantum computation and quantum computing is being used to speed up AI. One aspect of AI that has gained attention in the last decade, namely artificial curiosity or intrinsic motivation, has yet to be integrated with quantum computing. Moreover, recently, the curiosity loop was introduced, which includes a machine learning algorithm that provides intrinsic reward for a reinforcement learning agent, thereby optimizing the learning process. The curiosity loop has been used in the Curious Data Scientist Framework, including curious feature selection, curious instance selection and curiosity-based clustering. Here we propose an extension of this framework to include both quantum machine learning and quantum reinforcement learning algorithms within the curiosity loop architecture. We present a novel quantum curious feature selection algorithm within this framework as a first step in the introduction of Quantum Curiosity. Discussion and future extensions of this quantum framework are presented.

Keywords: Feature selection · artificial curiosity · quantum machine learning · quantum reinforcement learning

1 Introduction

The progress of quantum computing has reignited interest in the practical adoption of quantum computation algorithms, while the rapid ascent of AI has provoked curiosity about the interaction between the two disciplines. AI-for-Quantum involves applying machine learning and AI techniques to enhance the efficiency of quantum computations. Meanwhile, Quantum-for-AI focuses on employing quantum computers to accelerate machine learning and AI processes [44].

In the realm of machine learning (ML) and artificial intelligence (AI), there is growing interest in the subfield of artificial curiosity or intrinsic motivation algorithms [12,13,31,33], particularly in deep learning applied to complex scenarios. Artificial curiosity refers to a reinforcement learning agent that obtains intrinsic rewards derived from learning advancement. Consequently, in settings where

D. Cavar et al. (Eds.): QNLPAI 2025, CCIS 2659, pp. 316–328, 2026.
https://doi.org/10.1007/978-3-032-13883-5_17

rewards are sparse, algorithms like the intrinsic curiosity module [33], supply dense intrinsic rewards that enables the agent to learn about the environment in a faster way.

An additional area where artificial curiosity has demonstrated potential is the Curious Data Scientist Framework [27–30]. In this framework, the curiosity loop is employed: a machine learning model (Learner) attempts to learn from data while providing intrinsic rewards to an actor. This actor uses a reinforcement learning algorithm to adjust and filter the training set, thereby optimizing the Learner's learning progress. Notable developments within this framework include Curious Feature Selection and its extension, Deep Curious Feature Selection, where the Actor's decisions involve selecting features, as well as Curious Instance Selection and Curious Feature-based Clustering.

In the realm of quantum computation, Quantum Machine Learning (QML) is becoming an exciting method for improving data-driven tasks with quantum algorithms. Nevertheless, a constant challenge exists at the junction of classical data and quantum circuits: encoding classical features into quantum states demands substantial computational resources. Furthermore, near-term quantum computers, also known as NISQ devices, have strict limitations on qubit numbers and fidelity, which renders the direct encoding of high-dimensional data unfeasible. Consequently, effective feature selection is especially crucial in quantum environments.

In this paper, we present a new framework termed *Quantum Curious Feature Selection* (QCFS), which is a hybrid classical-quantum algorithm that employs reinforcement learning complemented by curiosity-driven exploration to determine key feature subsets suitable for quantum processing. Our methodology is grounded in the Curious Feature Selection framework initially developed for classical applications, but it is modified to guide quantum models under qubit constraints. Hence, it fulfills a dual role: from an AI-for-Quantum viewpoint, QCFS utilizes the curiosity loop to enhance feature selection, addressing the current constraints of quantum computers; from a Quantum-for-AI viewpoint, the curiosity loop is leveraged to optimize quantum machine learning, accelerating and enhancing classical data-focused learning.

Here, we present the QCFS algorithm. We "quantize" both aspects of the curiosity loop, namely, we substitute the Learner with a Quantum Learner [10] and the Actor with a Quantum reinforcement learning algorithm [35].

2 Related Works

This work builds on the curiosity-driven learning frameworks introduced by Moran and Gordon. The original Curious Feature Selection (CFS) algorithm [28] framed feature selection as a reinforcement learning problem guided by intrinsic reward, which was later extended to Deep Curious Feature Selection (DCFS) [30], incorporating recurrent neural networks in the reinforcement learning architecture. This framework was later extended to instance selection in the Curious

Instance Selection (CIS) algorithm [27], where clusters of examples are evaluated for their contribution to predictive accuracy. Most recently, the framework unified CFS and CIS into a novel curiosity-based Clustering algorithm [29].

2.1 Quantum Machine Learning

Quantum Machine Learning (QML) explores how to devise and implement quantum software that could enable machine learning that is faster than that of classical computers [4,38,42]. While QML encompasses many domains, here we focus on QML with *classical* data, i.e., using quantum machine learning algorithms with classical input-output pairs to speed up and improve accuracy compared to their classical counterparts [43]. This use of QML has initiated several important real-world applications [15], such as in healthcare [40].

However, there are many challenges before QML can attain its desirable goal [6]. Current quantum hardware remains limited in both the number of available qubits and the depth of circuits that can be reliably executed [1]. These constraints place practical limits on the execution of quantum algorithms, especially in machine learning contexts where quantum circuits must be repeatedly evaluated. Quantum machine learning (QML) models, including subset-based quantum neural networks, must therefore be designed to operate within these limitations [9,10]. This challenge has motivated structure-aware design choices and qubit-efficient models that are compatible with near-term hardware. To ensure compatibility, most QML circuits adopt compact encoding schemes and minimize entangling operations [3]. However, reducing depth and qubit usage can restrict model expressivity. Prior work has shown that structure-aware circuit design—such as sparse entanglement or modular feature interactions—can help mitigate these issues and support effective learning despite hardware limitations. Moreover, foundational reviews of QML emphasize that quantifying gate and query complexity remains critical to understanding practical advantages [4]. As such, feature selection becomes not only a performance optimization, but a hardware necessity. Identifying the most relevant features enables the model to stay within qubit budgets while preserving predictive accuracy [34].

2.2 Feature Selection

There are several methods for feature selection. Filter methods choose variables regardless of the machine learning model and are based on general metrics such as correlation, information-based metrices or statistical tests [23]. Embedded methods integrate the feature selection as part of the machine learning model training process and it is based on machine learning models with built-in feature selection methods, such as LASSO regression or tree-based models [5,16]. Wrapper methods search for subsets in the variable space and evaluate each of them by training a learning model based on each of the subset on a training set, evaluate each of the trained models on the test set and select the subset with the best performance [19,22]. Wrapper methods use several search techniques, the most exhaustive technique evaluates all subsets and selects the subset with maximum performance. This type search is not computationally effective for datasets with many variables [7].

2.3 Curiosity Algorithms

The field of artificial curiosity has started more than three decades ago [2,37], and has been gaining traction in the last ten years [17,24,25,31], with many applications, especially in the field of deep learning [18,33].

The basic intrinsically motivated learning [32], also known as artificial curiosity [36] or more specifically the curiosity loop [11–13], is based on the reinforcement learning framework and contains a learner (predictor) and an intrinsic reward.

As the basic curiosity loop's goal is to learn a correlation autonomously and actively in the best way possible, the core of each loop is the learner, which maps presented input–output pairs via an internally supervised learning algorithm. The agent in the curiosity loop actively learns via the reinforcement of the change in prediction errors. For each presented example, the learner gets a prediction error (i.e., the difference between the expected output and the correct output) and the reward value is set to this error's decrease over time [11–13,32]. The agent determines which new example is presented to the learner by selecting an appropriate action. The calculated reward is then used to update the agent's policy, which is then used in the next loop to determine the next appropriate action to select [11–13].

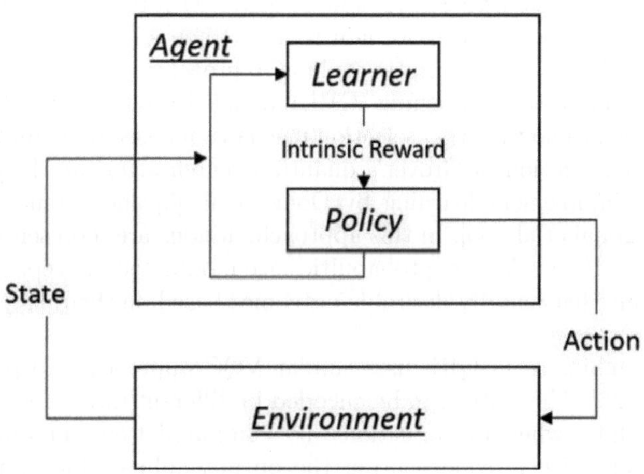

Fig. 1. The curiosity loop [28].

This idea underlies the Curious Feature Selection (CFS) algorithm, which frames feature selection as a reinforcement learning (RL) problem. An agent incrementally selects features from a dataset to maximize an internally generated reward signal—specifically, the reduction in prediction error achieved by adding a new feature. At each time step t, the agent selects an action a_t (a candidate feature), trains a predictive model, and receives a reward: $r_t = e_{t-1} - e_t$,, where e_t is the error of the model trained on the selected feature subset up to step t. The agent then updates a Q-value function using temporal-difference learning: $Q(s_t, a_t) \leftarrow (1 - \alpha)Q(s_t, a_t) + \alpha [r_t + \gamma \cdot \max_a Q(s_{t+1}, a)]$, with learning rate α and discount factor γ. Over multiple episodes, the agent converges to a feature selection policy that maximizes long-term reductions in prediction error. This process yields not only a single feature subset but a learned ranking of features based on their expected contribution to model performance (Fig. 1).

2.4 Reinforcement Learning

Reinforcement learners in curiosity-driven frameworks do more than optimize fixed feature sequences; they develop adaptive strategies for exploration that generalize across tasks and datasets. Rather than relying on external supervision or hand-tuned heuristics, these agents acquire policies through repeated interaction with the learning environment, adjusting their behavior based on the observed utility of past selections [28,39]. Classical reinforcement learning frameworks separate the value update mechanism (e.g., Q-learning) from the action selection rule, the latter governing the balance between exploration and exploitation [39]. Exploration is typically guided by stochastic policies—such as ϵ-greedy sampling or softmax over Q-values—that probabilistically favor high-reward actions while still exploring alternatives.

In deep variants like DCFS, the policy evolves with the agent's internal representation of past selections, allowing it to detect non-additive interactions that would be missed by greedy or static ranking approaches [30].

Quantum reinforcement learning (QRL) models introduce several interesting extensions. One is a novel action selection mechanism based on amplitude amplification, a generalization of Grover's quantum search algorithm [14], originally adapted for reinforcement learning by Dong et al. [8] and extended in recent work by Rajagopal et al. [35]. In this approach, actions are represented as quantum states, and their selection probabilities are modulated via repeated unitary transformations that amplify desirable outcomes based on their expected future rewards.

The more mainstream QRL uses similar VQC approaches to parameterize the policy [20,26]. The states can be encoded in different ways, e.g. either basis- or angle-encoding, whereas the actions are computed from the output of the quantum circuit, either by measuring the output qubits which represent the actions, thereby determining the RL selected action using quantum probability, or by obtaining the expectation value of the output qubits, that are then used with a softmax function to determine the selected action [20].

3 Quantum Curious Feature Selection (QCFS)

We present a quantum-enhanced version of the Curious Feature Selection (CFS) algorithm, originally introduced by *Moran & Gordon (2019)* [28], which retains the core architecture of curiosity-driven RL but replaces key components with quantum-native analogues.

QCFS integrates feature selection directly into the quantum modeling pipeline, thereby helping to alleviate two core quantum bottlenecks: the overhead of classical-to-quantum state preparation, and the scarcity of qubit resources. By using curiosity-driven policies to prioritize informative features, QCFS enables quantum circuits that are both more compact and more effective.

For prediction, QCFS employs a quantum neural network (QNN), a variational quantum circuit (VQC). The circuits encode classical feature subsets into quantum states via angle-encoding, followed by parameterized rotational gates and entangling gates (e.g., CNOT or CZ). The circuit parameters are optimized to minimize classification error, and internal rewards are computed based on measurement-derived loss.

The exploration strategy is also quantum-enhanced. Instead of classical RL, we implement a quantum RL algorithm based on [20], where the states and actions represent the features, and are basis-encoded with scaling parameters, followed by layers of parameterized rotation gates and entangling gates. The qubit probabilities are mapped to the Q-function, which, using softmax, determines the action, i.e. the next selected feature.

Despite these architectural upgrades, QCFS preserves the underlying CFS structure: features are selected incrementally, rewards reflect internal learning progress, and the agent learns a long-term selection policy. The use of quantum subroutines enables a richer encoding of feature correlations and a fundamentally different search dynamic, potentially improving both efficiency and generalization in high-dimensional feature spaces.

3.1 Learners

One suggested implementation of a quantum machine learning algorithm within the QCFS framework, is using a VQC. We used a variational quantum circuit (VQC) composed of input qubits as the number of selected features, N initialized in $|0\rangle^{\otimes N}$. The data is angle-encoded via single-qubit rotations $R_y(x_k)$ applied to each qubit $k \in \{1, ..., N\}$.

Following data encoding, the circuit implements a sequence of parametrized entangling layers. Each layer consists of:

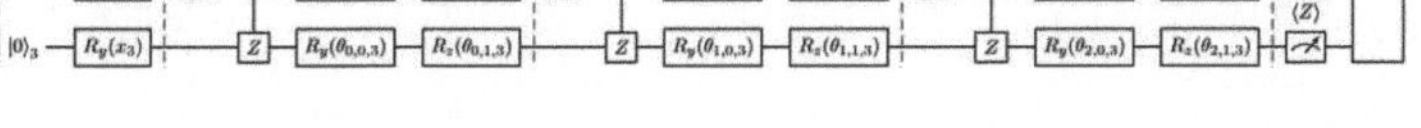

Fig. 2. VQC circuit as the Learner in the Quantum Curious Feature Selection.

1. **Entangling block**: A chain of controlled-Z (CZ) gates arranged in a linear topology to generate qubit correlations, $\mathrm{CZ}(q_i, q_{i+1}) \quad i = 1, ..., N-1$
2. **Parameterized single-qubit rotations**: On each qubit, an $R_y(\theta_{l,0,k})$ rotation followed by an $R_z(\theta_{l,1,k})$ rotation, where l denotes the layer index and k the qubit index.

The VQC in Fig. 2 implements three such layers ($l = 0, 1, 2$), with independent trainable parameters $\{\theta_{l,m,k}\}$, where $m \in \{0, 1\}$ denotes the rotation axis (y or z). This layered structure alternates between generating entanglement and applying locally tunable unitaries, enabling the circuit to approximate a broad class of functions over the input feature space.

At the output stage, each qubit is measured in the Pauli-Z basis, yielding expectation values $\langle Z_k \rangle$. These expectation values serve as the input features to a linear, input-output neural network layer, with weights $w_{j,k}$ $j = 1, ..., N$, $k = 1, ..., C$, in order to convert the N-dimensional VQC-output to C, the number of classes in the classification problem.

This architecture corresponds to a hardware-efficient ansatz [21], where parametrized single-qubit rotations and nearest-neighbor entanglement are alternated to balance expressivity with experimental feasibility.

3.2 Reinforcement Learners

The quantum reinforcement learning (QRL) policy ansatz follows the hardware-efficient encoding and variational structure proposed by Jerbi *et al.* [20].

The policy's states represent the features of the dataset, f_i, $i = 1, ..., n$ plus an additional f_0, which represents the initial state, before choosing the first feature. These $n+1$ states are encoded by a one-hot binary code, with $N = \lceil \log_2(n+1) \rceil$ qubits. These qubits are initialized in the $|0\rangle$ state, followed by a Hadamard gate to create an equal superposition.

The circuit then implements a sequence of parametrized layers, Fig. 3.

1. **Parameterized single-qubit rotations**: On each qubit, an $R_y(\theta_{l,0,k})$ rotation followed by an $R_z(\theta_{l,1,k})$ rotation, where l denotes the layer index and k the qubit index.
2. **Entangling block**: a chain of controlled-NOT (CNOT) gates arranged in a linear topology to generate qubit correlations, $\mathrm{CZ}(q_i, q_{i+1}) \quad i = 1, ..., N-1$
3. **State-dependent rotations**: The binary, one-hot encoded states are center-angled encoded, with scaling parameters $\lambda_{l,k}$, using $R_y(\pi\lambda_{0,k}(s_k - 0.5))$ and then $R_z(\pi\lambda_{1,k}(s_k - 0.5))$.

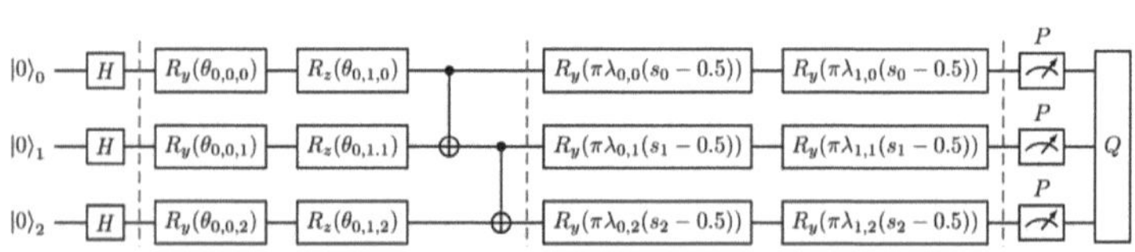

Fig. 3. QRL circuit as the Policy in the Quantum Curious Feature Selection.

The final quantum state's qubits' probabilities are calculated, and are used as the Q-value for the policy. The action is then selected based on a temperature-dependent $softmax$ function, to enable the exploration-exploitation tradeoff, with a decreasing temperature with episode number.

Another important implementation that ensures a smooth exploration-exploitation transition, was the use of the scaling parameters. Due to the fact that the same qubits are used as input and output (albeit with many gates in between), the $Q(s, a)$ has high $s - a$ correlations even in its initialization. However, RL should start with a uniform distribution over actions, *for all states*, since there is no inherent information before the first interaction with the environment. This was solved by setting the scaling parameters λ to a very low initial value, $\lambda = 0.01$, which "flattened" the initial $Q(s, a)$ values and resulted in a uniform action distribution for all states.

4 Results

We tested our proposed setup on two simple datasets, namely the *Iris* [41] dataset and *Breast cancer* dataset from Kaggle. For each dataset, we compared two-by-two, classical-quantum curiosity loops, namely, a classical or quantum Learner and a classical or quantum RL.

For the classical Learner, we used an ANN, with the same input-output layers as the VQC. It had two hidden layers, each with 10 neurons, with a ReLU function. For the quantum Learner, we used a VQC with three layers as described above. Both Learners used the same Adam optimizer and MSE loss function for training.

For the classical RL, we used a tabular Q-learning algorithm. For the quantum RL we used a QRL as described above, with three layers. Both RLs used softmax with the same episode-dependent temperature decrease from $\tau_0 = 0.9$, $\tau_T = 0.1$, and the same discount factor $\gamma = 0.9$.

4.1 Iris Dataset

For the *Iris* dataset, which has four features, we used the following parameters: Number of selected features: $N_{features} = 3$. Number of episodes for the curious loop: $N_{episodes} = 1000$. Number of batch instances per episode: $N_{batch} = 100$. Each algorithm was repeated $N_{repeats} = 10$. This results in the learnable parameters for each Learner and RL: ann - 183; vqc - 36; q-table - 20; qrl - 12.

Table 1 summarizes the mean accuracy, standard deviation, and best observed accuracy for each configuration across 10 runs, Fig. 4. Overall, the VQC–QRL combination achieved the highest mean accuracy (0.746) and the highest best-case performance (0.958), outperforming both its classical counterpart and the VQC with tabular Q-learning. The ANN models achieved lower mean accuracies, with QRL yielding slightly reduced performance compared to tabular Q-learning in the classical setting.

Table 1. Accuracy statistics for each learner type and RL approach.

Learner	RL type	Mean acc.	Std. dev.	Best acc.
ANN	Q-table	0.617	0.205	0.900
ANN	QRL	0.547	0.192	0.900
VQC	Q-table	0.633	0.221	0.833
VQC	QRL	**0.746**	0.165	**0.958**

4.2 Breast Cancer Dataset

For the *breast cancer* dataset, which has 32 features, we used the following parameters: Number of selected features: $N_{features} = 3$. Number of episodes for the curious loop: $N_{episodes} = 10000$. Number of batch instances per episode: $N_{batch} = 100$. Each algorithm was repeated $N_{repeats} = 2$. This results in the learnable parameters for each Learner and RL: ann - 172; vqc - 30; q-table - 930; qrl - 60.

Table 2. Accuracy statistics for each learner type and RL approach.

Learner	RL type	Mean acc.	Std. dev.	Best acc.
ANN	Q-table	0.601	0.167	0.719
ANN	QRL	**0.754**	0.186	0.886
VQC	Q-table	0.567	**0.044**	0.598
VQC	QRL	0.741	0.215	**0.893**

Table 2 reports the mean accuracy, standard deviation, and best observed accuracy for each configuration, Fig. 5. In the classical setting, QRL markedly improved performance over tabular Q-learning, with the ANN–QRL combination achieving a mean accuracy of 0.754 and a best accuracy of 0.886. For the quantum learner, QRL also yielded higher mean accuracy (0.741 vs. 0.567) and best-case accuracy (0.893 vs. 0.598) compared to tabular Q-learning, although with a higher standard deviation.

5 Discussion

These results demonstrate that the quantum subroutines introduced in **QCFS**—namely the quantum reinforcement learner and the VQC—can serve as effective drop-in replacements for the classical components used in the original CFS framework [27]. Despite their differing internal mechanisms, both quantum learners successfully converged to the signal features and outperformed their classical baselines in terms of final accuracy, despite having less learnable parameters. This reinforces the feasibility of hybrid quantum-classical pipelines for feature

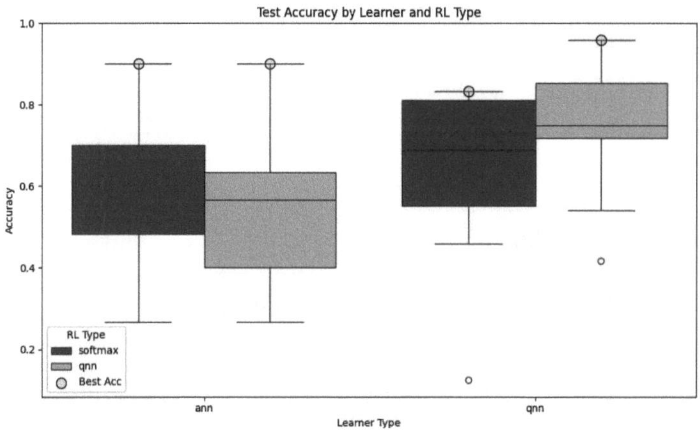

Fig. 4. Comparison of classical and quantum Learners and RL. Color denote RL type: classical (q-table) or quantum (qrl), x-grouping denote Learner type: classical (ann) or quantum (vqc).

selection and provides a promising template for future extensions of curiosity-driven search to quantum models.

VQC Variable Circuits. In the QCFS algorithm, each time-step within each episode represents a different combination of features, with an increasing feature numbers, e.g. the first time-step has 1 feature, the second has 2 features, etc. This represents a challenge since it necessitates a *different* circuit for each time-step, which may deter its implementation on a real quantum computer. More innovative running architectures may be required to address this challenge, e.g. running the first time-step for many episodes before moving to the second time-step.

Quantum Feature Encoding. In our QRL implementation, we used a one-hot binary centered angle encoding for the feature-space. This encoding enables a logarithmic scaling with the number of features, which can facilitate a large feature-space, even in NISQ devices. The simple examples presented above, a 32-feature dataset was easily encoded and ran with a small-qubit number, small-depth quantum circuit, and achieved impressive results.

Generalizability of the Framework. The paper presented the novel framework of Quantum Curiosity, where the (classical) curiosity loop is augmented by quantum Learner and RL. However, the specific implementation of the QCFS only hints to the potential of the framework, as several other instantiations of the curiosity loop have been previous studied [27–30]. Moreover, even within the QCFS implementation, we have only suggested a specific implementation for the quantum Learner and quantum RL. Other, more sophisticated QML algorithms can be implemented [15], as well as more complex QRL algorithms [26].

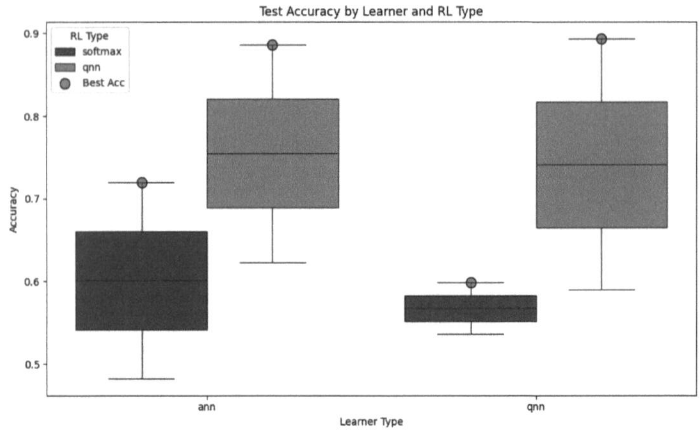

Fig. 5. Comparison of classical and quantum Learners and RL. Color denote RL type: classical (q-table) or quantum (qrl), x-grouping denote Learner type: classical (ann) or quantum (vqc).

Limitations. The paper presented a new framework, yet its implementation and results have several limitations. All results were run using simulations on a classical computer. Running the QCFS algorithm on a quantum computer may be challenging due to the highly interleaved classical-quantum hybrid nature of the curiosity loop. Furthermore, the results presented here are preliminary and only show improvement on small datasets.

6 Conclusion

We introduced QCFS, a quantum-enhanced extension of the Curious Feature Selection framework that integrates quantum reinforcement learning and quantum neural networks into the feature selection process. By selecting informative subsets prior to encoding, QCFS addresses critical bottlenecks in quantum learning, including qubit constraints and costly state preparation. Future work may explore other curiosity loop-based algorithms' quantum extensions.

References

1. Barends, R., et al.: Digitized adiabatic quantum computing with a superconducting circuit. Nature **534**(7606), 222–226 (2016). https://doi.org/10.1038/nature17658
2. Barto, A.G., Singh, S., Chentanez, N.: Intrinsically motivated learning of hierarchical collections of skills. In: International Conference on Developmental Learning (ICDL) (2004)
3. Benedetti, M., Grant, E., Wossnig, L., Severini, S.: Parameterized quantum circuits as machine learning models. Quantum Sci. Technol. **4**(4), 043001 (2019)

4. Biamonte, J., Wittek, P., Pancotti, N., Rebentrost, P., Wiebe, N., Lloyd, S.: Quantum machine learning. Nature **549**(7671), 195–202 (2017). https://doi.org/10.1038/nature23474
5. Blum, A.L., Langley, P.: Selection of relevant features and examples in machine learning. Artif. Intell. **97**(1), 245–271 (1997). https://doi.org/10.1016/S0004-3702(97)00063-5
6. Cerezo, M., Verdon, G., Huang, H.Y., Cincio, L., Coles, P.J.: Challenges and opportunities in quantum machine learning. Nat. Comput. Sci. **2**(9), 567–576 (2022). https://doi.org/10.1038/s43588-022-00311-3
7. Chandrashekar, G., Sahin, F.: A survey on feature selection methods. Comput. Electr. Eng. **40**(1), 16–28 (2014)
8. Dong, D., Chen, C., Li, H., Tarn, T.J.: Quantum reinforcement learning. IEEE Trans. Syst. Man Cybern. Part B Cybern. **38**(5), 1207–1220 (2008)
9. Farhi, E., Goldstone, J., Gutmann, S.: Quantum algorithms for fixed qubit architectures. arXiv preprint arXiv:1703.06199 (2017)
10. Farhi, E., Neven, H.: Classification with quantum neural networks on near term processors. arXiv preprint arXiv:1802.06002 (2018)
11. Gordon, G., Ahissar, E.: Hierarchical curiosity loops and active sensing. Neural Netw. **32**, 119–129 (2012). https://doi.org/10.1016/j.neunet.2012.02.024
12. Gordon, G., Fonio, E., Ahissar, E.: Emergent exploration via novelty management. J. Neurosci. **34**(38), 12646–12661 (2014). https://doi.org/10.1523/JNEUROSCI.1872-14.2014
13. Gordon, G., Fonio, E., Ahissar, E.: Learning and control of exploration primitives. J. Comput. Neurosci. **37**(2), 259–280 (2014). https://doi.org/10.1007/s10827-014-0500-1
14. Grover, L.K.: Quantum mechanics helps in searching for a needle in a haystack. Phys. Rev. Lett. **79**(2), 325–328 (1997). https://doi.org/10.1103/PhysRevLett.79.325
15. Gujju, Y., Matsuo, A., Raymond, R.: Quantum machine learning on near-term quantum devices: current state of supervised and unsupervised techniques for real-world applications. Phys. Rev. Appl. **21**(6), 067001 (2024). https://doi.org/10.1103/PhysRevApplied.21.067001
16. Guyon, I., Elisseeff, A.: An introduction to variable and feature selection. JMLR **3**, 1157–1182 (2003)
17. Hafez, M.B., Weber, C., Wermter, S.: Curiosity-driven exploration enhances motor skills of continuous actor-critic learner. In: 2017 Joint IEEE International Conference on Development and Learning and Epigenetic Robotics (ICDL-EpiRob), pp. 39–46 (2017). https://doi.org/10.1109/DEVLRN.2017.8329785
18. Huang, S.H., et al.: Learning gentle object manipulation with curiosity-driven deep reinforcement learning. arXiv preprint arXiv:1903.08542 (2019)
19. Jain, A., Zongker, D.: Feature selection: evaluation, application, and small sample performance. IEEE Trans. Pattern Anal. Mach. Intell. **19**(2), 153–158 (2002). https://doi.org/10.1109/34.574797
20. Jerbi, S., Gyurik, C., Marshall, S., Briegel, H., Dunjko, V.: Parametrized quantum policies for reinforcement learning. Adv. Neural Process. Syst. **34**, 28362–28375 (2021)
21. Kandala, A., et al.: Hardware-efficient variational quantum eigensolver for small molecules and quantum magnets. Nature **549**(7671), 242–246 (2017)
22. Kittler, J.: Feature set search algorithms. https://ci.nii.ac.jp/naid/80014031027
23. Kohavi, R., John, G.H.: Wrappers for feature subset selection. Artif. Intell. **97**(1), 273–324 (1997). https://doi.org/10.1016/S0004-3702(97)00043-X

24. Kompella, V.R., Stollenga, M., Luciw, M., Schmidhuber, J.: Continual curiosity-driven skill acquisition from high-dimensional video inputs for humanoid robots. Artif. Intell. **247**, 313–335 (2017)
25. Kulkarni, T.D., Narasimhan, K.R., Saeedi, A., Tenenbaum, J.B.: Hierarchical deep reinforcement learning: integrating temporal abstraction and intrinsic motivation. arXiv preprint arXiv:1604.06057 (2016)
26. Meyer, N., Ufrecht, C., Periyasamy, M., Scherer, D.D., Plinge, A., Mutschler, C.: A survey on quantum reinforcement learning. arXiv preprint arXiv:2211.03464 (2022)
27. Moran, M., Cohen, T., Ben-Zion, Y., Gordon, G.: Curious instance selection. Inf. Sci. **608**, 794–808 (2022)
28. Moran, M., Gordon, G.: Curious feature selection. Inf. Sci. **485**, 42–54 (2019)
29. Moran, M., Gordon, G.: Curious feature selection-based clustering. IEEE Trans. Artif. Intell. **607**, 763–779 (2022). https://doi.org/10.1016/j.ins.2022.06.115
30. Moran, M., Gordon, G.: Deep curious feature selection: a recurrent intrinsic-reward reinforcement learning approach to feature selection. IEEE Trans. Artif. Intell. **5**(3), 1174–1184 (2023). https://doi.org/10.1109/TAI.2023.3282564
31. Oudeyer, P.Y., Gottlieb, J., Lopes, M.: Intrinsic motivation, curiosity, and learning. Prog. Brain Res. **229**, 257–284 (2016). https://doi.org/10.1016/bs.pbr.2016.05.005
32. Oudeyer, P.Y., Kaplan, F., Hafner, V.V.: Intrinsic motivation systems for autonomous mental development. IEEE Trans. Evol. Comput. **11**(2), 265–286 (2007)
33. Pathak, D., Agrawal, P., Efros, A.A., Darrell, T.: Curiosity-driven exploration by self-supervised prediction. In: Proceedings of the 34th International Conference on Machine Learning. pp. 2778–2787. PMLR (2017). https://proceedings.mlr.press/v70/pathak17a.html
34. Power, L., Guha, K.: Feature importance and explainability in quantum machine learning. arXiv preprint arXiv:2405.08917 (2024)
35. Rajagopal, V., Niu, M.Y., Yuen, H.: Quantum reinforcement learning via amplitude amplification, vol. 7, p. 918 (2023)
36. Schmidhuber, J.: Formal theory of creativity, fun, and intrinsic motivation (1990–2010). IEEE Trans. Autonom. Mental Dev. **2**(3), 230–247 (2010). https://doi.org/10.1109/TAMD.2010.2056368
37. Schmidhuber, J.: A possibility for implementing curiosity and boredom in model-building neural controllers. MIT Press (1991)
38. Schuld, M., Sinayskiy, I., Petruccione, F.: An introduction to quantum machine learning. Contemp. Phys. **56**(2), 172–185 (2015). https://doi.org/10.1080/00107514.2014.964942
39. Sutton, R.S., Barto, A.G.: Reinforcement Learning: An Introduction. MIT Press (1998)
40. Ullah, U., Garcia-Zapirain, B.: Quantum machine learning revolution in healthcare: a systematic review of emerging perspectives and applications. IEEE Access **12**, 11423–11450 (2024). https://doi.org/10.1109/ACCESS.2024.3353461
41. Unwin, A., Kleinman, K.: The iris data set: in search of the source of Virginica. Significance **18**(6), 26–29 (2021). https://doi.org/10.1111/1740-9713.01589
42. Wang, Y., Liu, J.: A comprehensive review of quantum machine learning: from NISQ to fault tolerance. Rep. Prog. Phys. **87**(11), 116402 (2024). https://doi.org/10.1088/1361-6633/ad7f69
43. Zeguendry, A., Jarir, Z., Quafafou, M.: Quantum machine learning: a review and case studies. Entropy **25**(2), 287 (2023). https://doi.org/10.3390/e25020287
44. Zhu, Y., Yu, K.: Artificial intelligence (AI) for quantum and quantum for AI. Electronics **55**(8), 697 (2023). https://doi.org/10.1007/s11082-023-04914-6

Objective-Free Local Learning and Emergent Language Structure in Thinking Machines

P. Myles Eugenio(✉)

Department of Physics, Indiana University, Bloomington, IN 47405, USA
pamyeuge@iu.edu

Abstract. We present a neuro-symbolic framework for generative language modeling based on local, event-driven emergent learning in hierarchical Hopfield memory chains. These act as both a compositional short-term memory and a dynamic meta-tokenizer ("retokenizer"), building multi-scale tokens from scratch without predefined vocabularies or global objectives. Structure emerges through Hebbian updates that imprint local correlations, hierarchically composed into projection tensors with intrinsic gauge redundancy. Trained even on noise, the model produces synthetic languages whose morphological statistics match human language. Brief exposure of new neurons to the retokenizer binds multi-scale features into symbolic embeddings, forming emergent long-term keyvalue memories. This framework offers a scalable, interpretable route to neuromorphic, generative language systems where tokens, grammar, and reasoning arise as compressed memory traces in a fully unsupervised Hopfield hierarchy.

Keywords: Exotic AI · Hebbian · Physics-inspired Neural Nets · Hierarchical Compression · Neuro-symbolic · Neuromorphic · Matrix Product States

Objective-free local learning is the paradigm by which much of the observed structure and organization of the universe arises. Nature does not learn structure in a coordinated way, such as by minimizing a loss, but as a series of accidents made likely due to constraints governing local interactions. Cognition, chemical self-assembly, and even simple automata like Conway's Game of Life evolve through such decentralized processes. In this work [1,6], we present a model that follows this same principle: a locally interacting memory system in which symbols, grammar, and memory structures emerge through discrete events, not optimization. Structure is not imposed by training objectives, but unfolds from local updates that encode correlations into memory over time.

Each learning event in the model consists of a pair $(\tilde{v}, v)$, where $\tilde{v}_\mu^{(n-1)}$ is a projected context feature and v_k the next token. This event imprints a local Hebbian correlation into memory via the update $g_{\mu,k}^{(n)} \leftarrow g_{\mu,k}^{(n)} + \tilde{v}_\mu^{(n-1)} v_k$.

D. Cavar et al. (Eds.): QNLPAI 2025, CCIS 2659, pp. 329–334, 2026.
https://doi.org/10.1007/978-3-032-13883-5_18

The total energy of the system is given by a sum over these local interactions across layers,

$$H = \sum_{n\geq 2} \sum_{\mu,k} g^{(n)}_{\mu,k} \tilde{v}^{(n-1)}_{\mu} v_k,$$

and inference proceeds by gradient ascent on H with respect to v_k, yielding fast autoregression driven by stored multi-scale correlations.

Although each layer stores only local 2-point correlations, the recursive definition of projected tokens induces effective n-point interactions. Each projection acts as a discrete coarse-graining step:

$$\tilde{v}^{(n)}_{\mu_n} = \sum_{\mu_{n-1},k} P_n^{\mu_n,\mu_{n-1},k} \tilde{v}^{(n-1)}_{\mu_{n-1}} v_k,$$

so that the deepest features expand into full sequences via contraction:

$$\tilde{v}^{(n)}_{\mu_n} = \sum_{j_1,\dots,j_n} (P_n \cdots P_2)^{\mu_n}_{j_1\cdots j_n} v_{j_1} \cdots v_{j_n}.$$

This composition induces an effective n-point interaction,

$$H_n = \sum_{j_1,\dots,j_n} g^{(n)}_{j_1\cdots j_n} v_{j_1} \cdots v_{j_n},$$

with coefficients defined by contractions of the memory and projection tensors.

The projection hierarchy can be understood as performing a renormalization group flow (*def.* retokenization group), where higher-order (n-point) correlations are encoded via a hierarchy of local (2-point) interactions. This effective n-point description is possible because the tensor product structure of the P_n

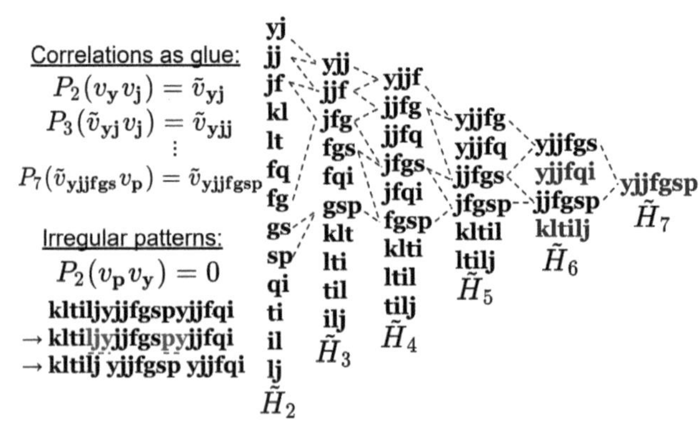

Fig. 1. The projector onto the gauge-invariant tokenset is equivalent to enforcing a hierarchical directed acyclic graph (DAG) over the feature space. It is a closed structure, where each n-gram is formed entirely from $(n-1)$ grams below it. This produces a word-forming/non-word-forming distinction, where non-word forming (i.e. statistical incompatible) patterns carry word boundaries.

chain defines a matrix product state (Fig 2), which admits a gauge redundancy corresponding to different tokenization orderings (e.g. $\tilde{v}^{(n)} \to \tilde{v}^{(n-1)}v$) (Fig. 1).

Once learned, the gauge redundancy can be exploited to perform a type of dynamic tokenization (retokenization), and allows the model to discern word boundaries from statistical compatibility alone, without the need for specialized stop or space tokens. This allows the $g^{(n)}$-hierarchy to act as a compositional short-term memory, which stores specific strings in its ground state, and which can be exactly retrieved by combining retokenization with next-token prediction. The learned words correspond to the accepted strings of a finite automaton – defined not through symbolic rules, but defined implicitly as a consequence of enforcing locality.

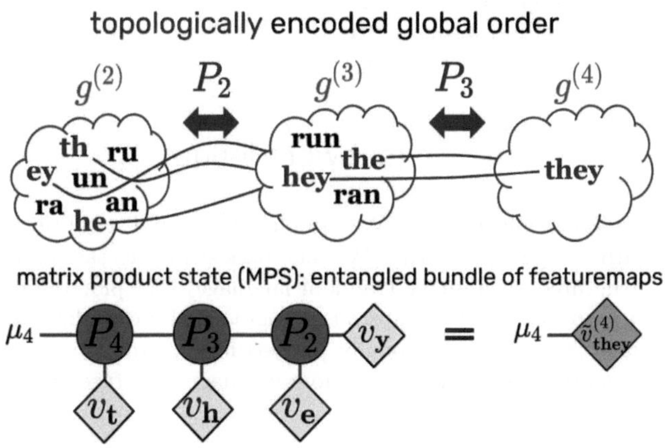

Fig. 2. Local interactions ($\tilde{v}^{(n-1)} \otimes v$) drive new model growths ($\tilde{v}^{(n)}$) when input events align with the allowed hierarchical DAG structure. Stored strings are induced global order parameters ($v \otimes v \otimes \cdots \otimes v \to \tilde{v}^{(n)}$), each living as a terminal node of the DAG. Each growth is compressed/decompressed as a matrix product state (MPS).

This approach not only respects the microscopic locality observed in the brain, but demonstrates how those constraints lead directly to universal human language structure [2–5]. We demonstrate this [1,2,6] by training the model against noise, which produces finite word length with a distribution of patterns observed universally across human language [2–5]. It teaches us that there is a lowest level of human memory (the retokenizer) which is a compositional n-gram model over a hierarchical DAG, where complete word patterns live at terminal DAG nodes. Such a model is limited to (in formal language terms) *regular* language. Word length is finite because of this limitation [1,6] (Fig. 3).

Because the model has no global objective and no predefined token boundaries, it exhibits a form of plasticity uncommon in conventional language models: By introducing a single new neuron a_α, and exposing it to the hierarchy during memory retrieval, the entire compositional feature trace of the sequence becomes

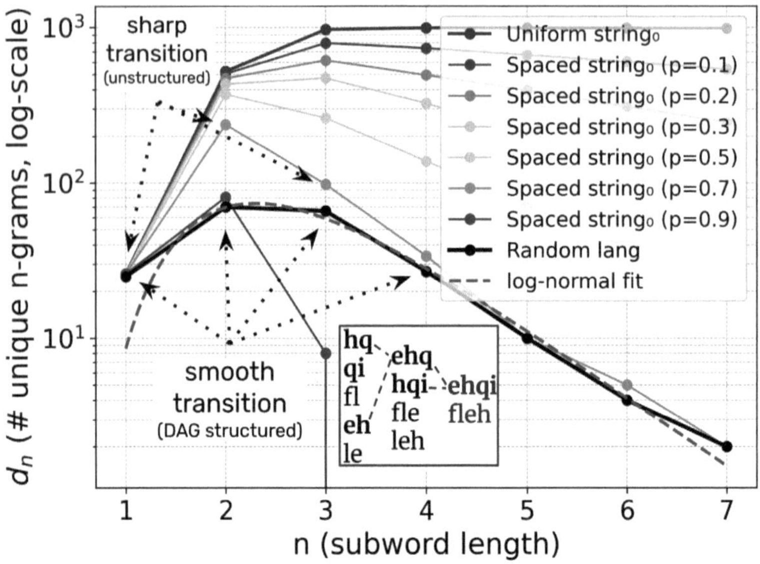

Fig. 3. Learning structure from noise. We sample a uniform distribution to generate a random string without spaces (string_O). We then pass string_O to the retokenizer, which grows a DAG structured vocabulary (random language). We plot the distribution of unique sub-word patterns, which collapses as a log-normal for random language, same as human language [3–5]. We additionally plot string_O w/ randomly inserted spaces (frequency p), to contrast with learned random language structure.

bound to it. This occurs via a Hebbian update, $m^{(n)}_{\alpha,\mu_n} \leftarrow m^{(n)}_{\alpha,\mu_n} + \eta\, a_\alpha \tilde{v}^{(n)}_{\mu_n}$, modifying H

$$H = \sum_n \sum_{\mu_{n-1},k} g^{(n)}_{\mu_{n-1},k} \tilde{v}^{(n-1)}_{\mu_{n-1}} v_k + \sum_\alpha a_\alpha \Big(\sum_n \sum_{\mu_n} m^{(n)}_{\alpha,\mu_n} \tilde{v}^{(n)}_{\mu_n} \Big).$$

This new neuron behaves as a long-term memory embedding, which can participate in future inference via an emergent associative key-value memory dynamic. This extends its inference class beyond the initial n-gram statistics, and makes continual learning possible since information stored in $g^{(n)}$'s can be forgotten.

In our work [1,6], we discuss how these dynamic learning processes lead to even further emergent inference types. Recursively performing cycles of learning & relearning drives self-organization of an increasingly complex tokenset (Fig 4). Such local-dynamic driven plasticity is not possible in AI whose architecture is fixed in order to do global learning (back propagation). It is a data-free structural emergence, similar to how a Turing machine can arise from the local cellular dynamics of Conway's Game of Life. Learning does not occur via a global fit, instead new information is retained by aligning it with emergent structure.

While this hints at a novel paradigm for language learning, it also makes the framework natively incompatible with modern NLP techniques. For instance,

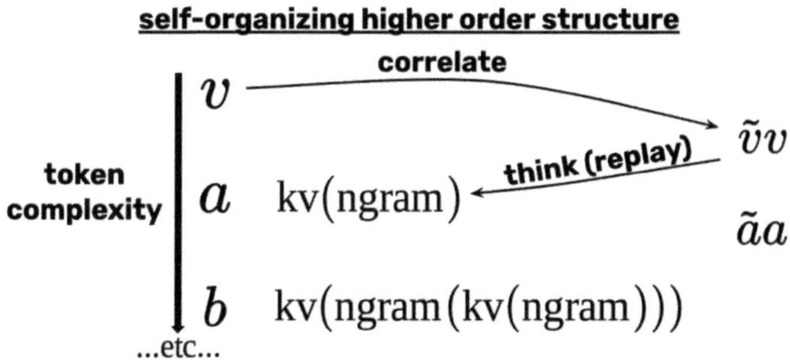

Fig. 4. Continual learning via memory retrieval (a.k.a replay, thinking). First, short-term memory generates new feature basis ($\tilde{v}^{(n)}$,$\tilde{a}^{(n)}$,...), whose entangled feature maps are then disentangled during replay by added long-term memory neurons (a,b,$\cdots$). Even in the absence of structured data (noise learning), the model self-organizes into an increasingly complex tokenset, with emergent attention mechanisms. The first of these mechanisms is a key-value memory wrapped around an n-gram model [1,6].

LLM's assume pretokenized input over fixed vocabularies, and a fixed embedding dimension. Thus tokenization is treated as a preprocessing step. The retokenizer is not a preprocessing step, but instead is an engine for generating new feature bases in a non-static architecture. Attempts to treat the retokenizer as a standard tokenizer break the model [1,6]. Hence the need for replay in order to do continual learning, so that the retokenizer memory can be erased, allowing new feature bases to be formed.

Scaling up in this framework means overcoming new challenges toward model scaling and experimentation, which live outside the global learning paradigm dominating modern artificial neural nets.

Retokenizing Short-Term Memory (STM).

- **Local Imprinting:** Events $(\tilde{v}^{(n-1)}, v)$ learned as local correlation $g^{(n)}_{\mu,k} \leftarrow g^{(n)}_{\mu,k} + \tilde{v}^{(n-1)}_{\mu} v_k$. No global objective nor loss.
- **Global Order from Local Interactions:** Multi-scale "magnetization" selects stored strings as ground states. Builds strings as n-point correlations $(v \otimes v \otimes \cdots \otimes v)$ from 2-point interactions $(\tilde{v}^{(n-1)} \otimes v)$ & learned mergers (P_n's).
- **Topological Memory:** Global order parameters (stored strings) encoded as terminal nodes of hierarchical DAG. Incompatibilities act as defects/domain walls (non-word forming patterns). Guarantees strong penalties against retrieval errors. Boundary-aware inference.
- **Inter-scale Entanglement:** Feature maps compressed as matrix product state (MPS). Allows for MPS/TensorTrain-based compression techniques.

- **Scientific Theory:** Model learns identical sub-word structure to human language when trained on noise. Demonstrates how microscopic locality is responsible for human language data and finite word length.

Long-Term Memory (LTM) Tokens.

- **Compression:** Projected features $\tilde{v}^{(n)}$ (from the P-chain) are capped by low-rank $m_\alpha^{(n)}$; activations $a_\alpha = \sum_n m_\alpha^{(n)} \cdot \tilde{v}^{(n)}$.
- **Decoupling:** $\{m_\alpha^{(n)}\}$ persist while STM synapses $g^{(n)}$ can be reset/forgotten.
- **Continual Learning:** New embeddings $(m_\alpha^{(n)})$ can be learned without over-writing existing ones. Model grows without retraining.
- **Parallelism:** Contributions from different α and depths n add linearly in H.
- **Emergent Computation:** The a_α contribution to inference generalizes beyond local n-gram statistics. Hierarchy of emergent compositional attention mechanisms.
- **No positional embeddings needed:** Each $\sum_n m_\alpha^{(n)} \cdot \tilde{v}^{(n)} = \sum_n m_\alpha^{(n)} \cdot P_n P_{n-1} \cdots P_2 (vv \cdots v)$ carries α-specific projectors, which encode morphological structure.

References

1. Eugenio, P.M., Beavers, A.F.: Self-organizing language. arXiv:2506.23293 (2025). https://arxiv.org/abs/2506.23293
2. Eugenio, P.M.: Hebbian learning the local structure of language. arXiv:2503.02057 (2025). https://arxiv.org/abs/2503.02057
3. Limpert, E., Stahel, W.A., Abbt, M.: Log-normal Distributions across the Sciences: Keys and Clues. BioScience **51**(5), 341–352 (2001). https://doi.org/10.1641/0006-3568(2001)051[0341:LNDATS]2.0.CO;2
4. Herdan, G.: The Relation between the dictionary distribution and the occurrence distribution of word length and its importance for the study of quantitative linguistics. Biometrika **45**(1–2), 222–228 (1958). https://doi.org/10.1093/biomet/45.1-2.222
5. Williams, C.B.: A Note on the statistical analysis of sentence-length as a criterion of literary style. Biometrika **31**(3–4), 356–361 (1940). https://doi.org/10.1093/biomet/31.3-4.356
6. Emergent Language Group (EmLa), Eugenio, P.M.: ababot: Code and Resources (2025). https://gitlab.com/emla-group/ababot

Author Index

D. Cavar et al. (Eds.): QNLPAI 2025, CCIS 2659, pp. 335–336, 2026.
https://doi.org/10.1007/978-3-032-13883-5

MIX
Papier aus verantwortungsvollen Quellen
Paper from responsible sources
FSC® C105338
FSC
www.fsc.org

If you have any concerns about our products,
you can contact us on
ProductSafety@springernature.com

In case Publisher is established outside the EU,
the EU authorized representative is:
Springer Nature Customer Service Center GmbH
Europaplatz 3, 69115 Heidelberg, Germany

Printed by Libri Plureos GmbH
in Hamburg, Germany